A William Appleman Williams Reader

A WILLIAM APPLEMAN WILLIAMS *Reader*

Selections from His Major Historical Writings

EDITED WITH AN INTRODUCTION AND NOTES BY

Henry W. Berger

IVAN R. DEE · CHICAGO

Grateful acknowledgment is made to the following publishers and individuals for permission to reprint copyrighted materials included herein:
Gerard McCauley Agency for excerpts from *The Tragedy of American Diplomacy*, copyright © 1959, 1962, 1972 by William Appleman Williams; *The Contours of American History*, copyright © 1961 by William Appleman Williams; *The Roots of the Modern American Empire*, copyright © 1969 by William Appleman Williams; *Some Presidents: Wilson to Nixon*, copyright © 1972 by William Appleman Williams; *America Confronts a Revolutionary World*, copyright © 1976 by William Appleman Williams; and *Empire as a Way of Life*, copyright © 1980 by William Appleman Williams.
Holt, Rinehart and Winston, Inc., for an excerpt from *American-Russian Relations, 1781–1947*, copyright © 1952, 1980 by William Appleman Williams.
Monthly Review Foundation for "A Second Look at Mr. X" from *Monthly Review* 4 (1952), copyright © 1952 by Monthly Review, Inc.; and for "Charles Austin Beard: The Intellectual as Tory-Radical," from Harvey Goldberg, ed., *American Radicals: Some Problems and Personalities*, copyright © 1957 by Harvey Goldberg.
Science & Society for "The Legend of Isolationism in the 1920's" from *Science & Society*, XVIII:1 (Winter 1954), copyright © 1954 by Science & Society, Inc.
Pacific Historical Review for "The Frontier Thesis and American Foreign Policy" from *Pacific Historical Review*, XXIV:4 (November 1955), copyright © 1955 by the Pacific Coast Branch, American Historical Association.
Random House, Inc., for an excerpt from *The Great Evasion*, copyright © 1964 by William Appleman Williams.
Center for Social Research and Education for "Confessions of an Intransigent Revisionist" from *Socialist Revolution* (now *Socialist Review*), III:5 (September–October 1973), copyright © 1974 by Agenda Publishing Company.

Library of Congress Cataloging-in-Publication Data:
Williams, William Appleman.
    A William Appleman Williams Reader : selections from his major historical writings / edited with an introduction and notes by Henry W. Berger.
        p. cm.
    Includes bibliographical references and index.
    ISBN 1-56663-008-8 (acid-free paper). — ISBN 1-56663-002-9 (pbk. acid-free paper)
    1. United States—Foreign relations. I. Berger, Henry W.
II. Title.
E183.7.W728 1992
327.73—dc20   92-17013

In memory of William Appleman Williams, 1921–1990,
and for Wendy Tomlin Williams

Where there is no vision the people perish.
Proverbs 29:18

We can as citizens deal with the
question of what to do, therefore,
only after we cope with the issues
raised by the meaning of the history.
William Appleman Williams, 1969

Acknowledgments

A number of individuals have, at important moments and in important ways, helped to make this book possible. Without them the effort would have suffered. Ms. Jeannie Williams of Scottsdale, Arizona, and Ms. Wendy Williams of Waldport, Oregon, were especially helpful with matters relating to William A. Williams's early years. Ms. Judith Cochran of the Department of History at the University of Wisconsin provided details of Williams's graduate school record, while William G. Robbins and Don E. McIlvenna, colleagues of Williams, supplied information about his career at Oregon State University. Professor Robbins also made available the text of the essay "The Annapolis Crowd," published here for the first time. Edward Crapol, professor of history at the College of William and Mary, who was first a student and then a colleague of Williams, made useful suggestions and provided me with a copy of Williams's address to the United States Naval Academy, also published here for the first time. Gerard F. McCauley, Williams's literary agent, was central to the success of the project by arranging for permission to reprint most of the selections included.

Finally, to my publisher and editor, Ivan Dee, who first proposed the book and my editing of it, special thanks are due for continuing encouragement, good humor, and, above all else, editorial wisdom and generous patience.

In the interest of readability I have omitted source notes from the selections included here, but I have retained those footnotes that amplify the text. I have also inserted descriptive information, in brackets or in footnotes, where I thought it would be helpful to the reader.

H. W. B.

*Washington University
at St. Louis
April 1992*

Contents

INTRODUCTION:
THE REVISIONIST
HISTORIAN
AND HIS COMMUNITY

History is a dialogue in the present with the past, about the future.
Douglas Adair, Fame and the Founding Fathers, *1984*

The revisionist is one who sees basic facts in a different way and as interconnected in new relationships.
William Appleman Williams, Confessions of an Intransigent Revisionist, *1973*

One can never forget that it is people who act—not the policy or program.
William Appleman Williams, The Shaping of American Diplomacy, *1956*

THIS book is designed to introduce the work of a revisionist historian whose perspectives about the United States and its relations with the world challenged and altered conventional interpretations of American diplomatic history. Defining a revisionist "as one who sees basic facts in a different way and as interconnected in new relationships," William Appleman Williams agitated debate, provoked denunciation, and invited dismissal of his writings over the course of more than three decades. But at his death, in March 1990, the impact of his teaching and publications—on both the writing of history and general intellectual discourse—could not be denied. The essence of his most important arguments may be found in the selections from his writings included in this book.

Reporting the passing of the often contentious and always outspo-

11

ken historian, the *New York Times* called Williams "an influential writer of a dozen revisionist books that questioned prevailing views of American history." The *Manchester Guardian Weekly* suggested he had exercised "an influence on American historiography probably greater than that of any of his contemporaries." At a memorial conference honoring him soon after his death, Williams's teacher and mentor, Professor Fred Harvey Harrington, observed with characteristic authority that "the field of U.S. diplomatic history is not the same because of what he did."[1] But, as Harrington noted, Williams had also been a dedicated political radical; political concerns had affected his decision to enter the historical profession in the first place. Both commitments were informed by family and community influences during his youth and by experiences of an earlier career in the United States Navy.

The only child of Mildrede Louise Appleman and William Carleton Williams was born in the small Midwestern town of Atlantic, Iowa, where he spent most of his boyhood. His father, who was raised on a farm near Atlantic, attended Iowa State College (now University) in Ames and joined the army air corps in 1917, training to become a demonstration test pilot during World War I. In November 1918 he married Mildrede and in June 1921 she gave birth to their son. Meanwhile, the elder Williams had held several different jobs, including a stint as pilot "barnstormer," but had tired of civilian life. He returned to service with the air corps at Fort Sam Houston in Texas where the family lived for a brief period. In early 1927, when Williams was not quite six years old, his father was killed in an airplane crash while taking part in war games exercises.

Williams's mother, "an independent lady," as he described her, was determined that the now fatherless youth should nonetheless enjoy a fulfilling childhood. Mildrede therefore returned with her son to Atlantic to live with her parents. While she attended college to earn a teaching certificate, Williams's grandparents provided "a good family life," tendering him affection, teaching him valuable skills, and promoting habits of good behavior.

Williams recalled that his personal development was substantially influenced by the exacting standards of individual performance and achievement demanded of him by his family. But communal obligations were equally if not more important, he remembered, and were

---

1. *New York Times,* March 8, 1990; *Manchester Guardian Weekly,* March 18, 1990; Fred Harvey Harrington, Remarks at a Conference to Honor William Appleman Williams, Washington, D.C., June 1990 (copy of text in editor's possession).

particularly tested during the depression years of his adolescence. Members of an extended family also provided fundamental role models, and Williams traced the beginnings of his political awareness to values set by their example. "The more I got out in the world," he observed, "the more I thought they were good values and that I was supposed to *do* something."[2]

The recipient of an athletic-scholastic award, Williams attended Kemper Military Academy in Booneville, Missouri, after completing his high school education. He then received a congressional appointment to the U.S. Naval Academy at Annapolis, Maryland, from which he graduated in the spring of 1944. By that time the United States had been involved in World War II for more than two and a half years. Williams volunteered for the amphibious corps and served as an executive officer on a landing ship in the Pacific theater of operations during the final fifteen months of the conflict. At the end of hostilities he was sent to Corpus Christi, Texas, to train as a naval aviator.

Williams took great pride in the education, formal and otherwise, that he acquired at the Naval Academy and during his tour of duty at sea. He spoke admiringly of the discipline and the excellence of instruction. And he discovered some things about power and its uses, and reinforced his beliefs about reciprocal responsibilities, whether in routine activities aboard ship or under fire in combat. His naval career also strengthened his convictions about the honoring of commitments and the moral necessity of accountability for one's views and actions.

At Corpus Christi these imperatives came together in an especially important episode of his life. He was drawn into direct-action politics, participating with blacks in a civil rights movement then rising in the area and joining other Annapolis graduates who sought to integrate the flight line at the adjoining naval base. As he told the story long after, "If you've never been a navy pilot you wouldn't have

2. "William Appleman Williams," interview by Mike Wallace in Henry Abelove, Betsy Blackmar, Peter Dimock, and Jonathan Schneer, eds., *Visions of History* (New York: Pantheon Books, 1984), p. 128. Biographical information about Williams has been reproduced in this introduction from materials in the Wallace interview, from William G. Robbins's essay in Lloyd C. Gardner, ed., *Redefining the Past: Essays in Diplomatic History in Honor of William Appleman Williams* (Corvallis: Oregon State University, 1986); "My Life in Madison," in Paul Buhle, ed., *History and the New Left: Madison, Wisconsin, 1950–1970* (Philadelphia: Temple University Press, 1990); from discussions with Jeannie Williams and Wendy Williams, and from letters and conversations between Williams and the editor during the years before his death.

any idea what heresy this is. What an outrage! To have blacks work on the engine of an airplane I'm going to fly?"[3]

The results of these agitations in Corpus Christi and at the naval air installation were predictable in the racial environment of the time. Williams was threatened several times by aggressive racists, evicted from his apartment, and harassed by the FBI. Officially reprimanded by his superior officer (who nonetheless refused to accept his protest of the forced resignation of a colleague), he was ordered transferred to Bikini Atoll in the Marshall Islands for the purpose of leading a mock amphibious exercise following a planned atomic testing in the area. But wartime injuries to his back resulting from an accident at sea and aggravated by training exercises at Corpus Christi landed him instead in several naval hospitals for more than a year. Doctors refused to allow him to be sent to Bikini or anywhere else. Even though he recuperated, Williams's back injuries troubled him periodically for the rest of his life.

The campaign in support of the rights of blacks in Corpus Christi was a major life experience for Williams. It was the moment of his political radicalization, when he was initiated into "the strategy and tactics of radical politics," and when he committed himself to "structural change as opposed to secondary reform."[4] Together with unanswered questions about America's involvement in World War II which had been troubling him, the Corpus Christi affair also raised issues in Williams's mind about the nature and purposes of American society. His enforced hospital stay of thirteen months allowed him to focus on such matters and intensified a desire for answers. He decided to turn to a study of history as the best means to make sense of his concerns. He received a medical discharge from the navy and was accepted in 1947 as a graduate student in history at the University of Wisconsin.

Madison in 1947 was an unusual place and time, and the twenty-six-year-old veteran thrived in the spirited intellectual and political atmosphere of the university and the state's capital. Attracted to Wisconsin chiefly because of the excellent reputation of its history department, he was not to be disappointed. Historians and scholars from other academic disciplines in the university introduced Williams to concepts that would shape his revisionist approach to historical study.

In addition to his own teacher and adviser Fred Harrington, the

3. "William Appleman Williams," in *Visions of History,* p. 127.
4. Williams, "My Life in Madison," p. 266.

American historians at Wisconsin (who included such prominent figures as Merle Curti, Paul Farmer, Merrill Jensen, William Best Hesseltine, Howard K. Beale, and Paul Knaplund) under whom Williams studied expected superior performance from their students. But they also encouraged them to investigate different kinds of sources and to explore new ways of evaluating history. Influenced by the legacy of an earlier generation of such "progressive" historians as Frederick Jackson Turner and Charles Austin Beard, Williams's teachers emphasized that an understanding of the past must take into account economic and social factors and their connections to politics and ideology.

It was an exhilarating learning experience, and Williams absorbed it all with great enthusiasm. No less important were his associations with graduate student colleagues, an uncommonly intelligent and intellectually daring group, many of whom would make their own mark on the historical profession in future years. Among them were Wayne Cole, Harvey Goldberg, John Higham, Jackson Turner Main (the grandson of Frederick Jackson Turner), David Shannon, Irvin Wyllie, and, at the end of Williams's graduate school years, Warren Susman. Their ongoing and often intense discussions of history, politics, and economics were carried on in a climate highly conducive to generating fresh perspectives on historical issues. Almost instinctively, Williams responded to such opportunities. Settling upon a study of American-Russian relations for his doctoral dissertation, he later acknowledged that his reservations about the reasons behind America's entry into World War II, the developing crises of the cold war, and the way in which the United States related to the world "prompted me to undertake an examination of American policy toward the Bolshevik Revolution and the Soviet Union. I was operating on an avowed argument that the study of history was relevant to our own time."[5]

When Williams was a graduate student, American diplomatic history was being written largely by "realists." The central actors determining foreign policy, according to the realist analysis, are (and should be) officials of the national state. Advocates of this perspective focus on bureaucratic decision-making, and the consequences of foreign policy are judged positively when political leaders respond to

5. "William Appleman Williams," in *Visions of History,* p. 130; Williams, *The Roots of the Modern American Empire: A Study of the Growth and Shaping of Social Consciousness in a Marketplace Society* (New York: Random House, 1969), pp. xiii–xiv.

national interests, international realities, and a correct understanding of power relationships.

Realist historians of the late 1940s and 1950s generally dismissed economic, ideological, and cultural factors in their assessments of foreign policy formulation and conduct. They also deplored the influence of domestic political pressures and public opinion (the latter usually described as uninformed or emotionally motivated), arguing that foreign policymaking ought to be left to elite decision-makers and their expert advisers. Such officials should exercise broad executive authority and resist moralistic and idealistic tendencies which, the realists said, impeded effective policymaking.

In the aftermath of World War II, members of the realist school were particularly anxious to combat any revival of prewar noninterventionism and what they regarded as insufficient awareness of dangers from communism and aggressive Soviet intentions. In their view, Americans who did not appreciate such threats and who evaded or questioned United States world power responsibilities were naive and unrealistic.[6]

Williams was not content with the realist approach to diplomatic history, nor with its definitions of national interests, and he disputed its analysis of both the nature of Soviet objectives and the motives of United States foreign policies. He wanted to explore alternative explanations for the tensions and conflicts that had come to dominate U.S.-Soviet relations. Using as a vehicle for his doctoral research the career of Raymond Robins, a social reformer and Progressive Republican who was sympathetic to Russia and thus a dissenter from policies that the United States adopted toward the Russian Revolution from its inception in 1917, Williams completed his study in 1950. He then expanded the focus back into time, situating the origins of Soviet-American antagonisms in the collision of U.S. economic expansion and tsarist Russian interests in northeast Asia at the turn of the century. The result of this historical survey was his first book.

American-Russian Relations, 1781–1947 (1952), the historian Walter

6. The realists are by no means a monolithic group of historians; they differ among themselves on many issues, including what constitutes realism, national interests, and U.S. responsibilities abroad. This brief discussion of the realists in the 1940s and 1950s reflects many of their writings during the period. George F. Kennan's *American Diplomacy, 1900–1950,* is the best known of the realist histories of the time, but historians as diverse as Thomas A. Bailey, Samuel F. Bemis, Foster Rhea Dulles, and Julius W. Pratt warned against a retreat from "world responsibilities," celebrated past examples of the uses of American power abroad, and sought to awaken Americans to the need for an activist foreign policy in the cold war.

LaFeber has pointed out, "recast our long-held and Cold War–ossified view of the entire U.S.-Russian-Soviet relationship [and] radically changed what we had been taught about American development in its crucial turn of 1890 to 1920."[7] The final chapter of Williams's book, a review of Soviet-American relations during and in the immediate aftermath of World War II, was no less controversial. In it he delivered a sharp critique of the postwar containment policy advocated by George F. Kennan, a discussion which attracted much attention and which he then extended and published as a separate essay, "A Second Look at Mr. X."

In analyzing the nature of American-Russian relations, Williams sought not only to explain American foreign policy but also to comprehend the overall meaning of America's history. To undertake this effort, he argued, the most productive method for him was to examine foreign relations. There, he maintained, the key elements defining American society in the past and present would likely reveal themselves most clearly in the way America dealt with others. From the outset, Williams rejected the traditional image of an isolationist America only reluctantly engaged in the world for a good part of its history. He vigorously challenged that view, for example, in several early essays about American foreign policy during the 1920s.[8]

He also reiterated the point that doing history was a way of integrating human experience, a perspective that was characteristic of the historical training he received at Wisconsin but which he formulated in his own way. Sometime later, in 1973, in an essay he called "Confessions of an Intransigent Revisionist," Williams elaborated his approach to researching and explaining history or, as he phrased it, "the process of choosing how I would make sense out of the world."[9] Acknowledging intellectual debts to Baruch Spinoza, Karl Marx, and Wilhelm Dilthey, Williams offered the view that society functions as an organic whole in which seemingly unconnected parts are in fact related to one another. People, he argued, act on the basis of how they perceive the parts both separately and in an ongoing relationship to one another within the whole. From Spinoza, Williams said, he had acquired ideas about organic unity; from Marx, insights about the relationships between ideological, political,

7. Walter LaFeber, Remarks at a Conference to Honor William Appleman Williams, Washington, D.C., June 1990 (copy of text in editor's possession).

8. See, for example, "The Legend of Isolationism in the 1920s," reprinted in this collection.

9. Williams, "Confessions of an Intransigent Revisionist," *Socialist Review,* 17 (September–October 1973), 93.

and economic factors that shape the historical process in specific time periods; from Dilthey, the late-nineteenth-century German philosopher-historian whose systematic interpretation of human experience stressed a comprehensive vision of knowledge, he derived the concept of a world-view, *Weltanschauung*, in which the Spinozist-Marxist assumption that "everything is internally related to everything else" operates to develop, sustain, modify, or alter the arrangement and structure formed by the individual parts and elements of existing reality. From this vantage point, then, the task was to explore how distinct elements of a historical event or development could together reveal the dynamic relationships of the reality in which they occurred. "Reality is not an issue of economics versus ideas, or of politics versus either," Williams contended. "Reality instead involves how a political act is also an economic act, of how an economic decision is a political choice, or of how an idea of freedom involves a commitment to a particular economic system."[1]

In that ultimate sense of things, knowledge ceases to be artificially segmented, reality becomes whole, and the way in which persons view the world can be understood. Men made decisions and acted according to their perceptions of reality, Williams insisted. "The issue has always been not whether they thought, but how and what they thought."[2] From this point of departure, stressing the significance of ideas shaped by interacting and intersecting political, economic, and cultural factors, Williams launched his revisionist reconstructions of American history. The most significant of them disputed existing interpretations of American foreign relations.

Williams's formulations carried him along, but also beyond, routes traveled by Charles A. Beard. Williams found impressive Beard's writings about the economic aspects of national affairs and the ethics of power politics even while differing with Beard's views in other respects. Williams denied, as had Beard, that foreign policy enjoys an existence separate from the economic and political system in which it develops and functions, or that policymakers conceive and execute foreign policy in a hermetically sealed, value-free environment unaffected by ideological commitments and economic interests.[3]

1. *Ibid.*, p. 94.

2. Williams, "A Profile of the Corporate Elite," in Ronald Radosh and Murray Rothbard, eds., *A New History of the Leviathan: Essays on the Rise of the Corporate State* (New York: E. P. Dutton, 1972), pp. 1–2.

3. See Williams's discussion of Beard in "A Note on Charles Austin Beard's Search for a General Theory of Causation," *American Historical Review,* LXII (October 1955), 59–80, and, reprinted in this volume, "Charles Austin Beard: The Intellectual as Tory-Radical," in Harvey Goldberg, ed., *American Radicals: Some Problems and Personalities* (New York: Monthly Review Press, 1957).

In the book that became the most widely read and probably the most influential of his published works, *The Tragedy of American Diplomacy* (1959), Williams claimed that the United States had embraced an expansionist, imperial foreign policy. It had done so because urban industrial corporate and political leaders at the end of the nineteenth century believed that national well-being required markets abroad for goods and capital and reliable access to raw materials in order to sustain the nation's developing industrial system. American imperialism was not, as most historians had previously suggested, an aberration or the result of an emotionally charged, psychically driven public forcing reluctant officials on a course of action they would otherwise have spurned. Americans endorsed expansion, Williams declared, because they believed overseas interests would satisfy their domestic needs and aspirations. He argued that such views were reinforced by ideas about the past that linked American democracy and prosperity to an expansion of America's frontiers across the continent. The most significant expression of this view in the 1890s—though by no means the only one—was articulated by the leading American historian of his generation, Frederick Jackson Turner, and by Brooks Adams, brother of the more famous Henry Adams, whose ideas and influence Williams first analyzed in an essay, "The Frontier Thesis and American Foreign Policy" (1955), before incorporating the discussions into the text of *The Tragedy of American Diplomacy* four years later.

In Williams's judgment, the frontier expansionist outlook became the source of perceived solutions to domestic crises and of programs and actions designed to meet the crises. The outcome of this process was the Open Door policy, conceptualized at the turn of the century as a means of assuring overseas markets. Describing it as "a brilliant strategic stroke" which sought to avoid the complications, burdens, and risks of traditional colonialism, Williams portrayed the Open Door as nonetheless imperial in nature, a policy that "led to the gradual extension of American economic and political power throughout the world." The Open Door concept "integrated and formalized the frontier thesis, the specific demands of businessmen, workers, and farmers, and the theory which asserted that the American economic system would stagnate if it did not expand overseas.... When combined with the ideology of an industrial Manifest Destiny, the history of the Open Door Notes became the history of American foreign relations in the twentieth century."[4]

4. Williams, *The Tragedy of American Diplomacy* (Cleveland: World Publishing, 1959), pp. 34–35, 38–40.

In subsequent writings, including later editions of *Tragedy,* Williams emphasized that "American imperialism was not forced on the majority by a domestic elite, any more than it was imposed on the country by outside forces or foreign nations." Many if not most Americans, he contended, "possessed the firm conviction, even dogmatic belief that America's domestic well-being depends upon sustained, ever increasing economic expansion." Success reinforced the ideology; failure only dictated the need for a more vigorous effort to make it work. Many Americans could and did benefit from the success of the system, Williams affirmed, but they did so at the expense of their democratic heritage and the welfare of the society as a whole.[5]

He deplored the "powerful and dangerous propensity to define the essentials of American welfare in terms of activities outside the United States." Doing so, he warned, resulted first of all in "an indifference toward, or a neglect of internal developments." Second, the "tendency to externalize the sources or causes of good things leads... to an even greater inclination to explain the lack of the good life by blaming it on foreign individuals, groups, and nations. This kind of externalizing evil serves not only to antagonize the outsiders but further intensifies the American determination to make them over in the proper manner or simply push them out of the way."[6]

When it first appeared, *The Tragedy of American Diplomacy* was ignored or damned by most reviewers. Critics charged that Williams was obsessed with economic explanations. Adolf A. Berle, Jr., a member of the elite corporate, political community Williams had discussed in his work, called *Tragedy* "brilliantly done," a book "that must be regarded with respect." But, Berle went on to say, "wrong is the apparent assumption that America could well have developed otherwise, and [Williams's] complete acceptance of economic determinism."[7] Other reviewers echoed Berle's objections and condemned Williams's imperialist characterization of American expansion.

Williams did not deny that he had accented the role of economic considerations in fueling America's expansionist drives. He had done so, he said, because in his view the integrative ideology of marketplace capitalism was central to the politics, economics, culture, and psychology of the society. Americans had come to identify their

5. Williams, *Tragedy* (1962), p. 11; (1972), p. 15; Williams, *Roots of the Modern American Empire,* p. 5.

6. Williams, *Tragedy* (1972), p. 15.

7. Adolf A. Berle review of *The Tragedy of American Diplomacy* in *New York Times Book Review,* February 15, 1959, pp. 3, 22.

freedom, security, and success with the continuing growth of the capitalist system. Whether this took the form of territorial acquisition (seldom the case after the 1890s) or of an informal empire constructed by means of the Open Door policy (the typical outcome in the twentieth century), the result was imperial behavior. The United States found itself opposing societies that resisted America's attempt to impose its power and its view of the world upon them. The effort, he said, had also led to war. The tragedy of American diplomacy, Williams averred, was that in its pursuit of freedom through empire, America violated its own avowed ideals, risking the destruction of others and its own ruin.

Yet Williams was not quite the determinist many of his detractors accused him of being. He did not so clearly attribute America's imperial expansionist career to a foreordained, inevitable consequence of capitalist requirements. Rather, he focused on the convictions of the nation's leaders and citizens who believed in the necessity of empire. He argued, therefore, that Americans should and could change their outlook and behavior—in direct and ironic contrast, for example, to Berle, who had denied that America could have developed differently or presumably that it should change. In contrast, Williams advocated a "radical but noncommunist reconstruction of American society," a cause he advanced with increasing fervor in his future writings.

In *Tragedy*, Williams also brought his interpretation of the Open Door policy into the period of World War II, a conflict he discussed as "the war for the American frontier." Buoyed by victory over its adversaries at the end of the global struggle, but haunted by the specter of renewed depression and a world once again susceptible to disorder, revolution, and war, American leaders "saw the future in terms of continued open-door expansion," according to Williams, "and embarked upon a program to force the Soviet Union to accept America's traditional conception of itself and the world." That kind of foreign policy, Williams observed, would not only meet with a likely Soviet resistance but also ran the danger of a devastating military confrontation. "Another effort to stabilize the world as an American frontier will," he warned, "very likely lead to a nuclear war."[8]

Clearly a reaction to the cold war policies of the United States, Williams's treatment of the origins and character of the Soviet-American confrontation attempted to counter the dominant view of

8. Williams, *Tragedy* (1959), pp. 150, 210.

Soviet expansionist designs. While he did not deny Russian acts of repression in Eastern Europe (or, for that matter, in the Soviet Union itself), Williams depicted a Soviet Union distinctly inferior to the United States at the conclusion of World War II. He stressed the defensive and limited nature of Soviet policies toward the West. The United States had not alone begun the cold war, he conceded, but it bore the major responsibility for the dangerous and costly way in which it had developed and was continuing, including the extension of the conflict into the rest of the world where America sought acceptance of its version of order.

Defenders of American cold war policies quarreled with Williams's interpretations of Soviet motives and actions and United States intentions and uses of power. But the arguments and issues he and other cold war revisionists introduced (often while disagreeing among themselves) ignited and energized debate over the origins of the historic encounter and over the fundamental purposes and consequences of United States interests and actions in the world.

In a passionate conclusion to *Tragedy*, Williams called upon the United States to take the lead in deescalating the cold war and to abandon the Open Door policy and the *Weltanschauung* that had given rise to it. The problem, as he defined it, was "how to sustain democracy and prosperity without imperial expansion." As a first step he recommended a disengagement from confrontation with the Soviet Union, China, and other communist nations, a strategy he believed would encourage reform within those societies. He urged the adoption of new programs and policies which would permit the United States to cooperate with the world instead of trying to Americanize it. Doing so, he concluded, would orient American foreign policy toward helping other peoples to realize their own identity in their own way. "The essence of such a foreign policy would be an Open Door for revolutions...and Americans would no longer find it necessary to embark upon crusades to save others."[9] Far from advocating an isolationist foreign policy as a prescription, Williams was instead proposing a different kind of relationship with the world based upon an alternative vision of America itself.

By the time he completed *The Tragedy of American Diplomacy* in 1959, Williams had returned to the University of Wisconsin as a faculty member after teaching at Washington and Jefferson College, Ohio State University, and the University of Oregon. At Wisconsin

9. Williams, *Tragedy* (1959), p. 210–212.

he succeeded his teacher, Fred Harrington, who had entered university administration.

Williams established his national reputation as a radical historian during the eleven years (1957–1968) he spent at Madison. The setting helped him attain such a distinction. At the time Wisconsin was one of a handful of universities and colleges in the country employing radical teachers. The commitment to high intellectual standards on the campus and a progressive tradition in the community, which Williams had experienced as a graduate student nearly a decade earlier, still prevailed. In a period of growing political and social turmoil and dissent throughout the country, Madison quickly became a center of activity in the civil rights and anti–Vietnam War movements in which students, faculty, and community residents participated.

Williams took an active role in these activities. And he began to draw into his courses more and more students, most of whom left his lectures perplexed or stunned by interpretations of American foreign relations different from any they had heard or read before. Lloyd Gardner and Walter LaFeber, his teaching assistants at the time, recalled how Williams forced students to think about history in a different way, "from a broader perspective and more critical in context." An undergraduate remembered years later that Williams's "impact was enormous.... [He] made history come alive."[1]

Graduate students were also attracted to him. Together with some who had begun their work under his predecessor, about thirty-five completed their Ph.D's under Williams's direction. They earned a reputation nationally as the Wisconsin School of Diplomatic History. Several of the graduate students also played a key role in creating an innovative radical journal, *Studies on the Left,* which began publication in 1959. As two of its editors noted, *Studies on the Left* "was both a product of the disenchantment with the old left and a forerunner and participant of the new."[2] Its scholarly articles examined American political and economic institutions and ideology and offered analyses of American history, society, and foreign policy. When it moved from Madison to New York City in 1963, *Studies on the Left* extended its influence considerably beyond the intellectual boundaries of the University of Wisconsin, affecting the development of

1. Robbins, "Doing History Is Best of All...," in Gardner, *Redefining the Past,* p. 11; Nina Serrano, "A Madison Bohemian," in Buhle, *History and the New Left,* p. 82.
2. James Weinstein and David W. Eakins, eds., *For a New America: Essays in History and Politics from 'Studies on the Left,' 1959–1967* (New York: Vintage Books, 1970), p. 6.

radical scholarship and politics and attracting articles from across the country and abroad. Williams disclaimed a major role in its affairs, but his own work clearly inspired its creation and much of its focus.

Two years after *Studies on the Left* appeared, Williams completed *The Contours of American History* (1961), in which he linked the sources of American expansion to the nation's capitalist development. The book was both a broad overview and a searching critique of how American elites had struggled with the problems and possibilities of national development. Williams began this survey by exploring the nature of British mercantilism, a system of nation-state regulation and restraint of the political economy for the common good. Adapting and modifying traditions derived from the mother country, he explained, Americans ushered in their own "Age of Mercantilism, 1740–1828." In turn it was succeeded—subverted, in Williams's view—by "The Age of Laissez-Nous Faire, 1819–1896." Commitments to the general welfare gave way to avaricious individualism, with an increasing reliance on expansion as the certain means of resolving internal contradictions and conflicts. The "new reality" and the dynamics of expansion, however, also provoked a terrible civil war, and in its aftermath new ideas began to transform the old order.

In response to the challenges and crises of a rapidly industrializing society, Americans developed the programs and institutions of the "Age of Corporation Capitalism" of the current period. Its galaxy of ruling groups, increasingly identified with the culture of the large corporation, created a system dedicated to enlarging economic growth and insuring a political order sustained by overseas expansion.

As he had in *The Tragedy of American Diplomacy,* Williams argued that "frontier expansionism" was both a dangerous "gate of escape" and a false avenue for the fulfillment of America's promise. "The central question facing Americans in the second half of the 20th Century," he declared, was "could they define their existence without recourse to the expanding frontier that had formerly provided them with the private property they used to prove their existence?" Williams replied affirmatively but did so by challenging Americans to transform the existing system into a new reality. It was a morally charged vision inspired by the early twentieth-century American socialist Eugene V. Debs. Debs, Williams submitted, "understood that expansion was a running away, the kind of escape that was destructive of the dignity of men," and had advocated instead "the creation of a socialist commonwealth." Williams now pursued Debs's dream into the late twentieth century. Americans, he proclaimed, "have the chance to create the first truly democratic socialism in the world."[3]

This, as Williams very well knew, was a highly unlikely event anytime soon, if only because most Americans believed in and accepted the system under which they lived. But in *Contours* he called attention to those earlier American leaders who he said had at least attempted to build "a community—a commonwealth—based on private property without relying on imperial expansion."[4] These individuals had tried to honor the system and make it work better by using its power more fairly and equitably. Men like Jonathan Edwards, Henry Clay, John Quincy Adams, Charles Evans Hughes, and Herbert Hoover were the kind of people Williams was talking about. In the course of researching and writing *The Tragedy of American Diplomacy* and *The Contours of American History,* he reevaluated their place in the nation's past. Many of them were conservatives, and several, in particular Hoover, had been harshly criticized in traditional historical accounts. None, Williams admitted, were without faults; all had accumulated failures. But, he insisted, they had confronted the system in which they lived and had attempted to improve it, and their efforts must be taken seriously.

Hoover, especially, attracted Williams's attention. One suspects this was partly because he was the perfect foil to the kind of liberal hypocrisy and imperial behavior Williams decried. "Hoover," he announced, "was against the Empire," a capitalist leader who "knew the system better than *any* other President" and saw the need "to overcome the classic inequities of capitalism without at the same time moving toward fascism or bureaucratic statism."[5]

Williams's often startling estimates of individuals like Hoover contrasted sharply to his appraisals of other American heroes whose ideas and performances he judged in far more negative terms. Thomas Jefferson and Andrew Jackson were attacked for their undelivered promises, aggrandizements, and transgressions. So were those among the abolitionists who, Williams argued, had viewed blacks as inferior human beings and who had failed to offer a plan for dealing with the results of emancipation, leaving freed slaves to

3. Williams, *The Contours of American History* (Cleveland: World Publishing, 1961), pp. 477, 487–488.
4. *Ibid.,* p. 485.
5. Williams, *Some Presidents: From Wilson to Nixon* (New York: Vintage Books, 1972), pp. 39, 45–46.

the mercies of an exploitative, inequitable, laissez-faire economic system. He also criticized Lincoln (increasingly so in later writings) because he seriously doubted Lincoln's commitment to self-determination. Added to the Great Emancipator's opposition to black equality, this defect diminished his reputation for Williams.

The giants of twentieth-century liberalism scarcely fared better. Williams condemned the political manipulations, duplicities, and consolidations of power by Woodrow Wilson and Franklin D. Roosevelt. Most of all, he denounced FDR's abuses in the conduct of foreign policy. Like Beard, Williams faulted Roosevelt for failing the moral tests of leadership, deceiving and lying to the public about the directions he was taking the nation in the years before America's entry into World War II. That course of events illustrated for Williams the resumption of a shift by the United States: from the use of economic power to increasing reliance upon military means as the way of defending America's system and expanding it into the world.

Whether he was examining the makers or critics of American society, Williams concentrated largely on elites in the system. He recognized that in foreign affairs the elites had made and executed policy since the late nineteenth century, testimony to the concentration of decision-making in the hands of urban corporate centers of power. But when he wrote *The Roots of the Modern American Empire* (1969), Williams—in what amounted to a modification of his earlier views—traced the dynamics of America's expansionist commitment to another source as well. During the nineteenth century, he now observed, it was the agricultural majority, the farm businessmen and their spokesmen, who in their search for markets had generated the expansionist imperial outlook that was accepted at the turn of the century by urban industrial leaders who were consolidating their dominion over the political economy. The imperial consensus thus created was carried into the twentieth century by means of the Open Door policy. The decision to pursue empire, Williams argued, could have been avoided if the agricultural majority and urban leaders had chosen differently.

Choosing differently, Williams believed, was now an urgent need. United States imperial actions in the second half of the twentieth century were becoming more extensive, expensive, and destructive because of American opposition to revolutions. He angrily disapproved, for example, of America's hostile policy toward the Cuban revolution, devoting one book-length indictment, *The United States,*

Cuba, and Castro (1962), to the subject. Writing in the aftermath of the failed Bay of Pigs invasion of 1961, Williams appealed to a conservative tradition of placing limits on empire. He dedicated the book, "From an American radical... to the memory of the most challenging conservative of them all: John Quincy Adams" who, as secretary of state more than a century earlier, had alerted Americans to the dangers and great costs of continued interventionism.

Fifteen years after the book on U.S.-Cuban relations, when he published *America Confronts a Revolutionary World, 1776–1976* (1977), Williams was voicing anguish as well as anger over America's assaults on revolutions in such places as Guatemala, Iran, Indonesia, Vietnam, and Chile. He was, he said, "weary under the burden of my knowledge of my country's dishonoring its once noble commitment to the right of self-determination." He had also come to lower his expectations that conservatives would reclaim the tradition. American conservatism had declined. Hoover, he lamented, had been "the last great conservative to honor the bedrock principle of self-determination." The former president knew "that crusades to self-determine other peoples in our image involved the fundamental denial of that ideal." Conservatives had not, Williams regretted, acted upon that kind of knowledge during the agony of the Vietnam War, and he saw little likelihood that they would do so now.[6]

Williams therefore reaffirmed his commitment to grass-roots citizen action aimed at fundamental structural change and the reshaping of existing institutions. He appealed to Americans of all political persuasions to acknowledge the truth of their imperial past, to repudiate empire, and to begin the task of creating an alternative world. Communal visions dominated the prescriptions of his later writings in which he stressed themes of decentralization, self-determination, and a redistribution of power from the state to regionally organized, democratically functioning communities. The vision was in the tradition of Greek membership in a *polis,* a small political community. The time had come. Williams implored, for "a sustained effort to organize a social movement dedicated to replacing the American Empire with a federation of regional communities. No euphemisms and no talk about reform. The objective is to create a federation of democratic socialist communities."[7]

This proposal for decentralized democratic socialism was an ideal

6. Williams, *America Confronts a Revolutionary World, 1776–1976* (New York: William Morrow, 1976), pp. 178, 180.

7. *Ibid.,* pp. 193–194.

that refined and elaborated ideas Williams first considered while attending a seminar on socialist economics for five months at Leeds University in England, when he was still a graduate student. He developed the concept as an essential ingredient of his alternative to Open Door imperialism and to the egoistic, avaricious, and dehumanizing character of marketplace capitalism he found so unacceptable.

This character of capitalism he addressed in *The Great Evasion* (1964), in which he asked readers to contemplate the contemporary relevance of Karl Marx's critique of capitalism to an understanding of the American capitalist ethos. In a controversial reading of Marx (in which he stressed the Kantian influences in Marx's philosophical writings) much disputed by Marxist scholars, Williams purposefully omitted a discussion of class formations and class conflict in applying Marx's insights to America. He concentrated on Marx's elaborations of the human and material costs of capitalism, the repressive character of capitalist expansion abroad (and the domestic sacrifices such expansion entailed), and the increasing alienation, misery, and antisocial behavior of individuals living in a capitalist system. Marx's analysis was thus relevant to America, Williams reasoned, because of his acute understanding that while capitalism created "a system of political economy and a society," it had failed to create an "ethical and equitable human community," precisely what Williams charged was missing in twentieth-century America.[8]

His alternative, the decentralized community, had as its basic premise a striving for quality rather than quantity of life. Williams was frank to say that the pursuit of affluence must be sharply curtailed if not altogether abandoned. He directed his message not only to liberals whose solutions to America's problems—increasing growth rates and more sophisticated global management—he rejected. He was also addressing radicals whom he accused of being "hooked on quantity of life as bad as anybody."[9] The left, he declared, had to rethink its own values, agendas, and commitments, not to mention strategies and tactics for effecting change.

Late in the 1960s, in the midst of frustrated opposition to the Vietnam War and increased domestic upheavals, Williams became

8. Williams, *The Great Evasion: An Essay on the Contemporary Relevance of Karl Marx and on the Wisdom of Admitting the Heretic into the Dialogue About America's Future* (Chicago: Quadrangle Books, 1964), pp. 124, 176. For an example of a leftist critique of Williams's interpretation of Marx, see Eugene D. Genovese, "William A. Williams on Marx and America," *Studies on the Left*, 6 (January-February 1966), 70–86.

9. "William Appleman Williams," in *Visions of History*, p. 139.

disenchanted with many in the New Left, protesting a number of their actions which he believed contradicted and damaged efforts to change American society and the nature of United States relations with the world. He especially deplored "random nonsocial violence" as self-defeating and was disturbed when members of the New Left "tried to *impose* [their] consciousness on the rest of society through what [they] considered 'vanguard' actions in a crisis situation."[1]

Clearly, more than a matter of style was involved. Williams opposed political behavior that he believed diminished possibilities for creating a general social consciousness, fragmented organizational and programmatic efforts, and ruptured the kind of inclusive, democratic coalition-building he felt was necessary even to begin to imagine changing the system. A new and different idea of freedom, he wrote in the last lines of *The Roots of the Modern American Empire* in 1969, "must be inclusive.... It is essential for radicals to devise workable plans and procedures for decentralization that will enable all of us to realize a richer and more creative conception of freedom." He did not think that radicals in the New Left had begun to do this, and their failure to do so during the late 1960s, he believed, had cost them the support of many. "I think it was we who lost them, instead of them abandoning us."[2]

In 1968 Williams left the University of Wisconsin to join the history department at Oregon State University in Corvallis. Personal and professional reasons accounted for his move. He had more than fulfilled his obligations to the training of graduate students and wished to devote more time and energy to undergraduate instruction. Oregon State had no graduate program in history, and the attraction of a less demanding professional career and of being able to live on the Oregon coast, sixty miles from Corvallis, greatly appealed to him. Among other advantages, the migration to Oregon put him and his family in touch with a more diversified community, something that had become increasingly difficult to achieve in Madison.

At Oregon State Williams quickly and conspicuously became involved in university affairs. He was particularly active in trying to improve the quality of undergraduate teaching and in expanding the university's humanities program by helping to develop interdiscipli-

1. Williams, "My Life in Madison," pp. 270–271.
2. Williams, *Roots of the Modern American Empire*, p. 452; Williams, "My Life in Madison," p. 270.

nary courses and establish a humanities center. Outside of the
university he delivered numerous lectures, participated in community
forums, and, in the early 1980s, began to write weekly and then
biweekly newspaper columns on current issues for two of the state's
larger newspapers, the *Salem Statesman-Journal* and the *Portland
Oregonian*.[3] He also published several more books, including a
twentieth-century history textbook, *Americans in a Changing World*
(1978).

In 1980 Williams wrote *Empire as a Way of Life*, his last major
effort. It was also the year in which he was elected president of the
Organization of American Historians (OAH), the leading professional association for teachers and scholars of United States history.
Both the book and the presidency of the OAH served as platforms
for his continuing efforts to raise historical consciousness, build
community, and reach beyond the historical profession to engage
others in the work of history.

Williams's ambitious plans in these regards as head of the OAH
went mostly unfulfilled, though some ideas and initiatives were
implemented in the decade following his one-year term in office. His
election as president of the traditionally staid organization, however,
reflected the change in his professional status. Gradually his work
had become recognized, albeit far more favorably abroad than in the
United States. He had achieved respectability if only because the
force of his ideas ultimately compelled historians to confront them.
While his sweeping revisionist framework and his morally charged
assertions often provoked controversy, his views had come to occupy
a central place in historiographical debates. What's more, they had
inspired a large body of revisionist and neorevisionist literature,
some of it couched in the parameters of his interpretations but much
of it beyond them.

A careful reading of his work shows that over time Williams
himself refined or changed some of his own revisions. He allowed,
for example, that American efforts to advance an Open Door world
order involved strategic, political, and cultural considerations as well
as economic drives, something he had never actually disputed, and a
more inclusive perspective accepted by many revisionists including
those influenced by him. In ascribing a singularity of purpose to
America's world outlook (regardless of disagreement about which
motive was controlling at any given time), Williams had successfully
punctured historical myths of American innocence, isolationism

3. Robbins, "Doing History Is Best of All...," pp. 16–17.

(especially between the two world wars), disinterested and altruistic behavior, and a purely reactive foreign policy. But in so doing he sometimes claimed too much for his interpretations of particular documents and events. The effect was to minimize differences among those making policy or seeking to influence the conduct of domestic and foreign affairs, even when those differences were tactical and might produce different, though perhaps unintended, consequences.

Williams could also be faulted, as he was constantly, for holding the United States chiefly responsible for America's involvements and conflicts abroad. This indictment carried with it the additional criticism that he depreciated real external threats against proclaimed American interests. Both accusations were true—and both missed or preferred to ignore the central point of Williams's approach to America and to its history.

He was, when it came down to it, intensely American in wishing the United States to honor cherished ideals which he believed the nation had not fulfilled for much of its history and could not achieve as an imperial capitalistic society. Throughout all his writings, none excepted, Williams asked why America had behaved as it had, whether its actions had truly been necessary, whether earlier policy conceptions—whatever their merits or success—were any longer realistic, beneficial, and, above all, morally justified. He passionately reaffirmed his dedication, as a historian and as a citizen, to "freedom and equality *within a community*" and unequivocally rejected the idea "that such a commitment can only be established by perpetual outrage against the faults of other societies.... I do not approve of imperial actions by Russia *or* by Israel, and I do not approve of repression in Brazil *or* in France; but," he maintained, "most of all I like them least by and in my own America."[4]

His concerns were thus with his own country. Most threats to America were exaggerated, he contended, and replies to them were far more dangerous and costly to America than the threats themselves. More fundamentally, he rejected the "imperial way of life" which had given rise to perceived interests abroad. A definition of democracy and freedom that relied on empire for its success was simply unrealistic and unacceptable to him. He disputed the relationship and urged its dissolution in favor of "community as a way of

4. Williams, "Confessions of an Intransigent Revisionist," p. 92.

life."[5] Not to do so, he feared, would lead to more tragedy, perhaps even nuclear catastrophe. In the last decade of his life Williams increasingly framed the issue in terms of the ethics and uses of power.

"The questions of how one acquires power, and the purposes for which one uses power, are at the center of our individual morality and our public virtue," he declared in 1986. He developed this theme through an interest he cultivated in comparative maritime history while living in Oregon. Citing fourteenth- and fifteenth-century China as an example of a society that had said no to imperial behavior even while possessing the power to engage in it, he observed that "the Chinese never used force to create a territorial or ideological empire" and instead had chosen an alternative vision for defining its existence and meaning.[6]

To the end of his life Williams advocated an alternative vision for America, an ever more insistent objective in view of the capacity for massive destruction held by the world's proliferating nuclear powers. True, he overstated in alarmist terms the prospects of nuclear war between the United States and the Soviet Union. And his proposals for a Soviet-American accommodation rather than a continuing strategy of containment were a lost cause before Mikhail Gorbachev rose to power.

But Williams and other critics of containment had not been wrong in calling attention to the enormous costs endured by their own country and other societies in waging the cold war. Whatever role America's foreign policies played in weakening the Soviet Union, it was Gorbachev and his allies who took the initiative in confronting the failures of *their* empire, and who set out to dismantle it in a vain hope of preserving the Soviet Union itself. And it was they who sought a new relationship with the United States. While American leaders and the media celebrated Gorbachev's actions as tantamount to surrender and a victory for the United States, the ex-leader of the now dissolved Soviet Union may have been closer to the truth when he recently concluded that both sides had lost the cold war.

William Appleman Williams was, however, less concerned with cold war victories or national superiority than with what Americans

5. Williams, *Empire as a Way of Life; An Essay on the Causes and Character of America's Present Predicament Along with a Few Thoughts About an Alternative* (New York: Oxford University Press, 1980), p. 213.

6. Williams, "Thoughts on the Comparative Uses of Power," George Bancroft Lecture, United States Naval Academy, September 1986, pp. 2, 6.

intended to do about the nation's conduct of its own affairs. It was perhaps fitting that his last essay, "The Annapolis Crowd" (1987), completed three years before his death from cancer, employed the example of the Naval Academy from which he had begun his excursions and commitments more than forty years before. Denouncing the Iran-Contra affair "which, far more than Watergate, created a fundamental threat to constitutional government in the United States," Williams condemned in particular the activities of naval officers Oliver North, John Poindexter, Robert McFarlane, and James Webb who played "central roles" in the operation. They had, he said, "confused loyalty with honor." They had failed "the tradition of an officer of the line and a gentleman." They had misused and abused the responsibilities of power. They had not said no and had transgressed their public duty to uphold the Naval Academy's doctrine of commitment to "honor, uprightness, and truth." They had violated the community by their imperial and imperious behavior. Williams asked and wanted Americans to do otherwise, applying doctrines of the moral use of power and public virtue to "the entire culture—civilians as well as the military."[7] He was, to the end, the revisionist historian speaking to the truth of community.

7. Williams, "The Annapolis Crowd," August 1987, pp. 5, 8.

A William Appleman Williams Reader

THE BIRTH OF
CONTAINMENT

[from *American-Russian Relations, 1781–1947*, 1952]

In 1917, the third year of World War I, Russia experienced two revolutions within eight months. The March Revolution, occurring only weeks before the United States entered the war, overthrew the tsar and established a Provisional Government, essentially liberal and bourgeois in character, which committed itself to continue the war against the Central Powers. This decision was strongly opposed by the radical Bolsheviks who were gaining support and who sought an immediate cessation of the war, if necessary by means of a separate peace treaty with Russia's enemies.

The United States welcomed the March Revolution and initially responded favorably to the Provisional Government, urging it to go on fighting the war and to crush the Bolshevik opposition. But confidence sagged in the ability of Alexander Kerensky, who became the leader of the Provisional Government in July 1917, to achieve American objectives, and Washington soon became indifferent to prospects for the survival of the regime. Kerensky was indeed weak, unable or unwilling to prosecute the war successfully, and U.S. officials believed he was allowing the Bolsheviks to gain strength and influence. American policymakers increasingly looked to other, more conservative, forces to "save Russia."

This policy was resisted by Raymond Robins, who was an important member of the American Red Cross Commission in Russia. Nominally a private relief agency distributing medicine, food, and other humanitarian aid to victims of war and revolution, the Red Cross Commission was promoted and financed by individuals closely associated with the House of Morgan. The investment firm held significant commercial interests in Russia as well as a substantial monetary stake in the Allied war cause.

Hoping to use its relief activities as a means of strengthening the

Provisional Government and preventing a Russian withdrawal from the war that would weaken or defeat the chances for an Allied victory, the Red Cross Commission secured the reluctant permission of President Woodrow Wilson to undertake its humanitarian and political assignment and arrived in Russia in August 1917. Once there, as Williams recounts, Robins tried in vain to win renewed U.S. support for Kerensky and to forestall a Bolshevik takeover. Robins encouraged Kerensky to preempt the Bolsheviks by redistributing land to the peasants, a recommendation most unwelcome to American officials and unfulfilled by the Provisional Government.

After the successful Bolshevik seizure of power in the November Revolution, Robins worked with Colonel William V. Judson, an American military attaché, to secure U.S. recognition of the new Soviet government in hopes of influencing the Bolsheviks (renamed Communists in March 1918) to remain in the war and creating a future relationship with Russia. But American foreign policy leaders were against the Bolshevik Revolution from the start, Williams argued, because of its radical nature and its challenge to Wilsonian visions of international order.

Refusal to deal with the Bolshevik leaders in 1917, as Robins and Judson advocated, was followed instead by American aid to counter-revolutionaries opposed to the Bolsheviks and by Allied military intervention in 1918. In Williams's view, the American response to the revolution at its inception created mutual distrust and generated tensions that seeded the bitter antagonisms of the cold war after World War II.

Any movement [against the Bolsheviks]...should be encouraged even though its success is only a possibility.

Secretary of State Lansing, December, 1917

The poorest service that can be rendered Russians by Americans, whether in Russia or at home, is to lose hope in her future, to stupidly and blindly turn back.

Raymond Robins, September, 1917

WASHINGTON was bewildered, confused, and angered by the Bolshevik coup. Rather than shake itself awake and come to grips with reality, the Administration at first tried to ignore the existence of Lenin's government. But the failure of the counterattacks by Kerensky[1] and the Moscow Committee of Safety indicated that the Bolsheviks could not be wished away. Yet the policy ultimately formulated by Washington was based in part on the assumption that Lenin would miraculously disappear, and that the Soviet Government would—because it should—collapse. The main points of American policy were quickly evolved and implemented. They were, moreover, consciously formulated.

These cornerstones were: (1) as long as the Bolsheviks remained in power the United States would refuse to establish normal intercourse and would under no circumstances recognize Lenin's government; (2) Washington would do all in its power to aid any serious and conservative leader or group whose aim was the destruction of the Soviet Government. The origins of this policy were obscured by publicity that presented Russia's withdrawal from the war as the product of Lenin's role as a German agent. The de-emphasis, almost to the point of exclusion, of Russia's economic collapse made it possible to type the Bolsheviks as unscrupulous representatives of German militarism. But in fact none of the policy makers based their antagonism to the Soviet Government on this argument. Their basic motivation was an intense opposition to what they considered an effort "to make the ignorant and incapable mass of humanity dominant in the earth"; and a steadfast refusal to admit the hard fact that the Russian Revolution of November, 1917, was a revolution—not a parliamentary election—or recognize the reality of the Bolsheviks' seizure of power, or to acknowledge that Lenin would not stand by and theorize about his defeat.

The sources of American policy are of especial significance when considered in relation to the armed intervention of the United States in Russia, both European and Siberian. For American intervention in Russia is usually explained as a move designed solely to forestall Japanese expansion in Manchuria and Siberia. Yet this analysis of the origins of intervention is gravely misleading. True, Washington did oppose Tokyo's efforts to exploit both American preoccupation in Europe and Russia's weakness during World War I; but to account for American intervention in Russia on that ground alone is to evade

1. Alexander Kerensky, minister of justice and then minister of war in the Russian Provisional Government headed by Prince Georgii Lvov and established by the Russian Duma in the aftermath of the March 1917 revolution which overthrew the tsar. On July 20, 1917, Prince Lvov resigned and was succeeded as prime minister by Kerensky who served until the Bolshevik Revolution in November of the same year.—ED.

the question of why Washington did not collaborate with Lenin, who took the initiative to seek an alliance with the United States for the specific purpose of opposing Japan. Instead, the United States delayed intervention until the Wilson administration found a Russian to support who was not only anti-Japanese but also anti-Bolshevik. Indeed, the search for an acceptable anti-Bolshevik—Admiral Aleksander Kolchak was finally chosen—was the factor that delayed American intervention from February to July, 1918.

This basic anti-Bolshevik character of intervention underlies, in turn, the failure of the United States to collaborate with the Soviet Union against Japanese expansion from 1920 to 1922, during Tokyo's invasion of Manchuria in 1931, and later, when Japan began to wage hostilities against China in 1937. For the corollary of Washington's opposition to the Soviet Union's economic and social programs was the old pre-World War I American policy of attempting to secure supremacy in Manchuria through economic penetration under the open-door policy. And though publicly explaining its actions as steps taken to help China against both Japan and the Soviet Union, Washington actually sought to assume control of the Chinese Eastern Railway. In the attempt, as will be seen, the United States even tried to deny China the right to participate in joint operation of the line.

Formulated in the first months of 1918, this policy of antagonism to Soviet Russia had three other important results. Any and all efforts to emphasize the national problems faced by the Bolsheviks in the early days of their rule—considerations which would restrict and modify the application of their theoretical program—were automatically discounted and ignored. Instead, antagonism led to intervention, which enabled the Bolsheviks to use nationalism as their own rallying cry. The consolidation of Bolshevik power, an event considerably abetted by intervention, only deepened the enmity of American policy makers and heightened their determination to outlast the Soviet state. The decision "to promote tendencies which must eventually find their outlet in either the breakup or the mellowing of Soviet power" was not reached in 1945 or 1947—it was an established policy as of January 31, 1918.

Many forces helped establish this policy toward Soviet Russia in the winter of 1917–18, but the men in Washington needed no prompting. As a political theorist, [Woodrow] Wilson, who believed in a "slow process of reform," considered revolution a "puerile doctrine"; and as President of the United States viewed actual revolutions as events that in "other states should be...prevented."

Neither Secretary of State [Robert] Lansing nor his career foreign-service assistants in the State Department made any move to quarrel with this estimate as applied to the Bolshevik Revolution. Long neglected in investigations of American foreign relations, these bureaucrats played important roles in policy formulation.

For by 1917 the United States was a highly industrialized nation, and one of the consequences of that development had been an increase in and an extension of the power of the national government. As the duties and responsibilities of the elected officials increased through the years after 1900, more and more authority was delegated to members of the appointive and civil service bureaucracy. By their day-to-day handling of routine affairs and through their function of supplying information to higher officials—who made the major decisions—these bureaucrats exerted a significant influence on the character of national policy. Nor was their importance restricted to instances where they had direct ties with special groups outside the government, as has been seen in the case of Willard Straight, who functioned as agent for the financial institutions of Kuhn, Loeb and Company and the House of Morgan at the same time he served as chief of the Far Eastern Division of the State Department. As men conscious of their power these bureaucrats made decisions both in terms of their personal attitudes and from the point of view of a special-interest group within the government.

In 1917, and thereafter, too, these men in the Department of State—unknown to the general public and tucked away safely beyond the reach of even an aroused congressman—formed a tightly knit team. With reference to American policy toward Soviet Russia, several of them deserve specific consideration because of their importance. The influence of Samuel Harper[2] has been noted, and when he returned from Russia he merely renewed old friendships with William Phillips, Frank Polk, Richard Crane, and Basil Miles. But Harper found himself considerably restricted by professional duties throughout the academic year 1917–18, and he was not intimately involved in policy decisions until June, 1918.

2. Samuel Harper was a University of Chicago professor who served as personal adviser to Ambassador David R. Francis in Russia from 1916 until early 1917. Harper had a close relationship with Charles R. Crane, a wealthy Chicago businessman who held investments in Russia and whose son, Richard Crane, was Secretary of State Robert Lansing's personal secretary. William Phillips was a State Department career officer who earlier served as the first chief of the Far Eastern Division at State and as a liaison between the department and key American financiers such as J. P. Morgan, E. H. Harriman, and Jacob Schiff.—ED.

Meanwhile the others functioned smoothly. Frank Polk, a graduate of Yale and Columbia, was a New York lawyer appointed counselor of the State Department when Robert Lansing was moved up from that job to replace William Jennings Bryan as Secretary of State. Phillips, of course, had been an important link between the Department and the financiers in the days of Dollar Diplomacy, and he continued to exercise a significant influence in the years after the Bolshevik Revolution. But while Polk and Phillips should not be underestimated, Basil Miles was the figure who gradually became the leader in the Department's day-to-day routine. His increased influence was in part a product of earlier experience in American-Russian relations. Miles dropped his business career to serve as private secretary to George von Lengerke Meyer (Theodore Roosevelt's businessman diplomat) when the latter was sent to Russia in 1905 as Roosevelt's special representative to the Tsar. Both Miles and Meyer, who viewed the great mass of Russians as "not much superior to animals with brutal instincts," were members of Roosevelt's social and political circle—and the President's intense dislike of Russia is well known.

This background became more important when, after Meyer was recalled from Russia in 1906, Miles stayed on in Russia as Third Secretary in the Embassy until May, 1907, when he returned to the United States to manage the Washington, D.C., office of the United States Chamber of Commerce. He resigned that post to be appointed special assistant to Ambassador [David R.] Francis,[3] who later reminded Lansing that "the principal object of my appointment as advised by yourself and President Wilson was to negotiate [a] treaty on commerce and navigation." Miles was raised to Minister Plenipotentiary early in 1917, and after service as an aide to the Root Mission[4] was called home to be a special advisor on Russian affairs. Shortly after his return in September, 1917, he took over the Russian desk in the Department of State and was designated chief of the

3. David R. Francis had been a prominent St. Louis businessman, publisher, and Democratic politician before President Woodrow Wilson named him Ambassador to Russia in 1916. Francis served until 1918 and thus was the last U.S. ambassador to tsarist Russia and the only American representative to the short-lived regime established in the wake of the March revolution.—ED.

4. The Root Mission was headed by Elihu Root, former secretary of state in the administration of Theodore Roosevelt. President Wilson ordered the Root Mission to Russia after the March revolution in order to gather information, offer policy recommendations, and encourage the Russians to remain in the war against the Central Powers.—ED.

Division on Russian Affairs. President Wilson considered him a "capital" member of the State Department.

Russian affairs were also of vital concern to the Departments of War and Treasury, but "most everything" was handled by the State Department and decisions were "largely influenced by the recommendations of its ambassadors and its chiefs." Within the State Department Miles, Phillips, and Polk reigned supreme. The Secretary turned to them constantly. Polk "worked closely" with Phillips and "made a good team" with Lansing. These aides screened all the reports from abroad, made oral and written summaries to the Secretary and other departments, and filtered the stream of people who provided additional information or endeavored to influence policy. In most instances they drafted the messages to American representatives in Russia. No matter what the Secretary's personal inclinations, he was limited in large measure by the interpretations and decisions of these advisors. But there was no conflict between Lansing and his advisors in the matter of policy toward Russia.

Both President Wilson and Secretary Lansing received a steady stream of cables that reported and verified the Bolsheviks' consolidation of power and the continued demonstrations for peace. Burleson[5] and [Secretary of War Newton D.] Baker both supplied Wilson with Judson's[6] analysis of the situation. The crisis might well, warned Judson, "put Russia...out of the war," and pointed out that this would "lead everywhere to an accentuated struggle between extreme socialism and severe reaction." Colonel House[7] and other diplomatic representatives all wrote similar, if less acute, dispatches. But the State Department blandly announced that Lenin would soon be overthrown and that Russia would remain active in the war. Secretary Lansing assured the Ambassador of the Provisional Government that the United States would recognize him indefinitely. Later a report hinted that a blockade would be established until "a stable government" was effected. This report was officially denied, but the Treasury Department suspended further cash advances and all shipments to the Provisional Government were halted.

By the end of November the Administration had outlined its policy toward Russia. Francis was brought up to date by a report

5. Albert Burleson was postmaster general in the Wilson administration.—ED.

6. Colonel William V. Judson was an army engineer who served as an American military observer during the Russo-Japanese War (1904–1905) and as a military representative in the Root Mission to Russia in 1917.—ED.

7. Colonel Edward M. House was an adviser to and confidant of President Wilson.—ED.

from Lansing on his talks with Jules J. Jusserand, the French Ambassador to the United States. Lansing considered him the "most accomplished" foreign diplomat in Washington, and one with whom it was "never...necessary to guard against tricks or deceptions." They discussed the question of a general agreement not to recognize the Bolsheviks, and the French drive for intervention, launched with a gentle probing action in the west, found a soft spot. In Petrograd more resistance was encountered. American representatives in Russia proved themselves far more resilient than the group in Washington. Immediately following the actual coup they renewed their efforts to keep Russia in the war. At the same time they began to organize into two groups with reference to the Bolshevik Government.

The immediate objective of the Robins group was to keep the Eastern Front intact. The morning after the Bolsheviks occupied the Winter Palace Robins[8] began an exploratory trip through the city. His first objective was to check the rumors that Kerensky had gathered a strong force in the suburb of Gatchina and was about to depose Lenin. Neither that visit nor the remainder of his scouting trip impressed Robins with the strength of the counter-revolution. But Thompson,[9] bombarded with reports that Lenin and Trotsky were German agents, was not convinced, and Robins agreed to gather more information. He asked Thompson, however, for permission to change the guards at the Red Cross warehouse. Thompson refused. Robins asked him if that was an order. Reluctant to disregard Robins' advice, Thompson said no. On the way to Smolny,[1] Robins engaged the Red Guards to protect the supplies of food and medicine. As a result, the Red Cross "never lost a pound of anything" during the remainder of its work in Russia.

The second and last session of the Second Congress of Soviets opened at Smolny at eight in the evening. Robins was an interested observer. He stayed until five the next morning, through all the

8. Raymond Robins, a key member of the American Red Cross Commission to Russia in 1917–1918, was a prominent Chicago progressive and supporter of Theodore Roosevelt. His wife, Margaret Dreier, was also an active progressive and president of the Women's Trade Union League.—ED.

9. William Boyce Thompson was a mining magnate associated with financial interests of the House of Morgan which held substantial investments in Russia and tendered large loans to the allies during World War I. Thompson sponsored, paid for, and headed the Red Cross Commission to Russia in 1917.—ED.

1. Smolny Institute had been an aristocratic ladies' school until the March revolution. It then became the headquarters of the Petrograd Soviet until the Bolshevik Revolution after which, for a time, it housed the offices of Lenin and the Bolshevik party.—ED.

debates on peace, the land question, and the fierce struggle to establish a coalition. Back at the Hotel Europa he reviewed the meeting for Thompson.

"Chief, we have got to move pretty fast. Kerensky is as dead as yesterday's 7,000 years."

Thompson was still bothered by the German agent thesis, and Robins was unable to satisfy his doubts. Robins pointed out, however, that the Bolsheviks were in power and that a decision must be reached as to whether the Red Cross would stay in Russia or abandon the field. Robins argued that the only way to find out where the Bolsheviks stood was to talk to them. Thompson agreed, and authorized Robins to visit Smolny. Robins was handicapped, however, by the violent anti-Bolshevism of his interpreter, Sasha Kropotkin. Not only was she a political enemy of those in power, but she was deeply involved emotionally in the counter-revolution. Her contacts, so valuable during Kerensky's days in office, were now a definite handicap. After long consideration Robins selected Alexander Gumberg, a Russian-American from New York.

Gumberg was an important if quiet member of the American colony in Russia from the date of his arrival in the early summer of 1917. Long a resident of New York's East Side, Gumberg had a "deep love" for America, even though it had offered him most of its worst and little of its best. Although many of his friends developed a romantic and emotional attachment to the November Revolution, Gumberg's central purpose was, and remained, to help build strong relations between the two nations. The limitations imposed upon him by America thwarted him at every turn. Automatically associated with the extreme left wing, and discriminated against in other ways, Gumberg had been denied the opportunity to make an individual contribution. When he returned to Russia as the representative of a New York manufacturing concern, however, it appeared that his unique background would be utilized.

His "thorough understanding of the situation in both" Russia and America made him of the "greatest possible assistance" to Charles Edward Russell[2] and the rest of the Root Mission. When Russell was denied permission to remain in Russia, he strongly recommended Gumberg to John F. Stevens of the Railroad Commission. Stevens declined to avail himself of Gumberg's services, but Gumberg

2. Charles Edward Russell, an American socialist and successful businessman, was a member of the Root Mission to Russia.—ED.

became an observer who occasionally did work for Bullard[3] of the Committee on Public Information and Charles Smith of the Associated Press.

Robins and Gumberg knew each other through the long discussions among the American group during the months of August, September, and October. Gumberg provided more accurate information than the others who had reported to Robins, and was the only American to warn of the impending collapse of the Provisional Government. Though not a Bolshevik, Gumberg did have access to Smolny through his brother and by virtue of his acquaintance with [Leon] Trotsky, who published a Russian-language newspaper in New York before his return to Russia. Robins turned to Gumberg for help in securing his first appointment with Trotsky and then, on November 10, employed him as a personal secretary. The two men complemented each other to an unusual degree. Robins accepted Gumberg as an equal, valued his advice, but made his own decisions. Gumberg, on the other hand, was given an excellent opportunity to use his knowledge and experience to help build a bridge between Russia and the United States. The association thus formed lasted until Gumberg's death in 1939.

Robins held his first interview with Trotsky on either the tenth or the eleventh of November. Robins, a devoted follower of Theodore Roosevelt and himself no further left than any enlightened reformer, did not discuss the fine points of Marxism with one of its high priests. But both men were political realists. "I won Trotsky," Robins recalls, "by putting my case absolutely on the square. By not hiding anything." Robins advised Trotsky that he was there because he would be dealing with those in power, no matter who they were, because he wanted to continue Red Cross activities and keep Russia in the war. He also wanted to gauge Bolshevik power and determine whether Lenin and Trotsky were German agents or sympathizers.

Robins verified the fact of Bolshevik control and concluded that they were "very peculiar" German agents. Dealing directly with Trotsky, Robins secured the transfer of some thirty boxcars of Red Cross supplies to Jassy, Rumania; and had a large quantity of condensed milk and other supplies conveyed from Murmansk to

3. Arthur Bullard, correspondent of the magazine *Outlook* and a declared socialist, served in the Russian office of the Committee on Public Information, a government agency created by the Wilson administration to promote prowar sentiment and activities. Bullard, a close friend of Colonel House, soon became a strong critic of the Bolsheviks and an opponent of Raymond Robins's efforts to establish relations with the new revolutionary regime.—ED.

Petrograd, after General Frederick C. Poole, head of the British Economic Mission, told him to write them off as lost. Later, Trotsky co-operated with Robins to hold up a large contraband train destined for Germany at Viborg, and on Robins' request sent the material to Murmansk where it was guarded by the British Fleet. Thompson was convinced. "My emphatic belief," he cabled Davison,[4] "is that [the] present Russian situation is not hopeless for the Allies."

Official American representatives were not of the same mind. Francis, who originally hoped the Bolsheviks would try to form a government because "the more ridiculous the situation the sooner the remedy," refused to have any contacts with Smolny; and on November 19 appealed to the people of Russia to "remove the difficulties that beset your pathway." Consul [Maddin] Summers was likewise concerned with "all classes of Russians standing for law and order." Judson first sided with this group and notified the chief of the old Russian General Staff that the newspaper report of an embargo "correctly states the attitude" of the United States. Lieutenant Colonel Monroe C. Kerth joined the French and British military representatives to protest "categorically and energetically" against any separate armistice.

Meanwhile Thompson prepared to return to the United States and attempt to modify American policy. The decision was made soon after the Bolsheviks consolidated their power in Petrograd and Moscow, and on November 19 Robins provided Thompson with a long letter of introduction to Theodore Roosevelt. The letter symbolized Thompson's determination to effect a shake-up in Washington, for in earlier years the financier bitterly opposed Roosevelt on the grounds that he was too radical. Thompson originally planned to leave via Siberia and proceed directly to Washington. But Thomas W. Lamont, also of the House of Morgan, strongly advised Thompson to come to London and confer with Colonel House; and at the last moment Thompson agreed to this plan. He left Petrograd on November 28, 1917, having promoted Robins to the rank of colonel in command of the Red Cross unit. Thompson's last official act was to deny Judson's statement that supplies from America would be stopped and to dissociate the Red Cross from the American military's ultimatum.

Judson, however, had already concluded that the Bolsheviks were

4. Henry P. Davison was a member of the House of Morgan and head of the American Red Cross Association. He and William Boyce Thompson sponsored the American Red Cross Mission to Russia.—ED.

without question the de facto government of Russia. He also realized
that his primary objective—to prevent peace on the Eastern Front—
could hardly be gained by a policy of blind antagonism to the
Bolsheviks. Knowing of Robins' success in dealing forthrightly with
Smolny, Judson turned to him for advice. On November 27 they had
a long conference during which Judson requested Robins to question
Trotsky on the proposed armistice with Germany. On the same day
Judson also wrote a second and more conciliatory note to Trotsky.

Several factors contributed to the establishment of this relationship
between Robins and Smolny and of the close co-operation between
Judson and Robins. First was the fact that Sisson,[5] who arrived on
November 25, found the Ambassador "without policy except anger
at the Bolsheviks." But for the time Francis failed to implement his
policy. So intense was his emotion than he could not bring himself to
share the realism of George Buchanan, the British Ambassador and
a fellow conservative. Buchanan hated the Bolsheviks with a deep
malice, but saw and admitted that Russia should be released from
her war commitments. "Every day we keep Russia in the war against
her will," he warned, "does but embitter her people against us." In
no sense, of course, did Francis agree with William Chapin Hunt-
ington, American commercial attaché, who recognized that the
Bolsheviks touched "a deep yearning," and that the embassies "with
their fear" of recognition were "making fools of themselves." But in
the early days of the revolution Francis did not commit himself so
thoroughly and effectively to the cause of counter-revolution as did
his Consul General, Maddin Summers.

Summers entered the Foreign Service shortly after he completed
his schooling at Vanderbilt and Columbia. He switched from bank
clerk to consular clerk in July, 1899, and remained in the Foreign
Service. Save for one brief stint in Belgrade he served exclusively in
Spain and South America until August, 1916, when he was detailed
to Moscow. Shortly thereafter he married Natalie Goraynoff, the
daughter of a Russian noble. Summers was a highly competent and
efficient officer of the Foreign Service; but as a man to interpret and
maintain relations with a revolutionary government he was less than
qualified. The limitations imposed by his narrow conservatism were

5. Edgar Sisson, former *Chicago Tribune* editor, was appointed in 1917 by
President Wilson as head of the Russian department of the Committee on Public
Information. Strongly anti-Bolshevik, Sisson purchased and arranged forged docu-
ments alleging that Lenin and Trotsky were German agents. He prevailed upon the
Wilson administration to publish the documents in October 1918 under the title *The
German-Bolshevik Conspiracy*—ED.

further increased by associations stemming from his marriage. Summers' opposition to the Bolsheviks hardened when Natalie's family lost both its land and laborers through the November Revolution. Ruin and Bolshevism were "synonymous" to Consul Summers; and he drove himself without limit in an effort to destroy Smolny.

The Embassy itself, moreover, suffered from serious demoralization. The cause was the Ambassador's conduct. The fact that Charles Crane spoke "well" of Francis did not alter the fact that the Ambassador was both indiscreet and exceedingly indifferent to the responsibilities of his position. The Ambassador's failure began, according to Harper, on the trip to Russia. Aboard the *Oscar II* bound for Petrograd was a group of passengers "distinctly open to suspicion" as German agents. One of these was an especially attractive and intelligent woman, Madame Matilda de Cram, who was "very friendly" with Francis by the time the group reached Russia. Her continued association with the Ambassador caused the Embassy staff "much anxiety." Francis refused to hear the charges or modify his conduct.

Through the months of October and November, 1917, the relationship between Madame de Cram and Francis continued and, possibly, matured. She was constantly in the Embassy. She heard policy discussed, and was many times in the rooms where cables were coded and deciphered. At least one letter report was given to her by Francis for her perusal. When she was detained for some cause, the Ambassador called on her. Madame de Cram's influence was greater than that of any official member of the Embassy staff—and probably exceeded that of the combined group. Judson, J. Butler Wright, Embassy counselor, Colonel Kerth, Captain E. Francis Riggs, and Robins all knew the situation firsthand. When Francis was careless with cipher codes and the secret material disappeared, these men launched their own investigation. They quickly discovered that Madame de Cram was on the secret suspect list of the Inter-Allied Passport Bureau. Some member of the Embassy staff then notified the State Department. The Department fired back a blunt warning that Madame de Cram was suspected both of espionage and connection with the Black Tom Plot, and directed Francis to suspend all relations with the woman immediately.

Francis was enraged. He termed the informer a "willful liar" and continued the association. Finally Judson, acting in desperation, called on the Ambassador personally. Judson recited the long record of evidence and even showed Francis the dossier from the Passport

Bureau. Francis was personally pleasant, but Judson left knowing that he had made absolutely no impression. The matter became the "subject of gossip" in Washington, but Francis continued the relationship on through 1917 and well into 1918.

These important considerations were re-enforced by Robins' growing insight into the Revolution itself. Familiar with the writings of Marx long before he arrived in Russia, Robins assumed, in the early days of November, that Smolny would follow the guidebook. Indeed, he was quite aware that Lenin's speeches and writings were filled with exhortations to the workers of the world and promises of the revolution to come. These developments, coupled with Trotsky's co-operation on the questions of Red Cross supplies and contraband, convinced Robins that the cry of German agent was misleading.

This did not mean that Robins was in sympathy with Bolshevism. His record of opposition to socialism, and of support for Theodore Roosevelt and Charles Evans Hughes,[6] was long and vigorous. Robins' analysis of the Revolution did indicate, however, that Germany would be denied any large-scale exploitation of Russian resources unless they conquered the nation. As he continued to press Trotsky on this question of contraband, Robins began to see the full implications of the dilemma in which Smolny found itself. Although theoretically and ideally committed to world revolution, the principal problem faced by the Bolsheviks was the consolidation of their power in a nation state. Trotsky acknowledged the seriousness of the situation when, later in November, he approached Robins and suggested the use of American troops to stop the contraband traffic. For all their huzzahs for international revolt, the Bolsheviks knew that to survive they must capitalize on one of three opportunities: war fatigue in Russia, the conflict between Germany and the Allies, or the struggle between the United States and Japan in the Far East. Though the Allies "refused" this first offer from Trotsky it was renewed several times as German aims in Russia became clearer.

Robins, in turn, realized that Smolny's problem presented a great opportunity to Allied diplomacy. Two main options presented themselves. Full-scale opposition might well destroy Smolny. But that was militarily well-nigh impossible: American resources were committed on the Western Front. And on another level the Congress had declared war against Germany—not Russia. On the other hand, Bolshevik weakness could be exploited, not only in terms of world

6. Charles Evans Hughes, Republican presidential candidate in 1916, secretary of state 1921–1926, and chief justice of the U.S. Supreme Court 1930–1941.—ED.

politics, but to modify the Bolsheviks' domestic program. This, to Robins, presented the only realistic possibility. He felt it would be more productive to work for firm American-Russian relations, which would serve both to stabilize world politics and to give the United States the greatest influence with the Revolution, than to allow reactionary forces to triumph or to muddle through and be confronted by a Soviet government that had won out on its own.

This estimate of the situation led both Robins and Judson into a diplomatic no-man's land where they were useful but expendable. After his long talk with Judson on November 27, Robins saw Trotsky about the armistice proceedings. Trotsky exhibited considerable interest in the possibility of reaching some agreement; and Judson went back to Francis and reopened their old argument about establishing some working contact with Smolny. Judson insisted that the Bolsheviks were the de facto government, and argued that the peace sentiment would force them at least to negotiate with the Germans. Given that situation, the only realistic policy was to attempt to insert a clause in the settlement that would immobilize German troops in the East. Francis, under pressure from Sisson and others who supported Judson's plan, and aware that the British were considering a similar move, granted Judson's request and gave him official authorization to talk with Trotsky. Judson first approached the British and French for their support. General Knox,[7] at first "rather favorable" to the idea, was overruled by [British Ambassador] Buchanan. The French had no sympathy for the idea. They were "implacable," noted Judson, and appeared to be "more bent upon expressing their opinion than upon substantial accomplishments." As a result, Judson made the trip alone.

On December 1, 1917, Judson held a forty-minute interview with Trotsky. Judson, who "made it clear at the outset that at the present time he had no right to speak in the name of the American Government," desired "to clear up certain misunderstandings" and exert some influence on the scheduled peace talks between Russia and Germany.[8] Trotsky voluntarily recognized that Russia had "a

7. General Alfred Knox, British general sympathetic to and supportive of the counterrevolutionary army of Russian General Lavr Georgievich Kornilov which, in September 1917, tried and failed to overthrow the Kerensky government in Petrograd (St. Petersburg).—ED.

8. On November 28, 1917, the new Bolshevik regime proposed an armistice and peace negotiations with the Germans. Discussions commenced at Brest-Litovsk on December 3, an armistice was concluded on December 15, and a treaty was signed on March 3, 1918.—ED.

certain obligation to her Allies," and was further "very amiable and
very responsive" to Judson's program to hold German troops on the
Eastern Front. The armistice commission, agreed Trotsky, "would be
given instructions accordingly." In parting, Trotsky assured Judson
that the "allies of Russia would have further opportunity to examine
into and offer suggestions as to said terms."

Judson and Robins were enthusiastic and prepared to exploit the
opportunity. Judson's experience convinced him that Robins' interpretation of the Revolution was accurate, and he prepared a vigorous
program to take advantage of the fact that the United States was the
"only Allied nation possessing the confidence of Russia sufficiently to
act." His aim was to "extract a broadening of its foundations from
the Soviet Government" and at the same time keep Russia in the
war. Judson requested authorization to express the United States'
"friendly appreciation" of the "desperate situation" and to make it
meaningful by offering to co-operate in the operation of the trans-
Siberian railway system and to carry through with "assistance on a
larger scale of every other character."

Judson's optimism was not warranted. For on the day of his
interview with Francis, the Ambassador was advised that it was
"most unwise" for him to "take any sort of initiative." After the
Department reacted unfavorably to the news of Judson's talk with
Trotsky, the Ambassador was to save face by denying that he
authorized the visit; on December 3, meanwhile, Francis refused
Judson's request to see cables between Washington and the Embassy.
Judson assumed that the information contained in the State Department cables would enable him to "better advise" the War Department and to make his communications "more harmonious" with
those of the Ambassador—a state of affairs Judson thought might be
of "obvious advantage to our Government." Ambassador Francis did
not agree.

Washington also had other ideas of what constituted its obvious
advantage. "By the first of December" the Administration forced
itself to acknowledge the "temporary success" of the Bolsheviks.
Three days later the President and Lansing found themselves united
in "disappointment and amazement" against the "class despotism" in
Petrograd. Lansing prepared and submitted to Wilson a long memorandum on Russia. In essence it was an embittered attack on Smolny
that concluded with a strong recommendation not to recognize the
Bolshevik Government because of its class origin and structure. The
President (who thought that "a great menace to the world had taken

shape") "approved in principle," but "did not think that it was opportune to make a public declaration of this sort."

This decision was made *before* the reports of Judson's trip to see Trotsky reached Lansing. When the Secretary did learn of the interview, on December 4 and 6, he acted with more dispatch than at any time since the March Revolution. He talked with Secretary of War Baker "on recalling Judson from Petrograd," conferred with Phillips on the same problem, and also discussed the situation with Wilson. The result was the following cable sent to Francis on December 6, 1917:

> Referring press reports received here last few days concerning communi-
> cations of Judson with Trotsky relative armistice, President desires
> American representatives withhold all direct communication with Bol-
> shevik Government. So advise Judson and Kerth. Department assumes
> these instructions being observed by Embassy.

The following day Lansing again conferred with Wilson on Judson's "conduct in Petrograd," and then unburdened himself to his diary. "The correct policy for a government which believes in political institutions as they now exist and based on nationality and private property," he wrote, "is to leave these dangerous idealists alone and have no direct dealings with them." The Secretary was appalled at what he termed an effort "to make the ignorant and incapable mass" dominant in the world. Nor did he grasp the counter-revolutionary import of nationalism. The "only possible remedy," he decided, was for a "strong commanding personality to arise … gather a disciplined military force … restore order and main-tain a government." Generals Alexei Kaledin and Mikhail Alexeev, formerly the Tsar's Chief of Staff, who had gone to South Russia immediately after the Bolshevik coup, were noted as the most promising candidates for the position of savior. *As these events of early December, 1917, make unmistakably clear, neither Lansing nor Wilson formulated policy toward Russia on the premise that Lenin was a German agent.* This fact cannot be overemphasized, for later com-mentary, both official and scholarly, presented intervention as either anti-German or anti-Japanese in origin.

These counter-revolutionary forces in South Russia rapidly be-came the focus of American interest. Phillips, Polk, and Miles all shared Lansing's opposition to Smolny and supported his December 10 recommendation to Wilson. The best "hope" was a "military dictatorship"; and the "only apparent nucleus … sufficiently strong to supplant the Bolsheviks" appeared to be the group around Kaledin. Further conferences, during which Secretary McAdoo[9] indicated his support of the project, resulted in the preparation of a highly confidential memorandum outlining American policy in support of the counter-revolutionary forces.

This document, to which Wilson gave his "entire approval," was sent on to Oscar T. Crosby, Treasury representative on the Inter-Allied Finance Council, for the guidance of American representatives in Europe. The problem had been "carefully considered," Crosby was advised, to the conclusion that "any movement" against the Bolsheviks "should be encouraged even though its success is only a possibility." [Former tsarist Generals] Kaledin and Kornilov were singled out for special consideration. As yet it was "unwise" and impossible to give open financial aid, Crosby was cautioned, but Kaledin should be advised that Washington was "most sympathetic with his efforts." Britain and France, furthermore, should be approached on the matter of finances. Obviously, Crosby was warned, it was of particular importance to act "expeditiously" and secretly. This policy decision, it should be noted, was made on December 12, 1917, ten days *before* a similar decision was made by England and France during a conference in Paris. Of especial significance is the fact that Wilson and Lansing both acted, not from a belief that Lenin was a German agent, but from an avowed opposition to what they considered the goals of the November Revolution.

The dates in question become even more important when considered in relation to the activities of William Boyce Thompson after he left Russia. The House of Morgan's influence in England became readily apparent when Thompson was taken aboard H.M.S. *Vulture* at Bergen, Norway, after he missed his regular connections. Lamont, who arranged the battleship ride for Thompson, was upset when the latter arrived in London too late to catch Colonel House and Vance McCormick,[1] but did arrange conferences with high members of the British Government. After his initial interview with Ambassador Page, Thompson saw Lord Reading; Admiral Hall, head of British Naval Intelligence; Sir George Clark, Balfour's[2] representative; John Buchan, British propaganda chief; and Lord Carson of the War Office. All were impressed with Thompson's knowledge and analysis

9. William Gibbs McAdoo, secretary of the treasury in the Wilson administration.—ED.

1. Vance McCormick was chairman of the U.S. War Trade Board.—ED.

2. Arthur H. Balfour, British foreign minister.—ED.

of the situation. Carson told Thompson to inform Wilson that he would "go just as far as he will and further," and that finances were no problem.

On either December 13 or 14 Thompson had lunch with Prime Minister David Lloyd George at 10 Downing Street. He was in no sense awed by the Welshman's high office. "Because of their short-sighted diplomacy," Thompson told Lloyd George, "the Allies since the Revolution have accomplished nothing beneficial, and have done considerable harm to their own interests." It promised little, he continued, to treat Russia as an outcast; for very possibly the Bolsheviks were the key to the entire war. Firm contacts with them should be established, Thompson argued, for two reasons. Any chance to reconstitute the Eastern Front must be exploited to the limit. Equally important was the fact that the Bolsheviks were fighting for their very existence, and as yet had been unable to translate their theories into action. Internally they were struggling with necessities; and internationally they were searching for security. "Let's make them our Bolsheviks," Thompson suggested.

Lloyd George seemed to accept the proposal. He expressed agreement with Thompson's suggestions to send representatives "democratic in spirit," and to constitute an inter-allied commission to carry on relations with the Bolsheviks as a de facto government. Thompson was also asked to express Lloyd George's agreement to President Wilson. Thompson and Lamont left for the United States the next day as guests aboard a British transport. They arrived in New York on Christmas Day and hurried on to Washington to complete their errand.

But Lloyd George, meanwhile, followed Thompson's advice in a peculiar manner. True, he selected Robert Bruce Lockhart, who served in the British Embassy in Russia during 1904–5, to go to Russia; and Lockhart, who had been trying to influence Lord Alfred Milner to adopt a policy similar to Thompson's, appeared to be a logical selection. He was, moreover, charged with the "responsibility of establishing relations." But, in Lockhart's words, "I was to have no authority." This is not surprising, for on December 22, 1917, Lord Milner agreed, on behalf of England, to support the forces of counter-revolution. Lockhart's mission would appear to have been part of the plan "to avoid the imputation as far as we can that we are preparing to make war on the Bolsheviki." On December 23, 1917, England and France signed a formal agreement to support Alexeev and to split Russia into respective spheres of influence. Thompson's advice became a mite distorted in its execution.

In Russia a similar situation existed. Robins and Judson continued their work to keep Russia in the war. Consul Summers led the forces of containment and destruction. The prize at stake was the concurrence of Ambassador Francis who had yet effectively to implement any policy—even his own anger. For a time it appeared that Robins and Judson would succeed in their efforts to have the United States take advantage of Smolny's tenuous position and endeavor to establish a firm relationship with Russia on the basis of mutual self-interest.

Sisson offered his support to Robins and Judson immediately upon his arrival in Petrograd. He approved the policy that motivated Judson's visit to Trotsky and cabled Creel[3] so to advise the President. Creel found Lansing and Wilson unreceptive, and was ordered to rebuke Sisson. But in the meantime Sisson had received Creel's advice to "co-ordinate all American agencies in Petrograd and Moscow." To Sisson this was a "plain order," and he began to interpret the cable liberally. Apparently he was "taking himself quite seriously," for he continued to irritate Francis. Lansing again brought the matter to Wilson's attention; and the President seems to have reminded Creel of his earlier orders. In any event, Creel took occasion to assure the President that Sisson understood that he was "not to touch the political situation."

Sisson did not evidence this understanding. Robins shared with Sisson the services of Gumberg and secured for him Bolshevik co-operation in the distribution of various speeches and other propaganda. Some time during the middle of December Robins proposed the use of Bolshevik propaganda against German troops. With Sisson he worked out the plan and put it into operation. During this period Sisson gave every indication that he shared Robins' determination to "use the possibilities yet remaining" to establish "an authoritative Allied co-operation in Petrograd."

Consul Summers viewed the situation in a slightly different manner. On December 15, following private talks with right-wing General A. A. Brusilov, Summers personally dispatched De Witt Clinton Poole, consul at Moscow, to approach Alexeev and Kaledin. Summers acted on his own initiative, and before he received any word of Washington's decision of December 12. Poole spent the rest of December sounding out these White [anti-Bolshevik] leaders. Both he and F. Willoughby Smith, American consul at Tiflis, gave

3. George Creel, a journalist and head of the Committee on Public Information.—ED.

Alexeev, Kornilov, and Kaledin strong moral support. Lansing ordered Smith, who was "in close touch and working unanimously with" these leaders, to make duplicate reports to Crosby in London. Summers and Poole recommended that the United States "should immediately" support this movement as the "only salvation." "The Russia we welcome as a democratic nation," wrote Summers, "is in the South."

This performance by Summers may have contributed to Francis' mid-December failure of nerve. The Ambassador, for all his antagonism to the Bolsheviks, realized that Wilson's policy of non-intercourse with Smolny placed the United States in a ridiculous position. When the Washington cable arrived he promised Robins that he would "stand between you and the fire." Almost immediately his courage wavered; and he asked whether Red Cross personnel were included in the President's order. The Department quickly advised Francis that they were, and so to advise Robins.

Working in close co-operation with Judson, Robins meanwhile received "assurances from Trotsky" that Russia would insist that Germany hold her troops on the Eastern Front if the armistice was extended. They scored again when Trotsky gave the United States credit for holding up a rumored Japanese intervention in the Far East. In view of these developments, both men considered Summers' policy extremely dangerous. Judson, whose cables were ignored by the War Department, viewed the mission to Kaledin as "absolutely futile and ill-advised." Robins thought the move would "simply mean civil war," and might well develop to Germany's advantage. The United States was "becoming isolated," warned Judson, by its "position of apparent repulsion of the Soviet Government."

This fact, coupled with his own regretful admission that Bolshevik power was "undoubtedly" supreme in Russia, made Francis willing to overlook the Department's non-intercourse order to Robins. The Ambassador was willing "to swallow pride, sacrifice dignity, and with discretion" establish regular contact with Smolny. Judson, realizing this was a key opportunity, wrote a vigorous letter to the Ambassador urging him to take the lead. German influence is unopposed, Judson began, principally because the United States had no communications with the Bolshevik Government. "The terrible responsibility for this deplorable condition, fraught with untold danger" to the world, rested, declared Judson, upon himself and the Ambassador. It was their responsibility, he pointed out, to inform Washington and to recommend appropriate action. "Do not stand on dignity," he concluded. "It is necessary that the United States adopt at once a broad Russian policy."

For the moment Francis agreed, and requested permission for Robins to continue his relations with Smolny. The request officially appeared to be dictated by Red Cross requirements, but the true purpose was as indicated. It was fortunate that the façade was employed, for Phillips was upset by Francis' earlier willingness to establish working relations with the Soviets. Noting that the Ambassador appeared to be "thoroughly depressed," Phillips warned Lansing that Francis needed "a tonic in the form of a Departmental instruction." The Secretary agreed, and on December 29 Francis was advised that recognition was "not considered" a present possibility. The same day Lansing authorized Robins to continue his visits to Smolny on Red Cross business.

Francis interpreted the approval in the same sense as the request. This was important, for on December 27 the negotiations at Brest-Litovsk were disrupted over the question of occupied territories. Adolf Joffe expressed Soviet willingness to withdraw from Poland, Lithuania, Courland, and other Baltic areas pending local plebiscites unhampered by occupying forces. Germany retorted, through Richard von Kuhlmann, that she considered those nations to have signified their preference for Germany. The plebiscite, Kuhlmann amplified, would "ratify the will already expressed." The meaning was clear, and Smolny realized it was being forced to choose between a German-dictated peace or a renewed war, which without help would mean the destruction of Bolshevik power.

Robins' entire forecast was being verified, and he hurried to Smolny to exploit the break in the weather. Trotsky was "enraged" and exceedingly worried by the German proposals. His primary concern was "what America will do" if negotiations terminated. Robins immediately informed Judson, and together they "hastened" to the Embassy to inform Francis. After hearing their report, the Ambassador gave them full authority to "go to Trotsky and inform him that [the United States] would render all assistance possible." Even the British and French admitted it was a great opportunity and agreed to support the decision.

The opportunity thus offered to the United States by virtue of Smolny's primary concern with its own existence was so challenging that both Francis and Washington momentarily overcame their fundamental antagonism and considered the possibility of reaching some *modus vivendi* with the Bolsheviks. Despite evidence of the benefits that would thereby be gained, the United States refused to abandon its program of support for counter-revolution. That active intervention would be the final decision was indicated in Francis' cable of January 1, 1918. On that afternoon and evening Sisson, after conferences at the Embassy, attended the meeting of the Central Executive Committee of the Soviets of Workers', Soldiers', and Peasants' Deputies called to discuss the crisis. He reported to Francis, Robins, and Judson that "the speeches all indicated a spirit of readiness to resume the war if the Germans did not yield." Francis agreed to cable Washington that he would "take any step...necessary to prevent separate peace."

Unknown to Robins and Judson, the Ambassador was "inclined" to think that if such a peace proved unavoidable "it should favor Germany to [the] extent possible in order to make it the more unacceptable not only to the allies but to pacifist and proletariat throughout the world." Francis then inquired if the Department agreed. The arrival of the cable in Washington prompted Basil Miles to write a short note to Phillips. "I had not thought this last sentence requires answer," he remarked. Neither did Phillips, Polk, or Lansing. Nor, in the last analysis, did President Wilson.

On the same night the long arm of Lansing reached Russia in the form of Judson's unconditional recall. The interview with Trotsky on December 1, 1917, aroused the Secretary's intense anger; and at his request Secretary of War Baker agreed to withdraw Judson. Always one "eager to say what seemed to be the truth," Judson paid a high price for his integrity. It is possible that Secretary Lansing's personal satisfaction was extracted at a rather high cost to the interests of the United States.

Judson was stunned, and for more than a week took little vocal part in the rapid sequence of events. Robins continued the effort to conclude an understanding with Smolny on his own. His arguments still reached Francis, but Judson's withdrawal unnerved the Ambassador. "Surely our interest is to prevent peace," cabled Francis to Lansing; but he "would not presume to commit [the] Department." Still, the Ambassador "might consider it advisable to commit myself to recommend assistance...for sincere rigorous prosecution of war." The Ambassador did just that on January 2, promising Robins that he would cable for help if Smolny was forced into war. Two cables were drafted and initialed by Francis for Robins' use in discussion with Trotsky.

These stand-by messages gave both Robins and Trotsky definite reason to believe that the United States was seriously interested in agreement. Francis signed the following statement, drafted by Robins, which would appear to be reasonably definite.

> If upon the termination of the present armistice Russia fails to conclude a democratic peace *through the fault of the Central Powers and is compelled to continue* the war I shall urge upon my government the fullest assistance to Russia possible, including the shipment of supplies and munitions for the Russian armies, the extension of credits and the giving of such advice and technical assistance as may be welcome to the Russian people....

Two days later the Ukrainian Rada, a separatist government, opened negotiations with Germany; and on January 5, 1918, Kuhlmann informed Trotsky that Germany would no longer negotiate on the basis of no annexations and no indemnities.

The Bolsheviks were desperate. Trotsky argued to Lenin that the negotiations had to be dragged out to provide time for either a revolution in Germany and Austria, or for the Allies to promise assistance. Lenin was very skeptical, and agreed to the plan only on condition that Trotsky himself did the delaying. "At his insistence" Trotsky left for Brest-Litovsk on the night of January 5. Events likewise moved toward a climax in Washington. Acting at least partially under the immediate pressure of Colonel House, Lansing, Lord Balfour, and Sisson—who cabled Creel that there was a need for "internal evidence" of Wilson's concern for the Russian situation— President Wilson delivered his Fourteen Points Speech on January 8, 1918.

With pointed reference to the parleys "in progress at Brest-Litovsk," Wilson enunciated his conception of the "only possible program" for world peace. The subsequent struggle over the implementation of this program and the development of Washington's policy toward Russia have tended to obscure the character of Wilson's references to Russia. In view of the President's later actions these are of particular interest. It is clear, for example, that Wilson viewed the Bolsheviks as the legitimate "Russian representatives" who were speaking as the "voice of the Russian people" at Brest-Litovsk. The President considered, moreover, that they "were sincere and in earnest." Aware that Russia was "prostrate and all but helpless" before "the grim power of Germany," Wilson carefully specified his policy.

> The evacuation of all Russian territory and such a settlement of all questions affecting Russia as will secure the best and freest co-operation

of the other nations of the world in obtaining for her an unhampered and unembarrassed opportunity for the independent determination of her own political development and national policy and assure her of a sincere welcome into the society of free nations under institutions of her own choosing; and, more than a welcome, assistance also of every kind that she may need and may herself desire. The treatment accorded Russia by her sister nations in the months to come will be the acid test of their good will, of their comprehension of her needs as distinguished from their own interests, and of their intelligent and unselfish sympathy.

The President's remarks indicate a momentary disagreement with Lansing on Russian policy. Or more exactly, perhaps, an occasion when Wilson's sympathy with the deep urge for economic and social reform actually influenced a policy statement. For on January 2, 1918, Secretary Lansing repeated his earlier argument that the Bolsheviks could not be recognized in any manner because they were "a direct threat at existing social order." The Secretary viewed their *Appeal to the Toiling, Oppressed, and Exhausted Peoples of Europe* as a call "to the ignorant and mentally deficient"—to Lansing a "very real danger in view of the social unrest throughout the world." He was also opposed to any broad program of national self-determination. It was, in Lansing's opinion, "utterly untenable" to hold that either Ireland or India should break away from the British Empire. This long and urgent memorandum did not—quite obviously—set the tone for Wilson's address. But the Secretary's loss of influence was only temporary.

Shortly after the President expressed his "heartfelt desire and hope that some way may be opened whereby we may be privileged to assist the people of Russia," Lenin wrote his analysis of Smolny's predicament and, feeling that aid from the Allies was no more than a foolish hope, concluded that Russia had to sign the peace. On January 11, however, Gumberg managed to obtain an interview with Lenin for Robins and Sisson. The two men requested Lenin's co-operation in spreading Wilson's speech across Russia and into Germany. Lenin considered the statement "a great step ahead toward the peace of the world" and assured them that he had no objection to its distribution. He also asked as to the implementation of the speech—an inquiry not answered. Lenin, faced with the reality of German military might, was aware that words are not immediately effective against bullets. But for the time being the Bolsheviks refused to accept the dictates of Germany—and Lenin did not publish his views on the matter.

Beyond the fact that it secured the distribution of Wilson's speech in Russia, this interview was important because it exerted a critical influence on the division of American personnel in Russia. Sisson emerged from the conversations with the conviction that it was a "mistake for anyone to believe that our political democracy can merge with this industrial democracy." Trusting to the always-dangerous procedure of thinking other people's thoughts, Sisson concluded that Lenin considered himself "the Great Destroyer." Sisson shortly embarked on a vigorous campaign to fight Lenin as a German spy, but by his own admission the label was composed of "only popular catchwords." Sisson's opposition to the Soviet Government was grounded in his conviction that industrial and political democracy were irreconcilable.

Robins emphatically dissented from this interpretation. The result, in Sisson's mind, was the "Robins grouch." Within three weeks the disagreement resulted in Sisson's switch to the side of counter-revolution. Robins, on the other hand, proceeded to exploit the initial contact with Lenin in every possible manner. During the remainder of his stay in Russia, Robins became one of the few foreigners to gain Lenin's trust. It was established, by Lenin's own admission, on the same terms as Robins' relationship with Trotsky. "Robins represents," remarked Lenin in 1918, "the liberal bourgeoisie of America." Neither Lenin nor Robins had any delusions as to the other's position—but they were not hypnotized by ideology.

At Brest-Litovsk, meanwhile, Trotsky delayed the negotiations by insisting on the principle of self-determination. Germany's Major General Max Hoffman angrily pointed out that "the victorious German armies [were] on Russian territory"—an argument difficult to refute—and on January 18 Trotsky suspended further talks and returned to Petrograd. On January 21 and 22, 1918, the situation was debated at length by Bolshevik party leaders.

"The situation in which the Socialist Revolution in Russia finds itself," Lenin began, "is to be taken as the point of departure for every definition of the international task confronting the new Soviet Government.... It would be a mistake," he amplified, "for the Soviet Government to formulate its policy on the supposition that within the next six months, or thereabouts, there will be a European, to be more specific, a German Socialist revolution." That, declared Lenin, would be a "blind gamble." "The only true inference to be drawn from this is that from the time a socialist government is established in any one country questions must be determined not with reference to preferability of any one imperialistic group but solely from the point of view of what is best for the development and consolidation of the socialist revolution which has already begun."

The arguments for a revolutionary war might give "satisfaction to those who crave the romantic and the beautiful," Lenin concluded, but they had no relation to reality. The only policy was to sign the peace and save the revolution. Joseph Stalin, then no more than a second-level member of the policy-making group but the man who was to become Lenin's ultimate successor, supported the latter's interpretation in 1918 as well as in later years. "There is no revolutionary movement in the West," Stalin argued in January, 1918, "there are no facts; there are only potentialities, and we cannot take into account potentialities." With this and other support Lenin stalled those who counseled a revolutionary war. But Trotsky's policy was also supported, and he prepared to test the project of "no peace, no war."

The Constituent Assembly, meanwhile, was dissolved. The Bol-sheviks' determination to push the revolution through to what they considered the socialist phase was implemented in this instance by an intense campaign against the Assembly among the soldiers and workers of the capital. That the workers "rather inclined to an indifferent skepticism" toward the meeting was a measure of their success; as was the fact that although the Second Baltic Squadron "swore not to go against it," the sailors viewed an active defense of the Assembly as "another question." Small wonder, then, that there was no resistance when the Assembly was dissolved on the pretext that "the guard is tired."

Despite his opposition to Lenin, Sisson concurred with Robins' report that the act was accepted "without important protest." The judgment was verified by the Bolsheviks' political opponents. As members of the Conservative as well as the moderate Socialist parties agreed, the people seemed "equally unwilling to rescue the Provi-sional Government or to join the Bolsheviks." More forthright was a leader of the latter group's admission, a few years later, that "we could not drive them against the Bolshevik movement." Actually, the dissolution of the Constituent Assembly was a reflection of the existing situation in Russia, and not a call to civil war. The Allies, despite their public claims to the contrary, had a very intimate knowledge of that fact.

Perhaps aware that his policy was somewhat unrealistic, Trotsky asked Robins as to the chances of American recognition before he left for Brest-Litovsk. Robins told him frankly that there was no such possibility, and Trotsky was left to sally forth to attack the Germans with oratory. Meanwhile Judson prepared to leave, his requests to remain unanswered. To the last a voice unheard, Judson cabled on the day of his departure that the United States might "lose many chances to serve [its] own interests" unless "friendly inter-course...not involving recognition" was quickly established.

This farewell warning was ignored in Washington. Wilson's interest in the proceedings at Brest, so evident in his speech of January 8, proved to be limited to verbal concern. The President acknowledged that Russian power appeared to be "shattered"; but when the Bolsheviks were forced by that very fact to continue the negotiations he exhibited no interest in extending material aid. Brest-Litovsk was rationalized as further proof of Bolshevik treach-ery. The President chose to remain passive until there was "some-thing definite to plan with and for." This choice, coupled with the State Department's view that statements of principle answered any requests for aid, and their decision to avoid any acts that would damage the cause of counter-revolution, meant that Washington had turned its back on any policy designed to influence developments within the Soviet Government—save in a negative sense.

The decision was due neither to a misunderstanding nor to a lack of information. When Wilson prepared his warning that policy toward Russia would be the "acid test" of Allied diplomacy, he had at hand a multitude of reports and suggestions. In addition to the advice of Colonel House, Lord Balfour, and Creel that some statement on Russia was needed, the President had similar messages from Lansing, William C. Bullitt, another State Department advisor, Phillips, Robins, and a long letter from William Boyce Thompson. Phillips viewed Bullitt's conclusion that "Today the iron is hot!" as of "great importance," and considered the primary issue to be "how best to take advantage of the present hostility of the Bolsheviks to the German Government." House, after conferences with Thompson and Lamont, advised "an expression of sympathy" and the offer of "our financial, industrial, and moral support in every way possible." Creel forwarded Thompson's letter, a long review of his talks in London—including Lord Carson's message to the President—that closed with the argument to influence the Soviets in the direction and interests of the United States. All these arguments were discussed at the White House on January 7, 1918, and clearly helped shape Wilson's speech of the following day.

During the same period the United States took the first steps toward intervention and acquiesced in the British blockade of Russia. The arguments of John K. Caldwell, consul of Vladivostok, Richard Washburn Child, another of the President's many advisors, and the British for some show of strength in the Far East were thoroughly discussed by Wilson, Baker, Lansing, and Secretary of the Navy Josephus Daniels. Caldwell wanted military action to comply with the "numerous requests" he had received "from better-class Russians for foreign intervention and protection to enable them to organize." Lord Robert Cecil of the British Foreign Office was "uneasy" about the military stores at Vladivostok. Child argued that the Germans would soon overrun Siberia—an area some 4,000 miles from Brest-Litovsk—and proposed that Japan be allowed to intervene *"at once."* The President seems to have followed the advice of the Department's own Basil Miles. Miles's plan was to "continue...support of elements of law and order in the south, but...not exploiting Russia to carry on a civil war." The inherent contradictions of this advice would appear obvious, but Wilson thought it "a sensible program." In any event, the cruiser *Brooklyn* was ordered north on January 3, 1918.

Lansing's reply to the French proposal for direct intervention made it apparent that Miles had convinced everybody. The "anarchy" in Siberia moved Paris to suggest, on January 8, a "military mission" to protect the supplies at Vladivostok form "German influence." Lansing did not think armed action would be wise in view of the "present conditions in Siberia." It might, the Secretary pointed out, "result in uniting all factions in Siberia against" the White Russian forces. Clearly, the decision was reached not in terms of the danger of German occupation, but on the basis of what action would offer the most support to the forces of counter-revolution. The Department's decision to co-operate with the British embargo on goods to Russia was reflected in the American Red Cross order "to hold up all orders for Russia which have not yet been placed." "Our neglect to place additional orders," explained George W. Hill, assistant director of Foreign Relief, "will automatically stop shipments to Russia."

Spurred on by Robins, William Boyce Thompson opened the long campaign to gain a hearing for the argument that intervention was not in the best interests of the United States. Wilson professed himself "much interested" in Thompson's argument, but the initial effort to gain a personal audience through the offices of Secretary of the Treasury McAdoo, Polk, and Supreme Court Justice Louis D.

Brandeis was unsuccessful. But Thompson was encouraged by the President's message of January 8 and redoubled his efforts to reach the White House.

Far more significant than his public speeches was Thompson's success in organizing a group of interested public figures. He called on Theodore Roosevelt and reviewed the Russian situation in detail. Roosevelt was momentarily convinced, writing Robins that he would, "of course, govern my conduct and my utterances hereafter absolutely by it." This was not quite true, as events proved—Roosevelt later wrote "that the United States should join with Japan and support the White Russians"—but for the time being the former President passively supported Thompson. More important was the support Thompson gained from United States Senators William E. Borah, William M. Calder, Robert L. Owen, William J. Stone, and other prominent figures including Hugh A. Cooper, director of a large engineering corporation, and later important in relations with Russia.

"Night after night" these men discussed the critical need to revise American policy. Thompson hammered away at the futility and danger of the Administration's recent decision. Borah, who earlier objected "to the Hamletic program of thinking too much upon the deed," led Owen, Calder, Stone, and Cooper in a direct assault on the White House. Others wrote of Robins' significance and urged that his important associations with the Bolshevik leaders be extended. As a result of this pressure, Senator Owen—who broke party ranks to support Robins in the latter's campaign for United States senator in 1914—was asked to prepare a written policy recommendation. Owen suggested that the Bolsheviks be acknowledged as a de facto government, and implied that the efforts of Robins should be given full support. Thinking that the tide was about to turn, Thompson wrote again for an interview. But Wilson's request for a departmental opinion on Owen's suggestions was answered by Basil Miles, who thought it "quite impossible" to follow the senator's recommendations. Thompson was advised that the President had a "cold," which limited conversation. Evidently Lansing was likewise handicapped, for he abruptly ended his substitute interview before Thompson had a chance to present his views.

Robins, meanwhile, extended his contacts with Lenin and extracted surprising concessions from the Soviet Government. His talks with Lenin during the week of Owen's offensive in Washington resulted in the transfer to Switzerland of Ivan A. Zaklind, Trotsky's assistant, who had co-operated with anarchist threats against the American Embassy. He also negotiated the cancellation of John Reed's appointment as Soviet consul in New York.[4] But Robins, growing more hopeless as the days dragged by without word from the United States, was only mildly encouraged by the arrival of Bruce Lockhart from England on January 30, 1918. It was well that Robins was groping in the dark, for had he known of Wilson's "cold" he might well have given up entirely.

For it is apparent that by the end of January, 1918, President Wilson had accepted—"for other than military reasons"—the principle of intervention as the basis of American policy toward Russia. It is likewise clear that the other reason, which Secretary of War Baker later chose to "refrain from discussing," was a decision to implement a policy designed to support counter-revolution against the Soviet Government. At the time, the policy was not clearly revealed because armed intervention did not follow immediately. Later, when that tactical step was taken, the basis of the original decision was obscured by the fact that Washington also desired to prevent further Japanese expansion on the mainland of Asia. But, as Wilson's interest in the various anti-Soviet governments in Siberia—and active support to one of them—indicated, intervention was an attempt to restrict Japan within the limits imposed by the decision to oppose the Soviets.

4. John Reed, American radical journalist, was in Russia in 1917 and wrote a classic account of the Bolshevik Revolution, *Ten Days that Shook the World* (1919). Reed died in Soviet Russia in 1920 and was buried in Red Square.—ED.

A SECOND LOOK
AT MR. X

[from *Monthly Review,* 1952]

George Frost Kennan's proposals for containment of the Soviet Union first appeared publicly in the influential journal *Foreign Affairs* in July 1947 under the pseudonym "Mr. X." Originally communicated to Washington as the "long telegram" of February 22, 1946, from Moscow, where he was then serving as an attaché in the American embassy, Kennan's analysis of Soviet behavior and his policy recommendations were received by U.S. officials convinced of the need to confront the Soviet Union after World War II. Kennan's containment strategy became the basis of American conduct toward the Soviet Union for the next four decades.

Williams, however, dissented from the containment doctrine and subjected Kennan's appraisal of American-Russian relations to major criticism. Observing that containment had resulted in a "sterile and negative" American foreign policy and that the author himself was having serious reservations about its application, Williams called upon Kennan—and the United States—to abandon the containment policy altogether.

GEORGE Frost Kennan's appointment as United States Ambassador to the Soviet Union was a move of vital significance in the Cold War. For the choice of Kennan, self-acknowledged author of the policy of containment and publicly proclaimed "inside strategist" of the Cold War, reemphasized Washington's determination to press the original policy of containment—even though Kennan himself has hinted at the grave fallacy of his master plan. And while the Truman administration has yet to take note of its own expert's apparently changed views, the Republicans, under the guidance of John Foster Dulles, bid fair to push containment to its logical conclusion— preventive or provoked war. Clearly, these aspects of current American policy toward Russia point up the need to take a second look at Kennan.

The errors of fact, violations of logic, and cases of judgment by double standard that may be found in Kennan's published writings comprise a total far beyond the scope of a single paper. But the fundamental character of his work is apparent in the famous "X" article, first printed in *Foreign Affairs* in July, 1947, and later republished in Kennan's volume on *American Diplomacy, 1900–1950.* Ostensibly an article on the Soviet political structure, Kennan's "X" article was originally written as a policy document for Secretary of Defense James Forrestal—and actually was but a condensation of the views Kennan had expressed as early as the first part of 1946. This background is important, for it reveals that Kennan's policy of containment was the product of long-term reflection on American-Russian relations; and Kennan was the leader of that small coterie of State Department personnel specifically trained in that field.

Despite the care that went into its preparation, the "X" article contains two signal weaknesses: Kennan's failure to probe the relationship between economic forces and foreign policy; and his attempt to analyze the history of the world since 1917 (and make recommendations for the present) without acknowledging, or addressing himself to, the fundamental challenge that the Bolshevik Revolution presented to the western world in general, and to the United States in particular. For the challenge of contemporary Russia is far more than that of a giant military machine: the Soviet Union is equally potent as the symbol of a fundamental critique of capitalistic society that is currently the basis of action in many non-Russian areas of the world.

To evade or ignore this aspect of American-Russian relations is to explain the past inadequately and to formulate current policy without comprehending the basic forces that condition day-to-day actions and decisions. It would require one to account for the non-Russian centers of Communism, for example, *solely* on the basis of pre-1917 concepts of political treason or a quite inexplicable index of psychiatric maladjustment. And that pattern of causation (while apparently accepted by many in the western world) has little relevance to the rise of Russian influence in China.

Even within his own frame of reference, however, Kennan's

review of American-Soviet relations is open to serious question. There was "little" that the United States "could have done," he observes in *American Diplomacy,* "to moderate" the Soviet's "burning hostility" toward the West. Begging the question of what foundation in fact that antagonism might have had (both during and after the Bolshevik Revolution), Kennan concludes that "it was hardly to be altered by anything" the United States could have done directly, and observes that the "best reaction to it on our part would have been at all times an attitude of great reserve, consistency, and dignity." (P. 81.)

That is certainly not a unique view of American-Soviet relations, but since Kennan is an expert on the question, his omission of several key aspects of history is difficult to understand. Surely Kennan is aware that Secretary of State Robert Lansing was avowedly and militantly opposed to the Bolshevik Revolution because of its economic and social goals; that the Wilson administration ignored several specific overtures from Lenin for collaboration against Germany and Japan; and that President Wilson openly "cast in his lot with the rest" and actively supported counter-revolutionary forces in an attempt to overthrow the Soviets.

Hard to comprehend, in short, is Kennan's decision to ignore the fact that from the early days of the November Revolution to the failure of the 1937 Brussels Conference on Japanese aggression in China, the Soviet Union persistently wooed the United States in search of an understanding that would serve to decrease the probability of a conflict that Kennan describes as "at best a war of defense" for the West. Since Kennan is apparently unaware that Tsarist Russia made three overtures of a similar nature to the United States between 1905 and 1912, his failure to place these Soviet advances in a broad framework is perhaps understandable; but even considered as purely post-1917 moves, they can hardly be explained as examples of "burning hostility." Indeed, they document a remarkable Marxist heresy by the very torchbearers of the faith. For economic and political collaboration with the United States designed to preserve Moscow would also preserve Washington—a fact that could not have been missed by the men in the Kremlin. Far from being forced to alter unmitigated antagonism, as Kennan implies, the United States had a standing opportunity to respond to positive advances.

Nor does Kennan deal candidly with American foreign policy as a whole during the interwar years. Far from isolationism, Washington's policy is perhaps best described as an attempt to exercise dominant power within a framework of "freedom without responsi-

bility." Political and economic (and in some cases military) intervention in Latin America, Europe, and China is not isolationism. And
the Roosevelt administration's disinterest in the terms of appeasement offered to Mussolini and Hitler as long as they did not touch
American interests is striking evidence of the refusal to accept
responsibility. These are but the most glaring examples of Kennan's
failure to grapple with basic problems in their entirety. The result is
clear: Kennan's recommendations lack validity. That these conclusions can be accepted as a basis for action is a matter of record, but
to expect them to promote the "national interest" (a well-worn
generality that Kennan declines to define) is neither logical, necessary, nor possible.

Kennan's statement of the policy of containment is major evidence
in support of this judgment. For when he came to apply his
"theoretical foundation" to the specific problem of policy-making,
the result was a recommendation for action designed to effect either
a definitive change in, or the actual destruction of, the Soviet Union.
To be sure, his point of departure is an admission that the sincerity
of Soviet leaders cannot be questioned—that they do desire the
betterment of life in Russia—but he immediately concludes that they
have explained what Kennan takes to be lack of progress in that
direction by the prior necessity to establish the security of the
government.

Kennan's first problem, therefore, is to establish the validity of this
thesis. For a review of the facts, however, he substitutes a statement
that enables him to label the security argument as no more than a
rationale by which the Soviet leaders maintain themselves in
power—no more, in short, than a technique of control. "Tremendous
emphasis," Kennan writes, "has been placed on the original Communist thesis of a basic antagonism between the capitalist and Socialist
worlds." But, he continues, "it is clear, from many indications that
this emphasis is not founded in reality. The real facts concerning it
have been confused by the existence abroad of a genuine resentment
provoked by Soviet philosophy and tactics and occasionally by the
existence of great centers of military power, notably the Nazi regime
in Germany and the Japanese Government of the late 1930's, which
did indeed have aggressive designs against the Soviet Union." There
is, Kennan then concludes, "ample evidence that the stress laid in
Moscow on the menace confronting Soviet society...is founded not
in the realities of foreign antagonism but in the necessity of explaining away the maintenance of dictatorial authority at home."(P. 113.)

These comments and interpretations require further examination. Two notable omissions are Kennan's failure to point out that capitalist leaders militantly opposed socialism (both verbally and more actively) long years before the existence of the Soviet state, and his like failure to note Soviet overtures to the United States from 1917 to 1937. He also neglects to mention the fact and character of allied intervention in Russia. Nor does the reader find any reference to the avowed policy aims of Herbert Hoover (the "abandonment of their present economic system" on the part of the Bolsheviks) and Charles Evans Hughes (who conditioned recognition on "fundamental changes" in the Soviet economic system). Likewise peculiar is the use of the word "occasionally " and the chronology "in the late 1930's" to characterize the threat to Russia from Germany and Japan.

"Occasionally" can hardly be applied to an armed challenge that concerned the world for the majority of the interwar years. And the phrase "in the late 1930's" does not take account of Japan's activities in the intervals from 1917 to 1922 and from 1931 to 1941—or Hitler's from 1934 forward. Kennan's argument that neither Japan's occupation of eastern Siberia and subsequent attacks along the border between Manchuria and Russia nor Hitler's expansion in Central Europe was a threat to Soviet security contrasts strangely with his claim that Moscow was a dire threat to America at a time when the United States had the only stockpile of atom bombs. Yet upon this questionable foundation Kennan proceeds to build his entire argument.

Kennan goes on to deal with two other factors that are central to an analysis of his policy recommendation. "The theory of the inevitability of the eventual fall of capitalism," he writes, "has the fortunate connotation that there is no hurry about it." (P. 116.) And again, "the Kremlin is under no ideological compulsion to accomplish its purposes in a hurry." (P. 118.) He points out, however, that the Soviet Government, "like almost any other government...can be placed in a position where it cannot afford to yield even though this might be dictated by its sense of realism." (P. 119.)

For this reason, Kennan emphasizes, "it is a *sine qua non* of successful dealing with Russia that the foreign government in question should remain at all times cool and collected and that demands on Russian policy should be put forward in such a manner as to leave the way open for a compliance not too detrimental to Russian prestige." (P. 119.) This statement would appear to indicate that Kennan (despite his inaccurate and misleading presentation of past policies toward Soviet Russia) envisaged some careful effort to establish a basic security accommodation with Moscow. His actual conclusion, however, can hardly be described in that manner.

Rather does Kennan prescribe the use of "unanswerable force," a coupling of words that has no meaning save in a military sense. Nor is his formulation vague. The United States, he concludes, "has it in its power to increase enormously the strains under which Soviet policy must operate, to force upon the Kremlin a far greater degree of moderation and circumspection than it has had to observe in recent years, and in this way promote tendencies which must eventually find their outlet in either the break-up or the gradual mellowing of Soviet power." (Pp. 126–127.) And Kennan's choice of words further emphasizes his resort to force: had he meant "a result to be expected," he would have used the phrase *will eventually*. Instead he wrote *must eventually,* an expression of obligation under "physical or logical necessity." But men do not surrender nations or social systems to the dictates of logic, as Kennan himself admits.

Thus Kennan disregards both his own warning about "tactless and threatening gestures" and his concern "to leave the way open for a compliance not too detrimental to Russian prestige." For his policy calls for the application of a steadily rising military pressure to challenge existing Soviet leadership. (Pp. 119, 120.) To this the Soviet leaders can hardly be expected to reply other than by preparations for a short-range showdown. This will hardly bring a "mellowing" of internal controls in Russia. By the same token, Kennan's proposals destroy the "fortunate connotation" in Soviet theory that there is "no hurry." A more classic *non sequitur* could hardly be conceived—even as an exercise in mental gymnastics. But the responsibility for the future of American-Russian relations cannot be classed as intellectual amusement, for upon their character depends the immediate future of the world. And freedom is not nurtured by nations preparing for war.

There is considerable evidence that Kennan later came to realize the fallacy of his 1946 policy recommendations. In 1951, while on leave of absence from the Department of State, he was a bit less disingenuous—and considerably more moderate—in his statements. First, he cautioned that no war (a more candid substitute for his earlier phrase "unanswerable force") with Russia "could be more than relatively successful" (pp. 129–130); took care to point out that even a defeated Russia would not emerge in the image of America (p. 131); sharply redefined the character of the role that the United

States could play—from "has it in its power to increase enormously the strains" to "our role can be at best a marginal one"; and finally warned that any attempt "at direct talking by one nation to another about the latter's political affairs is a questionable procedure." (Pp. 130, 53, 152.)

Later still, on the eve of his departure for Moscow, Kennan more openly indicated doubts about his earlier analysis. "I want to assume that everything I've thought up to now is wrong," he is reported to have observed, "and see whether I come out at the same place this time." He remarked, however, that any change in his earlier conclusions was "improbable"—an admission that raised serious questions as to Kennan's ability to free himself from the thought patterns of the "X" article. Kennan left no doubt, though, that he was worried by the consequences of containment, for he expressed a fear that it was "a lesson that Americans have learned rather too well." (The New Yorker, May 17, 1952, pp. 111, 112.) His concern is well founded, but nothing can alter the fact that it was Kennan himself who served as their tutor.

Central to Kennan's shift was his belated realization that the United States will never have enough power to force Russia to "unquestionably yield to it." Once he awoke to this basic error of his "X" article, Kennan quickly saw that his policy in action could well "increase [the Russians'] fear of being warred upon." (The New Yorker, pp. 112, 116.) Small wonder that he seemed to be giving expression to a fear that his policy of containment is one for which he does not relish ultimate responsibility.

But Kennan cannot escape that responsibility. If he has in fact abandoned containment, he owes the world a formal statement of his decision—for his was the conception and the early implementation of the policy. To date, it has not been abandoned by the United States. If its author now finds it lacking in validity and dangerous in its consequences, then his is the responsibility to throw his weight on the side of revision.

Yet Kennan's greatest failure lies in his inability to define that "something which goes deeper and looks further ahead"—without which containment, by his own admission, "can only remain sterile and negative." (American Diplomacy, p. 153.) That "something" is no less than the courage to acknowledge the broad challenge of the Bolshevik Revolution. One must conclude that so far, at any rate, Kennan is unaware of the challenge, and until he faces that issue candidly he cannot be expected to formulate an effective response to the challenge of Soviet power.

THE LEGEND OF
ISOLATIONISM
IN THE 1920's

[from *Science and Society*, 1954]

Few myths held a firmer and longer grip on American history than that of isolationism. Until it was challenged by historians in the late 1950s, the prevailing view claimed that the United States remained largely aloof from foreign affairs until the 1890s and then retreated once again from the world after World War I—until rudely and forcibly thrust into renewed involvement during World War II. The 1920s was particularly vulnerable to the description of isolationism, and the "lost" decade became a special reference point for scholars as well as politicians seeking to discredit those critical of more recent American activism in the world.

In the first of four articles he wrote about the diplomacy of the twenties, Williams reexamined the record and argued that "far from isolation, the foreign relations of the United States from 1920 through 1932 were marked by...involvement with—and intervention in the affairs of—other nations of the world." He introduced into his discussion the concept of American "corporatism," an alliance during the twenties of government and private institutions seeking and connecting social order and stability at home with the achievement of similar goals abroad.

\

THE widely accepted assumption that the United States was isolationist from 1920 through 1932 is no more than a legend. Sir Francis Bacon might have classed this myth of isolation as one of his Idols of the Market-Place. An "ill and unfit choice of words," he cautioned, "leads men away into innumerable and inane controversies and fancies." And certainly the application of the terms *isolation* and *isolationism* to a period and a policy that were characterized by vigorous involvement in the affairs of the world with consciousness of purpose qualifies as an "ill and unfit choice of words." Thus the purpose of this essay: on the basis of an investigation of the record to suggest that, far from isolation, the foreign relations of the United States from 1920 through 1932 were marked by express and extended involvement with—and intervention in the affairs of—other nations of the world.

It is both more accurate and more helpful to consider the twenties as contiguous with the present instead of viewing those years as a quixotic interlude of low-down jazz and lower-grade gin, fluttering flappers and Faulkner's fiction, and bootlegging millionaires and millionaire bootleggers. For in foreign policy there is far less of a sharp break between 1923 and 1953 than generally is acknowledged. A closer examination of the so-called isolationists of the twenties reveals that many of them were in fact busily engaged in extending American power. Those individuals and groups have not dramatically changed their outlook on foreign affairs. Their policies and objectives may differ with those of others (including professors), but they have never sought to isolate the United States.

This interpretation runs counter to the folklore of American foreign relations. Harvard places isolationism "in the saddle." Columbia sees "Americans retiring within their own shell." Yale judges that policy "degenerated" into isolation—among other things. Others, less picturesque but equally positive, refer to a "marked increase of isolationist sentiment" and to "those years of isolationism." Another group diagnoses the populace as having "ingrained isolationism," analyzes it as "sullen and selfish" in consequence, and characterizes it as doing "its best to forget international subjects." Related verdicts describe the Republican party as "predominantly isolationist" and as an organization that "fostered a policy of deliberate isolation."

Most pointed of these specifications is a terse two-word summary of the diplomacy of this period: "Isolation Perfected." Populizers have transcribed this theme into a burlesque. Their articles and books convey the impression that the Secretaries of State were in semi-retirement and that the citizenry wished to do away with the Department itself. Columnists and commentators have made the concept an eerie example of George Orwell's double-think. They label as isolationists the most vigorous interventionists.

The case would seem to be closed and judgment given if it were not for the ambivalence of some observers and the brief dissents filed by a few others. The scholar who used the phrase "those years of isolationism," for example, remarks elsewhere in the same book that "expansionism...really was long a major expression of isolationism." Another writes of the "return to an earlier policy of isolation," and on the next page notes a "shift in policy during the twenties amounting almost to a 'diplomatic revolution'." A recent biographer states that Henry Cabot Lodge "did not propose... an isolationist attitude," but then proceeds to characterize the Monroe Doctrine—upon which Lodge stood in his fight against the League of Nations treaty—as a philosophy of "isolation." And in the last volume of his trilogy, the late Professor Frederick L. Paxton summed up a long review of the many diplomatic activities of the years 1919–1923 with the remark that this was a foreign policy of "avoidance rather than of action."

But a few scholars, toying with the Idol of the Market-Place, have made bold to rock the image. Yet Professor Richard Van Alstyne was doing more than playing the iconoclast when he observed that the "militant manifest destiny men were the isolationists of the nineteenth century." For with this insight we can translate those who maintain that Lodge "led the movement to perpetuate the traditional policy of isolation." Perhaps William G. Carleton was even more forthright. In 1946 he pointed out that the fight over the League treaty was not between isolationists and internationalists, and added that many of the mislabeled isolationists were actually "nationalists and imperialists." Equally discerning was Charles Beard's comment in 1933 that the twenties were marked by a "return to the more aggressive ways...[used] to protect and advance the claims of American business enterprise." All these interpretations were based on facts that prompted another scholar to change his earlier conclusion and declare in 1953 that "the thought was all of keeping American freedom of action."

These are perceptive comments. Additional help has recently been supplied by two other students of the period. One of these is Robert E. Osgood, who approached the problem in terms of *Ideals and Self-Interest in American Foreign Relations*. Though primarily concerned with the argument that Americans should cease being naive, Osgood suggests that certain stereotypes are misleading. One might differ with his analysis of the struggle over the Treaty of Versailles, but not with his insistence that there were fundamental differences

78 A William Appleman Williams Reader

between Senators Lodge and William E. Borah—as well as between those two and President Woodrow Wilson. Osgood likewise raises questions about the reputed withdrawal of the American public. Over a thousand organizations for the study of international relations existed in 1926, to say nothing of the groups that sought constantly to make or modify foreign policy.

Osgood gives little attention to this latter aspect of foreign relations, a surprising omission on the part of a realist. But the underlying assumption of his inquiry cannot be challenged. The foreign policy issue of the twenties was never isolationism. The controversy and competition were waged between those who entertained different concepts of the national interest and disagreed over the means to be employed to secure that objective. Secretary of State Charles Evans Hughes was merely more eloquent, not less explicit. "Foreign policies," he explained in 1923, "are not built upon abstractions. They are the result of practical conceptions of national interest arising from some immediate exigency or standing out vividly in historical perspective."

Historian George L. Grassmuck used this old-fashioned premise of the politician as a tool with which to probe the *Sectional Biases in Congress on Foreign Policy*. Disciplining himself more rigorously in the search for primary facts than did Osgood, Grassmuck's findings prompted him to conclude that "the 'sheep and goats' technique" of historical research is eminently unproductive. From 1921 to 1933, for example, the Republicans in both houses of Congress were "more favorable to both Army and Navy measures than...Democrats." Eighty-five percent of the same Republicans supported international economic measures and agreements. As for the Middle West, that much condemned section did not reveal any "extraordinary indication of a...tendency to withdraw." Nor was there "an intense 'isolationism' on the part of [its] legislators with regard to membership in a world organization." And what opposition there was seems to have been as much the consequence of dust bowls and depression as the product of disillusioned scholars in ivory towers.

These investigations and correlations have two implications. First, the United States was neither isolated nor did it pursue a policy of isolationism from 1920 to 1933. Second, if the policy of that era, so generally accepted as the product of traditional isolationist sentiment, proves non-isolationist, then the validity and usefulness of the concept when applied to earlier or later periods may seriously be challenged.

Indeed, it would seem more probable that the central theme of American foreign relations has been the expansion of the United States. Alexander Hamilton made astute use of the phrase "no entangling alliances" during the negotiation of Jay's Treaty in 1794, but his object was a *de facto* affiliation with the British Fleet—not isolation. Nor was Thomas Jefferson seeking to withdraw when he made of Monticello a counselling center for those seeking to emulate the success of the American Revolution. A century later Senator Lodge sought to revise the Treaty of Versailles and the Covenant of the League of Nations with reservations that seemed no more than a restatement of Hamilton's remarks. Yet the maneuvers of Lodge were no more isolationist in character and purpose than Hamilton's earlier action. And while surely no latter-day Jefferson, Senator Borah was anything but an isolationist in his concept of the power of economics and ideas. Borah not only favored the recognition of the Soviet Union in order to influence the development of the Bolshevik Revolution and as a check against Japanese expansion in Asia, but also argued that American economic policies were intimately concerned with the extension of one or more aspects of American influence, power, and authority.

Approached in this manner, the record of American foreign policy in the twenties verifies the judgments of two remarkably dissimilar students: historian Richard W. Leopold and Senator Lodge. The professor warns that the era was "more complex than most glib generalizations...would suggest"; and the scholastic politician concludes that, excepting wars, there "never [was] a period when the United States [was] more active and its influence more felt internationally than between 1921 and 1924." The admonition about perplexity was offered as helpful advice, not as an invitation to anti-intellectualism. For, as the remarks of the Senator implied, recognition that a problem is involved does not mean that it cannot be resolved.

Paradox and complexity can often be clarified by rearranging the data around a new focal point that is common to all aspects of the apparent contradiction. The confusion of certainty and ambiguity that characterizes most accounts of American foreign policy in the twenties stems from the fact that they are centered on the issue of membership in the League of Nations. Those Americans who wanted to join are called internationalists. Opponents of that move became isolationists. But the subsequent action of most of those who fought participation in the League belies this simple classification.

And the later policies of many who favored adherence to the League cast serious doubts upon the assumption that they were willing to negotiate or arbitrate questions that they defined as involving the national interest. More pertinent is an examination of why certain groups and individuals favored or disapproved of the League, coupled with a review of the programs they supported after that question was decided.

Yet such a re-study of the League fight is in itself insufficient. Equally important is a close analysis of the American reaction to the Bolshevik Revolution. Both the League Covenant and the Treaty of Versailles were written on a table shaken by that upheaval. The argument over the ratification of the combined documents was waged in a context determined as much by Nikolai Lenin's *Appeal to the Toiling, Oppressed, and Exhausted Peoples of Europe* and the Soviet *Declaration to the Chinese People* as by George Washington's Farewell Address.

Considered within the setting of the Bolshevik Revolution, the basic question was far greater than whether or not to enter the League. At issue was what response was to be made to the domestic and international division of labor that had accompanied the Industrial Revolution. Challenges from organized labor, dissatisfied farmers, frightened men of property, searching intellectual critics, and colonial peoples rudely interrupted almost every meeting of the Big Four in Paris and were echoed in many Senate debates over the treaty. And those who determined American policy through the decade of the twenties were consciously concerned with the same problem.

An inquiry into this controversy over the broad question of how to end the war reveals certain divisions within American society. These groupings were composed of individuals and organizations whose position on the League of Nations was coincident with and part of their response to the Bolsheviks; or, in a wider sense, with their answer to that general unrest, described by Woodrow Wilson as a "feeling of revolt against the large vested interests which influence the world both in the economic and the political sphere." Once this breakdown has been made it is then possible to follow the ideas and actions of these various associations of influence and power through the years 1920 to 1933.

At the core of the American reaction to the League and the Bolshevik Revolution was the quandary between fidelity to ideals and the urge to power. Jefferson faced a less acute version of the same predicament in terms of whether to force citizenship on settlers west of the Mississippi who were reluctant to be absorbed in the Louisiana Purchase. A century later the anti-imperialists posed the same issue in the more sharply defined circumstances of the Spanish-American War. The League and the Bolsheviks raised the question in its most dramatic context and in unavoidable terms.

There were four broad responses to this reopening of the age-old dilemma. At one pole stood the pure idealists and pacifists, led by William Jennings Bryan. A tiny minority in themselves, they were joined, in terms of general consequences if not in action, by those Americans who were preoccupied with their own solutions to the problem. Many American business men, for example, were concerned primarily with the expansion of trade and were apathetic toward or impatient with the hullabaloo over the League. Diametrically opposed to the idealists were the vigorous expansionists. All these exponents of the main chance did not insist upon an overt crusade to run the world, but they were united on Senator Lodge's proposition that the United States should dominate world politics. Association with other nations they accepted, but not equality of membership or mutuality of decision.

Caught in the middle were those Americans who declined to support either extreme. A large number of these people clustered around Woodrow Wilson, and can be called the Wilsonites. Though aware of the dangers and temptations involved, Wilson declared his intention to extend American power for the purpose of strengthening the ideals. However noble that effort, it failed for two reasons. Wilson delegated power and initiative to men and organizations that did not share his objectives, and on his own part the president ultimately "cast in his lot" with the defenders of the status quo.

Led by the Sons of the Wild Jackass, the remaining group usually followed Senator Borah in foreign relations. These men had few illusions about the importance of power in human affairs or concerning the authority of the United States in international politics. Prior to the world war they supported—either positively or passively— such vigorous expansionists as Theodore Roosevelt, who led their Progressive Party. But the war and the Bolshevik Revolution jarred some of these Progressives into a closer examination of their assumptions. These reflections and new conclusions widened the breach with those of their old comrades who had moved toward a conservative position on domestic issues. Some of those earlier allies, like Senator Albert J. Beveridge, continued to agitate for an American

century. Others, such as Bainbridge Colby, sided with Wilson in 1916
and went along with the president on foreign policy.

But a handful had become firm anti-expansionists by 1919. No
attempt was made by these men to deny the power of the United
States. Nor did they think that the nation could become self-
sufficient and impregnable in its strength. Borah, for example,
insisted that America must stand with Russia if Japan and Germany
were to be checked. And Johnson constantly pointed out that the
question was not whether to withdraw, but at what time and under
what circumstances to use the country's influence. What these men
did maintain was that any effort to run the world by establishing an
American system comparable to the British Empire was both futile
and un-American.

In this they agreed with Henry Adams, who debated the same
issue with his brother Brooks Adams, Theodore Roosevelt, and
Henry Cabot Lodge in the years after 1898. "I incline now to
anti-imperialism, and very strongly to anti-militarism," Henry
warned. "If we try to rule politically, we take the chances against
us." By the end of the first world war another generation of
expansionists tended to agree with Henry Adams about ruling
politically, but planned to build and maintain a similar pattern of
control through the use of America's economic might. Replying to
these later expansionists, Borah and other anti-expansionists of the
nineteen-twenties argued that if Washington's influence was to be
effective it would have to be used to support the movements of
reform and colonial nationalism rather than deployed in an effort to
dam up and dominate those forces.

For these reasons they opposed Wilson's reorganization of the
international banking consortium, fearing that the financiers would
either influence strongly or veto—as they did—American foreign
policies. With Senator Albert B. Cummins of Iowa they voted
against the Wilson-approved Webb-Pomerene Act, which repealed
the anti-trust laws for export associations. In the same vein they tried
to prevent passage of the Edge Act, an amendment to the Federal
Reserve Act that authorized foreign banking corporations. Led by
Borah, they bitterly attacked the Versailles Treaty because, in their
view, it committed the United States to oppose colonial movements
for self-government and to support an unjust and indefensible status
quo. From the same perspective they criticized and fought to end
intervention in Russia and the suppression of civil liberties at home.

Contrary to the standard criticism of their actions, however, these anti-expansionists were not just negative die-hards. Senator Cummins maintained from the first that American loans to the allies should be considered gifts. Borah spoke out on the same issue, hammered away against armed intervention in Latin America, played a key role in securing the appointment of Dwight Morrow as Ambassador to Mexico, and sought to align the United States with, instead of against, the Chinese Revolution. On these and other issues the anti-expansionists were not always of one mind, but as in the case of the Washington Conference Treaties the majority of them were far more positive in their actions than has been acknowledged.

Within this framework the key to the defeat of the League treaty was the defection from the Wilsonites of a group who declined to accept the restrictions that Article X of the League Covenant threatened to impose upon the United States. A morally binding guarantee of the "territorial integrity and existing political integrity of all members of the League" was too much for these men. First they tried to modify that limitation. Failing there, they followed Elihu Root and William Howard Taft, both old-time expansionists, to a new position behind Senator Lodge. Among those who abandoned Wilson on this issue were Herbert Hoover, Calvin Coolidge, Charles Evans Hughes, and Henry L. Stimson.

Not all these men were at ease with the vigorous expansionists. Stimson, for one, thought the Lodge reservations "harsh and unpleasant," and later adjusted other of his views. Hoover and Hughes tried to revive their version of the League after the Republicans returned to power in 1920. But at the time all of them were more uneasy about what one writer has termed Wilson's "moral imperialism." They were not eager to identify themselves with the memories of that blatant imperialism of the years 1895 to 1905, but neither did they like Article X. That proviso caught them from both sides: it illegalized changes initiated by the United States, and obligated America to restore a status quo to some aspects of which they were either indifferent or antagonistic. But least of all were they anxious to run the risk that the Wilsonian rhetoric of freedom and liberty might be taken seriously in an age of revolution. Either by choice or default they supported the idea of a community of interest among the industrialized powers of the world led by an American-British entente as against the colonial areas and the Soviet Union.

This postwar concept of the community of interest was the first-generation intellectual offspring of Herbert Croly's *Promise of American Life* and Herbert Hoover's *American Individualism.* Croly's opportunistic nationalism provided direction for Hoover's "greater mutuality of interest." The latter was to be expressed in an alliance between the government and the "great trade associations and the powerful corporations." Pushed by the Croly-Hoover wing of the old Progressive Party, the idea enjoyed great prestige during the twenties. Among its most ardent exponents were Samuel Gompers and Matthew Woll of the labor movement, Owen D. Young of management, and Bernard Baruch of finance.

What emerged was an American corporatism. The avowed goals were order, stability, and social peace. The means to those objectives were labor-management co-operation, arbitration, and the elimination of waste and inefficiency by closing out unrestrained competition. State intervention was to be firm, but moderated through the cultivation and legalization of trade associations which would, in turn, advise the national government and supply leaders for the federal bureaucracy. The ideal was union in place of diversity and conflict.

Other than Hoover, the chief spokesman of this new community of interest as applied to foreign affairs were Secretaries of State Hughes and Stimson. In the late months of 1931 Stimson was to shift his ground, but until that time he supported the principle. All three men agreed that American economic power should be used to build, strengthen, and maintain the co-operation they sought. As a condition for his entry into the cabinet, Hoover demanded—and received—a major voice in "all important economic policies of the administration." With the energetic assistance of Julius Klein, lauded by the National Foreign Trade Council as the "international business go-getter of Uncle Sam," Hoover changed the Department of Commerce from an agency primarily concerned with interstate commerce to one that concentrated on foreign markets and loans, and control of import sources. Hughes and Stimson handled the political aspects of establishing a "community of ideals, interests and purposes."

These men were not imperialists in the traditional sense of that much abused term. All agreed with Klein that the object was to eliminate "the old imperialistic trappings of politico-economic exploitation." They sought instead the "internationalization of business." Through the use of economic power they wanted to establish a common bond, forged of similar assumptions and purposes, with both the industrialized nations and the native business community in the colonial areas of the world. Their deployment of America's material strength is unquestioned. President Calvin Coolidge reviewed their success, and indicated the political implications thereof, on Memorial Day, 1928. "Our investments and trade relations are such," he summarized, "that it is almost impossible to conceive of any conflict anywhere on earth which would not affect us injuriously."

Internationalization through the avoidance of conflict was the key objective. This did not mean a negative foreign policy. Positive action was the basic theme. The transposition of corporatist principles to the area of foreign relations produced a parallel policy. American leadership and intervention would build a world community regulated by agreement among the industrialized nations. The prevention of revolution and the preservation of the sanctity of private property were vital objectives. Hughes was very clear when he formulated the idea for Latin America. "We are seeking to establish a *Pax Americana* maintained not by arms but by mutual respect and good will and the tranquillizing processes of reason." There would be, he admitted, "interpositions of a temporary character"—the Secretary did not like the connotations of the word intervention—but only to facilitate the establishment of the United States as the "exemplar of justice."

Extension to the world of this pattern developed in Latin America was more involved. There were five main difficulties, four in the realm of foreign relations and one in domestic affairs. The internal problem was to establish and integrate a concert of decision between the government and private economic groups. Abroad the objectives were more sharply defined: circumscribe the impact of the Soviet Union, forestall and control potential resistance of colonial areas, pamper and cajole Germany and Japan into acceptance of the basic proposition, and secure from Great Britain practical recognition of the fact that Washington had become the center of Anglo-Saxon collaboration. Several examples will serve to illustrate the general outline of this diplomacy, and to indicate the friction between the office holders and the office dwellers.

Wilson's Administration left the incoming Republicans a plurality of tools designed for the purpose of extending American power. The Webb-Pomerene Law, the Edge Act, and the banking consortium were but three of the more obvious and important of these. Certain polishing and sharpening remained to be done, as exemplified by Hoover's generous interpretation of the Webb-Pomerene legislation, but this was a minor problem. Hoover and Hughes added to these implements with such laws as the one designed to give American customs officials diplomatic immunity so that they could do cost accounting surveys of foreign firms. This procedure was part of the plan to provide equal opportunity abroad, under which circumstances Secretary Hughes was confident that "American business men would take care of themselves."

It was harder to deal with the British, who persisted in annoying indications that they considered themselves equal partners in the enterprise. Bainbridge Colby, Wilson's last Secretary of State, ran into the same trouble. Unless England came "to our way of thinking," Colby feared that "agreement [would] be impossible." A bit later Hughes told the British Ambassador that the time had come for London's expressions of cordial sentiment to be "translated into something definite." After many harangues about oil, access to mandated areas, and trade with Russia, it was with great relief that Stimson spoke of the United States and Great Britain "working together like two old shoes."

Deep concern over revolutionary ferment produced great anxiety. Hughes quite agreed with Colby that the problem was to prevent revolutions without making martyrs of the leaders of colonial or other dissident movements. The dispatches of the period are filled with such expressions as "very grave concern," "further depressed," and "deeply regret," in connection with revolutionary activity in China, Latin America, and Europe. American foreign service personnel abroad were constantly reminded to report all indications of such unrest. This sensitivity reached a high point when one representative telegraphed as "an example of the failure to assure public safety...the throwing of a rock yesterday into the state hospital here." Quite in keeping with this pattern was Washington's conclusion that it would support "any provisional government which gave satisfactory evidence of an intention to re-establish constitutional order."

Central to American diplomacy of the twenties was the issue of Germany and Japan. And it was in this area that the government ran into trouble with its partners, the large associations of capital. The snag was to convince the bankers of the validity of the long range view. Hoover, Hughes and Stimson all agreed that it was vital to integrate Germany and Japan into the American community. Thus Hughes opposed the French diplomacy of force on the Rhine, and for his own part initiated the Dawes Plan. But the delegation of so much authority to the financiers backfired in 1931. The depression scared the House of Morgan and it refused to extend further credits to Germany. Stimson "blew up." He angrily told the Morgan representative in Paris that this strengthened France and thereby undercut the American program. Interrupted in the midst of this argument by a trans-Atlantic phone call form Hoover, Stimson explained to the president that "if you want to help the cause you are speaking of you will not do it by calling me up, but by calling Tom Lamont." Stimson then turned back to Lamont's agent in Europe and, using "unregulated language," told the man to abandon his "narrow banking axioms."

Similar difficulties faced the government in dealing with Japan and China. The main problem was to convince Japan, by persuasion, concession, and the delicate use of diplomatic force, to join the United States in an application of its Latin American policy to China. Washington argued that the era of the crude exploitation of, and the exercise of direct political sovereignty over, backward peoples was past. Instead, the interested powers should agree to develop and exercise a system of absentee authority while increasing the productive capacity and administrative efficiency of China. Japan seemed amenable to the proposal, and at the Washington Conference, Secretary Hughes went a great distance to convince Tokyo of American sincerity. Some writers, such as George Frost Kennan and Adolf A. Berle, claim that the United States did not go far enough. This is something of a mystery. For in his efforts to establish "cooperation in the Far East," as Hughes termed it, the Secretary consciously gave Japan "an extraordinarily favorable position."

Perhaps what Kennan and Berle have in mind is the attitude of Thomas Lamont. In contrast to their perspective on Europe, the bankers took an extremely long-range view of Asia. Accepting the implications of the Four and Nine Power treaties, Lamont began to finance Japan's penetration of the mainland. Hughes and Stimson were trapped. They continued to think in terms of American business men taking care of themselves if given an opportunity, and thus strengthening Washington's position in the world community. Hughes wrote Morgan that he hoped the consortium would become an "important instrumentality of our 'open door' policy." But the American members of the banking group refused to antagonize their Japanese and British colleagues, and so vetoed Washington's hope to finance the Chinese Eastern Railway and its efforts to support the Federal Telegraph Company in China.

In this context it is easy to sympathize with Stimson's discomfort when the Japanese Army roared across Manchuria. As he constantly reiterated to the Japanese Ambassador in Washington, Tokyo had come far along the road "of bringing itself into alignment with the methods and opinion of the Western World." Stimson not only wanted to, but did in fact give Japan every chance to continue along that path. So too did President Hoover, whose concern with revolution was so great that he was inclined to view Japanese sovereignty in Manchuria as the best solution. Key men in the State Department shared the president's conclusion.

Stimson's insight was not so limited. He realized that his predecessor, Secretary of State Frank B. Kellogg, had been right: the community of interest that America should seek was with the Chinese. The Secretary acknowledged his error to Senator Borah, who had argued just such a thesis since 1917. Stimson's letter to Borah of February 23, 1932, did not say that America should abandon her isolationism, but rather that she had gone too far with the wrong friends. The long and painful process of America's great awakening had begun. But in the meantime President Hoover's insistence that no move should be made toward the Soviet Union, and that the non-recognition of Manchukuo should be considered as a formula looking toward conciliation, had opened the door to appeasement.

THE FRONTIER THESIS
AND AMERICAN
FOREIGN POLICY

[from *Pacific Historical Review*, 1955]

Central to Williams's interpretation of American foreign policy was his emphasis on the conscious and steady expansion of the United States abroad. He had first called attention to this impulse in the early chapters of *American-Russian Relations*, where he located the decline in friendship and the beginnings of animosity between the two societies in their confrontation in northeast Asia during the 1890s, when American economic interests collided with Russian imperial activities. Williams then set out to explore more fully the causes for U.S. expansion in general. He examined the ideas of Frederick Jackson Turner and Brooks Adams which provided central insights for his explanations. The influential concepts advanced by Turner and Adams in the 1890s, Williams asserted, "became the world view of subsequent generations of Americans and...important... to understanding America's imperial expansion in the twentieth century."

ONE of the central themes of American historiography is that there is no American Empire. Most historians will admit, if pressed, that the United States once had an empire. They promptly insist that it was given away. But they also speak persistently of America as a World Power. Whatever language is used to describe the situation, the record of American diplomacy is clear in one point. The United States has been a consciously and steadily expanding nation since 1890. This essay is an initial exploration of one of the dynamic causes behind that extension of varying degrees of American sovereignty throughout the world.

Three continuing and interacting processes produce foreign policy. First, the domestic and overseas activity of the citizenry, and of other countries, which forces a government to take action in the international area. Second, the nature of that official action. And third, the reactions that such policies provoke among its own people and on the part of the foreigners who are affected. The circle is thus closed and rolls on through time. In studying foreign policy it ultimately becomes necessary to break into this continuity and find out, if possible, what the people in question thought they were doing.

One way to do this is to reconstruct the reality with which given men were forced to deal, look at it through their eyes, interpret it with their ideas, and then conclude as to the consequences of such a world view. The argument here, based on such a methodology, is that a set of ideas, first promulgated in the 1890's, became the world view of subsequent generations of Americans and is an important clue to understanding America's imperial expansion in the twentieth century.

One idea is Frederick Jackson Turner's concept that America's unique and true democracy was the product of an expanding frontier. The other idea is the thesis of Brooks Adams that America's unique and true democracy could be preserved only by a foreign policy of expansion. Turner's idea was designed to explain an experience already ended and to warn of the dangers ahead. Adams' idea was calculated to preserve Turner's half-truth about the past for his own time and project it into the future. Both ideas did much to prevent any understanding of a wholly new reality to which they were applied, and to which they were at best inadequate and at worst irrelevant. But taken together, the ideas of Turner and Adams supplied American empire builders with an overview and explanation of the world, and a reasonably specific program of action from 1893 to 1953.

Turner's influence began when he was declared the parent of the frontier thesis by a star chamber court—the American Historical Association. His statement of the idea then became the central, if not the only, thesis of Everyman's History of the United States. His personal influence touched Woodrow Wilson and perhaps Theodore Roosevelt, while his generalization guided subsequent generations of intellectuals and business men who became educational leaders, wielders of corporate power, government bureaucrats, and crusaders for the Free World.

Adams preferred direct ties with the policy-makers. He did not achieve Turner's fame among laymen, but he passed his ideas on to Theodore Roosevelt and others who guided American expansion at the turn of the century. Fifty years later he was discovered by two groups of intellectual leaders. Scholars awarded him intellectual biographies and estimates of his influence. Those more immediately concerned with public policy, like columnist Marquis Childs and foreign service officer George Frost Kennan, introduced him to the public and applied his ideas to later problems.

Turner and Adams first offered their ideas on the marketplace of opinion and influence between 1893 and 1900, the years of crisis at the end of three decades of rough and rapid progress. American society had undergone, in the space of a generation, an economic revolution in each of four critical areas: steam, steel, communications, and agriculture. The coincidence and convergence of these upheavals produced a major crisis. Bewildered by its quadruple triumph, the United States momentarily panicked. Then, reassured by illusions of ideological purity and international omnipotence, it embarked upon a second industrial revolution. But in that frightening pause between culmination and renewal Turner and Adams looked out upon a harsh and disturbing reality.

The basic steel industry and transportation system of the country were completed. The rate of national economic growth was falling off. New technological advances had yet to be applied in wholesale fashion. Instead, it seemed that the giants of the economic community had turned aside from their conquest of nature to despoil their own kind. Trusts, holding companies, and corporations began to wolf down the individual business man in a feast of consolidation and concentration. Farming was ceasing to be a family affair. Development of the public domain was coming more and more to be controlled by large capital. The Census Director emphasized the sense of foreboding when he announced, in April, 1891, that "there can hardly be said to be a frontier."

This, to Turner and Adams, was the most dangerous omen of all. Both men grew up believing in the traditional conservative philosophy that the key to American democracy was the dynamic competition between men and groups who had a stake in society. They shared the conviction, or more probably the assumption, that this stake had been, for capitalist and farmer alike, the readily available and extensive supply of land. Railroads, steel plants, and wheat production were all similar in being based on control of landed resources and wealth. Now the life blood of American democracy was gone.

The consequences seemed appalling. Men looked to be making capital out of each other. Real estate speculation rapidly collapsed, even in the South. Wheat prices declined steadily. But the rate of interest seemed immune to the laws of economic gravity. Men were no longer going west as hired hands and becoming land owners. Tenancy, not ownership, seemed the institution with a future. One hundred eighty thousand people retreated eastward from Kansas. Those who stayed raised more cain than corn. Even the cowboy went on strike in parts of Texas.

Workers were no happier. The relative rate of increase in real wages slacked off, and then, from 1889 to 1898, wages lost ground in an absolute sense. "Strike!" became the rallying cry. Miners came out of the ground in Idaho, Colorado, and Virginia. Switchmen became pickets in Buffalo. Eugene V. Debs led his American Railway Union to the relief of the industrial peons of the Pullman Company. The Army of the United States countermarched with fixed bayonets against American civilians in Chicago. Debs saw in the polished steel of those bayonets the vision of American socialism. But other men were too preoccupied with the mirage of a square meal. They roamed the country looking for jobs. Their wives stayed home to scavenge the garbage cans. And in Pennsylvania the heroes of Homestead could not buy shoes for their children.

In the molten flux of this crisis, on July 12, 1893, Frederick Jackson Turner undertook to explain what was happening to America. His interpretation also contained an implicit recommendation for action. His famous paper on "The Significance of the Frontier in American History" was Turner's application of his philosophy of history to American problems. History, for Turner, was nothing if not utilitarian. *"Each age,"* he had emphasized two years earlier, *"writes the history of the past anew with reference to the conditions uppermost in its own time."* For Turner his was the "age of machinery, of the factory system, and also the age of socialistic inquiry." Present-minded concern with the crisis which coincided with his intellectual maturity conditioned Turner's entire frontier thesis.

Thus Turner consciously sought a dynamic explanation of America's more happy history in the eighteenth and nineteenth centuries. He had the answer by 1891. "The ever-retreating frontier of free land is the key to American development." Then, in 1893, he changed the formulation of that thesis from a negative to a positive construction, and in the process used a vigorous, active verb—expansion. "This perennial rebirth, this fluidity of American life, this expansion westward with its new opportunities, its continuous touch with the simplicity of primitive society, furnish the forces dominating American life." Expansion, he concluded, promoted individualism which "from the beginning promoted democracy."

Expansion, Individualism, and Democracy was the catechism offered by this young messiah of America's uniqueness and omnipotence. The frontier, he cried, was "a magic fountain of youth in which America continuously bathed and rejuvenated." Without it, "fissures begin to open between classes, fissures that may widen into chasms." But he was confident that these dangers could and would be avoided. "American energy will continually demand a wider field for its exercise." Ultimately he lauded the pioneer as the "foreloper" of empire. And to drive home the lesson he quoted Rudyard Kipling, the laureate of British imperialism. Turner had explained the past and implied a program for the present. Materialistic individualism and democratic idealism could be married and maintained by a foreign policy of expansion.

Turner gave Americans a nationalistic world view that eased their doubts, settled their confusions, and justified their aggressiveness. The frontier thesis was a bicarbonate of soda for emotional and intellectual indigestion. His thesis rolled through the universities and into popular literature as a tidal wave. Expansion a la Turner was good for business and at the same time extended white Protestant democracy. Patrician politicians like Theodore Roosevelt and Woodrow Wilson could agree with railway magnate Edward H. Harriman, financier J. P. Morgan, and the missionaries on the validity of Turner's explanation of America's greatness. Turner's thesis thus played an important role in the history of American foreign relations. For his interpretation did much to Americanize and popularize the heretofore alien ideas of economic imperialism and the White Man's Burden.

Meanwhile, in that same month of July, 1893, another student of the frontier came to the same conclusion reached by Turner. Within a month he, too, read a paper which stated the same thesis but in a different manner. But Brooks Adams was tucked away in America's ancestral home in Quincy, Massachusetts. The public knew nothing of his work. Astringent and argumentative, he was forty-five and fed

up with America's professional intellectuals. He read *his* paper to a
peer, brother Henry Adams. Together they shared it with a few of
their fellow New England noblemen, like Henry Cabot Lodge, John
Hay, and Theodore Roosevelt, who did what they could to translate
the implications of its thesis into official American policy.

The paper that Brooks read to Henry was the manuscript copy of
The Law of Civilization and Decay. It was a frontier thesis for the
world. Adams, like Turner, sought meaning and significance for the
present from his study of history. "The value of history lies not in the
multitude of facts collected, but in their relation to each other."
Unlike Turner, Brooks Adams took the world as his subject and
studied it with the aid of psychology and economics. He concluded
that the centers of world civilization followed the frontiers of
economic wealth and opportunity westward around the globe. The
route was unmistakable: from the Mediterranean Basin through
Western Europe to Great Britain. And to him the crisis of the 1890's
was the turmoil incident to its further movement across the Atlantic
to New York.

Brooks Adams was confronted with the same gloomy report of the
Census Director that had so disturbed Turner. The continental West
was filled up. America no longer had a frontier. As with Turner, this
was a body blow to his early and easy assumption of steady
evolutionary progress. He did not duck the truth. The thesis, he
wrote brother Henry, worked out "in such a ghastly way that it
knocks the stuffing out of me." He counterpunched with a policy of
aggressive expansion designed to make Asia an economic colony of
the United States. Russia was the most dangerous opponent; but
Japan also needed to be watched. The strategy was to play them off
against each other. America would be left as mistress of the vast
frontier of Asia. "I am an expansionist, an 'imperialist,'" if you
please," he told a Boston newspaper man, "and I presume I may be
willing to go farther in this line than anyone else in Massachusetts,
with, perhaps, a few exceptions."

Thus did Turner and Adams reach the same conclusions in their
separate studies of the frontier. Adams said that civilization followed
the frontier of economic wealth. Turner agreed. Adams called the
frontier the zone between "barbarism and civilization." Turner used
"savagery and civilization." Adams maintained that American industry's "liberal margin of profit" had been "due to expansion" across
the continent. Turner argued that America's true democracy was the
product of this same expanding frontier. Both men saw the end of

the continental frontier as the cause and symbol of crisis. Both dreaded the revolution—be it socialistic or monopolistic—that seemed to threaten at every turn. Adams chimed in that dissolution and decay might also follow. And implicitly or explicitly both men agreed on the program to avert chaos. Further expansion was the Kentucky rifle with which to cut down the night riders of catastrophe—Socialists, Robber Barons, and Barbarians.

Turner's thesis became America's explanation of its success and the prescription for its own and others' troubles. His interpretation of the American experience reassured and then inspired the millions. This is not to say that Turner had no influence on those who sat at the desks of decision. He did. Possibly with Theodore Roosevelt; certainly with Woodrow Wilson, and the generations of business men and bureaucrats whose teachers assured them that an expanding frontier was the cause of America's democratic success. But primarily he was the apostle of a revival movement that restored the faith of the conquerors of North America and made them international crusaders.

A far-western newspaper editor, writing in the summer of 1955, provided one of the clearest statements of this function and influence:

> The idea, our forefathers believed, was to "push the Indians back to the frontier." Then, with the Indians pushed back to the wilderness, all would be well.... Well, remember Kaiser Bill? He rather replaced the Indians.... Then, while World War I's doughboy was still wearing out pieces of his uniform, it became obvious that the woods, out along the frontier, were still full of Indians. The thing to do, we figured, was to push back the Indians.

Novelists of the frontier have used Turner's insight as the central theme of their work. Indeed, their protagonists often seem more Turnerian than human. Consider, for example, an impromptu speech delivered by one of Ernest Haycox's Oregon pioneers:

> We grew up in the American notion that we could start from nothing and become rich or get elected president. That's our religion, much as any we've got—that we could turn a dream into beefsteak and prosperity and happiness, leave our children more than we had, and so on. When we got older we saw that it wasn't that sure a thing. But we couldn't admit the dream was bad, for that would be saying hope is an illusion. So we saw empty land out here and we've come here to make a fresh start, hoping that what was wrong back East won't be wrong here.

Such examples suggest that the history of Turner's thesis may well offer a classic illustration of the transformation of an idea into an ideology.

Adams, for his part, became something of a Marx for the influential elite. He lost much of his direct personal significance after Theodore Roosevelt stepped down as President in 1909, though he did continue to have the ear of Senator Henry Cabot Lodge. But thirty years later Charles Austin Beard revealed that Adams, as well as Turner, was one of the men who had changed his mind. Beard even republished *The Law of Civilization and Decay* with a long introduction praising Adams as a penetrating and original thinker. A bit later Adams was discovered by a new group of policy-makers. State Department officials, columnists and commentators, and other advisors to the powerful began to cite him in footnotes and—more often—to paraphrase his ideas as their own. One even reissued his foreign policy recommendations of the 1890's as a guide for the United States in the Cold War.

Adams always exercised his more personalized influence within the mainstream of Turnerism. He caught Theodore Roosevelt after the last battles of *The Winning of the West.* Turner had meanwhile encouraged Roosevelt to continue his interpretation of the westward movement as the civilizing conquest of the savage by the Anglo-Saxon democrat. He also may have sharpened Roosevelt's uneasiness about the close of the frontier. Roosevelt was "very much struck" by Turner's essay on the significance of the frontier. He thought it contained "some first class ideas" which came "at *the* right time." Turner's ideas were "so interesting and suggestive" that Roosevelt wrote a blind letter to open the correspondence. But Roosevelt's great awakening came in his seminars with Brooks Adams.

Fellow aristocrat though he was, Adams rudely frightened Roosevelt. The strenuous life connected with destroying the Indian and winning the West had been fun. Not so with the battle to break down the powerful arguments and demolish the dreary logic of *The Law of Civilization and Decay.* Perhaps Roosevelt never quite forgave Adams for having written and published the book. And once, probably in a moment of anger with him for having thrown human nature into the perpetual motion machinery of evolution, he went so far as to call Adams "half-crazy." But the best that Roosevelt could do with *The Law* was to admit that it would be hard work to repeal it and ask Adams for advice on strategy and tactics.

Adams thus became something of the chairman of an informal policy-planning staff for the executive department in the years from 1896 to 1908. His was not, of course, the only influence brought to bear on President Roosevelt, Secretary of State John Hay, and other leaders. Exporters of cotton, capital, and kerosene all demanded that the government open the door to consumers around the world. Protestants and Populists wanted to export their respective brands of Americanism to the emotional and intellectual markets of colonial areas. But Adams, even more than Alfred Thayer Mahan, offered an interpretation of such pressures and a program for using them to control Asia.

For the foreign policy section of his first presidential message, Roosevelt borrowed a magazine article written by Adams and paraphrased it for the Congress. The recommendation was an Adams classic: use economic and military power to expand the frontier of the United States westward to the interior of China. Quite in keeping with Adams' plan, Roosevelt backed Japan in its war against Russia. But the maneuver went awry. Russia threatened to retaliate with social revolution. Adams feared this possibility more than anything else. He was afraid that such a revolution would turn into a secular reformation that would halt American expansion. Roosevelt and Adams frantically did what they could to prop up the old regime and left the problem for their successors.

Woodrow Wilson was ultimately to try his hand at controlling such a revolution in Russia. But first he had to contend with Mexican and German challenges to American democracy. Throughout these years Turner was an unseen intellectual roomer in the White House. Wilson and Turner had been close friends as well as visiting professor and student at Johns Hopkins University in the 1880's. Long walks after classes gave them a chance to learn from each other. Wilson knew and loved the aristocratic South. Turner told him about the West, and explained how it had made America democratic. And they talked about "the power of leadership; of the untested power of the man of literary ability in the field of diplomacy."

Wilson relied extensively on Turner's frontier thesis in presenting his own interpretation of American history. "All I ever wrote on the subject came from him." A comment overgenerous, perhaps, but not misleading. Read Wilson on American expansion after 1896: "The spaces of their own continent were occupied and reduced to the uses of civilization; they had no frontiers.... These new frontiers in the

Indies and in the Far Pacific came to them as if out of the very necessity of the new career before them."

Wilson did not miss or fail to act on the economic implications of the frontier thesis, but he was the very model of Turner's crusading democrat. Indeed, Wilson's religious fervor called him to this duty even before the First World War. Earlier Americans had taught the Mexicans the meaning of Manifest Destiny and Dollar Diplomacy. Later, in the midst of revolution, the Mexicans seemed to forget American ideas about constitutional government and property rights. Wilson stepped in and became an enthusiastic tutor in moral imperialism. Vigorous though this instruction was, the President's former pupil was a bit critical of his old professor. "I hadn't his patience with Mexico," admitted Turner.

He likewise felt that Wilson was a bit too slow to act against the Germans. But he recognized the need for a perfect moral posture before the world. He devoutly supported the war to make the world safe for democracy. Fourteen years earlier Turner had observed that America's duty was "to conserve democratic institutions and ideals." Small wonder that he was "warmly in favor" of Wilson's Fourteen Points and the League of Nations. Wilson called his own proposals the "only possible program for peace" which "must prevail." Even more than in the case of Theodore Roosevelt, the policies of Woodrow Wilson were classic Turnerism.

It has been suggested that so also were the early policies of President Franklin Delano Roosevelt. Professors Curtis Nettels, James C. Malin, and Richard Hofstadter advance strong arguments in support of this view. Roosevelt's speech at the Commonwealth Club of San Francisco during the campaign of 1932 is the basis of this interpretation. "Our last frontier has long since been reached," Roosevelt announced. "There is no safety valve in the form of a Western prairie.... Our task now is not discovery or exploitation of natural resources, or necessarily producing more goods. It is the...less dramatic business of administering resources and plants already in hand, of seeking to reëstablish foreign markets for our surplus production...of distributing wealth and products more equitably."

The extent to which Roosevelt wrote and understood what he said is debatable, but immaterial to the discussion at hand. One group of his advisors certainly acted within this framework. The N.I.R.A., the A.A.A., and other similar legislative measures were clearly based on the idea that the frontier was gone. But this relationship does not mean that Turner was the intellectual father of the New Deal's regulatory legislation. The fact of the frontier's disappearance was not the burden of the Turner thesis, but rather of the Census Director's dissertation. Turner's frontier thesis made democracy a function of an expanding frontier. The idea that the national government should use its power to rationalize, plan, and control the corporate development of the country had been Americanized and promoted by Herbert Croly, not Frederick Jackson Turner. Croly's *Promise of American* Life would seem more the intellectual handbook of the New Deal than Turner's essay on the frontier.

But there was a Turnerism in Roosevelt's speech at the Commonwealth Club. It was the remark about "seeking to reëstablish foreign markets for our surplus production." No single phase of the New Deal was pushed harder than Secretary of State Cordell Hull's campaign to expand trade. The real Turnerians among the New Dealers were those who converted a thesis about landed expansion into one about industrial expansion. Thus the inner history of the New Deal, and later administrations, can fruitfully be studied as a three-way tug-of-war between the Croly planners, the Turner inflationists and expansionists, and the Adamites, a group which sought to synthesize the two ideas. The planners lost much of their influence during the recession of 1937–1939. Recovery came only through expanded production for war. And it was during this period that Roosevelt and others began openly to apply Turner's thesis to the new economic situation. An expanding economy became the dogma of an industrial America.

Roosevelt had always been, at heart, a Turnerian in foreign policy. He was sure, save for a short interlude during the years between the wars, that America's frontier was the world. This attitude does much to explain Charles Beard's attacks on Roosevelt. Beard was a brilliant student of history keenly aware of the consequences of imperial expansion. He also understood, and had written about, the influence of the expansionist ideas of Turner and Adams. His study of these men led him to develop a Beardian antithesis on foreign policy. *In a closed world the attempt to maintain an expanding national frontier, be it ideological, political, or economic, would lead to war and tyranny. Democracy would be negated.* Thus he approved much of the early domestic program of the New Deal while militantly opposing Roosevelt's foreign policy. Self-containment and development comprised Beard's program. His motivation, his logic, and his conclusions were disdainfully dismissed or angrily assaulted until, a dozen years later, the Soviet Union began to manufacture hydrogen bombs.

Roosevelt's Turnerism was meanwhile blended with the *Realpolitik* of Adams. Roosevelt made much of his desire to end nineteenth-century colonialism. The Good Neighbor Policy, developmental projects for the Near East, and the plan to elevate China to the rank of a great power were offered as demonstrations of this democratic purpose. Little was said of the somewhat patronizing attitude and the more materialistic objectives of this approach. While the left hand reformed, however, the strong right was to serve as the mailed fist. Thus at the Atlantic Conference the Four Freedoms were matched by an understanding with Great Britain to police the world after the war. Russia would be admitted to this Anglo-American coalition if circumstances made that necessary. They did. Russia had been rejuvenated by the very revolution so feared by Brooks Adams, and its new strength was essential if Hitler was to be defeated. This face delimited America's frontier. And to further complicate the situation the Russians, in Marx and Lenin, had an Adams and a Turner all their own.

At this point, and no doubt unconsciously, Roosevelt took the worst from Turner and Adams. He seemed, from the spring of 1942 to the fall of 1944, to base his plans for the postwar era on the idea of a concert of power. Then, in October, 1944, he in effect reaffirmed the Open Door policy of John Hay. First he gave the impression of accepting Russian predominance in Eastern Europe. But at the same time he claimed "complete freedom of action" in the future. The Russians either declined or were unable to acquiesce in such unilateral reassertion of the frontier thesis. For the leaders of the frontier communities of the world had heard of Marx as well as Turner. And if the doors of the world were to be thrown open in one direction, why not in the other? The temptations and the pressures inherent in that question did much to produce the Cold War.

At some hour in the early years of the Cold War someone rediscovered Brooks Adams. Who it was and when it was may remain one of those tantalizing secrets of history. But done it was. Perhaps it was Marquis Childs, a newspaper columnist whose intellectual friends included many New Deal bureaucrats. In late 1945 or 1946 Childs wrote a long, laudatory introduction for a new edition of *America's Economic Supremacy*, Adams' old handbook for empire builders. Childs left no doubt as to the reason for his action. "If Adams had written last year, for publication this year, he would have had to alter scarcely anything to relate his views to the world of today."

Or perhaps it was George Frost Kennan, looking into the past for guidance after he became chief of the policy planning division of the Department of State. Kennan, in explaining and defending the policy of containment, mentioned Adams as one of the small number of Americans who had recognized the proper basis of foreign policy. Later, as in one of the few State Department policy discussions of which there is current public record, and in his estimate of the *Realities of American Foreign Policy*, Kennan's analysis and argument was in many respects remarkably similar to that of Adams. Only the as-yet-unopened files in the archives can reveal whether these corre-lations were initially patterns of causation. But it is not unknown for an idea first picked up and used as a rationalization to become an engine of later action.

Turnerism, meanwhile, retained its vigor during these years. The Truman Doctrine seemed an almost classic statement of the thesis that the security and well-being of the United States depended upon the successful execution of America's unique mission to defend and extend the frontier of democracy throughout the world. Another of President Harry S. Truman's major speeches spelling out certain aspects of this obligation was indeed entitled *The American Frontier*. But there were critics who insisted that the President was too conservative. Perhaps the leader of this group was John Foster Dulles, who was so dissatisfied with the limitations of Truman's formulation that he termed it positively "un-moral." And Dulles might well claim that his plan to liberate all people not ruled according to the precepts of individualistic democracy was the definitive statement of the thesis.

Yet as was the case when the United States liberated the Philip-pines in 1898, it was sometimes hard, in the years of the Cold War, to determine just what definition of freedom was being used by the Turnerians. A somewhat strange assortment of political theories and social institutions seemed to qualify as individualistic and democratic if they facilitated American expansion. This imperial standard of judgment stemmed in considerable part from the ideological na-tionalism of Turner's frontier and the nationalistic materialism of the Adams analysis of the world frontier. But these characteristics were synthesized in the concept of an expanding economy, which became the new American credo in the years after 1935, and particularly during the Cold War.

The argument that continually expanding industrial production was the basic remedy for the economic and social ills of industrial society was not, of course, originally advanced by either Turner or Adams. Nor is the idea itself irrelevant to the problem of keeping up with—and ahead of—the increasing minimum demands of a growing population. This essay is not concerned with such a historical and theoretical critique of the idea. But it is suggested that the manner in which American leadership accepted the proposition that an expanding economy provided the key to "building a successfully functioning political and economic system," in the words of Secretary of State Dean Acheson, was not unrelated to the milieu established by Turner and Adams.

Walter Prescott Webb has outlined the general nature of this intellectual association in his study of *The Great Frontier.* It does seem necessary to recapitulate the evidence which illustrates the manner in which Americans refer to Latin America and other areas as their new frontiers. It is more fruitful to review the discussions incident to the formulation of American foreign policy since 1945. Much emphasis has rightly been placed on the extent to which these programs were conceived within a framework of increasing tension with the Soviet Union. But this is only part of the story. One of the most striking themes to emerge from the multiplicity of hearings on this legislation is the degree to which it was motivated by the effort to solve American and world problems through the medium of an expanding economy.

Dean Acheson outlined this approach very carefully in May, 1947, as background for the forthcoming Marshall Plan. Three years later, after becoming Secretary of State, he emphasized the same idea even more directly. He explicitly denied that the situation of the United States vis à vis the Soviet Union was in any sense as desperate as that faced by Great Britain in 1940. "I do not imply," he concluded, "that the only reason for continuing the European recovery program is the threat of further expansion by the Soviet Union. On the contrary, the free world, even if no threat of this kind existed, would face the same hard task of building a successfully functioning system."

William C. Foster, an early administrator of the European Recovery Program, provided the neatest statement of the underlying assumption. "Our whole philosophy in the United States," he explained, "is that of an expanding economy and not a static economy to produce more, and not divide up what you have." W. Averell Harriman, who exercised general supervision over this program, shared this outlook. Nelson Rockefeller, another leader in the effort, tied the approach directly to the frontier thesis. "With the closing of our own frontier," he pointed out, "there is hope that other frontiers still exist in the world." So, too, did Harriman, when he was questioned on the relationship between American aid to European nations and the efforts of those countries to strengthen and maintain themselves in Africa, the Near East, and Asia. "It is, in a sense," he explained, "their frontier, as the West used to be with us."

Harriman further maintained, completing the analogy, that the United States, in order to sustain its expanding economy, had to support such action and develop its own position in those areas. Point IV assistance was described and defended as "absolutely essential" within this framework. Secretary Acheson agreed. And from one "heavily indebted to George Frost Kennan for much stimulation and guidance" came the most candid summary of all. America's interests in colonial territories "coincide with the interests of European metropolitan countries.... The best possible situation is a series of 'happy' colonial relationships.... We should not let our 'rabbit ears' ...dominate decisions in which a substantial degree of the national interest is at stake and in which there are no clear moral 'rights' and 'wrongs.'"

Such testimony offers considerable support for Webb's generalization that Americans viewed the frontier "not as a line to stop at, but as an *area* inviting entrance." And this attitude, whether held by the public or its elite, would seem to have been generated in part by Turner's thesis that democracy was a function of an expanding frontier and Adams' argument that the frontier was also the source of world power.

But it began to appear, after 1952, that Turner and Adams had met their match in Einstein and Oppenheimer. The General Theory of Relativity seemed likely to antiquate the frontier thesis. For armed with hydrogen bombs the messiahs become gladiators whose weapons will destroy the stadium. Their battle would make the world a frontier for fossils. Even the Russian followers of Marx and Lenin gave signs of becoming aware that their version of the thesis needed to be revised to accord with this new reality.

Perhaps Charles Beard can now rest easy. He was a better historian than either Turner or Adams. Yet he never found his Roosevelt or Wilson. Beard was always a bit too sharp and tough-minded for America's professional and intellectual politicians. He would chuckle to know that his idea of self-containment was reintroduced to Americans by Winston Spencer Churchill. Churchill's intellectual migration from aggressive imperialism to reluctant coexistence chronicled the demise of the frontier thesis. And Beard might ultimately have an American spokesman. The followers of Turner and Adams remained numerous and influential in the councils of state, but they hesitated to take the awful responsibility for acting on their theses. They seemed dimly aware that the United States had finally caught up with History. Americans were no longer unique. Henceforward they, too, would share the fate of all mankind. For the frontier was now on the rim of hell, and the inferno was radioactive.

CHARLES AUSTIN BEARD: THE INTELLECTUAL AS TORY-RADICAL

[from *American Radicals: Some Problems and Personalities*, 1954]

No American historian provided greater inspiration for Williams than Charles A. Beard. Williams admired Beard's intellectual independence and political courage. He was particularly impressed with the famous scholar's attempts to articulate a general theory of American historical development, an effort in which Williams himself was engaged. Williams contended that Beard, political conservative though he was, had developed important insights relating economic issues to political ethics, a linkage essential to historical understanding and social change. The connection dominated Beard's intellectual concerns and guided his controversial political involvements. Beard's academic career, Williams declared, was that of a revisionist committed to change in light of revelations derived from radical analysis and anchored in moral principles of political behavior. He was, therefore, in Williams's judgment, "a worthy example for American radicals."

I

Late one night in 1929, aboard a train clickety-clacketing northward along the Atlantic coast from the Carolinas, Charles Beard gave away a vital insight into his intellectual and public career. He was cornered in the smoker, defending himself against, and explaining himself to, some professional historians who challenged his emphasis on economics in history. One can imagine him: his patience gone, his blue eyes sparking like high-voltage electricity, and a scalpel's edge on his voice.

"I never said that economic motives explain everything!" he roared. "Of course, ideas are important. And so are ethical concepts. What I have always said and all I have said is that, among the various motives impelling men to action, the struggle for food, clothing, and shelter has been more important throughout history than any other. And that is true, isn't it?—*Isn't it?*"

Here, in one piercing paragraph, is the essence of Beard's intellectual personality. He was a radical in rooting to the heart of the matter and insisting that man's economic struggle was the "most important" part of history. But his conservative's caution was equally apparent. He refused to stereotype the relationship between the economic struggle and other phases of man's activity, or the future nature of the struggle itself. He declined, in short, to grant the inevitability of any pattern of development. Spengler's *Decline of the West* left him as unconvinced and as unsatisfied as Darwin's middle-class utopia or Marx's prophecy of a communal Eden. Beard accepted only the certainty of change and conflict.

This suggests that Beard may most aptly be described as the intellectual as Tory-Radical. He had little, if any, confidence in revolutionary efforts to wrench mankind out of its historical continuity. For this reason some radicals have said that he was short-sighted and worse, that he lacked the nerve of failure. But he did believe that people could improve their lives by controlling more rationally and more equitably the economic system under which they lived. And for this the conservatives have called him subversive.

The right-wingers are far closer to the truth. Beard contributed much to the currently neglected intellectual foundations of an American radicalism. He insisted that economic conflict and development is unending, and that it must constantly be analyzed, whatever the institutional organization of society. The American Left may be aware of this truth. It has failed, by and large, to act upon it since the days of its ideological romance with the New Deal's *noblesse oblige*. Beard also maintained that rulers who say one thing and do another, whatever the legal framework within which they act, undermine democracy. This morality is as important to those of the Left who close their ethical eyes while defending Franklin Delano Roosevelt's *conduct* of foreign affairs from 1938 to 1941 as it is to those who do likewise when discussing Soviet purges.

Thus Charles Beard's great legacy to American radicalism was not programmatic. Rather was it his persistent assertion, with great personal courage, that economics and morality are, respectively, the cornerstone and the keystone of the good life. Economic maladjustment will undermine morality; but the lack of ethical integrity will corrupt the best economic system. Beard never wholly neglected either of these propositions at any time during his career. Nor did he separate his intellectual and political activity. But he did tend to stress economic factors from his early maturity through the first years of the Great Depression. Thereafter he emphasized the ethics of power. Thus it may be helpful to review Beard's career within this framework: first his development and employment of a theory of social change; then his efforts to warn of the disastrous consequences of amoral politics.

II

Throughout both periods, of course, Beard's actions were in keeping with his analyses and morality. He considered the ivory tower as a refuge for the intellectual and moral coward—or scoundrel. The unity of theory and practice was to Beard a bit of Indiana common sense, not an alien philosophy to be disparaged or damned. In the earlier years, for example, he committed himself to educational and pragmatic efforts designed to increase his fellow citizens' understanding of causal forces, and to instruct them in the use and control of such forces to build a better society. Thus his vigorous work within the British working-class movement, his efforts to improve and extend American education, and his extremely practical proposals for rationalizing existing political institutions. During these years he worked primarily with other men, whether informally or in organized groups. But when he saw what seemed to him the rise of an essential immorality in American politics, Beard withdrew from group agitation to stand alone, unencumbered by conflicting loyalties, and to unmask in his writing the self-deceptions and public fabrications which he saw.

In a sense, of course, Beard stood so straight and so tall that he always stood alone. But he was not the lone wolf that some have pictured him. Only once before his attack on Roosevelt's foreign policy did he stand so much apart. That was in a similar situation, when, on October 8, 1917, he resigned from Columbia in defense of the principle of academic freedom. From the perspective of 1956 that act looms even larger than it did at the time.

"I am sure," he declared, "that when the people understand the true state of affairs in our universities they will speedily enact legislation which will strip boards of trustees of their absolute power over the intellectual life of the institutions under their management." For it will not do to blame the people. The trouble was, and is, that Beard overestimated the extent to which his colleagues were concerned with discovering "the true state of affairs"—let alone communicating that knowledge to the people and acting on it themselves.

But Beard was a different kind of academic man. His troubles were always caused by his efforts to establish and publicize "the true state of affairs." His resignation from Columbia, for example, was the first major consequence of his dedication to the task of developing and using a theory of social change. He left Columbia as the final act in a series of events which began with the publication, in 1913, of *An Economic Interpretation of the Constitution.* Thus the *New York Times* (October 10, 1917) discussed Beard's resignation in a representative fashion—burying the issue of academic freedom in a diatribe against that book. And in this instance the *Times* is a source of accurate information, for the top levels of Columbia's administration had been fighting Beard ever since the publication of the volume. Their attacks on academic freedom were but a specific demonstration of their general antagonism to Beard's ideals and objectives.

A later generation of conservatives, realizing that the search for a general theory of social change is not in itself proof of radicalism, has acted less hysterically, though not necessarily less effectively. A theory of social change can be used to oppose radical innovations and reforms as well as to encourage them. Most recent research along this line has been motivated and financed, in fact, by those who have such a negative purpose. But Beard's early opponents thought that his case study of the origins of the Constitution established his desire for radical change, and so struck back vigorously and viciously. Beard never wholly committed himself, however, to using a theory of change in any one manner. He wanted to save what was best, yet improve it along with all the rest. Hence the ambiguity of his career.

III

Basically, though, Beard was more of a radical than he sometimes found it easy to admit to himself. For the commitment to search for a theory of social change undercuts the assumption of uniqueness upon which the theory and practice of the majority of American liberals and conservatives have been based. Such a denial that the

United States is unique confronts those who understand it with a private and a general problem. It lays bare the uncomfortable truth, so personally pleasant to camouflage, that the evasion of basic issues ultimately becomes a terribly expensive flight from reality. And it thereby forces one either to continue such escape knowingly or else to grapple directly with the question of how to limit individual liberty without also destroying freedom.

Beard understood this. Prior to 1929 he was able to deny American uniqueness in theory while enjoying it in practice. But the Great Depression put an end to this idyll. And from that time forward Beard can only be understood in terms of a man wrestling with this central dilemma. These considerations also explain the changing nature of the criticism of Beard. His early opponents fought him because of his specific intellectual and political acts. His later critics, aware that he confronts them with the basic issue, assault the entire body of his work.

Save perhaps for a brief period early in the depression, Beard never came to grips directly with the theoretical and practical problems arising from the curtailment of individual liberty which was implicit in the idea of America living with and within itself. But Beard's own thesis that politics follows economics forced him, after the depression, to project two alternate paths for America's immediate future: rapid involvement in another general war, or self-containment within existing continental boundaries or, at most, the Western Hemisphere. This is not a happy choice for a man (or a society) who matured in the tradition of "anything is possible," and the shock of its harshness may do much to account for Beard's seeming shift to relativism during the early '30s. Yet Beard always returned to the central question of whether it necessarily follows that freedom is lost when liberty is curtailed. He never worked out a simple, programmatic solution for this problem. But he never denied, and only briefly evaded, the issue, and his basic answer was negative.

Beard's concentration on these key issues of causation and freedom does much to account for his interest in, and debt to, Karl Marx and James Madison. Those men labored all their lives over the same questions. But those who hope for a precise bookkeeping-style analysis of Beard's debt to these men will wait in vain. Beard was an on-going intellectual, concerned primarily with understanding and improving the world. He had little interest in, and even less time for, analyzing and defending himself.

Combined with his early experience in Chicago during the 1890s, Beard got from Marx a deep consciousness of change and an abiding sense of the importance to that change of the latent, long-run consequences of decisions made on the basis of short-term analyses. This emphasis on long-term generalized patterns helps to explain, for example, Beard's tendency to overlook immediate functional conflicts between economic groups. Beard's over-all interpretations, like those of Marx, are extremely difficult to destroy, whereas specific aspects of their analyses can be seriously modified or disproved.

Such weaknesses can not be inflated into proof of intellectual failure. It is possible, as several scholars have recently done, to demonstrate that some details of Beard's analysis of the origins of the Constitution are wrong. Thus, as a case in point, his stress on the role and importance of the men who held obligations of the Continental Congresses can be interpreted to deny Beard's entire interpretation. But such concentration on functional analysis can lead the critics even further from the mark. For there is a very considerable difference between saying that Beard was mistaken about bond-holders, and going on to argue that economic alignments were not the central dynamic of the movement for the Constitution. Critics who attempt the second assertion would seem to be forgetting that a historical generalization is not an answer to every specific question.

Beard's intellectual relationship to Madison is also easy to confuse or misconstrue. Some scholars have taken Beard's sometime assertion that he was a Madisonian at face value. More of them have claimed that he merely used Madison as camouflage for Marx. Both judgments seem a bit wide of the mark. It is more probable that Beard viewed Marx and Madison as complementary thinkers. An analysis of his famous essay on *The Economic Basis of Politics* (1922) supports this view. The over-all prognosis of Marx and Madison is very similar, as attested by Madison's famous forecast, in 1829, that the United States would suffer a serious economic and social crisis a century later. Beard also realized that Madison's system of factions was nothing less than an unsystematized anticipation of the functional school of sociological analysis. And, in some instances, Beard followed Madison's model in his own work.

At times Beard failed to use these ideas of Marx and Madison as well as he might have. He was always in a hurry, for one thing, and seldom took the time to dig out the facts on every faction. Sometimes his insights as to which groups were the most important were correct, and the finished essay was brilliant. In other cases, however, his research hypothesis was awry, and the error was compounded in the completed work. It was not that Beard ignored or monkeyed with the evidence, for he was fanatically honest. But he tended, in his concern and haste to find clues for the present, to work *with* his hypothesis instead of *from* it. But for Beard specific mistakes were of far less concern than the validity of his general analysis of American history. For he considered himself not so much an ivory-tower historian as a functioning student of history.

IV

What did Beard mean when he called himself a student of history, not a historian? The crucial difference between them lies in the former's emphasis on his study as a means, whereas the latter considers his work as an end in itself. True, the historian's work may be the means to a personally satisfying life, but such an argument either misses or begs the issue. So, too, does the claim that all historians are also students of history. A difference of degree does lead to a difference of kind. Beard studied history to equip himself to comprehend and change his own society: to understand the direction and tempo of its movement, and to pinpoint the places at which to apply his energy and influence in an effort to modify both aspects of its development.

Analyzed from this perspective, it becomes very difficult to demolish his two central interpretations, *The Rise of American Civilization* (1927) and *The Idea of National Interest* (1934). For what Beard did in these books was to confront his readers with the hard fact that it was specific Americans who made American history, and that for the most part they had acted on the basis of a materialistic calculus. He ripped aside the appearances and the rationalizations to reveal the realities. No wonder he was attacked, for his lesson was quite outside any connection with existing politics. It was radical in the deepest sense of the term. And so it remains.

Though obviously pointing the moral of responsibility, and spelling it out in case after case, Beard's writing prior to the Great Depression was not characterized by any overriding sense of urgency. Neither were his actions. A man anticipating and dreading imminent and catastrophic crisis does not center his efforts on educational and political reform. Save for the academic freedom episode, the tenor of Beard's writings and actions was that of a concerned and responsible man who assumed that there was plenty of time to go slowly. It seems probable that this outlook was a product of Beard's American experience reinforcing his awareness that Marx's sense of time was quite foreshortened.

But the depression brought Beard up short. Here was deep and general crisis. And there is little doubt that his intellectual and personal outlook responded immediately. The tone of his "'Five Year Plan' for America," written in 1931, was markedly different from that of his volume on *Public Service in America* (1919), or the concluding pages of *The American Party Battle* (1928). The earlier work is characterized by the assumption that there is plenty of time. His essay on a five year plan is urgent, and probes far deeper in an effort to suggest new and significant changes.

Beard did not, however, launch any frontal attack on private property. His proposal was no more, in essence, than an intelligent and rather extensive development of the idea of a corporate society, previously advanced in America by such men as Herbert Croly and Herbert Hoover. This concept of a corporate society is based on the proposition that every individual holds membership in two of the three basic units of all industrialized societies. All people are citizens, hence are part of the government. And, in addition, they belong either to capital or labor. Thus the state, in theory at least, is at once the common ground where both parties adjust their differences, and an independent power capable of enforcing judgments on both groups.

But corporatism is not a radical concept, for it is tied intimately to the principle of private property. And this weakens both its theoretical and its practical value. For unless the power to control investments, so vital to balanced economic growth, is exercised on the basis of a public choice between alternate programs and policies, one half of the economic life of society remains in the hands of a tiny minority.

Thus Beard's radical insights into the malfunctioning of the existing system were never matched by an equally fundamental program for its renovation. His predilection for such a corporate solution does explain, however, his support for much of the New Deal's domestic legislation. Beard and Roosevelt did see eye to eye on one point: they saw through the myth of rugged individualism. But when it came to the question of what to put in its place they turned first to a vague sort of corporatism, and then back to the dream of restoring competition. Neither of them looked forward to socialism.

V

The same disparity between radical analysis and conservative preference and program bedeviled Beard on foreign policy. Few short analyses, for example, match the quality of Beard's treatment of foreign affairs in *The Rise of American Civilization*. It is even more difficult to name a volume more rewarding in insights and suggestions than *The Idea of National Interest*. Beard stressed three points in these analyses of foreign policy: (1) it is intimately connected with domestic affairs, (2) empires are not built in fits of absent-mindedness, and (3) expansion does not in and of itself solve problems, and often complicates and deepens them.

These conclusions forced Beard to deal with several related problems. Both as a student of history and as an acting citizen it was vital for him to comprehend the system of ideas which first rationalize, and in turn further motivate, imperial expansion. In conjunction with his intrinsic intellectual ferment, and the shock of the depression, this need makes sense out of his sudden concentration on the work of German historians who were working on the general problem of *Weltanschauungen*, or conceptions of the world. This study was of key importance to Beard, for if he could come to grips with the general view of the world that was held by the expansionists, then he could attack it more directly and effectively.

He never carried through on this phase of his intellectual pursuits. It is, indeed, the weakest of all his performances. The reason that Beard never gave full attention to these studies, and rather shortly dropped them, lies in his growing concern over the drift of Roosevelt's foreign policy. Thus, after 1937, Beard gave less and less attention to the narrowly academic aspects of his work. It was not that his mind slowed down, but rather that his heart speeded up. Beard cared too deeply about America to bother with the formal rigmarole of the professional intellectual. And his love for his homeland brought him, deep in emotional turmoil, face to face with the multiple contradictions between his radical analyses, his strong concern for his fellow man, and his personal and philosophic commitment to private property. It would appear, on a close reading of his last books, that he sought a way out of this difficulty by emphasizing the primacy of moral integrity in public life.

One can only sympathize with Beard as he confronted his cruel dilemma. He realized, to start with, that the depression threatened the entire fabric of American society. This led him to cut through the cant of the claims of recovery and propose some serious modifications in the American economic system. He was quite aware, of course, that it was too late to "save capitalism" in the sense that the phrase was used by the New Dealers. Beard's fear was that the old order, though dying, would dominate the future. And he grew ever more disturbed as he realized that the New Deal was not economically successful. Nor could the failure be blamed only on the businessmen, for the New Dealers had few ideas about—let alone for—the future.

Then worse yet: he came to feel that the people in power were submerging the basic domestic problem in a foreign crisis, and defending this shift of emphasis by defining the new issue as the central danger. Here Beard confronted himself, for he too had to give an answer to this question of which was the crucial issue. It has been said, and often, that Beard failed this test. But the judgment is not that simple. Several things need to be kept in mind when appraising Beard's reaction. There was no radical program backed by organizational strength. Beard's position has often been misunderstood or misrepresented. And finally, the implicit import of Beard's criticism of Roosevelt is usually evaded.

It is possible to argue that an American socialism, structured around political and civil liberties and centralizing none but the economic power necessary to plan and administer balanced economic growth, leaving other property untouched, would have won Beard's support. Beard can hardly be blamed for the lack of such a choice. Indeed, a psychological analysis might well point to the conclusion that the New Deal intellectuals' attack on Beard is really indicative of their own sense of failure.

It will not do, furthermore, to argue that Beard would have opposed such a program because it carried the strong probability of entering the war. For Beard did not oppose the war that was fought. He did oppose the way that Roosevelt led this country into war, and the New Deal's strong inclination to think it was America's job to reform the world. This vital difference demands considerable emphasis because it is central to an understanding of Beard's thought and his importance. Beard made three central points in his attack on Roosevelt: the domestic crisis was being "solved" in a manner that only postponed and deepened it; this "solution" was being carried out in a manner—deceptively—that undercut democratic morality and practice; and the assumption by the United States of the right, or obligation, to police the world would compound both crises.

It is extremely difficult to deny the force of these arguments. Recovery and prosperity at the price of an extremely poor strategic position in World War II, a police action in Korea, and an atomic diplomacy based on cultivating the cold war *have* deepened the basic crises of the '30s. Nor were any of these developments inevitable. The consequences of Roosevelt's deceptive methods are perhaps less obvious, but perhaps even more dangerous. The practice of protecting the people from the truth in order to save them from themselves damages the fiber of a society. And, as Beard knew, no society can survive its own hypocrisy.

Thus Beard lived by the creed of grappling directly, honestly, and democratically with any problem, be it economic, social, or moral. And he fought hypocrisy and political chicanery with all the militance he could muster, a worthy example for American radicals.

IMPERIAL ANTICOLONIALISM

[from *The Tragedy of American Diplomacy,* 1959]

The Tragedy of American Diplomacy established Williams's reputation as a revisionist historian. In the first of three selections drawn from this work, he developed the concept of the Open Door Policy as the strategy devised by American leaders to promote overseas economic expansion in response to the domestic crises of the 1890s. The frontier expansionist ideas of Turner and Adams provided important ingredients for the emerging view that expansion would resolve domestic problems and ensure the prosperity and political success of American society. This outlook, Williams argued, played a significant role in the coming of the war with Spain in 1898 and the associated drive for markets in Asia. The result, he wrote, was the Open Door Policy and "the gradual extension of American economic and political power throughout the world." But the success of the policy, he maintained, "engendered the antagonisms created by all empires, and it is that opposition which has posed so many difficulties for American diplomacy in the twentieth century."

A continuance of the present anarchy of our commerce will be a continuance of the unfavorable balance on it, which by draining us of our metals... [will bring our ruin]. In fact most of our political evils may be traced up to our commercial ones, and most of our moral to our political.
James Madison to Thomas Jefferson, 1786

[Our recent policies] have hastened the day when an equilibrium between the occupations of agriculture, manufactures, and commerce, shall simplify our foreign concerns to the exchange only of that surplus which we cannot

consume for those articles of reasonable comfort or convenience which we
cannot produce.   *Thomas Jefferson, 1809*

American factories are making more than the American people can use;
American soil is producing more than they can consume. Fate has written
our policy for us; the trade of the world must and shall be ours.
                                            Albert J. Beveridge, April, 1897

Even protectionist organs are for free trade in China, where freedom is for
the benefit of American manufacturers. Even anti-Imperialists welcome an
Imperial policy which contemplates no conquests but those of commerce.
                                                    London Times, 1900

A MERICA's traditional view of itself and the world is composed of
three basic ideas, or images. One maintains that the United States
was isolationist until world power was "thrust upon it," first to help
Cuba, then twice to save the world for democracy, and finally to
prevent the Soviet Union from overwhelming the world. Another
holds that, except for a brief and rapidly dispelled aberration at the
turn of the century, America has been anti-imperialist throughout its
history. A third asserts that a unique combination of economic
power, intellectual and practical genius, and moral rigor enables
America to check the enemies of peace and progress—and build a
better world—without erecting an empire in the process.
   Not even Joseph Stalin maintained that America's record in world
affairs was exactly the reverse of this common view, and for
Americans to do so would be to mistake a candid and searching
re-examination of their own mythology for a tirade of useless
self-damnation. The classical ideas about American foreign policy
are not all wrong: the United States did come to full, active
involvement in international affairs by degrees; it has been anti-
imperialist in some respects at certain times; and periodically it has
consciously acknowledged various limitations on its power. But the
need for critical self-appraisal seems apparent upon considering the
implications of the accepted interpretation. For if America were in
fact all and nothing more than the traditional ideas declare it to be,
then it would experience but minor difficulties and suffer no crises.
Such a combination of power, morality, and technique would have
established the millennium long before the Bolshevik Revolution.
   In beginning such a re-evaluation of twentieth-century American

diplomacy it is illuminating to recall that Americans thought of themselves as an empire at the very outset of their national existence—as part of the assertive self-consciousness which culminated in the American Revolution. Though at first it may seem surprising, when contrasted with the image of isolationism which has been accepted so long, in reality that early predominance of a pattern of empire thought is neither very strange nor very difficult to explain. Having matured in an age of empires as part of an empire, the colonists naturally saw themselves in the same light once they joined issue with the mother country.

However natural, attractive, and exhilarating, such a commitment to empire nevertheless posed a serious dilemma for the founding fathers. Political theory of that age asserted the impossibility of reconciling democratic republicanism with a large state. Up to the time of the American Revolution at any rate, the British could remain ignorant of—or evade—that issue. Self-governing Englishmen never had to cope with the problem of integrating their conquests into their domestic social and political economy. Americans were not so fortunate, for any expansion they undertook immediately enlarged the mother country. Led by James Madison, they sought to resolve the contradiction between their drive for empire and their politics by developing a theory of their own which asserted that democratic republicanism could be improved and sustained by just such an imperial foreign policy.

Probably taking his cue from David Hume, an Englishman who attacked Montesquieu's argument that democracy was a system that could work only in small states, Madison asserted that expansion was the key to preventing factions—themselves primarily the result of economic conflicts—from disrupting the fabric of society. Institutional checks and balances could help, and were therefore necessary, but they were not enough in and of themselves. Expansion was essential to mitigate economic clashes by providing an empire for exploitation and development and to interpose long distances (and thus difficulties and delays in sustaining initial antagonisms) between one faction and the rest of the nation and the government itself.

Madison thus proposed, *as a guide to policy and action in his own time,* the same kind of an argument that the historian Frederick Jackson Turner formulated a century later when he advanced his frontier thesis which explained America's democracy and prosperity as the result of such expansion. Madison's theory was shared (or borrowed) by many other American leaders of his time. Thomas

Jefferson's thesis that democracy and prosperity depended upon a society of landholding and exporting freemen was a drastically simplified version of the same idea. Perhaps Edward Everett of Massachusetts most nearly captured the essence of the interpretation and argument in his judgment that expansion was the *"principle* of our institutions." In 1828–1829, Madison himself prophesied a major crisis would occur in about a century, when the continent had filled up and an industrial system had deprived most people of any truly productive property. His fears proved true sooner than he anticipated. For in the Crisis of the 1890's, when Americans *thought* that the frontier was gone, they advanced and accepted the argument that new expansion was the best, if not the only, way to sustain their freedom and prosperity.

The Crisis of the 1890's was a major turning point in American history. It marked the close of the age of Jacksonian laissez faire and provided the setting for the death scene of the individual entrepreneur as the dynamic figure in American economic life. At the same time, it was the cultural coming-out party of a new corporate system based upon the corporation and similar large and highly organized groups throughout American society.

Since it affected all Americans in one way or another, most of them either offered or accepted some kind of an explanation of the crisis. A great many, perhaps the majority, took the somewhat fatalistic view that the American system was so successful that it produced more than it could use, causing it to slow down every so often until the slack was taken up. Another large group argued that the system was somehow out of kilter, but disagreed over what could and should be done to improve it. Most of the critics thought a few modifications and reforms would take care of the trouble. A much smaller number, composed of socialists and other radicals, asserted that the existing system ought to be scrapped for a new one. Though the radicals never mustered enough strength to act on their proposal, they did provide some helpful ideas for the reformers.

It is often argued, therefore, that the history of the Crisis of the 1890's (and subsequent American development) revolves around a struggle between those who stressed the need to reform the system and others who argued that conditions would improve faster if it was left alone. Carried over into the realm of foreign affairs, that interpretation points to the conclusion that Americans were not very concerned with questions of foreign policy. The difficulty with that part of the analysis is that it does not correspond with the facts.

Americans were very agitated about foreign policy in the 1890's and sustained their interest after the depression ended. While it is apparent that much of American history in the twentieth century concerns purely domestic issues, it also is true that foreign affairs are a significant part of the story.

Perhaps the most important aspect of the relationship between domestic and foreign affairs is the fact that both the reformers and the conservatives agreed that foreign policy could and should play an important—if not crucial—part in recovering from the depression and in preventing future crises. This broad consensus was based upon two ideas. The first, held by manufacturers, bankers, farmers, and most other specific groups in the economy, explained the depression and social unrest as the result of not having enough markets for their specific product—be it steel, capital, or wheat. Hence each group looked at foreign policy as a means of getting markets for their merchandise or services. The second idea was much broader and took account of the particular outlook of all special interests. It explained America's democracy and prosperity in the past as the result of expansion across the continent and, to a lesser degree, overseas into the markets of the world. Either implicitly or explicitly, depending on the form in which it was presented, the idea pointed to the practical conclusion that expansion was the way to stifle unrest, preserve democracy, and restore prosperity.

The generalization about the relationship between expansion, democracy, and prosperity became most well-known as the frontier thesis advanced by Frederick Jackson Turner in 1893. But the most fascinating aspect of the idea was that it was put forth, in slightly different versions, by other intellectuals at just about the same moment that Turner published his essay. One of them was Brooks Adams, brother of the famous Henry Adams and close friend of such political leaders as Theodore Roosevelt, Henry Cabot Lodge, and John Hay. Another was William Graham Sumner, an economist and sociologist who believed almost fanatically in the virtue and viability of the old order of laissez-faire individualism.

In response to the Crisis of the 1890's, therefore, Americans developed a broad consensus in favor of an expansionist foreign policy as a solution to their existing troubles and as a way to prevent future difficulties. Special interests pushed expansion from their particular point of view, while the intellectuals unified such separate analyses in one general interpretation. The idea of expansion became even more pervasive because Turner, Adams, and Sumner evoked responses from different ideological and political groups in the country. Turner's statement of the frontier thesis, for example, appealed to the wing of the reform movement which favored using antitrust laws and political reforms to preserve democracy and prosperity. Adams, on the other hand, had his largest following among other reformers who accepted the large corporation and the giant banks but wanted the national government to regulate and control them in behalf of the general welfare.

Sumner's role is more difficult to judge. For one thing, his influence was connected with that of Herbert Spencer, the British philosopher of laissez faire. For another, and unlike Turner and Adams, Sumner did not himself advocate an expansionist foreign policy. But one of his central ideas asserted that it was "the opening of the new continents and the great discoveries and inventions which have made this modern age.... The chief source of new power, however, has been the simplest of all, that is, an extension of population over new land." This explanation implied further expansion, just as his defense of laissez faire sanctioned such action as a natural right. In any event, Sumner's influence—whatever it amounted to—affected the more conservative section of American society which insisted that the principles and practices of laissez faire offered the best answers to all economic and social problems.

Those specific pressures and general ideas in favor of expansion rapidly gained strength after 1890. By 1895, many individuals and groups were stressing the importance of expansion as a way to solve domestic economic problems. The editors of *Harper's* magazine outlined the approach rather bluntly as early as 1893. "The United States will hold the key," it explained, "unlocking the gates to the commerce of the world, and closing them to war. If we have fighting to do, it will be fighting to keep the peace." Others saw expansion as a way to avoid labor unrest—or even revolution. "We are on the eve of a very dark night," warned businessman F. L. Stetson in 1894, "unless a return of commercial prosperity relieves popular discontent." A bit later, Senator William Frye was even more specific. "We must have the market [of China] or we shall have revolution."

By the winter of 1897–1898, the expansionist outlook dominated American thinking on foreign affairs. Western farmers who wanted markets for their unsold produce and commodities joined forces with silver miners and railroad magnates. Jerry Simpson, a sometime radical politician from Kansas, expressed such concern in one anguished cry: "We are driven from the markets of the world!" Along with many other Populists, Simpson also supported the campaign for a big Navy. Midwestern flour millers and Southern cotton growers agitated for the same kind of diplomacy favored by giant oil corporations, steel barons, and textile manufacturers. James J. Hill sought to provide regular freight shipments (and hence revenues) for his railway system by lining up such interests in a general campaign for expansion across the Pacific.

Even the traditional policy of tariff protection was questioned and modified by Americans who saw reciprocity treaties as a way of getting into foreign markets. When it was organized in 1895, for example, the National Association of Manufacturers devoted over half its original program to the problems of expanding foreign markets. One of its specific proposals favored reciprocity treaties as a "practical method of extending our international commerce." And within a year the organization had established special commissions to push business expansion in Latin America and Asia. Its leaders also emphasized the role of such expansion in preventing labor unrest and in making it possible to obey the laws on child labor and yet earn a profit.

While he was president of the N.A.M. in 1897, Theodore C. Search summarized the general feeling within the business community. "Many of our manufacturers have outgrown or are outgrowing their home markets," he explained, "and the expansion of our foreign trade is their only promise of relief." Similar organizations, such as the Pan American Society and the American Asiatic Association, concentrated on promoting an expansionist foreign policy in one particular area. As the *Journal of Commerce* observed in 1897, more and more American economic leaders were fixing their eyes on "the industrial supremacy of the world." A growing number of bankers also began to consider overseas economic expansion as a way of putting their idle capital to work. Some favored direct loans to foreigners while others preferred to finance the operations of American firms. That difference of opinion led to conflict between some bankers and the industrialists over the question of what kind of expansion to undertake, but both groups did agree on the need for overseas activity.

Such general and active support for economic expansion is often neglected when considering the coming of the Spanish-American War. It is customary to explain the war as a crusade to save the Cubans, or to interpret it in psychological terms as a release for national frustrations arising from the depression. But while it may be granted that economic leaders preferred not to go to war as long as they could attain their objectives without it, and although it may be useful to talk about Americans developing a national compulsion to punish Spain for mistreating Cuba, it is equally apparent that such interpretations do not take account of several key aspects of the coming of the war. For one thing, it is clear that various groups saw war with Spain over Cuba as a means to solve other problems. Many agrarians viewed it as a way to monetize silver at home and thus pave the way for a general expansion of their exports to the sterling areas of the world. Some labor groups thought it would ease or resolve immediate economic difficulties. And many important businessmen, as contrasted with the editors of some business publications, came to support war for specific commercial purposes as well as for general economic reasons.

Although there were other reasons for the businessmen's attitude, four factors appear to have played the most important part in the developing outlook within the business community. First, the businessmen were convinced by the late summer of 1897 that recovery was being generated by overseas economic expansion. The jump in agricultural and manufactured exports (which actually began in October, 1896) and the turn of the international gold balance in favor of the United States during 1897 provided the basis for that interpretation. Hence they became even more convinced of the need for an active foreign policy. Second, changes in the Cuban situation affected some of them directly. Not only had the rebels come to appear less reliable to deal with in connection with American interests, but the Cuban conservatives (some of whom were Spaniards) began to change their anti-American position. Crystallized (and symbolized) by Senator Redfield Proctor's trip to Cuba which ended with a dramatic interventionist speech to the Congress, these two considerations prompted many American businessmen to replace their earlier indifference about saving the Cubans with vigorous support for action to protect American enterprise in the island. The irony was that many influential Americans now came to favor intervention as a counterrevolutionary move designed to prevent radicals from controlling Cuba.

Third, and perhaps most important of all, the large group of American leaders who saw economic expansion as the solution to social and economic problems were deeply agitated by indications that the European powers and Japan were going to divide China among themselves. Most Americans looked to Asia, and to China in particular, as the great market which would absorb their surpluses. It is beside the point that this did not happen; at issue is the nature of American thought and action at that time. As a result, a growing number of Americans began to think about a war with Spain more in terms of the Philippines than Cuba itself. To some extent, moreover, other businessmen who concentrated their activity in Latin America saw a more vigorous European diplomacy as a threat to their interests in that region, and so became more interested in taking Cuba as a move to forestall that possibility. Finally, those who viewed the situation in any of these ways were eased in their fears of a major war by the indications that the European powers did not agree among themselves.

These considerations help explain why, by November, 1897, many economic and political leaders were agitating for "improved trade conditions in Cuba" and for action to prevent the partitioning of China—and also dropping their objections to war as the court of last resort. As early as April, 1897, Albert Beveridge asserted that "the trade of the world must and shall be ours." The next month August Belmont (who was financing rebel bonds) and other key businessmen began to carry their campaign for intervention directly to President McKinley.

Though such businessmen acquiesced in McKinley's request to phrase their public agitation in terms of humanitarian purposes, that does not alter the fact that they were concerned with economic matters. And by March 15, 1898, a special agent sent to New York to sound out the business community found it "feeling militant." He reported that there was "nothing but war talk." Among those so engaged were John Jacob Astor, Thomas Ryan, William Rockefeller, Stuyvesant Fish, and spokesmen for the House of Morgan. It seems clear, therefore, that the specific and general consensus in favor of economic expansion played a significant role in the coming of the war with Spain. President McKinley did not go to war simply because the businessmen ordered him to do so; but neither did he lead the nation into battle against their economic wishes—as often is asserted.

Perhaps even more important to an understanding of twentieth-century American diplomacy is the manner in which the underlying bipartisan agreement on overseas economic expansion resolved the debate over whether or not America should embark upon a program of colonialism. Beginning with Admiral George Dewey's victory at Manila Bay and ending shortly after the election of 1900 (if not sooner), the argument is usually interpreted as a battle between the imperialists led by Theodore Roosevelt and the anti-imperialists led by William Jennings Bryan. It is more illuminating, however, to view it as a three-cornered discussion won by businessmen and intellectuals who opposed traditional colonialism and advocated instead the policy of an open door for America's overseas economic expansion.

Discounted in recent years as a futile and naive gesture in a world of harsh reality, the Open Door Policy was in fact a brilliant strategic stroke which led to the gradual extension of American economic and political power throughout the world. If it ultimately failed, it was not because it was foolish or weak, but because it was so successful. The empire that was built according to the strategy and tactics of the Open Door Notes engendered the antagonisms created by all empires, and it is that opposition which has posed so many difficulties for American diplomacy in the middle of the twentieth century.

At the outset, it is true, the debate between imperialists and anti-imperialists revolved around an actual issue—colonialism. Touched off by the specific question of what to do with Cuba and the Philippines, the battle raged over whether they should be kept as traditional colonies or established as quasi-independent nations under the benevolent supervision of the United States. Though the differences were significant at the beginning of the argument, it is nevertheless clear that they were never absolute. The Open Door Notes took the fury out of the fight. And within five years the issue was almost non-existent. The anti-imperialists who missed that changing nature of the discussion were ultimately shocked and disillusioned when Bryan became Secretary of State and began to practice what they thought he condemned.

Such critics were mistaken in attacking Bryan as a backslider or a hypocrite. Bryan's foreign policy was not classical colonialism, but neither was it anti-imperial. He had never shirked his share of the white man's burden, though perhaps he did shoulder a bit more of the ideological baggage than the economic luggage. He was as eager for overseas markets as any but the most extreme agrarian and industrial expansionists. As with most other farmers, labor leaders, and businessmen, economic logic accounts for much of Bryan's anti-colonialism. Looking anxiously for markets abroad as a way of improving conditions at home, all such men feared and opposed the competition of native labor. It was that consideration, as much as racism and Christian fundamentalism, that prompted Bryan to assert that "the Filipinos cannot be citizens without endangering our civilization."

Bryan's program for the Philippines symbolizes the kind of imperial anticolonialism that he advocated. Once the Philippine insurrection was crushed, he proposed that the United States should establish "a stable form of government" in the islands and then "protect the Philippines from outside interference while they work out their destiny, just as we have protected the republics of Central and South America, and are, by the Monroe Doctrine, pledged to protect Cuba." Opposition spokesmen gleefully pointed out that this was the substance of their own program.

Bryan also supported the kind of expansion favored by such Democrats as ex-President Grover Cleveland and ex-Secretary of State Richard Olney. "The best thing of the kind I have ever heard," remarked Cleveland of Olney's famous assertion that the United States "is practically sovereign on this continent, and its fiat is law upon the subjects to which it confines its interposition." As for Hawaii, Cleveland (and Bryan) wanted to control "the ports of a country so near to Japan and China" without the bother and responsibilities of formal annexation. Informal empire is perhaps the most accurate description of such a program. Both Cleveland and Bryan favored the overseas expansion of the American economic system and the extension of American authority throughout the world.

So, too, did such men as Roosevelt, Hay, and Lodge. At first, however, they stressed the acquisition of colonies, if not in the traditional sense of colonialism, at least in the pattern of administrative colonialism developed by Great Britain after the Indian Mutiny of 1857. Thus the early arguments between Roosevelt and Bryan were to some point. But the Roosevelt imperialists rather quickly modified their position in line with the argument advanced by such men as Brooks Adams. None of these leaders were motivated by a personal economic motive, but by concentrating on the economic issue, other more important considerations were overlooked. The Roosevelt group defined their economic interest in terms of preventing the stagnation of the American economic system, and their program to accomplish that objective was vigorous overseas economic expansion.

Following the thesis developed by Adams, they argued that the American system had to expand or stagnate. Businessmen agreed, interpreting that general economic analysis in terms of their specific and immediate economic motive for more markets. Imperialism or no imperialism, the nation agreed, our trade must be protected. But defined in that fashion, trade was no longer the exchange of commodities and services between independent producers meeting in the market place; it became instead a euphemism for the control of foreign markets for America's industrial and agricultural surpluses.

Secretary of State John Hay's Open Door Notes of 1899 and 1900 distilled this collection of motivations, pressures, and theories into a classic program of imperial expansion. Based on the assumption of what Brooks Adams called "America's economic supremacy," and formulated in the context of vigorous pressure from domestic economic interests and the threatening maneuvers of other nations, the policy of the open door was designed to establish the conditions under which America's preponderant economic power would extend the American system throughout the world without the embarrassment and inefficiency of traditional colonialism. Hay's first note of 1899 asserted the right of access for American economic power into China in particular, but the principle was rapidly generalized to the rest of the world. His second note of 1900 was designed to prevent other nations from extending the formal colonial system to China, and in later years that also was applied to other areas.

The Open Door Notes ended the debate between imperialists and anti-imperialists. The argument trailed on with the inertia characteristic of all such disagreements, but the nation recognized and accepted Hay's policy as a resolution of the original issue. In a similar fashion, it took some years (and further discussion) to liquidate the colonial status of the territory seized during the Spanish-American War. It also required time to work out and institutionalize a division of authority and labor between economic and political leaders so that the strategy could be put into operation on a routine basis. And it ultimately became necessary to open the door into existing colonial empires as well as unclaimed territories. But Secretary of State Hay's policy of the open door synthesized and formalized the frontier thesis, the specific demands of businessmen, workers, and farmers, and the theory which asserted that the American economic system would stagnate if it did not expand overseas.

America and the world shared this interpretation of the Open Door Policy at the time it was enunciated. Brooks Adams eulogized Secretary Hay as the realist who industrialized the Monroe Doctrine. The Philadelphia *Press* agreed: "This new doctrine established for

China is destined to be as important as the Monroe Doctrine has been for the Americans in the past century. It protects the present, it safeguards the future." Quite aware of the grand design, the Boston *Transcript* spelled it out in blunt accents. "We have an infinitely wider scope in the Chinese markets than we should have had with a 'sphere of influence' in competition with half a dozen other spheres." Many European commentators acknowledged that the strategy "hits us in our weak spot." Agreeing with the Boston analysis, a Berlin paper summed it up in one sentence: "The Americans regard, in a certain sense, all China as their sphere of interest."

Ex-Secretary of State Olney made it bipartisan. Prepared for the presidential election campaign of 1900, in which he supported Bryan, Olney's statement of the new imperial consensus was at the same time an excellent review of America's new foreign policy. "The 'home market' fallacy disappears," he explained, "with the proved inadequacy of the home market. Nothing will satisfy us in the future but free access to foreign markets—especially to those markets in the East." As one convinced at an early date by Brooks Adams that noncolonial economic expansion was the best strategy, Olney regretted the acquisition of the Philippines. It would have been wiser to have followed Washington's advice of 1796 and the principles of the Monroe Doctrine. "The true, the ideal position for us," Olney explained, "would be complete freedom of action, perfect liberty to pick allies from time to time as special occasions might warrant and an enlightened view of our own interests might dictate." But he was confident that the policy of the open door provided the very best approximation to that ideal.

Americans of that era and their European competitors were basically correct in their estimate of the Open Door Policy. It was neither an alien idea foisted off on America by the British nor a political gesture to the domestic crowd. Latter-day experts who dismissed the policy as irrelevant, misguided, or unsuccessful erred in two respects. They missed its deep roots in the American past and its importance at the time, and they failed to realize that the policy expressed the basic strategy and tactics of America's secular and imperial expansion in the twentieth century. When combined with the ideology of an industrial Manifest Destiny, the history of the Open Door Notes became the history of American foreign relations from 1900 to 1958.

The most dramatic confluence of these currents of ideological and economic expansion did not occur until the eve of American entry into World War I. For this reason, among others, it is often asserted that the United States did not take advantage of the Open Door Policy until after 1917, and some observers argue that the policy never led to the rise of an American empire. In evaluating the extent to which Americans carried through on the strategy of the Open Door Notes, there are two broad questions at issue with regard to statistics of overseas economic expansion, and they cannot be mixed up without confusing the analysis and the interpretation. One concerns the over-all importance of such expansion to the national economy. The answer to that depends less upon gross percentages than upon the role in the American economy of the industries which do depend in significant ways (including raw materials as well as markets) on foreign operations. Measured against total national product, for example, the export of American cars and trucks seem a minor matter. But it is not possible at one and the same time to call the automobile business the key industry in the economy and then dismiss the fact that approximately 15 per cent of its total sales in the 1920's were made in foreign markets.

The other major point concerns the role of such foreign enterprises and markets in the making of American foreign policy. This effect can be direct in terms of domestic political pressure, or indirect through the results of the American overseas economic activity on the foreign policy of other nations. In the broadest sense of gross statistics, moreover, the overseas economic expansion of the United States from 1897 to 1915 is more impressive than many people realize. Loans totaled over a billion dollars. Direct investments amounted to $2,652,300,000. While it is true that the nation also owed money abroad during the same period, that point is not too important to an understanding of American foreign policy. For the loans and the investments had a bearing on American foreign policy even though balance of payment computations reduce the net figure. Businessmen with interests in Mexico or Manchuria, for example, did not stop trying to influence American policy (or cease having an effect on Mexican or Asian attitudes) just because their investments or loans or sales were arithmetically canceled out by the debt incurred by other Americans in France.

Another misleading approach emphasizes the point that America's overseas economic expansion amounted to no more than 10 or 12 per cent of its national product during those years. But 10 per cent of any economic operation is a significant proportion; without it the enterprise may slide into bankruptcy. In that connection, the most recent studies by economists reveal that exports did indeed spark recovery from the depression of the 1890's. In any event, the businessmen and other economic groups *thought* the 10 per cent made a crucial difference, and many of them concluded that they could not get it in any way but through overseas expansion.

Other considerations aside, the conviction of these groups would make the figure important if it were only 1 per cent. Or, to make the point even clearer (and historically accurate), it would still be significant if all an entrepreneur did was to pressure the government to support an effort that failed. In that case the economic indicators would be negative, but the relevance to foreign policy might be very high. Such was precisely the case, for example, with the America-China Development Company. It ultimately disappeared from the scene, but before it died it exerted an extensive influence on American policy in Asia during the first decade of the twentieth century.

In another way, overseas economic operations which seem small on paper may mean the difference between survival and failure to a given firm. Faced by the near monopoly control over key raw materials exercised by the United States Steel Corporation after 1903, Charles Schwab had to go to Chile to get the ore supplies that were necessary to sustain the Bethlehem Steel Company. Schwab's investment was only 35 million dollars, but it played a vital role in his own affairs and exercised a significant influence on Chilean-American relations. Or, to reverse the example, economic activity which seems incidental judged by American standards is often fundamental to a weaker economy. This aspect of the problem can be illustrated by the situation in Manchuria between 1897 and 1904, where approximately one-tenth of 1 per cent of America's national product gave the Americans who were involved a major role in the affairs of that region, and provoked them to agitate vigorously for official American support. Their efforts were successful and led to crucial developments in American foreign policy.

It is impossible, in short, to judge the bearing of overseas economic expansion upon American diplomacy—and thus to judge the importance and efficacy of the Open Door Policy—in terms of gross statistics. The important factors are the relative significance of the activity and the way it is interpreted and acted upon by people and groups who at best are only vaguely symbolized by abstract aggregate statistics. And by these criteria there is no question about the great relevance for diplomacy of America's proposed and actual

overseas economic expansion between 1893 and 1915—and throughout the rest of the twentieth century.

Still another interpretation which discounts the significance of the
Open Door Policy in the early part of the century is based upon
America's failure to control Japanese activity in Asia. Though
perhaps the strongest argument of its type, it nevertheless fails to
establish its basic thesis. Three weaknesses undermine its conclusions: (1) the Open Door Policy was designed to secure and preserve
access to China for American economic power, not to deny access to
other nations; (2) America's difficulties with Japan between 1899 and
1918 stemmed from a failure of judgment concerning the execution
of the policy, not from a flaw in the policy itself; and (3) the United
States acted with considerable effectiveness between 1915 and 1918 to
prevent Japan from exploiting America's earlier error.

To grasp the full significance of these points it is vital to realize
that the Open Door Policy was derived from the proposition that
America's overwhelming economic power would cast the economy
and the politics of the weaker, under-developed countries in a
pro-American mold. American leaders assumed the opposition of
one or many industrialized powers. Over a period of two generations
the policy failed because some industrialized nations, among them
Japan, chose to resort to force when they concluded that the Open
Door Policy was working only too well, and because various groups
inside weaker countries such as China decided that America's
extensive influence was harmful to their specific and general welfare.

While that result may be judged a long-term failure, such a
verdict should not be confused with an unfavorable conclusion about
the policy in Asia between 1900 and 1918. Once it is understood that
the Open Door Policy was neither a military strategy nor a traditional balance-of-power policy, then it becomes clear that the troubles
in Asia stemmed from President Theodore Roosevelt's confusion on
that very point. For in first taking sides with Japan against Russia in
1904 in an attempt to exhaust both nations and thereby open the way
for American supremacy, and then fumbling in an effort to correct
his error by controlling the peace settlement, Roosevelt gave the
Japanese the initiative and on top of that antagonized them.

Roosevelt's mistake stemmed in large measure from his aristocrat's
noblesse oblige and his reaction to the theories of Brooks Adams.
From a very early date Roosevelt viewed himself as something akin
to the country squire of the twentieth century. Adams convinced him
of the importance of economic expansion, and reinforced his existing

view that the businessmen needed to be controlled. But Roosevelt interpreted such advice in the context of his admiration for the squire in the role of knight of the Round Table, the aristocrat's basic contempt and antagonism toward the peasant who aspires to higher things, and his racist nationalism. Useful insights into the ideology of those prejudices (along with others which matured in connection with the Bolshevik Revolution of November, 1917), and into the way they affected Roosevelt's successors, can be gained by considering them as part of the benevolent American desire to reform the world in its own image.

THE NIGHTMARE OF
DEPRESSION AND THE
VISION OF OMNIPOTENCE

[from *The Tragedy of American Diplomacy*, 1972]

United States involvement in World War II and the awesome challenges confronting the nation as victory neared did not, in Williams's mind, change American leaders' basic approach to the world. They remained dedicated to the fundamental strategy of the Open Door Policy, transforming it from "an intellectual outlook for changing the world into one concerned with preserving it in the traditional mold." Such a commitment gained added force, Williams suggested, because of America's considerably enhanced economic and military power at the conclusion of the war. It also escalated tensions with the Soviet Union. The failure to negotiate a comprehensive settlement recognizing the primacy of Soviet concerns about security and recovery "crystallized the cold war," in Williams's opinion. This treatment of American-Soviet affairs, and in particular the intimate connections he established between foreign policy decision-making and domestic affairs in both the United States and the Soviet Union, identified Williams as a leading cold war revisionist. He expanded considerably his discussion of cold war developments in the 1972 edition of *The Tragedy of American Diplomacy*, from which this and the next selection have been taken.

The President [Roosevelt] ... said that he himself would not be in favor of the creation of a new Assembly of the League of Nations, at least until after a period of time had transpired and during which an international police force composed of the United States and Great Britain had had an

133

opportunity of functioning.   *Remarks to Winston Churchill, August 1941,*
as Reported by Sumner Welles

For unless there is security here at home there cannot be lasting peace in the
world.   *Franklin Delano Roosevelt, January 1944*

It is important that I retain complete freedom of action after this conference
[in Moscow] is over.   *Franklin Delano Roosevelt, October 1944*

We cannot go through another ten years like the ten years at the end of the
twenties and the beginning of the thirties, without having the most
far-reaching consequences upon our economic and social systems.... We
have got to see that what the country produces is used and sold under
financial arrangements which make its production possible.... My conten-
tion is that we cannot have full employment and prosperity in the United
States without the foreign markets.   *Dean Acheson, November 1944*

...if the Russians did not wish to join us they could go to hell.
Harry S Truman, Remark of April 23, 1945,
as Reported by Charles E. Bohlen

In Rumania and Bulgaria—and rather less decisively in Hungary—the
Russian Government has sponsored and supported Governments which are
democratic in the Russian rather than in the English-speaking connotation
of the term and whose friendship for Russia is one of their main qualifica-
tions. This policy would fit in well enough with a "zones of influence"
conception of the [peace] settlement; and it would be idle to deny that other
great nations, both in the remoter and in the recent past, have pursued the
same policy in regions of the world which they deemed vital to their
security. During the past few weeks, however, the English-speaking Powers
have adopted an attitude towards Balkan affairs which seemed to imply the
contrary view that any of the three Powers may claim a right of intervention
even in regions especially affecting the security of one of the others; and the
clash of these opposing views, each of which can be formidably sustained by
argument, underlay all the difficulties of the Foreign Ministers in their
discussion of Balkan affairs.   *London Times Editorial, October 3, 1945*

...the United States has it in its power to increase enormously the strains
under which Soviet policy must operate, to force upon the Kremlin a far
greater degree of moderation and circumspection than it has had to observe
in recent years, and in this way to promote tendencies which must
eventually find their outlet in either the break-up or the gradual mellowing
of Soviet power.   *George Frost Kennan, February 1946–July 1947*

The situation in the world today is not primarily the result of the natural difficulties which follow a great war. It is chiefly due to the fact that one nation has not only refused to cooperate in the establishment of a just and honorable peace, but—even worse—has actually sought to prevent it.

Harry S Truman, March 1948

ROOSEVELT AND STALIN CONFRONT THE DILEMMAS OF VICTORY

POLITICIANS become statesmen not by honoring pious shibboleths, nor even by moving men to action with inspiring rhetoric, but by recognizing and then resolving the central dilemmas of their age.

When measured against this demanding standard, Franklin Delano Roosevelt's performance after 1940 poses a difficult problem in judgment for the historian. On the one hand, he seems clearly enough to have sensed the contradiction between his intellectual, emotional, and policy commitment to America's traditional strategy of the open door, and the new circumstances arising out of World War II which called for the acceptance of limits upon American expectations and actions, and for the working out of a concert of power with other major nations. Though it was not in any sense unique, Roosevelt's recognition of that new reality does entitle him to a place of honor within the community of American policy-makers. It also explains and justifies the praise of his partisans.

On the other hand, Roosevelt did not resolve the dilemma posed by that contradiction between tradition and reality. He occasionally spoke candidly of the problem. He offered a few very general ideas about the kinds of things that could be done to adapt American thinking and policy to the new conditions. And he suggested a few concrete proposals for dealing with specific aspects of the developing crisis. But he never worked out, initiated, or carried through a fresh approach which combined necessary domestic changes with a fundamental re-evaluation of American foreign policy. He did not resolve the dilemma. At the time of his death, he was turning back toward the inadequate domestic programs of the New Deal era, and was in foreign affairs reasserting the traditional strategy of the Open Door Policy.

Explorations into the forest of conditional history are sometimes fruitful, for they occasionally suggest new insights into what did occur. This is perhaps the case with the debate over what would have happened if Roosevelt had lived. The most sympathetic interpretation explains Roosevelt's ambivalence as a result of his declining health. That was a relevant consideration, but there is little evidence that Roosevelt seriously entertained even the idea of initiating a re-evaluation of America's conception of itself and the world. For the further such an inquiry is pushed, the more it becomes apparent that Roosevelt had not abandoned the policy of the open door; and that, even if he personally had been on the verge of trying to do so, few of his advisors and subordinates had either the intention or the power to effect such a change.

The leaders who succeeded Roosevelt understood neither the dilemma nor the need to alter their outlook. A handful of them thought briefly of stabilizing relations with the Soviet Union on the basis of economic and political agreements, but even that tiny minority saw the future in terms of continued expansion guided by the strategy of the Open Door Policy. The great majority rapidly embarked upon a program to force the Soviet Union to accept America's traditional conception of itself and the world. This decision represented the final stage in the transformation of the policy of the open door from a utopian idea into an ideology, from an intellectual outlook for changing the world into one concerned with preserving it in the traditional mold.

American leaders had internalized, and had come to *believe*, the theory, the necessity, and the morality of open-door expansion. Hence they seldom thought it necessary to explain or defend the approach. Instead, they *assumed* the premises and concerned themselves with exercising their freedom and power to deal with the necessities and the opportunities that were defined by such an outlook. As far as American leaders were concerned, the philosophy and practice of open-door expansion had become, in both its missionary and economic aspects, *the* view of the world. Those who did not recognize and accept that fact were considered not only wrong, but incapable of thinking correctly.

The problem of the Soviet leaders was defined by the confrontation between the expansive prophecy of Marx about world revolution (which was supported by the traditional Great Russian and Slavic ideas of world leadership) and a realistic, Marxian analysis of world conditions (which was reinforced by sober calculations of nationalistic self-interest). Russian leaders clearly recognized their dilemma, and realized that rehabilitation and military security were the points upon which its resolution had to hinge. But American policy offered the Russians no real choice on those key issues. Particularly after the atom bomb was created and used, the attitude of the United States left the Soviets with but one real option: either acquiesce in American proposals or be confronted with American power and hostility. It was the decision of the United States to employ its new and awesome power in keeping with the traditional Open Door Policy which crystallized the cold war.

To say that is not to say that the United States started or caused the cold war. Nor is it an effort to avoid what many people apparently consider the most important—if also the most controversial and embarrassing—issue of recent and contemporary history. For, contrary to that general belief, the problem of which side started the cold war offers neither a very intelligent nor a very rewarding way of approaching the central questions about American foreign relations since 1941.

The real issue is rather the far more subtle one of which side committed its power to policies which hardened the natural and inherent tensions and propensities into bitter antagonisms and inflexible positions. Two general attitudes can be adopted in facing that issue. One is to assume, or take for granted, on the basis of emotion and official information, that the answer is obvious: Russia is to blame. That represents the easy, nationalistic solution to all questions about international affairs. That attitude also defines history as a stockpile of facts to be requisitioned on the basis of what is needed to prove a conclusion decided upon in advance.

The other approach is to consider history as a way of learning, of mustering the intellectual and oral courage to acknowledge the facts as they exist without tampering with them. If they are unpleasant or disturbing, then new facts—in the form of our ideas and actions—must be created that modify the unsatisfying scene. This is the more difficult and the more demanding method. Recognizing this, John Foster Dulles offered in 1946 a classic bit of encouragement to push on with the effort: "There is no nation which has attitudes so pure that they cannot be bettered by self-examination."

In undertaking such self-examination, the first and essential requirement is to acknowledge two primary facts which can never be blinked. *The first is that the United States had from 1944 to at least 1962 a vast preponderance of actual as well as potential power vis-à-vis the Soviet Union.* Nothing can ever change the absolute and relative power relationship between the two countries during that chronological period. This relative weakness of the Russians did not turn them into western parliamentary democrats, and it did not transform their every action into a moral and equitable transaction. But it does confront all students of the cold war, be they academicians or

politicians or housewives, with very clear and firm limits on how
they can make sense out of the cold war if they are at the same time
to observe the essential standards of intellectual honesty. For power
and responsibility go together in a direct and intimate relationship.
Unless it tries all the alternatives that offer reasonable probabilities of
success, a nation with the great relative supremacy enjoyed by the
United States between 1944 and 1962 cannot with any real warrant
or meaning claim that it has been *forced* to follow a certain approach
or policy. Yet that is the American claim even though it did not
explore several such alternatives.

Instead, and this is the second fact that cannot be dodged, the
United States used or deployed its preponderance of power wholly
within the assumptions and the tradition of the strategy of the Open
Door Policy. The United States never formulated and offered the
Soviet Union a settlement based on other, less grandiose, terms. For
that matter, it never made a serious and sustained effort even to
employ in dealing with the Russians the same kind of tactics that
had been used for a generation before World War II in relations
with the Japanese.

It is true that the offer to include the Soviet Union in the Marshall
Plan can be interpreted as a similar move. For, if the Soviets had
accepted the conditions set forth for receiving such assistance, the
United States would have been in a position to exercise extensive
influence over internal Soviet affairs, as well as over its foreign policy.
To cite but one known example, American leaders would have
demanded that the Russians allocate large quantities of raw materials
to western Europe. That in itself would have delayed and complicated Soviet recovery, let alone its further development. Even so,
American policy-makers greeted the Russian refusal to participate on
such terms with an audible sigh of relief. They never made the kind
of serious effort to negotiate a satisfactory compromise with the
Russians as they had done with the Japanese. If it be objected that
the effort would have failed anyway because it had not worked with
the Japanese, then those who advance that argument must go on to
confront one of three conclusions that are inherent in their logic. It
must be admitted either that the strategy itself cannot succeed
without war, or that it can succeed without war only if the other
country accepts and works within limits set by the United States.
Otherwise, the policy must be changed—formally or informally.

Instead of being changed, however, the traditional strategy was
merely reasserted and put into operation at the end of the war under

the famous and accurate phrase about "negotiation from strength." But negotiation from strength meant in practice that there would be no meaningful negotiations. The concept defined negotiation as the acceptance of American proposals, and American leaders acted upon that definition. The broad and fundamental failure of the policy demonstrated the basic misconception of man and the world inherent in the policy of the open door. For it established beyond cavil that the policy of the open door, like all imperial policies, created and spurred onward a dynamic opposition to which it forfeited the initiative. Not even a monopoly of nuclear weapons enabled America to prove itself an exception to that involuting momentum of empire.

Even before they formally entered World War II, American leaders assumed that the United States would emerge from the conflict in a position to extend, stabilize, and reform the empire of the open door. Roosevelt's assumption that Anglo-American forces would police the world for a "transition period" after the defeat of the Axis was given overt expression in August 1941. That was almost four months before Pearl Harbor but after the decision had been made to help the Russians defeat Hitler in Europe. His casually optimistic outlook foresaw the ultimate creation of an international organization committed to the policy of the open door, a circumstance that would enable the United States to proceed with the work of developing the world.

Supported by a thoroughly bipartisan assortment of liberals and conservatives, this reassertion of the traditional open door strategy guided the community of American policy-makers throughout the war and on into the cold war era. Ultimately it became, in the best tradition of the open door, and in the words of G. L. Arnold, a sympathetic British observer, a view of the world resting "upon the expectation of a prolonged era of peace, Anglo-American hegemony (with the aid of China) in the United Nations and in the world generally, free trade outside the Soviet orbit and gradual liberalization within, a weakened and profoundly pacific Russia far behind the Western powers in the utilization of atomic energy." The assumption of virtuous omnipotence, implicit in the Open Door Notes and formulated explicitly on the eve of American entry into World War I, reached full maturity in that image of an American Century. As with Theodore Roosevelt's concern to save civilization and Wilson's crusade to make the world safe for democracy, however, the urge to give the future a New Deal was powered by a persuasive sense of the necessity to expand economically in order to sustain democracy and prosperity in the United States.

In keeping with this outlook, the United States declined in the winter of 1941–42 even to consider the Soviet Union's bid to settle the postwar boundaries of eastern Europe on the basis of the situation as it existed just prior to Hitler's attack. Russia raised the question in conversations with the British during November and December 1941, at which time Soviet spokesmen made clear and pointed references to being left out of the Atlantic Conference discussions of August 1941, between Churchill and Roosevelt.

Stalin suggested five major areas for agreement: (1) the boundaries of the Soviet Union should be guaranteed largely as they existed just prior to Hitler's assault in June 1941 (including the Curzon Line in Poland); (2) Austria should be restored as an independent nation; (3) Germany's industrial and military base should be weakened by splitting off the Ruhr manufacturing complex, by incorporating East Prussia into Poland, and perhaps by breaking off one other large province; (4) Yugoslavia and Albania should be re-established as independent countries, and Czechoslovakia and Greece should have their prewar boundaries reaffirmed; and (5) Russia should receive reparations in kind from Germany.

These proposals pose a fascinating "iffy" question: what if Russia had been committed to those conditions, and they had been honored by both sides? Certainly the postwar era would have developed in a significantly different manner. Another consideration is more relevant to what did happen, because the Soviets continued in large measure to emphasize their proposals of 1941 during the war and on into the subsequent period.

At the time, however, the American response was wholly negative. [Secretary of State Cordell] Hull considered it "unfortunate" even to discuss such "commitments," and simply refused to agree to them. He first put strong pressure on the British to delay and then spurn the Soviet offer. There is no mystery about his adamance. American leaders did not want to negotiate any settlements until they were in the strongest possible position, and they thought that would be at the end of the war. And they were guided by the Open Door Policy, and they had neither the desire nor the intention to negotiate away any equality of opportunity in eastern Europe.

Stalin nevertheless continued to press his proposals during discussions with [British Foreign Minister] Anthony Eden in Moscow in December 1941, and on into 1942. Hull never gave way. He secured

Roosevelt's support in April 1942, for the view that such commitments were "both dangerous and unwise." A month later the Secretary and his advisors in the State Department prepared a protest "so strong that we were in some fear lest the President disapprove it." The concern was unfounded. Roosevelt, so Hull reported, "quickly returned it with his O.K." The Soviets were blocked. The postwar configuration of eastern Europe was left moot—to be settled by other means.

This episode was extremely significant in American-Soviet relations, and English and American leaders realized that at the time. In many ways, the crisis can be understood most clearly in terms of the paradoxical attitude of the United States toward the Baltic States. Before World War I, Estonia, Latvia, and Lithuania had been provinces of Russia. Then, at the time of the Bolshevik Revolution, Germany had forcibly annexed them. During the subsequent years of intervention, the Allies encouraged and finally established the three countries as part of the *cordon sanitaire* designed to contain the Soviet Union.

Acquiescing in, but not accepting, that loss of its traditional "window on the West," the Soviets signed peace treaties with the new states in 1920. But the United States did not recognize the independence of those nations for several years, insisting that they were legitimate parts of the Russian state. Ultimately, however, America gave way and established diplomatic relations with the three countries. Having re-established its traditional authority over the Baltic states in 1939, the Soviet Union fully expected and intended to retain that control after the defeat of Hitler. In the discussions that took place during the winter of 1941–42, however, the United States refused to return to its original position. Stalin's blunt reaction to being blocked on this issue by Hull and Roosevelt (and thereby the British) casts an exceedingly bright light on subsequent tension between East and West.

"It is very important to us," Stalin explained at the outset of the negotiations, "to know whether we shall have to fight at the peace conference in order to get our western frontiers."

The record of the discussions reveals that the Russians became convinced that such a battle would be necessary.

"Surely this is axiomatic," Stalin shot back when Eden continued, as the advance guard for Hull and Roosevelt, to balk at an agreement. "We are fighting our hardest and losing hundreds of thousands of men in the common cause with Great Britain as our ally, and I should have thought that such a question as the position of the Baltic states ought to be axiomatic.... [I] am surprised and amazed at Mr. Churchill's Government taking up this position. It is practically the same as that of the Chamberlain Government.... This attitude of the British Government toward our frontiers is indeed a surprise to me so I think it will be better to postpone the proposed agreements."

"It now looks," he added in a remark that implicitly tied Roosevelt and the United States to the British position, "as if the Atlantic Charter was directed against the U.S.S.R." Stalin was of course aware of America's responsibility for preventing an agreement. Any doubts are removed by Eden's blunt summary of the whole affair. The American attitude, he warned on March 12, 1942, "will surely appear to Stalin so uncollaborative a state of mind as to confirm his suspicions that he can expect no real consideration for Russia's interests from ourselves or the United States."

Roosevelt took an almost identical position three years later, in the fall of 1944, when the issue was reopened by the Russian counteroffensive against Hitler. The British repeated their warning about the dangers inherent in Roosevelt's efforts to avoid a commitment: the Russians were on the scene, and the only possible way of sustaining Western interests was through serious negotiations based on a series of *quid pro quos*. Instead, Roosevelt and Hull again stood by the strategy of the open door. They insisted that any agreement between Stalin and Churchill would have to be limited to a period of three months duration. It seems very probable that Stalin concluded that he would "have to fight at the peace conference in order to get our western frontiers."

In the meantime, the refusal to negotiate a basic settlement with the Soviet Union in the winter of 1941–42 was almost immediately followed by another serious difference between the two countries. For, later in the spring of 1942, the Russians were given ambivalent and confusing assurances about when a second front would be opened in Europe. By August, when it had become apparent that Allied troops would not land on the continent that year, relations with Moscow had encountered very rough sledding. Even so, several developments reduced the tension and produced an interlude of improved relations between America and Russia. Foremost was the Russian victory at Stalingrad. That triumph convinced everybody, including the Russians, that Hitler would be defeated. As a result, and even before they launched their major counter-offensive, the Soviets embarked upon a fundamental debate over what to do after the war. Their discussion ranged across political, philosophical, and economic lines, but its essential nature was defined by Russia's tremendous physical and human losses in the war.

After Stalingrad, the Russians knew they would survive, but as a terribly weakened nation. Hence they were aware that the way they handled the recovery problem would influence all other decisions. Perhaps the most revealing insight into Russia's basic outlook at that time was offered (unconsciously, in all probability) by [Foreign Minister V. M.] Molotov on February 18, 1956—after the Soviets had developed their nuclear weapons, and after the Chinese Communists had triumphed in Asia. "We now have an international situation," he remarked, "of which we could only have dreamed ten or fifteen years ago." Implicit in Molotov's comment was the fact that the Russians had viewed their position in the 1940s as one of weakness, not offensive strength.

Though there were various shades of opinion as to how the central issue of reconstruction should be dealt with, the Russians divided into three broad groups. One of them, occasionally called "our softies" by their Russian opponents, held that it was necessary and desirable to undertake reconstruction at a relatively moderate tempo, obtaining assistance from the United States. The softies stressed the need and desirability of relaxing the pervasive and extensive controls that had been exercised over Soviet life ever since the first Five Year Plan and the wisdom of revising, decentralizing, and rationalizing the industrial system that had been built. They also emphasized the danger of deteriorating relations with the United States. Perhaps most significant of all, they advanced the thesis that Western capitalism could probably avoid another serious depression, and hence the appeal and the safety of the Soviet Union depended upon its ability to improve the quality of life in Russia and thereby induce other peoples to accept communism by the force and persuasiveness of example.

Others within Russia argued that the softies were wrong in theory or in fact. Some of these men, who may be called the conservatives, agreed with the softies that it was desirable to ease up at home and were half convinced by the more favorable analysis of foreign capitalism, but they doubted that the Western nations, and in particular the United States, would help the Soviet Union solve its reconstruction problems. Hence they concluded that Russia would have to establish a basic security perimeter in Europe, the Middle East, and Asia and once again pull itself up by its own bootstraps.

Opposed to the softies and the conservatives was a group which may be called the doctrinaire revolutionaries. The diehards scoffed at the analysis and proposals advanced by the moderates and asserted that the only practical and realistic program was to secure a base for militant revolutionary activity throughout the world. Such doctrinaires stressed the need to force the pace of reconstruction while doing all that was possible to export revolutions.

Stalin's temperament and experience inclined him toward resolving the dilemma posed by the problem of reconstruction and the tradition of revolution in a conservative manner. But that approach depended on two things for success: (1) limiting and controlling revolutionary action by foreign communists, which otherwise would antagonize the United States, and (2) reaching an economic and political understanding with America, an agreement that would enable Russia to handle the problem of recovery and at the same time relax certain controls and pressures inside the country. To use the language of Wall Street, Stalin was a bull on communism. He was confident that if given a peaceful opportunity to develop its program in Russia, communism would gradually appeal to more and more countries of the world. He felt this was particularly likely in the underdeveloped areas and in poorer industrialized nations. If this could be managed by getting aid from America and by restraining foreign Communists from seizing power through revolutions, then the movement toward socialism and communism would move slowly enough to avoid frightening the United States into retaliation against the Soviet Union itself.

Two important aspects of this ferment and clash of views within the hierarchy of Soviet leadership must be kept in mind throughout any discussion of American-Soviet relations after 1941. They are particularly important to an understanding of the interaction between the two countries during the period between April 1945 and the summer of 1948.

The first is that this conflict over policy within the Soviet Union cannot be discounted or dismissed on the grounds that it did not produce Western-style representative government in Russia. Both the American public in general and its individual leaders tend very strongly to interpret the absence of Anglo-Saxon institutions in another country to mean that there is also an absence of significant or meaningful disagreement and debate about important issues. This is simply wrong. The ways in which differences of interest and opinion are organized and exert influence are many and varied. Even in the United States, for that matter, many crucial issues came increasingly after 1929 to be debated and decided by an elite almost wholly outside the institutions of local, state and national elections. Furthermore, as events since 1952 have demonstrated, such debate in Russia did continue and did begin to take on institutional form and substance. It also affected policy.

This development leads directly to the second main point. American policy exerted an early, continuing, and significant influence on the course of debate in the Soviet Union. Indeed, it had done so since the very first weeks of the Bolshevik Revolution in 1917. American policy therefore influenced Soviet policy and action. These considerations can not be re-emphasized every time they appear in the subsequent pages of this essay, but it is extremely important to understand them and use them as intellectual tools in thinking about later events.

In order to bypass all the misunderstanding that it is possible to avoid, let these points be stated as simply and as directly as possible. As Stalin made clear in the winter of 1941–42, the Soviet Union fully intended to re-establish what it considered to be its minimum natural and desirable frontiers in eastern Europe. He further concluded that the United States and England would resist that effort. His opposition raised in the minds of Soviet leaders the very natural question as to whether or not they did not need an even firmer security perimeter.

Hence the problem for American leaders was one of developing an attitude and a broad set of proposals involving such security and economic aid for the Soviet Union that would enable them to negotiate some kind of modus vivendi with the Russians. The failure of American leaders to do that is the central theme of American diplomacy after the abortive negotiations of 1941–42. If studied and written as a critique of Soviet policy, the emphasis involved in treating these matters would be different. In that case, the story might very well focus on the way that the breakdown of the talks of 1941–42 strengthened those Soviet leaders who laid primary stress on extending communism as the Red Army moved westward. That might very possibly be the real tragedy of Soviet diplomacy. But since this essay is about American diplomacy, and—even more— since it was the United States that refused to offer any clear and unequivocal basis for such fundamental negotiations, the essay has to concentrate on America's actions and the ideas behind them.

Returning, then, to the events of the winter of 1942–43, there were several developments which encouraged Stalin in his propensity to resolve his dilemma in a conservative (i.e., nationalist) fashion. One was the Western landing in North Africa, which did apparently modify his suspicion and anger over the failure to make an assault on the European continent. More important, however, was an American approach concerning postwar economic relations with Russia which seemed to suggest that the Soviet Union could obtain help in dealing with its reconstruction problems. Stalin responded quickly and decisively. But he was ultimately forced to conclude that the American overture did not represent a changed outlook on the part of the majority of America's corporate leaders.

In its origins the plan was a continuation of the old idea that America's economic system had to have a constantly expanding foreign market if it was to survive and prosper. At bottom, therefore, it was the fear of another depression (or the resumption of the old one) that prompted a few American leaders such as Donald M. Nelson[1] and Eric Johnston[2] to think of large-scale exports to Russia. Johnston, for example, was convinced after careful investigation in 1944 that the primary concern of Soviet leaders was "to rebuild Russia." They also worried about the depletion of certain raw materials and thought that Russia could continue to supply such items as manganese after the war. This small minority of American leaders began to realize that, whatever his many faults, Stalin was not another Hitler and that the Soviet Union had not developed by the same dynamic as Nazi Germany.

During 1943, therefore, Nelson and a few other Americans pushed the idea of a large loan to Russia. Stalin told Nelson that he was very much in favor of the plan and even gave him a list of priority needs as a first step in working out a specific program. Their negotiations had much to do with the improvement in political relations between the two countries, exemplified by Stalin's voluntary promise to Secretary of State Hull in October 1943 that Russia would enter the war against Japan. A bit later, in November, the conversations at the Teheran Conference also reflected the improved atmosphere.

For his part, Roosevelt was by that time revealing a more realistic attitude about including the Soviet Union as a full partner in any

1. Donald Nelson (1888–1959), vice president of Sears, Roebuck and Company, served in the administration of Franklin D. Roosevelt as head of the Office of Production Management (1941–1942), chairman of the War Production Board (1942–1944), and as FDR's personal representative to China (1944–1945).—ED.

2. Eric Johnston (1896–1966), businessman and president of the U.S. Chamber of Commerce (later president of the Motion Picture Association of America), was a wartime emissary to the Soviet Union and strong proponent of expanded U.S. trade.—ED.

plans for the postwar world. He did not talk any longer, for example, about the way that England and America would between themselves police the world at the end of the war. In a similar way, he apparently grasped the fact that Stalin was "most deeply interested" in Russian recovery problems, and indicated at least some recognition of the way that issue was tied in with Soviet foreign policy. The President also seemed to be gaining some awareness that more reforms were needed in the United States. He talked, at least to some extent, about the importance of an "economic bill of rights" to balance, supplement, and reinforce America's traditional political freedoms. In certain respects, he appeared to be echoing the argument of the speech he had read at the Commonwealth Club in San Francisco during the 1932 presidential campaign. "America's own rightful place in the world," he asserted, "depends in large part upon" its handling of domestic issues. "For unless there is security here at home," he explained, "there cannot be lasting peace in the world."

Such remarks can be interpreted to mean that Roosevelt was beginning to understand that America's traditional policy of open-door expansion had contributed significantly to its domestic and international difficulties. Even so, his concrete proposals for development at home were pale copies of old New Deal legislation. And while he said he was "sorry" that he did not have time to discuss Russia's postwar recovery problems with Stalin at Teheran, the fact is that he never took—or made—time to do so during the remaining sixteen months of his life. He did not even see to it that his subordinates committed and prepared themselves to discuss and negotiate the issue with the Soviets. Roosevelt's declining health may account in part for this, but in that event it is clear that such an approach to the Russians was very low on the President's list of priorities.

There is at least one account, moreover, which suggests that Roosevelt's position was very similar to those who wanted to use Russia's needs to win major political and economic concessions. The story is told by James Byrnes[3] in his second volume of memoirs, *All in One Life*. He reports that Leo Crowley,[4] who was to terminate

3. James F. Byrnes (1879–1972), former director of the Office of War Mobilization (1943–1945), served as secretary of state in the administration of Harry Truman from 1945 to 1947.—ED.
4. Leo Crowley (1889–1972), a prominent member of the banking community in Wisconsin, was chairman of the Federal Deposit Insurance Corporation from its creation in 1934 until 1945. During World War II he served as chief of the Office of Economic Warfare (1943–1945) and was also head of the Foreign Economic Administration during the same years.—ED.

Lend-Lease shipments to the Soviet Union as soon as Germany surrendered, told him of a conversation with Roosevelt that took place about April 1, 1945, shortly before the President died. "Crowley told me that...he told the President about a rumor that our government was considering a loan to the Soviets of $10 billion, and that he [Crowley] thought it wise to refrain from making any loan until more was known of their postwar attitude. He said the President agreed." This account should not be taken as full proof of Roosevelt's attitude. But it does, even when evaluated with caution, support the main point at issue. It is simply not possible to account for the continuance of the Open Door Policy by blaming Roosevelt's successors, for the President did not carry through on persistent Russian overtures for major economic assistance to help them rebuild their shattered economy.

Had Roosevelt done this, it would be more meaningful to charge his successors—or the Russians—with sabotaging his plan for the future; for it is quite true that the small group around Nelson favoring some rapprochement with the Russians was opposed by a much larger number of America's corporate leaders. It seems likely that Averell Harriman, one of the many wealthy industrial and banking leaders who supported Roosevelt, and who was one of the President's top advisors, was one of the more influential leaders of the anti-Russian group. Harriman's natural antagonism to the Soviets was reinforced by his vigorous belief in the necessity of open-door expansion, a belief that may have been heightened even more by an unhappy experience with the Russians in the 1920s, when his attempt to control a sizable segment of the world's manganese market by developing Russian supplies ended in mutual dissatisfaction. Harriman was but one of many corporate leaders, however, who had gone into the Roosevelt Administration with anti-Russian views. Others included James V. Forrestal[5] and Bernard Baruch.[6] All of these men were skeptical of Nelson's approach to dealing with the Soviets and were supported in their view by State Department experts such as George F. Kennan (who was in Russia much of the time with Harriman).

These men shared Harriman's extremely reserved reaction, early in 1944, to the news that the Russians "were anxious to come to a prompt understanding" about postwar economic relations. His view

5. James V. Forrestal (1892–1949), financier, was secretary of the navy 1944–1947 and the first U.S. secretary of defense 1947–1949.—ED.

6. Bernard Baruch (1870–1965), major American financier, was an adviser to presidents from Woodrow Wilson to Dwight Eisenhower.—ED.

became even clearer when, a bit later that year, Stalin made a formal request for a loan of six billion dollars. Harriman advised cutting the initial amount under discussion to one-tenth of that sum and proposed that the project should be defined as a credit, rather than as loan, so that if it ever actually went through, the United States could exercise extensive controls over Russia's use of the money. Thus, while he agreed with the Nelson group that "the question of long-term credits represents the key point in any negotiations with the Soviet Government," he also shared the State Department's view that the lever provided by Russian weakness and devastation could and should be used to insure a predominant role for America in all decisions about the post-war world.

Harriman and most American leaders knew precisely what kind of choice they made. One of the most unequivocal pieces of evidence on this point comes from Admiral William H. Standley, who served as American Ambassador to Russia during the first part of the war. Speaking publicly on November 14, 1944, he offered a candid review of the situation. Some kind of rivalry with the Russians was unavoidable simply because they would be the only other victorious power on the continent of Europe. But that tension could be kept within bounds, Standley argued, if the United States accepted its primary responsibility in the situation.

"We must assume two important premises," he pointed out. "First, that Russia's security is vital to her and that she cannot turn to industrialization and development of her raw material resources unless she has that security.... After victory, security is their next consideration.... [And unless we help establish it] they will have to proceed on their own to provide it."

Harriman based his policy on an identical analysis. He candidly acknowledged "that the sooner the Soviet Union can develop a decent life for its people the more tolerant they will become." That interpretation obviously implied a basic policy of helping the Russians recover from the devastation of the war. But quite unlike Standley, Harriman proposed instead to exploit Russian weakness and force them to accept American policies. The Russians "should be given to understand that our willingness to co-operate wholeheartedly with them in their vast reconstruction problems will depend upon their behavior in international matters." "I am opposed to granting her that credit," he stated flatly in May 1945. "I would apportion that credit out piecemeal, demanding in return concessions on the political field."

From the very beginning of the discussions with Stalin in 1943, Roosevelt was aware of the Soviet overtures for economic aid and of the importance Stalin attached to such negotiations. Yet the President never took the lead himself in handling the issue. Nor did he direct the State Department or a special committee to push the matter. In the end, therefore, there was no concerted American effort to match the Russian approach of handling related political and economic questions on an integrated basis.

Roosevelt's attitude, which so clearly reflected the traditional outlook of the Open Door Policy, was revealed even more vividly in the spring of 1944, when the Soviet Army began to advance into eastern Europe. Confronted by Churchill with the need to come to some clear arrangement with the Russians, Roosevelt at first agreed to the idea of a clear and precise division of authority. Then, in an abrupt turnabout, he asserted that he must have "complete freedom of action," whatever the agreement arranged by Churchill and Stalin. After considerable effort, Churchill and Stalin worked out an understanding—"a good guide," said Churchill, "for the conduct of our affairs"—whereby Russia would exercise predominant authority in southeastern Europe, Great Britain would do so in Greece, and the Allies would share responsibility in Yugoslavia. Roosevelt reluctantly accepted this division of power on the basis of a three-month trial.

During subsequent months, the British intervened to crush a revolution in Greece and prepare the way for the installation of a government they wanted and could control. Though he urged the British to take a more liberal line, Roosevelt went along with Churchill on the need to control affairs in Greece and acquiesced in the Prime Minister's action. *Both in fact and in the eyes of the Russians, that committed Roosevelt on the eve of the Yalta Conference to the agreement worked out between Churchill and Stalin.* For his part, Stalin refrained from attacking or blocking the British move in Greece. Churchill reported that Stalin "adhered very strictly to this understanding." Stalin also moved to forestall trouble with the Western Allies arising from foreign communist agitation and revolution. He advised, and apparently even warned, Tito and Mao Tse-tung to abstain from revolutionary action in their nations and instead to accept subordinate positions in coalition governments led by pro-Western parties.

Against this background, and in the context of Germany's imminent defeat, Roosevelt met Churchill and Stalin at Yalta in February 1945. In addition to their knowledge of the Churchill-Stalin agreement, and of Stalin's self-containment during the Greek episode, American leaders were aware that the Chinese communists, after a long debate, had concluded in September 1944, that they preferred to work with the United States rather than with Russia in the future development of China. Thus it is absolutely clear that Roosevelt and his advisors knew that the Soviet Union was prepared to negotiate seriously about the character of postwar relations with the United States and that America had an equally fruitful opportunity in Asia. But during the conference American leaders were not concerned to push such negotiations. They were not prepared to abandon, or even seriously to modify, the traditional strategy of American expansion.

Disturbed by America's ambivalence and Churchill's increasingly open opposition, which increased the difficulty Stalin had in controlling the doctrinaire revolutionaries within his own camp, Stalin went to Yalta with two approaches to the postwar world. One was based on receiving a large loan from the United States. His overtures in this direction were answered with vague and unrewarding replies. Stalin's alternative was to obtain, by agreement or by self-exertion, economic reparations from Germany and a strong strategic position in eastern Europe, the Black Sea area, and the Far East. America went to Yalta, on the other hand, guided by little except a sense of mission to reform the world, a growing fear of postwar economic crisis, and an increasing confidence that Russian weakness would enable America to exercise its freedom and solve its problems by further open-door expansion.

Commentators have criticized President Roosevelt very severely on the grounds that he was naive in believing he could persuade Stalin to co-operate with the West after the war. Such attacks are weak and misdirected in several important respects. In the first place, it is almost absurd to think—or charge—that a man with Roosevelt's mastery of political infighting was naive. He may have overestimated his power or his skill, but he was not naive. Significantly, too, Roosevelt had *not* abandoned, at the time of his death, the intention of reasserting American power and influence in eastern Europe. It was suggested to him that the United States should file a vigorous protest over the Soviet action early in 1945 of reconstituting the Rumanian Government along pro-Soviet lines. Roosevelt did *not* reply that the basic issue should be forgotten. His position was quite different. *He said merely that the Rumanian episode, because it involved supplies for the Red Army that was still fighting Germany, did not offer the best kind of ground upon which to take a stand.*

Roosevelt's idea of reaching an accommodation with Stalin was not based on some utopian dream of perfect and everlasting agreement on any and all issues. However, Roosevelt simply did not understand the nature and workings of a modern, complex industrial economy. The result in domestic affairs was that his political acumen and skill were never focused on the central and vital issues of getting the political economy into some kind of fundamentally dynamic balance. The same weakness plagued him in dealing with the Russians. He never got his priorities straight. Short of war, economic aid was the one effective tool he had in negotiations with the Soviets. But he never used it.

Roosevelt's successors understood and used that lever, but they treated it as a weapon to force the Soviets to accept American policies. The conflict over affairs in eastern Europe which developed out of that attitude is usually stressed in discussing the origins of the cold war. Yet it may be that the issues of German reparations and American expansion in the Middle East were equally important as determining factors. Failing to obtain a loan from America, Stalin had to decide among three possible courses of action.

He could give way and accept the American interpretation of all disputed points, abandoning foreign communists to their fate and attempting to control the extremists in his own nation. He could respond with an orthodox revolutionary program throughout the world. Or, relying on large economic reparations from Germany, he could continue the effort to resolve his dilemma in a conservative manner even though he did not have any formal understanding with the United States. This approach would also do much to keep Germany from becoming a threat to Russia in the immediate future. It left him, however, with the need to effect some basic settlement concerning eastern Europe, the Far East, and the Black Sea region.

Stalin was able to reach such an understanding with the United States in but one of those areas. This was in Asia, where he traded American predominance in China (and Japan) for strategic and economic rights in Manchuria. Concerning eastern Europe, however, Stalin accepted an ambivalent proposal on the Polish issue which represented America's unwillingness to acknowledge his agreement with Churchill as much as it did Russia's security needs. He was no more successful in the Middle East, where American oil companies had moved back into Iran in 1943. Supported by the State Department and special emissaries, the companies were well along in their efforts to obtain extensive concessions. Roosevelt was "thrilled" by the chance to work along with the oil companies and make Iran an example of what America could do for undeveloped areas of the world, an attitude which helps explain why the United States was not willing to allow the Russians to obtain oil rights in northern Iran. Stalin gave way on the issue at Yalta and also refrained from pushing his desire to gain more security for Russia in the Black Sea area.

Despite his failure to get any positive response from the United States on the question of a postwar loan, or a clear understanding on other vital issues, Stalin still hoped to effect a conservative resolution of his dilemma. Throughout the first half of 1945, for example, *Izvestia* stressed the vitality of the American economy (in striking contrast to the fears being expressed in Congressional hearings), emphasized the importance of resolving outstanding issues by negotiation, and reiterated the fruitfulness of economic co-operation. The British press attaché in Russia reported that Soviet comment remained restrained and hopeful until America initiated a campaign of vigorous criticism and protest aimed at Soviet predominance in eastern Europe.

But the most significant indicators of the predisposition to work out some modus vivendi with the United States, and then to concentrate on internal recovery and development, came in the debates within the Soviet hierarchy, and in the relatively restrained policies followed in eastern Europe after the Nazis were defeated. One of the earliest indications of Russian emphasis on domestic affairs appeared in 1943 in the form of a discussion (in the journal *Under the Banner of Marxism*) over the proper way to teach economics. This took special note, among other things, of Stalin's praise of the United States. The crucial feature was the heavy stress laid upon the extent of the recovery crisis, and upon the need to concentrate on domestic affairs. Many American observers immediately understood and pointed out the nonrevolutionary implications of the argument, but official policy-makers in the United States took little if any cognizance of the matter.

An even more revealing debate occurred after the publication in 1946 of a major study of capitalism by the Soviet economist Eugene Varga. The date of 1946 is significant in two respects. It means, in the first place, that the discussion had been going on at least since 1944, a consideration which underscores the ambivalent, undecided, and cautious nature of Soviet thinking at the end of the war. It also indicates that the Russians had not made a firm decision on their basic approach as late as 1946; even though, as will be seen, the United States had been exerting strong pressure on the Soviet Union ever since the London Foreign Ministers' Conference in September 1945.

Varga's central point was that capitalism in general, and in the United States in particular, was capable of stabilizing itself in the postwar era. He went on to argue that the role of the government could be positive and creative under capitalism, and in that fashion suggested that the classic Marxian prophecy about the inevitable collapse of capitalism might need to be revised and modified. Varga's argument pointed very directly toward the need to stabilize relations with the United States, and to concentrate on domestic Soviet development.

These examples point up a very important kind of continuity in Soviet affairs that is often missed or forgotten. The revisionist debate that erupted within and between communist countries in the mid-1950s was actually no more than a continuation of the discussion that began in 1943–44 within the Soviet Union, and which was pursued very vigorously as late as 1947 and 1948. The two illustrations mentioned here should not be taken as isolated, atypical events. Early in 1945, for example, a very long and strongly argued revisionist article appeared in the magazine *Foundations of Marxism*. Similar debates took place around short stories and novels. And the philosopher Aleksandrov, who had good things to say about Western capitalist thinkers, was in high favor as late as the first months of 1947. The popular idea that Soviet leaders emerged from the war ready to do aggressive battle against the United States is simply not borne out by the evidence. Varga himself was not attacked in public in any serious way, for example, until after Winston Churchill's militant Iron Curtain speech in 1946, and the enunciation of the Truman Doctrine in March 1947.

Soviet officials who later chose to live in the West often offered the same kind of evidence bearing on Russian policy at the end of the war. One of the American experts who interviewed many such men offered this general judgment about Soviet policy in Germany. "The paramount consideration was not the extension of the revolution to Germany and the establishment of a Soviet Government there, but the rehabilitation of the Soviet Union's war-ravaged industry and transportation...regardless of the effect this policy might have on...establishing a Soviet Germany." For that matter, the Red Army's railroad lines across Poland into Germany were ripped up in 1945. And in eastern Europe, the Soviet approach was modeled on the popular front governments of the 1930s rather than upon the existing Soviet system.

The point of these examples (and there are many more) is not to suggest, let alone try to prove, that Stalin and other Soviet leaders behaved either as Western democrats or as men uninterested in exercising influence in eastern Europe. The point is to indicate and to stress the importance of three quite different things: first, the very significant extent to which Soviet decisions from 1944 through 1947 were based on domestic Russian conditions; second, the degree to which the Soviets were assuming that capitalism would stabilize itself around the great and undamaged power of the United States; and third, the way in which those two factors pointed in the mind of many Russians—including Stalin—to the need to reach some kind of agreement with America. They never defined such an understanding on the basis of abandoning Russian influence in eastern Europe or acquiescing in each and every American proposal just as it first emanated from Washington. But neither did they emerge from World War II with a determination to take over eastern Europe and then embark upon a cold war with the United States.

Beginning in 1946, Stalin grew ever more skeptical about the possibility of negotiating any basic understanding with American leaders. But he never became a fatalist about war with the United States. And the so-called softies in the party were not finally downgraded, and then subjected to vigorous and extensive attacks (including imprisonment) until the late summer and early fall of 1947. It was not until even later that the Soviet Union moved ruthlessly to extend and consolidate its control over eastern Europe.

THE WISDOM OF
AN OPEN DOOR
FOR REVOLUTIONS

[from *The Tragedy of American Diplomacy*, 1972]

In the final chapters of *The Tragedy of American Diplomacy* Williams emphasized how the Open Door Policy evolved into an increasingly aggressive display of global power as a means of preserving the American empire. He contended, however, that the policy had not produced just or equitable results for the peoples of the areas into which the United States had extended its economic system and ideological precepts. Moreover, the effort violated traditionally proclaimed American ideas and ideals of freedom and self-determination. This, he argued, was the tragedy of American diplomacy. The Vietnam War exemplified and deepened it. United States resistance to revolutions and revolutionary movements perceived as threats to an American version of world order, he observed, meant endless interventions and wars with increasingly harmful consequences to the welfare and freedoms of Americans at home. He concluded that "American foreign policy must be changed fundamentally" and American society radically altered.

The tradition of all past generations weighs like an Alp upon the brain of the living.   *Karl Marx*

It is not my duty as a historian to predict the future, only to observe and interpret the past. But its lesson is clear enough; we have lived too long out of contact with reality, and now the time has come to rebuild our lives.

Callitrax, Historian of Lys,
In the City and the Stars, *by Arthur C. Clarke*

156

Yes, strictly speaking, the question is not how to get cured, but how to live.
Marlow to Stein, in Lord Jim, *by Joseph Conrad*

THE students, teachers, and other dissenters who initiated and led
the movement to end the war in Vietnam understood that the
pattern of intervention was ineradicably entwined with other inequitable and destructive aspects of American society. Many had been
early foot soldiers in the long-going battle to end racism and
discrimination against Black Americans. Others had concentrated on
the problem of poverty, or on the stultification of high school and
college education. A few were dedicated pacifists, and some had
given much effort to help workers improve their lives. Most of them
had become aware, whatever their age, of three other deeply disturbing developments in America: the steady loss by the individual of his
ability to self-determine himself in postwar society; the loss of almost
all sense—as well as the reality—of a community in an increasingly
managed and manipulated system; and the decline of a commitment
to being moral (or, conversely, the increasing hypocrisy).

The recognition of those failures gradually created, during the
long and difficult struggle to end the war, a conviction that existing
American society had to be changed. Otherwise there would be more
interventions and more deterioration at home. Not all of the millions
who came to oppose the war in Vietnam developed that kind of
understanding or commitment. But many did come to sense the
necessity of going beyond the question of ending the war. As a result,
the beginnings of a true social movement appeared for the first time
since the turn of the twentieth century.

Much of that process was reinforced by the continuing success of
revolutionary movements throughout the world. The dedication and
determination of the Vietnamese to truly self-determine their own
lives forced many Americans to confront the implications of trying to
sustain traditional American foreign policy. They sensed, even if they
did not fully understand, that such a course would involve its own
kind of drastic changes in the United States. It would mean ever less
freedom and ever more enforced work and privation. It would mean
living with the death of friends and loved ones as a routine
experience. And it might well mean the death of all.

Even in its existing unfocused and unorganized state, that awareness among the citizens first forced the elite to manifest a new degree of caution and circumspection. During that phase of its response, the elite clothed its maneuvers and manipulations in the traditional rhetoric of victory for a free and peaceful world. Then the reality of massive death-counts in Vietnam and the increasing strength of the opposition in the United States forced President Johnson to withdraw from the election of 1968. Finally, the growing recognition of the true nature of the terror began to affect the thinking of some erstwhile imperial-minded leaders (like Robert F. Kennedy) and led others (like President Richard M. Nixon) to attempt to stabilize the existing empire by cutting losses in Vietnam and by negotiating an interim *modus vivendi* with Russia, the Peoples Republic of China, and various other revolutionary governments.

Hence the meaning of the title of this chapter has changed since I wrote it in December 1961. Then I was primarily concerned, having tried to show how History offers a way of learning, to do what I could to break the terrifying momentum toward disaster that ultimately carried us into Vietnam. Thus I emphasized the methods by which we could change our traditional ways of dealing with other peoples. I see no reason to alter anything in the list of suggestions I offered at that time, except to drop the device of the rhetorical question.*

It is time to stop defining trade as the control of markets for our surplus products and control of raw materials for our factories. It is time to stop depending so narrowly—in our thinking as well as in our practice—upon an informal empire for our well-being and welfare.

It is time to ask ourselves if we are really so unimaginative that we have to have a frontier in the form of an informal empire in order to have democracy and prosperity at home. It is time to say that we can make American society function even better on the basis of equitable relationships with other people.

It is time to stop defining trade as a weapon against other people with whom we have disagreements. It is time to start thinking of trade as a means to moderate and alleviate those tensions—and to improve the life of the other people.

It is time to stop trying to expand our exports on the grounds that such a campaign will make foreigners foot the bill for our military

*Which I used, despite my strong dislike of the form, in the hope of giving the general reader a sense of the relevance of History, and of engaging him in a serious reevaluation of his existing outlook.

security. It is time instead to concern ourselves with a concerted effort to halt and then cancel the armaments race.

It is time to stop saying that all the evil in the world resides in the Soviet Union and other communist countries. It is time to admit that there is good as well as evil in those societies, and set about to help increase the amount of good.

It is time to admit that our own intelligence reports mean that the Russians have been following a defensive policy in nuclear weapons. It is time to take advantage of that attitude on their part, break out of our neurosis about a Pearl Harbor attack, and go on to negotiate an arms control measure.

It is time to admit, in short, that we can avoid living with communist countries only by embarking upon a program that will kill millions of human beings. It is time, therefore, to evolve and adopt a program that will encourage and enable the communist countries to move in the direction of their own utopian vision of the good society as we endeavor to move in accordance with our own ideals.

Nor do I see any reason to modify the following passages:

Once freed from its myopic concentration on the cold war, the United States could come to grips with the central problem of reordering its own society so that it functions through such a balanced relationship with the rest of the world, and so that the labor and leisure of its own citizens are invested with creative meaning and purpose. A new debate over the first principles and practices of government and economics is long overdue, and a statement of a twentieth-century political economy comparable to *The Federalist* papers would do more to enhance America's role in the world than any number of rockets and satellites. The configuration of the world of outer space will be decided on the cool green hills of earth long before the first colonizing spaceships blast free of the atmosphere.

Having structured a creative response to the issue of democracy and prosperity at home, the United States could again devote a greater share of its attention and energy to the world scene. Its revamped foreign policy would be geared to helping other peoples achieve their own aspirations in their own way. The essence of such a foreign policy would be an open door for revolutions. Having come to terms with themselves—having achieved maturity—Americans could exhibit the self-discipline necessary to let other peoples come to

terms with themselves. Having realized that "self-righteousness is
the hallmark of inner guilt," Americans would no longer find it
necessary to embark upon crusades to save others.

In this fashion, and through a policy of an open door for
revolutions, Americans would be able to cope with the many as yet
unknown revolutions that are dependent upon peace for their
conception and maturation. Only in this way can either the general
or the specific tragedy of American diplomacy be transcended in a
creative, peaceful manner.

To transcend tragedy requires the nerve to fail. But a positive
effort to transcend the cold war would very probably carry the
United States and the world on into an era of peace and creative
human endeavor. For the nerve to fail has nothing at all to do with
blustering and self-righteous crusades up to or past the edge of
violence. It is instead the kind of quiet confidence that comes with
and from accepting limits, and a concurrent understanding that
accepting limits does not mean the end of existence itself or of the
possibility of a creative life. For Americans, the nerve to fail is in a
real sense the nerve to say—and mean—that we no longer need what
Turner called "the gate of escape" provided by the frontier. It is only
in adolescence or senility that human beings manifest a compulsive
drive to play to win. The one does not yet know, and the other has
forgotten, that what counts is how the game is played. It would
actually be pathetic rather than tragic if the United States jumped
from childhood to old age without ever having matured. Yet that is
precisely what it will do unless it sloughs off the ideology of the
Open Door Policy and steps forth to open the door to the revolutions
that can transform the material world and the quality of human
relationships.

Perhaps it is by now apparent to the reader that there is a basic
irony involved in this conception and interpretation of American
foreign policy as tragedy. This irony arises from, and is in that sense
caused by, the truth that this essay is in two respects written from a
radical point of view.

First, it is radical in that it seeks to uncover, describe, and analyze
the character and logic of American foreign policy since the 1890s. It
is therefore critical in the intellectual sense of not being content with
rhetoric and other appearances, and of seeking instead to establish by
research and analysis a fuller, more accurate picture of reality.

Second, it is radical in that it concludes from the research and
reflection, that American foreign policy must be changed fundamen-

tally in order to sustain the wealth and welfare of the United States on into the future. This essay recommends that the frontier-expansionist explanation of American democracy and prosperity, and the strategy of the Open Door Policy, be abandoned on the grounds that neither any longer bears any significant relation to reality.

This essay also points toward a radical but noncommunist reconstruction of American society in domestic affairs. And it is at this point that the irony appears: there is at the present time no radicalism in the United States strong enough to win power, or even a very significant influence, through the processes of representative government—and this essay resets on the axiom of representative government. Hence, ironically, the radical analysis leads finally to a conservative conclusion. The well-being of the United States depends—*in the short-run but only in the short-run*—upon the extent to which calm and confident and enlightened conservatives can see and bring themselves to act upon the validity of a radical analysis. In a very real sense, therefore, democracy and prosperity depend upon whether the New Frontier is defined in practice to mean merely a vigorous reassertion of the ideology and the policies of the past or to mean an acceptance of limits upon America's freedom of action.

The issue can be stated as a very direct proposition. If the United States cannot accept the existence of such limits without giving up democracy and cannot proceed to enhance and extend democracy within such limits, then the traditional effort to sustain democracy by expansion will lead to the destruction of democracy.

We now know that the conservatives did not act upon a radical analysis. Yet the proposition remains true: that was the only way the disaster in Vietnam could have been avoided. And it remains true in the deeper sense that short-term palliatives devised from selected portions of the radical critique will serve at most to postpone—not avoid—further such terrors.

And so now we confront another irony. There is today the beginning of a social movement that could change America in a radical way, and thereby realize our most cherished ideals and aspirations. Hence we must recognize the wisdom of including in our outlook the idea of an open door for such a revolution in America.

Chile has demonstrated the possibility of choosing that course in a democratic election. Perhaps we Americans, whose votes have mattered increasingly less in recent decades, can restore the integrity of our own franchise through a similar display of self-determination.

THE AGE OF
MERCANTILISM,
1740–1828

[from *The Contours of American History*, 1961]

The Contours of American History, from which the next three excerpts are taken, was an ambitious effort to reinterpret the whole of American history in terms of capitalist development. Williams examined ideas and programs developed by individual members of elite groups during various stages of the process in each of the three major periods he identified. Integrating domestic events and foreign affairs, he employed the concept of *weltanschauung*, a basic view of the world, to show how the maturing ideas of the prevailing order in each era were confronted, shaped, and finally transformed by changes and conflicts and from the inception and challenge of new beliefs.

Williams located the roots of the first period, "The Age of Mercantilism," in the evolving British political economy and imperial system that preceded America's declaration and war of independence. American Revolutionary leaders, he argued, recast mercantilist principles as they first debated and then chose independence and the creation of an American empire. The ideals of mercantilism were, however, severely tested and undermined by expansionist drives and by failures to control excesses of private property against the public welfare. "Unwilling...to make a fuller commitment to social property in the name of a corporate commonwealth," Williams wrote, the mercantilist leaders yielded to those "who demanded that private property and interest be given full scope and unrestrained liberty in the name of individualism."

Private Vices, by the dextrous Management of a skillful Politician, may be turned into Public Benefits.   *Bernard Mandeville, 1714*

Mercantilism thus meant primarily that, under the pressure of new intellectual enlightenment in various spheres, people were, for the first time, directing their deliberate attention to aims which they had long cherished unreflectingly. *August Heckscher, 1935*

The Triumph of the Rising Order

Shall we whine and cry for relief, when we have already tried it in vain?
George Washington, 1773

We do not want to be independent, we want no revolution.
Joseph Hewes, 1775

We have it in our power to begin the world over again.
Thomas Paine, 1776

We must rebel some time or other, and we had better rebel now than at any time to come; if we put off for ten or twenty years, and let them go on as they have begun, they will get a strong party among us, and plague us a great deal more than they can now.
Joseph Hawley to Samuel Adams, 1776

THOUGH it might have seemed far-fetched in the 1670s, Shaftesbury's[1] strategy to subvert Spain's American empire by capturing its trade (and bullion) had proved its validity within two generations. His similar expectation that the commercial colonies would develop closer economic and social ties to England was also being verified. South Carolina and its southern neighbors were redirecting the Indian and Spanish trade down the Ashley and Cooper rivers towards the wharves of Charleston; Pennsylvanians and New Englanders were carrying Spanish pieces of eight to London in payment for manufactures; and British ships of the home marine were making regular trading voyages along the coast of South America.

Working within the frameworks of attitudes and policies established during the Restoration, the American colonies and England had constructed a complementary empire. Far more relaxed in tone

1. Shaftesbury was Anthony Ashley Cooper, First Earl of Shaftesbury (1621–1683), English statesman and a central figure in the history of British mercantilism who also played a major role in the founding of the colony of South Carolina.—ED.

and routine than it appeared to many later observers—and certainly not a tightly ruled imperialism—this mercantilism had produced a surprisingly close approximation to the idea, and even the ideal, of a commonwealth. Though he committed himself to independence sooner than most colonists, Samuel Adams began with nothing more than a determination to reform the affairs of Massachusetts. And even when he broadened his attack to include England's colonial policy, his initial objective was no more than to re-establish the old mercantilist system with the kind of liberal rule that Massachusetts had enjoyed under governor Thomas Pownall.

Pownall's outlook, like that of Benjamin Franklin, his friend and fellow speculator in Ohio lands, was that of the nabob. Such rising upper-class colonials assumed they would ultimately inherit the empire; in the meantime they sought to further their economic and social welfare by making alliances with various groups in English society and in the British government. Though they did not verbalize it as explicitly or as formally, and lacked the power to act on it overtly, the great majority of colonists shared the basic assumptions of the nabob and aspired to emulate him. Like their leaders, most of them were hesitant or indifferent toward independence until the morning of the break with England. And many of them never bothered to fight after the war began. As for Franklin and his fellow nabobs, it was only with great reluctance that they joined Adams and his revolutionary allies in Virginia in making a bid for an independent empire.

THE SOUTH AND THE RISE OF AN AMERICAN GENTRY

Further developed than any of its neighbors, Virginia was the symbol and the leader of the colonies south of Pennsylvania. Negro slavery was the mainspring of that society. Slaves handled the great crops of tobacco, rice, and indigo that provided the security for the wealthy indebtedness of the region, and their masters contributed leadership in social, political, and economic affairs. As a practice and as an institution, Negro slavery in the American colonies developed within the logic and politics of English mercantilism. Slavery was the gravest weakness of that system: the frayed and raveled end of the strand of mercantile economic theory which stressed the importance of a large, cheap, and controlled labor force that could produce a staple surplus for export. And in this instance, theory was eminently practical as well as persuasive. African chiefs proved only too ready to supply such human exports. They had been doing it for centuries. Scrambling for empire along every great circle route on the globe, English traders entered the dirty business in an organized fashion when Charles II chartered the Royal African Company in 1672. After that monopoly was broken in 1697 (as laissez faire put its foot in the English door), the industry became even more extensive and degraded as other Englishmen joined colonists from Salem and Rhode Island to parlay the normally narrow margin of profit into a lucrative and lamentable commerce.

Most 17th-century Englishmen were harsh and offhand about slavery. The vigorous nationalism and anti-foreignism of mercantilism reinforced the existing discrimination against the Negro because of his different color, religion, and culture. Yet at no time did the planters of Virginia or other southern colonies manage to convince themselves that slavery was beyond morality. For that matter, southerners were periodically assailed by questions about its economic advantages. Many thought that the cost of slaves (the "Profits arising thereon [are] so very great") explained the persistently unfavorable balance of trade, and hence indebtedness, of the region. Others questioned whether slavery was efficient, adding that the southern economy needed more men with diversified skills, industry, and initiative.

Such economic doubts were reinforced by the sense of social and corporate responsibility which was strong in the secular philosophy consciously modeled on that of the English gentry, and in the religious doctrines of the established Anglican church. George Washington and other planters of the late colonial era anticipated the demise of slavery long before the inspiring rhetoric of the Declaration of Independence reminded the colonists of their responsibilities as free Englishmen. As a leader who saw the need to diversify the economy of his region, Washington combined both an economic and a moral argument in his candid critique of slavery.

Yet many influences converged to sustain the dreadful institution. Though not as straightforward as Patrick Henry, many planters shared his preference for having someone else do the hard work; he spoke bluntly about "the general inconvenience of living without them." Others had frenzied imaginations which transformed legitimate (and intelligent) concern about the difficulties incident to emancipation into scenes of orgiastic violence, biological decay, and wholesale poverty. Yet—during the colonial era, at any rate—it was the economic arguments that seem to have been the most powerful.

Washington's program for developing a diversified agriculture and local industry made a great deal of sense, but the majority of the planters could not translate it into reality. Their debts to London middle-men, which Thomas Jefferson later spoke of as being inherited for generations, increased as the value of their tobacco declined. These economic scissors snipped away their freedom of maneuver. As even Washington admitted (and he was an exceptionally efficient and wealthy planter), "goods [were] for the most exceedingly dear bought." Probably most planters tried to raise more of their own food, and some experimented with a few acres planted for the West Indies market, but the majority continued to abuse their land with the same old commodity crops.

As tobacco declined in value on the European market, the planters sought a solution within the traditional framework of mercantilism. They proposed to limit production and improve quality. With virgin land lying open to the west, however, not many of them could command the discipline to restrict their output. But they did combine their efforts to raise more of the staple with the idea of quality controls and inspections, and with the traditional mercantilist system of centralized depots. Together with the steady exhaustion of the soil, this campaign to expand production reinforced the existing drive to the west for more land. When they did not simply elbow them out and onward, the planters and speculators leapfrogged over the yeomen and frontiersmen, and thus southerners of different classes came into common conflict with British regulations limiting expansion beyond the mountains.

Such an emphasis on expanding production steadily strengthened the conclusion drawn from earlier experience that gang labor provided the only way to make a profit on staple crops. Though it was possible to raise tobacco, and later cotton, on smaller units of cultivation, this profitableness of gang labor became one of the chief arguments—or excuses—for maintaining the slave system. It should not be imagined, however, that the planters were unique in defending slavery. Southern yeomen aspired to own their own slaves (many realized the ambition), and white workers in such cities as Charleston organized against free Negro labor (as in the shipbuilding yards) at an early date.

In later years, after coming under militant attack from the critics of slavery, southerners often replied by emphasizing the achievements of their culture. Though not justifying Negro slavery in America and often exaggerated, the argument had a certain validity. For the best of the south was exceptionally good; it was mature, responsible, respectful of learning, civilized, and urbane. Moral without being priggish, the planter aristocracy probably comprehended the verity of original sin at least as well as most of the New England theocracy. And though their reforms may have been weakened by an overly developed propensity to compromise, such men did avoid the arrogance of self-righteous crusading. Long before the tradition of the Cavalier was somewhat belatedly imported after 1660, southerners had begun to advance their own version of the life of the English gentry, and it evolved rapidly through the 18th century.

Like many other southern mansions, that of William Byrd at Westover, Virginia, was less elegant but nevertheless comparable to those of many English estates. Commanding a fine vista of the James River, its bold and imposing structure featured a mahogany stairway and housed a magnificent library of 4,000 volumes. And in the ports, such as Annapolis to the north, great homes like the Hammon-Harwood house designed by William Buckland typified a similar pattern of living. Though this southern architecture might be described rather as a solidly appropriate style rendered in good taste than as great art, it was justly admired.

St. Michael's church in Charleston was likewise an impressive symbol of the gentry's culture. Presumably because as a group they were far less prone than some other colonials to discuss every issue in a theological vocabulary, because they separated church and state by law, and because Thomas Jefferson came to be considered the symbol of the entire society, it has often been assumed that the southern aristocrats were Deists in all but name or men for whom sitting in church was one of the chores of their class. But James Madison and many others among the southern gentry were deeply, although not ostentatiously, religious in the Anglican tradition of the corporate church. While vigorously opposed to bishops running the state, and increasingly tolerant of dissent, they retained a strong sense of inclusive Christian social morality. Washington's Farewell Address, for example, emphasized that such an ethic was essential to sustaining the ideal and the practice of the general welfare.

Samuel Matthews of Virginia was typical of the many planters whose names do not get into every history book, but who nevertheless exhibited a strong sense of social responsibility. He managed his own affairs with care and success, took an active part in local government, and tried to anticipate and prepare for the development of the region. Although they may have sent their sons to England for

an education, men such as Byrd and William Fitzhugh also worked
to establish colonial colleges and lower schools. In all these respects,
they labored to improve life in the present as well as to develop
a tradition and found a family dynasty with its own coat-of-arms.
And as for the tradition, they proved so successful that some
back-country southerners ultimately rebelled against those who ignored or abused it.

This southern aristocracy developed several contrasting though
complementary styles of life. At one extreme, some of its merchants
and professional men represented an almost exclusively urban and
commercial influence. Joseph Hewes and James Iredel of North
Carolina typified that pattern. Further south, the Charleston merchants and factors like Henry Laurens revealed an even greater
similarity to their British counterparts. Indeed, many of them came
to feel that they had so much in common with their trans-Atlantic
prototypes that they were extremely disinclined to break the connection. Christopher Gadsden in Charleston was a notable exception,
becoming a vigorous advocate of independence.

On the other hand, many planters were practically pure agrarians.
Similar in their outlook to some of the patroons along the Hudson in
upper New York, these men stayed close to the land in thought as
well as in routine. This mode of life and its associated view of the
world ultimately prompted them to take up and adapt the basically
feudal philosophy of the French physiocrats. Though placing great
emphasis on individual freedom and local self-government, they
dominated the economic, political, and social life of their countries
and regions in an aristocratic style that was often benevolent and
almost always effective. In later years, the leaders of this group in the
south were Virginians like John Taylor of Caroline and John
Randolph of Roanoke; in the north, New York's George Clinton was
the outstanding figure.

Despite the difficulties in doing so, a significant number of
planters were by 1740 developing still another pattern of life which
resembled that of the English gentry. Whether in Maryland, Virginia, or other southern colonies, this group maintained city houses,
were governed as to their clothes and coaches, silver and lace,
manners and anecdotes by the latest London fashions, and similarly
extended their other interests and tastes. Charleston was perhaps the
exemplar of this more cosmopolitan existence; yet as the center of
government and society as well as of trade fairs, and boasting the
College of William and Mary founded in 1693, Williamsburg was

also a focus of the urban-commercial-agrarian life; and Annapolis, in those days a far more important port than Baltimore or Norfolk, developed along similar lines.

Like its English predecessor, this colonial gentry also diversified its economic activities. Virginia began offering bounties on cotton (and on linen cloth) in 1730, and within a few years some entrepreneurs were beginning to experiment with wheat and other crops as a supplement to their staples of tobacco, rice, and indigo. Local manufacturing emerged alongside this extended agriculture. Robert Carter invested in a Baltimore ironworks, Colonel Scarburgh produced shoes and malt, and George Washington loomed woolens as an integral part of his plantation enterprises as well as drawing up plans for the future of Virginia's iron industry. Such men as Thomas Johnson of Maryland and Robert Beverley of Virginia thought along the same lines and brought forward specific ideas, as with Johnson a plan for a Potomac Canal and Beverley a program for a Virginia mercantilism. Washington rapidly assumed the leadership of this group. It was by no means all talk; by 1775 Maryland and Virginia had 82 blast furnaces producing iron.

Men such as Washington made it evident that the image of the gentry and the ideal of a diversified and balanced society that was associated with it was steadily gaining strength and being translated into reality during the 18th century. In another way, the founding of Georgia in 1732 revealed the persistence of the mercantilism that Shaftesbury had done so much to consolidate almost three generations earlier. Beginning with the idea of a planned economy, Georgia's leaders emphasized the importance of corporate development. Undertaken for "the more direct and better convenience of the inhabitants," the colony's road-and-ferry legislation specified that the citizens recognize their responsibility to work on such projects. And commodity-inspection laws were instituted on the ground that it was "in the interest of the colony that all lumber exported be honestly and faithfully made." After slavery was legalized in 1750, the Georgia aristocracy moved even more rapidly toward their own version of the attitudes and policies which had been maturing in the older colonies.

Virginia and South Carolina had similar work laws underwriting labor on roads, canals, and public buildings. South Carolina's legislation of 1749 for "regulating the price and assize of bread" was an avowed manifestation of the corporate responsibility to control "covetous and evil-disposed persons" who acted only "for their own gain and lucre" and thus "deceived and depressed...especially the poorer sort of people." Virginia's law "to prevent the exportation of bad and trash tobacco" emerged from the mercantilist's basic conception of political economy; such conduct contributed directly "to the great decay of trade" and thereby weakened the entire colony. And Georgia's laws on price-fixing and its limitation on the rate of interest were likewise designed "to encourage trade."

Intellectual and policy responses to this increasing colonial maturity took two principal forms. Those who wholeheartedly accepted the framework of the British Empire maintained the outlook of the nabob who ruled at home through a combination of his local wealth and his connections in the Metropolis. Men of that view exhibited no particular impatience for the independence that they assumed would come in the future. Largely because of opponents in the colonies who stood ready to challenge his supremacy once independence arrived, the nabob was against a break with the mother country under all but the most extreme circumstances. As a classic figure of this group, Laurens of South Carolina once asserted that he "felt much more pain" over independence when it finally arrived than over the death of a son. This attitude reflected the normal political evolution of the upper class in a colonial system and occurred in India and other British possessions as well as in America. Most southern planters, as well as the majority of colonial leaders in Pennsylvania and New York, held and acted upon this conception of the world.

On the other hand, some southern mercantilists like Gadsden and Washington infused the attitude and role of the nabob with a vigorous self-consciousness that moved rapidly toward independence. Ultimately they were joined by planters like George Mason of Virginia and Willie Jones of North Carolina who entertained a more narrowly agrarian view of the world. The age, intelligence, and expanded interests of these native mercantilists all help to explain the difference in their outlook. It was not only that many of them were young, but also that they came to maturity when their society and their class had established a tradition and a style of their own. Richard Henry Lee, for example, was typical of a younger generation impatient for leadership in a vigorous society.

With the decline of the tobacco market, such men intensified and extended their interest in western lands and invested in nonagricultural enterprises. And for similar reasons, they also manifested an increasing desire to enter the general world market with their surpluses. Acutely aware of the possibilities of an undeveloped continent, they recognized the problems to be surmounted and faced up to them persistently and astutely. Both Johnson and Washington concluded that the diversified economic development of the Potomac waterway to the west would help to weaken the institution of slavery as well as to sustain the position and the power of the coastal gentry as the colonies expanded inland. As that argument implies, they had a vision of an American empire from an early date.

NEW YORK AND PENNSYLVANIA: FINISHING SCHOOLS
FOR THE AMERICAN NABOB

In contrast, no similar group of leaders in the middle colonies developed and committed itself to this emerging American mercantilism until just before the Declaration of Independence in 1776. Even then they were exceedingly reluctant revolutionaries. Many key figures in Pennsylvania and New York fought hard for a compromise with England. To many of them, reconciliation must have seemed a Jacob's ladder to safety from a rising sea of relentless competitors and lashing critics. Thus it is not surprising that the expansionists among them thought primarily in terms of mixed English and colonial companies, nor that a significant number of these nabobs ultimately left America to become important leaders in England and other parts of the empire. From their inception, these middle colonies were the home and hearth of the loyal nabob.

Established by the Dutch as a fur-trading depot in the 1620s, New York remained a comparatively small colony for many years. Extensive commitments in men, money, and interest were not forthcoming; both the government and the Dutch West India Company were initially more interested in an empire in Asia, Africa, and Brazil. Moving belatedly to salvage some of its investment by capturing more English and French trade in America, the Dutch government in 1638 made New York a free port in all but name. The strategy worked brilliantly but not immediately and not for the Dutch. Always a center of the fur trade, New York began to expand and diversify its commerce. Tenant farmers could accurately complain that many fields "lie fallow and waste," but agricultural surpluses and shipping services provided enough capital to launch the city's booming economic growth. In a short time the port attracted, and produced, an increasing population of sailors, merchants, and laborers. They were a wild ethnic mixture with a speculative outlook on life and a sometimes vulgar and unfocused cosmopolitanism that further weakened the colony's loyalty to the Dutch.

Had the French acted vigorously, pushing down the river valleys from Canada, the history of the world might have become a different story. But however poor an English king he became as James II, the Duke of York performed magnificently in seizing New York in 1664. Providing a sorry preview of what was in store for his subjects at home, the Duke then mismanaged the job of ruling his conquest. He was no match either for the entrenched landed aristocracy, the rising merchant interest, or the restive and aggressive lower class. Giving up in frustration and failure, he sold off great chunks of the original grant and went home to fail again.

Having defeated their second "mother country," the New York patroons proceeded to consolidate their local control. As they did so, they created an integrated gentry typical of the age of mercantilism. Thus, as they made economic investments in commerce and shipping, they married into the rising elite of merchants and lawyers in New York. Sitting astride one of the most extensive and rapidly expanding trade centers in the colonies, this New York gentry became highly prone to take its well-being for granted. It was not that they were lazy or lacked initiative; it was simply that their fortunes seemed to billow as naturally as the sails of their ships in a fresh trade wind. Handling everything from luxury furs to beeswax, dried venison, and porkers on the run, their exports of agricultural commodities and semi-finished raw materials provided the basis of a commerce with Europe and the West Indies that dramatized the general development of the colonies. And by the 1740s some of them had begun to invest in banking and manufacturing while others turned their attention to speculative opportunities in the west.

Since they at least acknowledged the same tradition of the corporate Anglican religion that guided many southerners, it might be assumed that the New York gentry evolved a similar conception of social responsibility. This was not the case. Under the impact of disorganized and shifting outside authority, extensive and mixed immigration, and almost unchallenged local power, the New Yorkers created a caricature of the gentry. Politics became a treacherous and generally pointless scramble within the aristocracy. James De Lancey commanded one faction dedicated to keeping the upstart lawyers and merchants in their place. He was opposed by William Livingston who attempted to rally support among the smaller merchants and even the laboring class. The primary result of his strategy was to create a growing sense of solidarity and organization among his ultimate opponents, led by such popular figures as Isaac Sears and Alexander McDougall. As for the upstate yeomen and tenant farmers, they were generally ignored by both factions and only slowly began to organize their own philosophical and practical opposition.

Though De Lancey played an important part in founding King's College, and a few others indicated some awareness of the responsibilities of the gentry, most New York aristocrats continued to devote most of their energies to trade and the gay life. De Lancey's son was something of an extreme, but nevertheless typical, example. Principally concerned with "cock-fighting, horseracing, and women," he once led such a carousing invasion of Philadelphia as to frighten the fathers of that city—as well as its mothers (and no doubt even some of its daughters). There was a more favorable side to such revelry, however, because, in conjunction with the great (albeit unnerving) tradition of the sailor on shore leave, it helped New York to establish a pattern of entertainment that was broader in every sense of the word than any to be found in the other colonial cities.

As might be expected in such a commercial center, New York also supported the evolution of the daily newspaper and the tradition of a free (if slandering and scandalous) press. Beyond that, the city was culturally backward. Cadwallader Coldens' *History of the Five Nations*, a review of the Indians and the wars incident to taking their land, was the only book produced in the colony that was worthy of serious attention. And while such painters as Lawrence Kilburn and John Wollaston provided many portraits for the elite, their subjects were seemingly averse even to the kind of tension that helps create a great graphic image. Yet, in a way that was revealing, the focus in most of their likenesses was the wide expanse of shimmering light ricocheting off the satin waistcoats that covered the full bellies; in this sense, at any rate, the artist did transmit a hint of the deeper reality, for many members of the New York gentry opposed independence even after the fighting began.

Though many of them reacted similarly, the Pennsylvania leaders included men of a vastly different style with a far broader image of the good life. For despite the fact that Benjamin Frankin's amatory abilities and adventures might indicate the opposite, William Penn founded Pennsylvania as what he always referred to as "The Holy Experiment." Under more appropriate circumstances, Penn might have been one of the great benevolent despots. Governing in that style, and guided by his Quaker faith in the goodness of men and his sophisticated mercantilism, he made the very best of the geographical and human resources at his disposal.

Established between 1680 and 1682, Pennsylvania rapidly overtook older colonies and by 1740 was challenging them for political and economic leadership. England's post-Restoration economic boom helped the colony get off to a quick start, and within two years Philadelphia boasted more than 350 dwellings. Political and religious controversies in England and on the Continent helped to maintain a steady flow of immigrants, and the early settlers encouraged others to share the bonanza. Penn exploited these favorable circumstances through judicious mercantile policies and astute propaganda. As a pioneering master of what later public-relations experts were to call the "soft sell," his advertising campaigns in Europe combined a promise of wealth and grandeur with a candid and psychologically clever warning that the lazy and untalented might better stay where they were. Western Europeans responded eagerly. Encouraged by leaders of their own such as Francis Daniel Pastorius, Germans (and some Dutch) arrived with an outlook sympathetic to the established Quaker religion. Unusually content with their own company and capable of building thriving communities by their own skill in carpentry, farming, weaving, wood-working, pottery, and shoemaking, these men and women were willing to accept the political and social leadership of the Quaker aristocracy on the eastern coast. This involved no great sacrifice, for they had their own society and culture, and those who became particularly successful managed to move quietly into the inner councils of government.

These experiences were so generally satisfying, and accounts of them so persuasive, that in Europe some Germans worried lest their sons abandon promising futures at home for the opportunities in America. Perhaps nothing is as revealing of the evolution of life in the colonies as a sharp letter of complaint written by a German family to a son in England. Trying to shame him into abandoning a plan to emigrate to Philadelphia, a brother disparaged the ambition. "From appearances," he wrote snidely, "you wish perhaps to become an English nabob." Apparently attracted by just that prospect, the errant brother sailed for Pennsylvania.

Other immigrants from Scotland and Ireland were less adaptable; they were more driven by religion, more harried by memories of earlier troubles, and less sophisticated in their image of success in America. Finding the seacoast and its immediate hinterland settled, they tramped on through to the frontier, some of them spilling down across the Appalachians into the southern uplands on the way. Hard-working as they were, many had reserves of energy which they turned toward politics and expansion. Far more aggressive than the Germans (from whom, ironically, they got their deadly long rifles), these predominantly Presbyterian settlers mixed religion and economic grievances into a back-country brew that finally fermented into overt opposition to Quaker rule.

Anything but radicals, they wanted little more than a greater share in the existing government. More representation was their general cry, and their specific complaints converged on taxes and Indians. Opposing some excises (such as those on the liquor they made), they concentrated on getting more help against the Indians who checked their freebooting advance into the Ohio valley. And as they began to produce surpluses from the rich land, they added the argument that farm-to-market roads and canals would serve to speed up the war against the red men.

Many of the shopkeepers and workers in Philadelphia, as well as the seaboard gentry, resisted such demands for economic and political reasons. Busily engaged in enjoying and developing existing opportunities, or organizing to win a greater share of them, they had little inclination to weaken their own position. But one group of Quaker leaders opposed aggressive western expansion (and the resulting violence against the Indians) for reasons of religious principle. One can quarrel with their assumptions but not with their logic or motivation. Their hospitals, secondary and higher schools, and philanthropic projects revealed a commitment to the spirit of *noblesse oblige* unsurpassed in America. When finally confronted with the ultimate choice of abandoning their central premise of non-violence or giving up political power, they chose the latter. Easy as it is to call such men impractical, and as conveniently persuasive as the label may be after the Indians are no longer a problem, a little reflection suggests that those Quakers bequeathed America one of its great moments of philosophic insight and moral courage. For the Indians were, after all, human beings, and they did have a society which the colonists and their sons destroyed.

Had the expansionists and such of their leaders as Benjamin Franklin and Robert Morris tried the Quaker program of gradual, equitable, and peaceful dealings with the Indians, they and the latter-day critics of the Quakers would seem more persuasive. A recent assertion that Americans enjoyed free security as well as free land throughout most of their history, and that these factors explain the nation's development is hardly half the story. What is missing is the pattern of total war developed and put into operation against the Indians and then transferred to later opponents. Initiated by the colonists in a mood of self-righteous arrogance out of gluttony for land they often never even cleared, let alone cultivated, such total war extracted a terrible physical and moral price for security. It also planted in the American mind an assumption of omnipotence that was to prove costly. The Quakers stood out against this policy and ethic at a time and in a way that does credit to their intelligence, their values, and their courage.

Poor Richard's aphorisms were faint echoes of that morality. For this very reason, no doubt, they appealed to many men who were rising to the top in Pennsylvania's bubbling pot of opportunity and success. But as in other colonies, the issue in political economy was not should there be any controls, but rather what kind. Pennsylvania regulated various phases of the market system, established government loan offices and land banks, and also encouraged local wage- and price-controls affecting butchers, innkeepers, bakers, and other concentrated or monopoly trades. A law of 1725 revealed the spirit that was so prevalent in the southern colonies; it was passed to prevent the export of inferior flour which would threaten "the credit of our trade and the benefits thence arising."

Combining (and controlling) the colony's natural resources and its ambitious, skilled labor force, Pennsylvania's seaboard gentry developed a highly diversified economy based on surplus food production (including processed flour), livestock breeding, rough manufacturing, and all phases of domestic and international trade. Guided by a generally mercantilist outlook, Philadelphia's leaders gained rapidly on their rivals in Boston and New York. This intracolonial competition played an important role in ultimately determining attitudes toward British policy after 1763. As the old leader falling behind, Boston proved to be the most militant and aggressive opponent of the Crown's decision to tighten up the empire. In the meantime, Pennsylvania's rapid progress provided context and springboard for Benjamin Franklin's fabulous career.

Though in some respects he appeared to be an advocate of laissez faire, Franklin was actually a nabob who wanted free trade in the same sense that the English gentry demanded greater access to the opportunities of the empire. A man who came so close to living by the what-is-is-right credo that on major issues he broke the rule but once, Franklin accepted the empire and set out to sustain, expand, and exploit its opportunities. He succeeded. His twenty-five years as a printer, culminating in his becoming publisher of *The Pennsylvania Gazette* and *Poor Richard's Almanac*, established his fortune. Along the way he had time to learn four languages, found the Philadelphia Library, the American Philosophical Society, and an academy, and organize the Junto, a private intellectual club in which many rising leaders developed their economic and political ideas. He retired from active business at an age when most men were just reaching for the top and turned to sophisticated scientific tinkering, empire politics, and majestic schemes of land speculation.

Franklin's famous experiments with electricity, as well as his more prosaic modifications of existing ideas and gadgets, were a tribute to his learning and to his speculative, almost childlike curiosity. There is nothing inherently wrong with such an attitude, but it should not be confused with that of science. To a scientist the design of the experiment is the essence of the discipline, and by this criterion Franklin was only a lucky, albeit clever, amateur.

This once-in-an-epoch combination of the dedicated amateur's *expertise* with the casual flair and style of the dilettante is what proved so irresistible. The frontiersman needing a better fireplace made Franklin into the same kind of hero as did the member of a European salon who was searching for proof that the scientist was a good fellow like himself. But praiseworthy though it is, an interest in the results of science is vastly different from an understanding of the method and a willingness to accept its discipline. Because of his role in blurring this vital distinction, it may very well be that America's later propensity to think that playing with nature, or technological facility, is the same thing as the scientific spirit goes back to Franklin.

In any event, it is difficult to think of Franklin as a scientist if only because he invested so much time and intelligence in land speculation. Along with his British allies, one of his regular associates in those enterprises was Thomas Wharton, whose name, appropriately enough, now graces a school of business at the University of Pennsylvania which originated as Franklin Academy. As the leader of such ventures, Franklin carried on an intricate and delicate—albeit militant—struggle for control of the Ohio frontier and hence the continent.

The essence of Franklin's outlook was the British mercantilism he borrowed from Sir William Petty. As a man who thought England's radical John Wilkes an "outlaw," and who maintained for many years that George III was "the best king any nation was ever blessed with," Franklin was in no sense a revolutionary. Working within the existing framework and in close association with English leaders, he hoped to outflank domestic rivals like the Virginians led by George Washington and place Pennsylvania in the direct line of succession as the center of a mammoth British Empire. In his view, sustained expansion would keep the people busy farming and in that way turn them from domestic manufacturing while creating a limitless market for British manufactures. It would also "continuously draw off" the unemployed in eastern cities and thus decrease the chance of urban unrest.

Franklin abandoned this truly magnificent strategy very late and with great reluctance. Only his broad mercantilist vision and his opportunism kept him from becoming a Loyalist along with so many other men in Pennsylvania, New York, and New England who had also developed their careers and ideas within the assumptions of the nabob. And as Franklin later admitted, the strength of those precepts made it difficult, even for a man with his perception of the main chance, to adapt his political economy to the circumstances of independence. This insight offers an important clue to the reason why the leaders of the revolution were younger men, or at any rate men with a clearer conception of a self-defined corporate society.

NEW ENGLAND AND THE IDEOLOGY OF CALVIN'S CORPORATE SOCIETY

Though they had insisted on their separateness and self-contained independence from the summer they stepped ashore on the wrong piece of real estate and managed to survive only with the help of the Indians, many New Englanders were just as slow as Franklin to accept the idea of a final break with England. For men who claimed to be the Children of God, most of them were strangely slow afoot when it came to striking out on their own. They seemed to prefer the garden of empire that the British Board of Trade had created and that the Royal Navy walled off from misguided interlopers.

Just such a vision of a City on the Hill had guided the founders of New England during their earlier efforts to purify the corporate society of England's late Tudors and early Stuarts. Only after failing in the effort did they decide that America was "the place where the Lord will create a new Heaven and a new Earth." Those early leaders understood and honored Calvin's thought with its strong emphasis on the integration of economic and other affairs in a corporate whole. Like the Virginians who were more religious than is sometimes realized, the New England Puritans were more concerned with problems of political economy than their theological polemics might indicate. For that matter, many of them came to America for immediate and personal economic reasons as well as to attain long-range ideological objectives.

Though carried to the near edge of fanaticism by their theology, such men nevertheless were Englishmen who had matured during the pre-Revolutionary consolidation of mercantilism. While still in England, they argued with considerable justice that their triumph would not upset the political economy of mercantilism but would only organize and administer it with greater rigor and success. As with Calvin, they distinguished aristocracy, monarchy, and democracy as the three forms of government and concluded in agreement with him that a mixture of aristocracy and democracy offered the best compromise.

John Winthrop's sense of the general welfare was strong and included the realization that the relationship between prices and wages had to be taken into account when working out a general system of economic regulation. John Cotton had a similar concern for the common good and the economic policies calculated to promote it, and Cotton Mather advanced a theory of taxation based on the principle of a progressive rate and the assumption that the receipts would be used for public benefits. Another New Englander sounded like Shaftesbury and other English mercantilists of the 17th century: "Whilst men are all for their private profit, the public good is neglected and languisheth." As his contribution to this discussion, Increase Mather emphasized the fact that social welfare is not the automatic product of profits. "Sometimes," he noted, "one man by seeking to advance himself has brought great misery on whole nations." And the persistence of this outlook was revealed a century later. "*Trade* or *Commerce*," concluded an essay on the good republic, "is an Engine of State, to draw men into business, for the advancing and enobling of the Rich, for the support of the Poor, for the strengthening and fortifying of the State."

Considered in this context, the characterization of Calvinism and Puritanism as philosophies based on making fine distinctions takes on a deeper significance. For as can be seen, there were two crucial decisions constantly demanding to be made. First, it had to be determined whether critics were attacking the idea and ideal of such a corporate community or merely proposing different means for building and sustaining it. Second, it was vital to decide when "enobling the Rich" began to subvert "the support of the Poor." Or, to illustrate the problem in a way which calls attention to the Puritan's less than puritanical outlook on life, consider the issue of liquor. Winthrop and Mather agreed that the "wine is from God, but the Drunkard is from the Devil." The difficulty was in deciding how to hinder the Devil without denying God.

Rather than to view New Englanders as either all ideology or all practicality, it seems more accurate to describe them as men living in terrible and unremitting tension between, on the one hand, the confidence that their ideal was correct and, on the other, the anxiety generated by a fear of destroying the ideal by enforcing it too rigorously or having it undone by outsiders. John Cotton came to face this dilemma as a result of his understanding and friendship with Anne Hutchinson. Winthrop had the same problems in his relationship with Roger Williams. Both men finally came down on the side of enforcing loyalty to the ideal. But they did so with a rending reluctance which, given their outlook and experience as committed men who had led the colony through extreme difficulties, is more a tribute to their consciousness of the dilemma than it is proof of their blind fanaticism.

The point is not that Williams and Anne Hutchinson were wrong. The issue is to get beyond the stereotype of the Puritan. However one chooses between the contestants, it should be apparent that the Puritans were a great deal more than bluenoses dedicated to spoiling everyone's good time. What they wanted was a good time with an equal emphasis on the good rather than a complete stress on the time. To say that they sought a chimera is to give up the intellectual and moral struggle: they asked the right questions and struggled for the right answers.

Nevertheless, like the little girl with a curl in the middle of her forehead, these early Puritans had a kink in their ideology; when they went wrong, they went very, very wrong. Devoted to the ideal of a corporate community guided by a strong moral sense, they developed a great talent for misinterpreting any opposition. From the outset, for example, they were prone to view the Indians as agents of the Devil waiting to test their convictions—even though their theology implied very strongly that the red men were members of the Invisible Church. But that definition externalized Evil, thus making it an object to be overpowered rather than an internal, human weakness to be contained until transformed (or, in the case of the Indians, to deal with them as co-equal Children of God).

This propensity to place Evil outside their system not only distorted the Puritans' own doctrine, it inclined them toward a solution which involved the extension of their system over others. Here was a subtle convergence of religious and secular ideas, for mercantilism also emphasized the necessity as well as the desirability of expansion in economic and political affairs. It externalized secular evil by arguing that domestic poverty could in the last analysis be overcome only by taking wealth away from others. Far from wanting no more than to be left alone, New Englanders developed a solution to their religious and secular difficulties which prompted vigorous action against an external cause.

Even so, and in the same way that they were at first ambivalent toward Williams and Anne Hutchinson, they were initially cautious in opposing the demand brought forward in the 1620s and 1630s for broader participation in political affairs. Raised by wealthy men as well as by the middle and lower classes, this attack on restricted government might easily have succeeded. But when the rulers hesitated, only a small number of the critics stepped forward and declared themselves free men. Convinced that such caution indicated a lack of conviction, the oligarchy swung shut the gate and slammed home the bolt. Not even the halfway covenant of 1662, by which the children of the converted were admitted to partial church membership, reopened it. For by that time the leaders had consolidated their position and altered the meaning of the old ideal.

Embarking upon a campaign of righteous persuasion which often became outright intimidation, and upon a bloody trail of persecution, the church fathers punished the courageous, exiled the bold, and terrified the timid. As early as the 1650s, an old man was doubled over in irons for 16 hours and then lashed 100 times with a tarred rope. Far from "enobling the Rich, and support[ing] the Poor," this horrible travesty on the ideal of a corporate community culminated some 20 years later in the witchcraft trials. It is of course true, and fortunate, that not many people were killed, but that is only half the ledger. None were saved. Unless, perhaps, it was Winthrop himself; there is a story about him which suggests that on his deathbed he saw his mistake. Asked to sign a warrant for the banishment of another heretic, he refused: "No, I have done too much of that work already."

During those same years, Winthrop and his successors consolidated their political position at home and within the empire. Winthrop's attitude is wonderfully revealed by an episode in which he had to borrow the royal ensign from a visiting ship so that the captain of the vessel could report in London that he had seen it flying over the colony. "Our allegiance binds us not to have the laws of England," explained Winthrop, "any longer than while we live in England." While he agreed with those Englishmen who thought it desirable to exercise more authority over New England, Shaftesbury refused to panic over the colony's freedom. His assumption that the colonists would come to accept the basic principles of the empire was generally correct. As in other colonial regions, New Englanders fought more or less effectively for local authority while accepting the restrictions of the Navigation Acts and the compensating rewards of trade and naval protection.

In the century that followed Winthrop's militant resistance, Massachusetts and its neighbors evolved a dynamic and stratified society led by the merchant aristocracy. Poor farm land, boundary restrictions in their charters, and the opposition of the French, Indians, and New Yorkers (and each other) combined to make New Englanders into miners of the sea. There was some agricultural farming, as well as tree harvesting, and some city men owned or speculated in land; but the boulders of New England produced more poets, pamphleteers, and politicians than landed gentry. Fishing, shipbuilding, processing operations in flour, lumber, and alcohol, and colonial and international trading created the private fortunes, the training grounds of decision makers, and the economic weather for the entire region.

Slave trading was an integral part of the system. Some old-time merchants even called it "the first wheel of commerce." Though an exaggeration, the profits on "black ivory" purchased many a prayer book and Bible and spilled into collection plates from Providence to Boston. "We have seen," cried one critic of the miserable business, "molasses and alcohol, rum and slaves, gold and iron, in a perpetual and unholy round of commerce." As that comment suggests, New Englanders developed a complex economy; it was simple only in essentials. Codfish were graded and exported to the appropriate market, top fillets went for flour and tobacco down the coast, and the rest to the Mediterranean for salt and wine or to the Indies. Whale-chasing was successful in its own right and ultimately created a young candlemaking industry in Rhode Island. Naval stores and ships were supplied on order for England as well as for traders in Boston. At the center of the whole system were the merchants who handled everything from marine insurance to retail sales across the counter, and the rising body of colonial lawyers who knew the ropes of such an economy in both senses of the term.

Considerable insight into New England can be gained by comparing it, instead of contrasting it, with the Southern colonies. The obvious differences can be overemphasized to the point of serious misunderstanding, for there were many similarities. Both were pocket-deep in the business of slavery. Both upper classes were opposed by the lower orders within their regions. And both groups of leaders valued artistic achievement. Thomas Hancock's great house on Beacon Street in Boston, for example, was the merchant's version of Mount Vernon. New England's John Singleton Copley, furthermore, was *the* colonial painter. Gifted among colonial artists with exceptional visual perceptiveness, Copley had a unique ability to create the illusion that is more real than reality. His portrait of Samuel Adams, for example, calls up an image of Calvin that reveals the essential Adams far better than does any written study of the man.

These two societies held yet other elements in common. Though both groups found it ever more difficult to maintain a rate of growth within England's mercantilist empire that they had grown accustomed to, neither of them reacted by embracing independence en masse. Finally, and perhaps most important of all, each had an outlook rooted in a religious conception of the good society as a balanced, corporate system originally shared by their Puritan and Anglican ancestors in England. Perhaps it is not as surprising as it sometimes appears, therefore, that Massachusetts and Virginia ultimately struck the alliance which defeated Great Britain. Or, in another way, that one of the great philosophic and literary documents of American history is the correspondence between John Adams and Thomas Jefferson.

As also in Virginia, moreover, the New Englanders who took the lead in the revolutionary movement were men committed to that ideal of corporate responsibility and welfare. Jonathan Edwards, Samuel Adams, and John Adams played particularly important roles in sustaining the morality of a corporate society and the political economy of a balanced mercantilist state. All were products of the educational system founded by the early theocracy and its secular leaders. Learning was not only a part of religion in the basic sense (how else could the Bible be emphasized?), but it was considered vital for the training of preachers and for the general prosperity of the society. Fines for the neglect of education were levied in Massachusetts as early as 1642, and within five years teachers were given special consideration. Whether Harvard was founded for secular or religious objectives is not really the issue; both were part of the corporate entity in 1636.

But this early devotion to the corporate ideal was weakened as Massachusetts and the other colonies in New England extended their boundaries and their prosperity. Religion was not abandoned, but the wealthy "river gods" of the Connecticut Valley and the merchants of Salem, Boston, and Providence gradually redefined the meaning of the crucial term, the elect. From signifying membership in Calvin's corporate religious community it came to mean the upper class of that society. Furthermore, since the leaders dominated the political system, they began to equate the elect with the elected. By this casuistry they gave themselves a happy aura of liberalism in an age when laissez faire was beginning to challenge the corporate emphasis in mercantilism.

Jonathan Edwards assaulted their outlook with tremendous vigor and passion. Professor Perry Miller's description of the campaign is appropriately bare and explicit: Edwards "demonstrated to New Englanders of 1734 that they had ceased to believe what they professed, and that as a result the society was sick. He did not merely call them hypocrites, he proved that they were." In defining religious commitment as an affair of the heart, in considering that only God is worthy of worship, in placing high value on the intellect and on education, in valuing and respecting self-government, and in asserting that there were positive, pragmatic consequences of being sober, honest, responsible, and willing to work—in all these respects Edwards was a man who left his life as a monument to the positive side of Puritanism. Perhaps even more important, having ultimately recognized that the principal danger of his outlook lay in turning politics into a crusade, he did all that he could to moderate that unhappy tradition.

Intellectually, or theologically, Edwards reasserted and insisted that Calvinism was a religion for none but the strong at heart; it confronted men with a harsh world and offered them no quarter. Either they lived together as the children of God or they lived together as animals. "Frauds and trickishness in trade," Edwards thundered, supplemented the casual callousness "in taking any advantage that men can by any means obtain, to get the utmost possible of their neighbor for what they have to dispose of, and their neighbor needs." Worst of all, men "take advantage of their neighbor's poverty to extort unreasonably from him those things that he is under a necessity of procuring." Edwards explained this decay by man's natural tendency to confuse his interests with those of the Lord, a propensity encouraged and even justified by the false theology of such English preachers as John Taylor and Daniel Whitby. Edwards was not alone among New England theologians in recognizing that these ideas emerged with the parallel economic progress of the mother country and the colonies. Jonathan Mayhew of Boston saw the connection and candidly tailored the corporate cloth of Calvinism to fit the individualism of John Locke and Adam Smith. Not so Edwards. Accepting the challenge to Christianity that was implicit in this evolving laissez-faire business ethic, he attacked its theological (and hence intellectual) premises.

Men like Taylor and their American admirers had done a very simple and effective thing; they raised once again the obvious question about Calvinism. If man is truly predestined, how then can he be asked to be good? For the doctrine to be tenable, they concluded, it had to grant that men were open to persuasion by God's agents and therefore had a will and volition of their own. As they admitted, theirs was a religion in which the disarming plea of insufficiency was enough to excuse any but the most blatant failure to honor the way of the Lord.

Edwards replied with a torrent of moral scorn directed by the hell-fire logic of a deep and brilliant believer. Neither cause and effect nor the experience of free will can be made intelligible and coherent, he insisted, without an inclusive conception of the universe. Suffering has no significance and no dignity outside such a world, and tolerance based on indifference, or the lack of any positive position, is nothing but an evasion of the whole point about toleration. For like suffering, toleration is meaningful only when the person involved truly cares about the issue; otherwise it becomes an insufferable arrogance. Hence the essential corporate character of Christian society: what belongs together belongs together, whether or not it is benevolent or pleasant. And to assert against this the claim that man is adequate is to commit the most grievous sin of all. No man is an end in and of himself.

Yet the other side of this religious conflict and revival that came to be known as the Great Awakening also had significant consequences for America's developing self-consciousness. For one thing, Edwards's targets were powerful figures in New England society, and their

vigorous faith in their own self-interest ultimately prompted many of
them to favor a war for independence. Having reached that conclusion, they made important contributions to its success. In a quite
different way, religious leaders like George Whitefield of England
influenced a large number of colonists. Whitefield had none of
Edwards's moral integrity or intellectual rigor. His sermons (a more
apt term might be performances) combined the free-will argument
that man could save himself with the idea that salvation meant a
return to Calvin's original ideas and ideals. Such a have-your-cake-
and-eat-it-too doctrine had a broad appeal. Scotch-Irish Presbyterians
and Congregationalists could join with men of the Dutch Reformed
Church in responding to this approach; it seems, for example, to
have inspired Patrick Henry in Virginia as well as Sam Adams in
Massachusetts.

"I was in my field at work," recalled one New Englander who
was roused by this theology. "I dropped my tool that I had in my
hand and ran home to my wife, telling her to make ready quickly to
go and hear Mr. Whitefield preach at Middletown, then run to my
pasture for my horse with all my might, fearing that I should be too
late." Having worked up such a lather on himself as well as on his
animal, the man was caked with a thin film of mud when he rode
into the cloud of dust raised by the arrival of other men and women
who had reacted in the same fashion.

Whitefield consciously spoke to "the rabble" as well as to "the
great and rich." In rhetoric and impact, if not in motivation, this was
an equalitarian Christianity, and some men like John Wise went on
to secularize it even more explicitly as a democratic political philosophy. In that very limited sense, therefore, the Great Awakening was a
colonial version of the Levellers' far more rigorous, and radical,
religious enthusiasm. But only an insignificant number of Levellers
developed in America, and to speak of colonial radicals in referring
to such men as Isaac Sterns or Sam Adams is to distort the term
beyond any serious or useful meaning.

COLONIAL MATURITY: THE ACHIEVEMENT OF BRITISH MERCANTILISM

But in a less rigorous way, as a movement based on the individual's discovery (or rediscovery) of self within a group, the Great
Awakening did reinforce and extend the rising self-consciousness
that the colonists were exhibiting in economic and political affairs.
By the 1740s, when the English government gave way before the

persistent entreaties and pressures of the South Sea Company and officially supported the penetration of Spain's empire in the New World, the American colonies were mature societies infused with an increasing confidence. When the war against Spain erupted into a general European conflict aimed at France, for example, Massachusetts planned, financed, and won a campaign against Louisburg. Costing more than £50,000, this assault captured the fort which commanded the trade routes and fishing grounds of the North Atlantic and controlled access to the St. Lawrence and the interior of the continent. When forced to give it up in 1748, Massachusetts gorged itself at the table of frustrated ambitions.

Similar clashes occurred during the next decade as Virginia, Pennsylvania, and New York disagreed with London's policies on the Indians and westward expansion. And with the outbreak of the French and Indian War in 1756, the conflict took on some of the characteristics of a struggle between two English-speaking empires. Following the mercantilist axiom that trading with the enemy was permissible if the opponent gave up more than he got, the colonials in Boston and Pennsylvania continued (and expanded) their commerce with the French West Indies. England was furious. Firing writs of assistance as one might use grapeshot, it moved in to enforce its restrictions. Hiring James Otis, a lawyer crony of Sam Adams, to defend them, the merchants accepted the challenge. As all good lawyers are wont to do, and doing it with "a torrent of impetuous eloquence," Otis transformed an earthy economic conflict into a noble constitutional issue.

British officials had warned of a rising militant self-consciousness fifteen years earlier. "Whether grown wanton by prosperity or whatever...," reported Lt. Gov. George Clark of New York in 1741, the colonists were by their acts reinforcing "a jealousy which for some years has obtained in England, that the plantations are not without thoughts of throwing off their Dependence on the Crown of England." As if to prove the point, William Bradford of Philadelphia started the *American Magazine* the same year, and by 1757 it was referring to the colonies "as a nation." Governor Lewis Morris of New Jersey agreed with Clark that some colonists were "grasping at the whole authority of Government."

Statistics help to explain this concern. Colonial population had mushroomed from 250,000 in 1700 to about 1,400,000 in 1750. And having produced an irrelevant one-seventieth of the world's pig and bar iron in 1700, the colonies were racing toward the one-seventh share they would turn out in 1775. By that time, their production was more than that of England and Wales combined. In a more general sense, the colonies had evolved an economic system. However compartmentalized it might be by the particularism of each colony, the resources, skills, and attitudes of the colonists had created a common and interdependent economy. They made shoes as well as iron, furniture as well as ships, and guns as well as rum. Their own lumber, livestock, and food could sustain a family or a settlement. And their trade with Europe, Africa, and the West Indies brought them other goods as well as capital. The colonies were so far along toward integration that one of the most common complaints concerned the lack of a compulsory system of weights and measures.

Such maturity was also revealed in the growing awareness of differences between classes and groups. This was not surprising: the colonies had been founded as sharply divided societies (consider the planter and the indentured servant), and a man with 1,000 acres or a ship to mortgage could always get wealthy faster than the man who had to stop and clear the trees from his family plot or save a stake while building ships for someone else.

A Plymouth tavern-keeper named Thomas Morton observed and protested such stratification less than a generation after the first settlements were established. William Davyes and John Pate led an unsuccessful rising in Maryland in 1676. Almost simultaneously, John Culpeper headed a similar movement in South Carolina and was saved from severe punishment only when Shaftesbury intervened in his behalf. New York artisans and small merchants organized protest movements further north. And in Massachusetts the struggle over the land bank revealed similar internal divisions as well as a conflict between the bank and the English government, a consideration which encouraged the supporters of the bank to feel that domestic welfare might depend on winning independence.

Far from being radical uprisings, these rebellions revealed a persistent concern to restore and strengthen the ideal and the practice of a corporate society in which responsibilities and benefits are shared. Led by Nathaniel Bacon in Virginia during 1676, the first major colonial uprising defined its objectives in exactly those terms. While the rebels complained with particular bitterness about the lack of support against the Indians, their list of grievances is anything but a call for laissez faire and most certainly not a program of Levellers. Rather did they damn the governor for "specious pretences of public works," for failing to initiate measures for "fortification, towns, or trade" or for "liberal arts, or sciences," for abusing the system of justice, and for violating the Crown's rights by making a *personal* monopoly of the beaver trade. Such fidelity to the accepted code of a corporate mercantilist state gave them every right to assert "we cannot in our hearts find one single spot of rebellion or treason."

Just a century later, the Regulator movements of the North and South Carolina backcountry manifested a similar outlook. Pointing out that men stole their horses and then sold them to the Dutch and the French, they demanded protection for their property and punishment for those who violated the regulations of the empire. They also petitioned for an equitable share in the government from which they requested such public benefits as schools, better poor laws, price-control and quality-inspection laws, and bounties for agriculture. Their attack on church leaders is particularly revealing, for they requested a vigorous reassertion of the corporate ideals and a wholesale distribution of Bibles. A program more typical of Anglican mercantilism would be difficult to imagine, and it is not surprising that such men supported the mother country when the revolution finally began.

That phrase, "the revolution," is in many respects a misnomer for there was no single decision to go to war. There were 13 different governments in America. Founded as separate colonies, developing different though complementary interests, and having waged their respective battles against Royal governors and the mother country, these governments were reluctant to give up any of their self-determination. Massachusetts typified their attitude when in 1754 it refused to support Franklin's proposed union on the grounds that "it would be subversive of the most valuable rights and Liberties of the several Colonies included in it." On the other hand, the colonists did have a vision of sharing a common future.

"What scenes of happiness we are ready to figure to ourselves!" cried a not atypical colonist in 1759. "You cannot well imagine," wrote another a year later, "what a Land of health, plenty and contentment this is among all ranks, vastly improved within the last ten years." And as early as 1755 an American geographer named Lewis Evans commented that Massachusetts was headed toward an empire of its own. But so was Virginia. Worried and upset "at the largeness" of his debts, delayed and frustrated in his plans for western development and land speculation as early as 1761, and anxious to diversify the economy of the entire region, George

Washington had begun to think as a leader of an American system. When he complained about poor or damaged imports from England, his London agents told him to send them back. Finally he exploded: it was impossible. How "can a person, who imports bare requisites only, submit it to be a year out of any particular article of clothing, or necessary for family use...It is not to be done. We are obliged to acquiesce."

IDEOLOGY AND INDEBTEDNESS: THE LEVER AND
FULCRUM OF INDEPENDENCE

As Washington and his peers like George Mason along the Potomac Valley grew ever more restive, the British government embarked upon a program to confine them further. Loyal Englishmen had been suggesting the virtue of that approach as early as 1747. "The colonies at this Time are arrived to a State of considerable Maturity," judged William Douglas in Boston: "perhaps it would be for the Interest of the Nations of Great Britain, and for the Ease of the Ministry or Managers at the Court of Great Britain, to reduce them to some general uniformity."

This concern with uniformity is the basic explanation of English policy after the final defeat of the French in North America in 1763. George III and his supporters (though not the mere hangers-on at Court) wanted a uniformity that had its roots in the doctrine of the divine right of kings. He sought it as a Patriot King for its own sake, and as a way to get money from the colonies in order to win his political battle in England. Others saw such control as the prerequisite for laissez faire in England: if policy was to be abandoned for interest at home, then policy had to triumph throughout the empire. Men could not pursue their enlightened self-interest unless there was a stable foundation on which to make their rational calculations, one which would withstand the violence of their competition and the shock of their mistakes. For quite different reasons, therefore, the king and many of his enemies agreed that the colonies had to be brought into line.

Having first placed restrictions on the settlement of the west in 1761, England announced on October 7, 1763, its decision to extend and enforce such limitation. Other edicts and laws followed in rapid succession during the next two years. Typical of the new approach was London's revocation of a controlled price system for the Indian trade as "doubtful in its principle"—a clear indication of the rising laissez-faire outlook in England. The colonists were more directly antagonized by a revenue law usually known as the Sugar Act (1764), which threatened to wipe out the margin of profit in the West Indies trade. It was followed by new restrictions on colonial money (1764), and demands that the colonists help finance the maintenance of British troops in North America (1765).

Then Parliament passed its first direct tax in the form of the Stamp Act, another revenue measure which raised the cost of legal documents, newspapers and Franklin's *Almanac*, and even playing cards. This not only threatened to raise the cost of business, but it soured a man's anticipation of a friendly game of cards—he had to ante up an extra time for the King. Finally, just when the colonists thought they had won a general victory in their bitter fight over the Stamp Act, England passed the Townshend Acts (1767). Consisting of taxes on colonial imports such as glass, lead, paint, paper, and tea (which was the national drink much as coffee is today), the legislation also erected special commissions and courts to enforce the collection of the money and punish offenders.

The colonists, whose self-consciousness and confidence had been intensified by the victory over the French, were affronted by the inclusive nature of these regulations and taxes. The new legislation also jarred their identification with the empire, and intensified the economic difficulties they were experiencing in a postwar depression. Massachusetts struck back on June 6, 1765, with a call for a meeting of the colonies to determine the strategy and organize the forces of a counterattack. Though not at that time the unchallenged leader of colonial resistance that he became in a few years, Samuel Adams was nevertheless the moving spirit of this first step toward independence and empire. Together with Virginians like Richard Henry Lee, Mason, and Washington, Adams and his New England allies made the Revolution.

Although he has been explained and interpreted as everything from a Leveller (and hence a radical of his time) to a neurotic haunted by a father image, Adams is best understood as a true Calvinist and thoroughgoing mercantilist. From an early age, he received religious training as a strict Congregationalist from his mother who had "severe religious principles." His father was a deacon of Boston's Old South Church. Emerging from this background, he developed views on the relationship between religion and politics that were subtle and complex. On the one hand, he staunchly

advocated and defended the "free exercise of the rights of conscience," and vigorously opposed any participation by the organized
church in secular affairs. Yet he was against allowing Catholics to
hold public office because of what he considered their divided
loyalties; either their commitment to Rome was meaningless, in
which case they were hypocrites, or they would follow the Pope in a
conflict of values with the electorate. At the same time, he defended
a modicum of state support to organized Protestantism on the
ground that the church played a vital role in maintaining a firm
corporate ethical system and in providing insurance against anarchy.

As with Calvin, Adams was a militant spokesman for the supremacy of civilian authority over military leaders and institutions. And
when ethical crises arose he was always willing "to step forth in the
good old cause of morality and religion." As he acknowledged in
later years, his central purpose was to make Boston "the *Christian
Sparta*" of the world. "I am *in* fashion and *out* of fashion, as the
whim goes," he commented in a revealing letter of 1768. "I will
stand alone. I will oppose this tyranny at the threshold, though the
fabric of liberty fall, and I perish in its ruins." Co-ordinated with the
other aspects of his thought, his very candid remarks about "the
Christian Sparta" and his willingness to pose the issue in terms of an
either-or choice indicate that Adams became a revolutionary in the
circumstances of his time precisely because he was a Calvinist
dedicated to the ideal and the reality of a corporate Christian
commonwealth. Calvin himself had followed that course, and his
ideas and logic would propel a true follower along the same path.
There seems little doubt that the words of Jonathan Edwards carried
the spirit of true Calvinism into the well-prepared mind of Samuel
Adams. Once there, it infiltrated the ideas of Shaftesbury, [John]
Locke, and [James] Harrington[2] to produce a man who signed many
of his militant polemics as "A RELIGIOUS POLITICIAN."

Though he accepted Locke's statement of natural rights and based
his political theory and practice on that principle, Adams also
stressed explicitly the dangers of individualism. Hence he set himself
firmly against men who defined liberty as "nothing else ... but *their*

2. James Harrington (1611–1677), British philosopher, advocated the creation of
independent political institutions within society as a means of stabilizing economic
relationships and checking arbitrary power. Harrington's ideas were succeeded by
those of John Locke (1632–1704), the political theorist of constitutional government
whose views, along with those of leaders of the English Puritan movement during
the first half of the seventeenth century, influenced American political thinkers of
the Revolutionary generation.—ED.

own liberty." Adams was not a laissez-faire individualist who thought that the competition between enlightened self-interests would produce the general welfare. "Liberty no man can truly possess," he amplified, "whose mind is enthralled by irregular and inordinate passions; since it is no great privilege to be free from external violence if the dictates of the mind are controlled by a force within, which erects itself above reason." "Religion and public liberty of the people are ultimately connected," he concluded: "their interests are interwoven; they cannot subsist separately."

Given the existence of a Christian corporate commonwealth, or the possibility of reforming such a society that had slipped away from the ideal, there is nothing in Adams's thought to justify a revolution. "The man who dares to rebel against the laws of a republic ought to suffer death," he asserted, because under those circumstances "sedition is founded on the depraved and inordinate passions of the mind; it is a weak, feverish, sickly thing." But if such a corporate Christian republic did not exist, or had decayed past the power of internal reform, then the same criteria enabled Adams to advocate revolution. Indeed, his principles forced him to do so. Thus any opponent of the true commonwealth became a public enemy. Adams ultimately cast Britain, and its agents and allies in the colonies, in that very role. Flatly declaring that "the Colonies were by their charters made different states by the mother country," Adams concluded that the new British policy was sedition against the original and true principles of the empire commonwealth.

Never sympathetic to "utopian schemes of levelling," Adams assumed a causal relationship between property and freedom. "These must stand and fall together." Thus Britain's move to tax the colonists was critically important: it "greatly obstructed" their trade and made the economic situation "very uneasy." As for Boston in particular, it "lived by its trade" and therefore had the "deepest concern" about the new policy. For Adams, the conclusion was obvious: acquiescence in such economic restrictions would make every colonist a "bond slave" by depriving him of the basis of his freedom. The Masters of Harvard agreed, asserting in 1765 that the new regulations "made it useless for the people to engage in commerce," and for that reason the laws could "be evaded by them as faithful subjects."

It seems doubtful that Adams sought *immediate* independence prior to 1770. His early polemics and letters stress the idea of forcing England to return to mercantilism. Take the natural and extensive profits of that system, he told them, and be satisfied. For that purpose (though perhaps from the outset for independence), Adams organized a propaganda network and a local political party supplemented by an extralegal police force known as the Sons of Liberty. Aided by such key allies as James Warren and John Adams, he used this machinery to maintain constant pressure (much of it in the form of physical intimidation by his street mobs) on Boston merchants. His purpose was to keep them in line on the economic embargo against British goods, and to make them do business without the stamps decreed in 1765. Counting on the pocketbook motive of the merchants, he assumed this would prompt the Boston traders to put similar pressure on the merchants in other colonial ports to keep them from taking all the profits. He also encouraged, prodded, and incited the Sons of Liberty and other similar groups throughout the colonies to exert their own power for the same purposes.

Lest the great importance of Adams be overemphasized, it should be made clear that each of the 13 colonies traveled its own road to independence. Adams could no more have singlehandedly bullied or bamboozled them into doing the same thing at the same time than he could have maneuvered his election as Pope. He had help, and lots of it, from several sources. Other lower- and middle-class leaders in the seaboard cities organized their own political clubs and street gangs, and deployed them as Adams used his own organization in Boston. Charles Thompson, for example, is often referred to as "the Sam Adams of Philadelphia." Isaac Sears and John Lamb were clever and militant leaders in New York, and in 1770 Alexander McDougall became a hero in jail for his role in opposing supplies to the British troops in the city. And further south, Patrick Henry and George Rogers Clark provided similar leadership for agrarian dissidents.

Upper-class leaders such as Joseph Galloway and John Dickinson of Philadelphia, Philip Schuyler and Robert Livingston of New York, and the majority of southern merchants were initially willing to support the kind of vigorous resistance to British policy advocated by Adams. But they never went beyond the idea of forcing England to restore the old order. "A little rioting," as one of them put it, "is a good thing." Beyond that point, however, such nabobs were openly afraid, as Gouverneur Morris explained, that the colonies would fall "under the worst of all possible dominions...the dominion of a riotous mob." Franklin was even willing, in the earlier years, to accept a tightening up of the empire and "make as good a night of it as we can."

Persuaded, prodded, and intimidated by its more militant elements, this coalition forced England to back down. Turning to the classic mercantilist weapon of economic sanctions, it adopted and ultimately enforced by extralegal (and strong-arm) organizations the strategy of refusing to import British goods. Led by Washington, Mason, Lee, and Henry, Virginia effected the general consolidation of this movement in 1769. This non-importation cut deeply into England's trade, which dropped almost a £1,000,000 in one year. As expected, British merchants and manufacturers reacted vigorously, demanding a modification or change of policy. It is more difficult to determine the effects of the concurrent agitation by Wilkes and other radicals in England, but since they were using the American issue for their own purposes it probably encouraged British leaders to retreat. Even more important than these effects in England, however, was the experience and organization that non-importation provided for the Americans.

Combined with the scrambling for position between and within the English parties, these direct and indirect results on non-importation produced successive repeal of the Stamp Act (1766) and of all but one of the Townshend Acts (1770). And though England kept a tax on tea, the American coalition collapsed. New York and Rhode Island abandoned non-importation, and the other colonies hurried to reopen their own trade. Unfortunately for those who favored such compromise, neither Sam Adams nor the British Government would leave them alone. Adams launched a determined campaign to establish a corporate Christian and mercantilist American empire.

Like his allies in Virginia, Adams was thus a revolutionary without being a radical. And while other popular leaders in the colonies spoke for interest groups that wanted a greater share of upper-class well-being and political authority, only a tiny and insignificant group of individuals offered anything remotely resembling a radical program. Some of Adams's counterparts in other colonies stressed an extension of popular government more heavily than he did, for example, but none challenged the assumptions of the existing order. Had the revolution come a generation later, it is very probable that one wing of the popular movement would have developed such an attack on established institutions. But whether judged within the predominant mercantilist outlook, or against the standards of the laissez-faire philosophy that was gaining power in England, the colonials were far from radical. In either case, the crux of the matter was the Levellers' demand that private property be replaced by social property so that the Christian concept of commonwealth could be fully developed. The colonials had not reached that point by 1776.

Hence they emphasized freedom of action and empire. "It is the business of America to take care of herself; her situation depends upon her own virtue," Adams declared at the end of 1770. "Arts and manufactures, ordered by commerce, have raised Great Britain to its present pitch of grandeur. America will avail herself of imitating her." A year later, Philip Freneau and Hugh Henry Brackenridge caught the spirit of that outlook in their militant *Ode to the Rising Glory of America*. And Adams's mercantilist emphasis on manufacturing was typified in the expanding enterprises that were developing in every colony. The Boston Society for Encouraging Industry and Employing the Poor (a mercantilist title if ever there was one) established a spinning school in 1769. The New York Society for the Promotion of Arts, Agriculture, and Oeconomy began to grant premiums for domestic production and apprenticeship schools in 1765. And by 1775 The United Company of Philadelphia for Promoting American Manufactures had 400 female employees. Even more significant was the way in which Americans reacted to the Tea Act of 1773 as a specific threat to American manufacturing as well as a general danger to the system.

Many Americans feared that the principle behind the East India Company's monopoly on tea would gradually be extended to other goods and thus give England control of all colonial wealth. Adams recognized and seized his chance: in December, 1773, his Boston Sons of Liberty chucked the tea into Boston Harbor. England retaliated in kind, combining the Coercive Acts against Boston itself with the Quebec Act directed against all the colonies. The latter law not only took part of the west north of the Ohio river and gave it to Canada, but it closed off the rest of the trans-mountain area and granted Catholics in Canada full religious freedom. This combination gave Adams everything he needed: a city as a martyr, a basic religious and ideological issue, and a fundamental economic grievance. Calling explicitly for "AN AMERICAN COMMON-WEALTH," he warned of English control over colonial Protestant churches, emphasized the danger of Catholic infiltration from Canada, and called flatly for continued westward expansion.

"An empire is rising in America," Adams exulted, calling for the annexation of Canada, Nova Scotia, and the fishing banks. "We can subsist independently of all the world." He was ready even then to "fight it out, and trust to God for success." Most other Americans were not. Without his allies in Virginia (and in the streets of Philadelphia and New York), Adams would have failed to defeat the nabobs and their compatriots—the loyal, the indifferent, the cautious, and the fearful among the general populace. Perhaps it is too much to say that the hinge of empire broke on the September day in 1774 when George Washington walked into the Continental Congress wearing his blue-and-buff uniform as commander of the Fairfax County Volunteers. Yet the symbolism of the act must have been almost as great to his contemporaries as it appears looking back at the scene with the knowledge that in less than two years he was to be commander-in-chief of an American army. Long before Jefferson had finished his last revision of the Declaration of Independence, Washington was in the field against the enemy. One frustrated loyalist had foreseen the result as early as February, 1775: "Adams, with his crew, and the haughty Sultans of the south juggled the whole conclave of the Delegates."

As a planter who had opposed the British years before 1763, and who had worked out broad and specific plans for American development, Washington concluded it "highly necessary that something should be done." Deeply concerned that Britain's policy was "starving" colonial manufactures, as well as draining the coffers of the trader and the farmer, Washington saw the issue in absolute terms. "Our all is at stake," he declared to George Mason on April 6, 1769. Other southerners came to share that conclusion during the next five years. Jefferson's witty definition of a planter as "a species of property annexed to certain mercantile houses in London" was accepted by Oliver Wolcott, Thomas Mason, and others, and caught the spirit of the growing support for freedom, property, and empire.

Thus it was that on July 17, 1774, Mason and Washington prepared the Fairfax County Resolves, the southern manifesto of independence. Objecting to being treated as "a conquered country" after a century of enjoying the "reciprocal" and "mutual benefits" of mercantilism, they described the new imperialism as a program "calculated to reduce us from a state of freedom and happiness to slavery and misery." Calling for a "firm union" of the colonies, they demanded an end to *all* trade with Britain by November, 1775, if the new policies were not revoked. Significantly, they included slaves in this total nonintercourse that was to be enforced by extralegal associations empowered to embargo violators in the colonies. Finally, they urgently recommended "temperance, fortitude, frugality, and industry, and... every encouragement in their power, particularly by

subscriptions and premiums, to the improvement of arts and manufactures in America."

On the next day, Washington served as chairman of the county
meeting called to consider the document. Exhibiting the same
determination he later showed in battle, he rammed it through
without discussion. And within a fortnight, the local militia which
had been drilling under his command was officially recognized.
Since it is true, despite one of the great myths of American history,
that Washington was a firm advocate of political parties based on
ideas and principles, it is perhaps useful to see him as the Shaftesbury of the American Revolution. In any event, he and Adams
symbolized the two mainstreams of colonial society that engulfed
England in defeat.

THE TRIUMPH OF AMERICAN MERCANTILISM

As they converged on Philadelphia in 1774, Adams and Washington caught the nabobs in a classic squeeze play. A New Jersey
merchant analyzed his (and his group's) dilemma with great perceptiveness on the eve of the Congress. He insisted that the colonies
could and should adjust their differences with the King in order to
preserve the imperial system and hence their own wealth and
welfare. "We ourselves," he pointed out, "have happily lived and
enjoyed all the liberty that men could or can wish." The alternative
was the "blood and destruction" that would be brought on by "the
sedition, nay treason that is daily buzzed into our ears" by the
advocates of independence. Yet the coming Congress, he concluded
fearfully, might be swayed by the men who wanted "a new empire."

As a member of the Congress thoroughly aware of its composition, Galloway agreed with "Mr. Z" from New Jersey. Magnificently
led by himself, one group of delegates sought a "remedy which
would redress the grievances justly complained of" and thereby lay
the basis for "a more solid and constitutional union between the two
countries." Supported by men like John Hancock, Silas Deane,
Robert Morris, and John Rutledge, Galloway's strategy suggests a
striking analogy with the policy of "No Peace—No War" advocated
by Leon Trotsky when the Bolsheviks were threatened by German
conquest in 1917 and 1918.

Opposing him, concluded Galloway, were men whose plan "was to
throw off all subordination and connection with Great Britain." Sam
and John Adams were the public heroes of this group, but they were

in fact partners with Gadsden, Washington, and Lee from the south, and men like Roger Sherman and George Clinton from the colonies around Massachusetts. Actually, both "Mr. Z" and Galloway over-simplified the composition of the Congress. There was a third bloc composed of men such as John Dickinson (Philadelphia), John Jay, James Duane, and Robert Livingston (all from New York) who wanted to negotiate a return to the system as it existed before 1763.

Galloway seized the initiative September 28, and presented his plan to co-ordinate the colonies and then establish a new union with Great Britain. A month of vigorous open debate and even more strenuous private negotiations (and intimidating rallies staged by Thompson) finally defeated it by one vote on October 23, 1774. In the tradition of all great revolutionaries, Adams, Washington, and Lee exploited their victory with ruthless *élan*. Declaring for "life, liberty, and property," they jammed through a militant attack on the Quebec Act, legislated into illegal law the principles (and some of the language) of the Fairfax Resolves, and established traditional mercan-tilist regulations on prices "so that no undue advantage" or suffering would result for any members of the new nation.

Massachusetts promptly set the pattern for other colonies with a formal legislative call for American manufactures. Arguing that the colonists were now a "family," the revolutionaries declared that the liberty, happiness, and welfare of families depended on "the less occasion they have for any articles belonging to others." Not only did those heirs of Calvin and the Puritans thus beat Thomas Jefferson to the idea of using "happiness" as a more felicitous synonym for "property" (one wonders if John Adams suggested the same substitu-tion to Jefferson), but they did so in a context of images that went back to early Tudor mercantilism. Specifically, the recipe for happi-ness included a call to improve "the breed of sheep"; to charge "only reasonable prices"; to manufacture nails, steel, tin-plate, salt-peter, paper, guns, powder, glass, buttons, and dyes, and to refine salt.

As this document suggests, British mercantilism bore a subtle and complex relationship to the American Revolution. It did not cause the conflict in the narrow sense because it had given way to the imperialism of laissez faire. But British mercantilism had provided the protection and the essential assistance by which a scattered group of pitiful settlements matured into 13 strong, militant, and self-conscious states. It also equipped the leaders of that society with a set of attitudes, assumptions, and ideas about policy that can only be understood as an American mercantilism. Thus when English leaders dropped mercantilism, the Americans picked it up and ran toward independence.

American leaders were very conscious of the crucial role played by imperial expansion in the mercantilist conception of the world. When he was only 20 (in 1775), John Adams thought it "likely" that "the great seat of empire" would soon be in the colonies. Members of Parliament sensed the vigor of this thinking among the colonists, and often asked their informants about the growth of this drive toward *"an independent empire."* British ministers anticipated Frederick Jackson Turner in explaining America by its drive to expand. Americans, wrote Lord Dunmore to Lord Dartmouth on December 24, 1774, "for ever imagine that the Lands further off are still better than those upon which they are already settled." Could any skeptics have heard John Adams exactly eight months later, their doubts would have vanished. Strongly implying that any nabobs who still hankered after a reconciliation with England had better get off the fence and either sail for London or see their tailors for a set of blue-and-buffs, Adams called for the Second Continental Congress to get on with the business of writing "a constitution to form for a great empire."

On January 9, 1776, Thomas Paine followed with *Common Sense*, the great propaganda document of the era, a truly artistic work. Like the *Federalist Papers* of the decade later, it was also an accurate guide to the general way in which colonists thought about the world. It was only common sense, Paine asserted, that there was "something absurd, in supposing a Continent to be perpetually governed by an island." Since more than one-third of the tonnage of Britain's trade empire was carried in ships built by colonists, it was obvious to him that farmers, planters, and other Americans would "always have a market while eating is the custom of Europe." Such magnificent sarcasm (perhaps produced by an extra decanter of brandy, since he never wrote without such medication for thinker's and writer's cramp) was followed by an outline for a mercantilist empire complete with a national debt, a national bank by which to measure and use it, and a navy.

Southerners quickly joined the chorus. "Empires have their zenith—and their descension to a dissolution," explained William Henry Drayton of South Carolina; "The Almighty... has made the choice of the present generation to erect the American Empire...[It] bids fair, by the blessings of God, to be the most glorious of any upon Record." Ever practical man that he was, Sam Adams had long before singled out Canada and the fishing banks for the early attention they received in the military campaigns (and in the Articles of Confederation which specifically mentioned Canada as an acceptable member). And even at that early date George Rogers Clark concentrated his attention on westward expansion.

"Prudence" might well dictate, as Jefferson explained in the Declaration of Independence (and as Locke made abundantly clear), that established governments should not be overthrown "for light and transient causes"; but then an independent empire was no light and transient cause. Following Locke like a schoolboy copying his lesson, Jefferson then recited the "long train of abuses and usurpations" which justified the act and saved the colonists from being classed as unnatural men. And as any good agrarian naturally would, particularly when he was a young revolutionary writing a manifesto, Jefferson equated property and happiness. The alliance between Massachusetts and Virginia could not have been symbolized more aptly or revealingly.

Distinguished and honorable advocate of reconciliation that he had been, Joseph Hewes had already acted on his appreciation of the facts: "Nothing is left now," he remarked on March 20, 1776, "but to fight it out." There was of course a great deal more left to do, and perhaps the most difficult task was to come to terms with the harsh fact that new empires were not welcomed by their elders in the 18th century.

The Fulfillment of the Passing Order

The [Missouri] question could be settled no otherwise than by a compromise.   *John Quincy Adams, 1821*

Whatever may be the abstract doctrine in favor of unrestricted commerce, [it]...has never occurred, and cannot be expected.

It is believed that the greater the expansion, within practicable limits, and it is not easy to say what are not so, the greater the advantage which the States individually will derive from it....It must be obvious to all, that the further expansion is carried, provided it not be beyond the just limit, the greater will be the freedom of action to both [National and State] governments.

James Monroe, 1822

The views and policy of the North Americans seem vainly directed toward
supplanting us in navigation in every quarter of the globe.

Lord Liverpool, 1824

Must we not say that the period which he [Washington] predicted as then
not far off has arrived?   *John Quincy Adams, 1826*

It is most desirable that there should be both a home and a foreign market.
But, with respect to their relative superiority, I cannot entertain a doubt.
The home market is first in order, and paramount in importance.

Henry Clay, 1824

CRISIS AND COMPROMISE IN A RENEWED STRUGGLE FOR THE WEST

SIGNIFICANT in its own right as the worst economic crisis yet
suffered by Americans, the panic and depression of 1819 also
marked the beginning of a decade of fundamental transition in
American society. On the one hand, the *Weltanschauung* of American
mercantilism was translated into a series of philosophic and practical
manifestations that documented its power and achievement. Even
when defeated by Andrew Jackson in 1828, for example, John
Quincy Adams was supported by 44 per cent of the voting public.
Yet Jackson's victory measured the extent to which the various
elements of the system created by American mercantilists had broken
into segments that were defining the common good in terms of their
own particularist interests.

The first collision of these conflicting developments produced the
crisis of 1819–1821 over the admission of Missouri as a slave state.
Representing the culmination of internal southern migration into the
old northwest, Missouri matured as an agricultural and commercial
political economy dominated by slaveholders and merchants who
were supported by yeomen accepting slavery. Since Alabama had just
been received into the Union as a slave state, Missouri leaders
anticipated no opposition. Instead, they walked onto glowing coals of
what was thought to be the dead ashes of the Hamiltonian faction.
To some extent that expectation was valid, for men such as Rufus
King[3] had stopped defining American problems in terms of relations
with England. They still leaned toward London, but primarily they

3. Rufus King (1755–1827) served as a delegate to the Constitutional Convention
and as minister to Great Britain. A leading Federalist, he was the party's losing
candidate for vice president (1804 and 1808) and for president in 1816, a contest won
by James Monroe.—ED.

were concerned to strengthen their place in the American political economy. The new group still composed a faction, but it was more broadly based in the maturing commercial-manufacturing sector of the economy and counted far more supporters outside New England than had its predecessor.

Thus a major crisis developed when, on February 13, 1819, James Tallmadge of New York introduced a resolution in Congress to prohibit the admission of Missouri as a slave state and to free all its existing slaves within a given period. Tallmadge was in many respects an innocent incendiary who apparently intended to start no more than a slow fire of humanitarian opposition to slavery that might illuminate his own career more brightly. Instead, it erupted into a blazing struggle between two sectors of the political economy.

King seized control of the issue with the idea of ending what he termed the southern monopoly of government. Candidly admitting that he was "very imperfectly acquainted" with the issue of slavery per se (upon which he had "not bestowed much consideration"), King's immediate objective was to re-establish the influence of the northern commercial-manufacturing interest in national affairs. He was not sympathetic to slavery, but that issue was not his primary concern. Nor did many of his associates and supporters give it a high priority. As men who were beginning to see the west as a practical reservoir of economic and political wealth, they were among the first eastern conservatives to redefine the west as a necessity and an opportunity instead of a liability. They were beginning to view the frontier as their utopia, just as had the gentry ever since the 1760s.

When it began, and even throughout its two-year life, the Missouri Crisis was more a fight among political leaders than a great national issue. It had some influence on the congressional elections of 1820, but obviously did not result in a mass attack on either slavery or the south. King turned to northern antislavery advocates for support *after* he launched his campaign. Even more important, it was the strength of the antislavery feeling among southern leaders that provided the key to the final compromise. They admitted that it was a "deplorable evil," and pointed to their active support of the colonization program as proof of their concern.

Concerned about the danger of upsetting the balance of the Constitution, and about the parallel adjustments between the various elements of the political economy, most southern leaders were not only contrite about slavery, but manifestly anxious to compromise. A good many of them agreed with a resolution from Kentucky which defined the danger as that of a congressional usurpation of power; a fear that Congress would emerge from the conflict with the power to subordinate any state "to perpetual vassalage, and reduce it to the condition of a province." And quite aware that the struggle was far more about control of the west than over the institution of slavery, most southerners were always ready to settle for dividing the continent along the latitude line 36° 30' westward from the Mississippi. That was the final result. Losing the support of northerners who were antislavery but not pro-faction, King was defeated.

Men such as John Quincy Adams and [James] Madison were nevertheless deeply disturbed by the implications of the crisis. "Should a state of parties arise founded on geographical boundaries, and other physical and permanent distinctions which happen to coincide with them," Madison fretted, "what is to control those great repulsive masses from awful shocks against each other?" Adams feared that nothing would. [Thomas] Jefferson agreed, but embarked upon a course of action that helped to destroy the very corporate ethic of mercantilism that might have averted the civil war. Recommending that the University of Virginia define education as teaching its students to be self-conscious southerners, and advising his compatriots to send their sons to such reliable schools instead of to northern institutions, he encouraged a thoroughly conservative, even negative, kind of regionalism. Repudiating his earlier support for manufactures, he denounced protection and emphasized the virtues of physiocracy. In view of his remark that John Taylor of Caroline followed the true philosophy but was unfortunately crying in the wilderness, Jefferson's actions suggest that he decided to join Taylor and transform the wilderness into a southern paradise. Certainly that was the impression and the advice that he bequeathed to his successors.

Implicitly, therefore, Jefferson finally provided a definition of the good society. It was a version of the physiocratic feudal utopia uncontaminated by outside influences and maintaining itself through the magic of the frontier and free trade. Together with Taylor, Jefferson thus created the illusion that ultimately became the romantic fiction of the ante-bellum south—a land of magnolias, mammies, and maidens watched over by benign and benevolent barons. Had he instead freed his slaves (even sending them to Africa), and thus honored the vision of a feudal utopia (for serfs were *not* slaves), the image of him as an apostle of American democracy would then have more substance. But in the end he was unable to define freedom save in terms of personal property in the form of other human beings.

ADAMS, MONROE, MARSHALL, AND CLAY—PROTAGONISTS
OF AN AMERICAN SYSTEM

For the time, however, the implications and the consequences of
the positions taken by King and Jefferson were overshadowed by the
last accomplishments of American mercantilism. Perhaps the most
striking of these was the role of internal improvements in sustaining
national development despite an extended period of economic slug-
gishness and rapidly increasing immigration. Roughly 14,000 people
entered America from abroad during every year of the 1820s. Their
spirit and skills no doubt put a floor under the confidence of
Americans at a time (e.g., 1824) when corn sold for eight cents a
bushel, wheat for twenty-five, and a barrel of flour brought $1.25.
Such figures can be misleading if read to mean a prolonged,
desperate depression. The country maintained and even extended the
development of its resources throughout the decade. But measured
against the rapid growth during the years of the embargo, and
particularly the immediate postwar years, the figures indicated a
slower rate of economic progress.

A good many mercantilists concluded that these conditions provided the best argument against laissez faire. "Whatever may be the
abstract doctrine in favor of unrestricted commerce," President
Monroe remarked in his annual message of December 3, 1822, the
necessary conditions have "never occurred, and cannot be expected."
Unlike an increasing number of southerners, Monroe also continued
to favor tariff protection for manufactures. Anticipating the day that
America would be "a manufacturing country on an extensive scale,"
and having given "full consideration" to the opposition arguments,
he recommended "additional protection" in December, 1823. And
despite the growing propensity of manufacturers to view the tariff as
a policy for them to manipulate for the narrow advantage of their
interest or faction, most supporters of the act of 1824 still viewed it as
within the framework of mercantilism.

Henry Clay also intensified his labors in behalf of the program of
internal improvements and tariffs that he began calling "an American System." "Commerce will regulate itself!" he sarcastically conceded to his critics. "Yes, and the extravagance of a spendthrift
heir...will regulate itself ultimately." Clay argued that the constitu-
tionality of internal improvements, as well as the delegation of
explicit powers such as those over commerce, was settled by prece-

dent, and his efforts in Congress were mainly directed toward holding enough southern votes to pass various pieces of legislation. He was aided by Hezekiah Niles and Matthew Carey, who advocated the American System incessantly in *Niles Weekly Register* and countless articles and pamphlets.

More sophisticated popular arguments were advanced by Frederick List, who was accurately described by a contemporary as a "high-class publicist." Probably the most respectable theoretical argument for the American System came from Daniel Raymond, whose *Thoughts on Political Economy* (1820) was the most systematic endeavor to recapitulate the ideas of British mercantilists and apply them to the American scene. In reality, the efforts of List and Raymond were feeble echoes of the English giants such as [Sir William] Petty, [Sir Josiah] Child, and [Sir James] Steuart,[4] and none of them could overcome the suspicion that they were spokesmen for an industrial faction that was merely using the rhetoric of mercantilism for furthering the objectives of an interest group.

Intellectually as well as politically, therefore, Clay received his most effective help from Monroe and Adams. Both men realized that there was more to mercantilism than economics. Monroe persisted in his conviction that "one system" of interrelated and balanced parts would accomplish "great national purposes" and "promote the welfare of the whole." Despite its rambling and redundant length, Monroe's special message of 1822 on internal improvements is one of the most illuminating and rewarding documents of the era. Written to explain his veto of a particular bill, the essay was a noble plea for a constitutional amendment that would save the whole idea of an interconnected and mutually responsible system.

Monroe warned of three basic dangers confronting the nation. Continued expansion without a sense of corporate responsibility would produce "sectional interests, feelings, and prejudices" that might disrupt "the bond of union itself." But undertaken without a constitutional amendment, internal improvements would also upset the balance of the Constitution and produce tyranny and ultimate violence. Furthermore—and here Monroe was clearly speaking for the southerners who had reacted so vigorously against the implications of the Missouri Crisis, as well as for all men of property—such action without a constitutional amendment would establish ominous precedents for outright seizure or infringement of private property.

4. Petty, Child, and Steuart were leading British mercantilists, the first two serving as advisers to the first Earl of Shaftesbury.—ED.

But Monroe's concern for the rights of private property should not be wholly attributed to the rising vehemence of southern concern for slavery. For one thing, his essay came four or five years before that outcry began its first crescendo. More importantly, the conflict between the rights of property and the common good was a dilemma implicit in mercantilist thought. Monroe put his finger on the conflict and asked for a public resolution. Without an amendment, there was no warrant to allow property "to be examined by men of science;...to authorize commissioners to lay off the roads and canals;...to take the land at a valuation if necessary, and to construct the works." Nor was there any sanction to go into business on such an extensive scale. Failing any such amendment, Monroe could only fall back on the magic of expansion to provide a way out of the impasse. America had a "system capable of expansion over a vast territory not only without weakening either [state or national] government, but enjoying the peculiar advantage of adding thereby new strength and vigor."

John Quincy Adams was more willing to devalue property rights in favor of the general welfare. His first annual message of December 6, 1825, was thus the great statement of the philosophy and the domestic program of American mercantilism. Two issues lay at the heart of the problem; "the dominion of man over himself" as well as over other people and nature, and the responsibility of the present generation for "the unborn millions of our posterity." Hence Americans "must still, as heretofore, take counsel from their duties, rather than their fears." Adams was unquestionably a Calvinist, and the rigors of that philosophy no doubt cramped his personal style, but he was also a man who belied the common assumption that a Calvinist lived in fear. He challenged America to become truly unique by mastering its fears. It was Jefferson and his followers who did not face up to the tension that freedom involved. They denied it was possible to be free *and* disciplined. Adams insisted that was the only meaningful definition of freedom.

"The great object of civil government," Adams declared in his first message, "is the improvement of the condition of those who are parties to the social compact." To that end he recommended "laws promoting the improvement of agriculture, commerce, and manufactures, the cultivation and encouragement of the mechanic[al] and of the elegant arts." His Secretary of the Treasury, Richard Rush, filed a support report which expanded on this "intimate connection" between manufactures "and the wealth, the power, and the happiness of the country," and proposed "timely and judicious measures" designed to "organize the whole labor" of the country in order "to lift up [its] condition." Speaking directly on his own, Adams concluded his message with a set of detailed proposals embracing roads and canals, a national university, scientific exploration and research, and literature. And as proof that men could put the common good above personal and party considerations, he proceeded to make presidential appointments (even in the cabinet) on the basis of quality rather than political allegiance.

Nor were the results of this movement for an American System limited to such rigorous and moving documents. Notwithstanding his reluctance to move very far without full constitutional sanction, and despite the growing opposition from southerners, Monroe did approve the General Survey Act of 1824, and that law introduced a period of extensive involvement. River and lighthouse appropriations were followed by a whole series of government interventions in the form of stock purchases in mixed enterprises. Government became an economic partner, for example, in the Chesapeake and Delaware Canal, the Louisville Canal (around the falls on the Ohio), the development of the Dismal Swamp route, and the Chesapeake and Ohio Canal.

In four years the Adams Administration spent almost as much on internal improvements as had been allocated in the previous twenty-four. Indeed, by 1826 the government was the largest single economic entrepreneur in the country. It handled more funds, employed more people, purchased more goods, and borrowed more operating and investment capital than any other enterprise. For generations that are reputed to have believed in weak and minimal government, the Founding Fathers and their first offspring created a rather large and active institution. A coincidence of ground-breaking ceremonies on July 4, 1828, was to symbolize both their accomplishments and the persistence of the pattern they established. Only a few miles away from where Adams turned dirt for the Potomac-Ohio Canal, other men were to begin the first railroad to the west. And the principle of government assistance to private companies was to know no greater application than in the pattern of land grants to railroads unless, perhaps, it was in the direct and indirect subsidies to corporation enterprise during World War I and World War II.

In their own time, Monroe and Adams also facilitated and approved the continued recovery and maturation of the national bank. Having saved it from its own worst enemies and rehabilitated its routine operations, Langdon Cheves resigned. He had taken as much abuse as he could stand and far more than most men would have endured. Nicholas Biddle of Philadelphia succeeded him. In Bray Hammond's recent words, "as naive as one to whom the world has been singularly kind may be," Biddle was somewhat like Adams in thinking that the effective and responsible performance of public duties was sufficient to its own perpetuation.

But Biddle was quite unlike Adams in being a man who reveled in the pleasures of life while discharging its duties. He could write a bit of witty, flirtatious doggerel to a casual female acquaintance that made Adams's labored efforts at poetry seem as brittle as baked raw clay. He could also be as unyielding as a granite crag to stockholders who complained that his profit reports were too skimpy. Biddle managed the bank to facilitate the development of the country without the wild ups-and-downs so often characteristic of an expanding economic system. He did a better job than the directors of the Bank of England. Under his leadership the bank not only established a national system of credit balancing which assisted the west as much as the east, and probably more, but sought with considerable success to save smaller banks from their own inexperience and greed. It was ultimately his undoing, for what the militant advocates of laissez nous faire[5] came to demand was helping without responsibilities. In their minds, at any rate, that was the working definition of democratic freedom.

Their first attempt to destroy the bank by bleeding it to death through local taxes was blocked by Chief Justice John Marshall, who wrote the principles of American mercantilism into the legal procedure and the law of the land. Even before Marshall laid down such guideposts, however, the lower courts had affirmed one of those principles in cases dealing with labor-union action. During the colonial and revolutionary periods, some local mechanics had organized by trades (in particular the shoemakers and tailors), and by 1799 they were bargaining collectively with employers and using such weapons as the strike and the social boycott to strengthen their position. A strike of this kind in Philadelphia raised the issue whether the mercantilist industrial code of Tudor England was to apply in America. At first upheld in all particulars, it was used to declare that even combinations to raise wages were illegal conspiracies against the common good.

5. A doctrine of individualism based on the belief that competition between enlightened self-interests will contribute to the general welfare.—ED.

That total proscription was modified by a New York court in 1809 by a decision legalizing organizations to improve wages. But further action which was "too arbitrary and coercive, and which went to deprive their fellow citizens of rights as precious as any they contend for" was defined as conspiracy. The distinction was reinforced by a Pittsburgh decision in 1815 which proscribed mechanics from acting "by direct means to impoverish or prejudice a third person, or to do acts prejudicial to the community." Later cases during the 1820s upheld that view. As in England, such an outlook was not only mercantilist in its explicit references to the corporate responsibility of labor organizations, and in its clear attack on the monopoly power of guilds, but its implicit meaning was very similar—labor would benefit with and from the general improvement of the political economy.

Marshall's Supreme Court decisions were important because he was concerned to strengthen such a national system and because he, too, ruled against monopolies in the economic sphere. As a member of the Virginia gentry with holdings in land, insurance companies, canals, banks, and even early railroad ventures, Marshall was a firm advocate of mercantilism. He favored a "paternal legislature" that would support internal improvements through mixed companies and in other ways encourage and regulate the economy. Thus he upheld the sanctity of contracts and included charters of incorporation within that definition.

On the other hand, he sensed the potential danger of corporations being given a certain kind of "immortality" and "individuality" by such rulings. He explicitly declared, in any event, that a corporation should "not share in the civil government of the country." Acts of incorporation did not confer an individuality that gave "political power or political character." It would appear that Marshall was trying through such specific restrictions to prevent the development of what later Americans described as the "invisible government" of large corporate enterprises. He also invalidated monopoly charters, as in the case of *Gibbons* v. *Ogden* (1824) concerning a steamboat franchise in New York. These decisions bear a striking resemblance to the key documents of the struggles in England to open up the system created by mercantilism, and yet at the same time prevent any one element from destroying the balance of the political economy.

Marshall had already pointed out in the case concerning the national bank (*McCulloch* v. *Maryland*, 1819) that "a corporation is never used for its own sake, but for the purpose of effecting something else." Thus the bank was constitutional because the government was "intrusted with such ample powers, on the due execution of which the happiness and prosperity of the nation so vitally depends." He added somewhat later that the purpose of the Constitution was "to maintain an uniform and general system." "Throughout this vast republic, from the St. Croix to the Gulf of Mexico, from the Atlantic to the Pacific, revenue is to be collected and expended, armies are to be marched and supported." Marshall's support for expansion, which became explicit in his decision in the case of *American Insurance Company* v. *Canter* (1828), was implicit in his mercantilism and sharpened by his fear of what would happen if it stopped. He fretted that "the price of labor will cheapen, until it affords a bare subsistence to the laborer."

Marshall's thoroughly mercantilist decisions were delivered in a prose that was as vigorous as his philosophy. For that matter, most of the great art of the Age of Mercantilism appeared in the constant discussions and debates over the problems of the political economy. Some of the speeches during the Missouri Crisis, for example, were magnificent rhetorical achievements. Rufus King and William Pinckney were particularly powerful and stylish. John Sergeant of Pennsylvania won a unique accolade from Randolph of Roanoke, who at his best could crack syntax like a whip. *"Never speak again! Never speak again!"* cried Randolph, half-persuaded by the performance.

John Quincy Adams also provided a good many documents of enduring literary significance. So had Madison, whose letter to Jefferson of October 24, 1787, in which he reviewed the proceedings of the constitutional convention, outlined the "feudal system of republics," and summarized his theory of expansion, provided a typical display of his abilities and set a high standard of performance. Adams nevertheless produced several items that were superior. His diary, for example, can be resisted only by those whose feeling for life is so underdeveloped as to count as nonexistent. And his *Report Upon Weights and Measures* is in many respects the classic document of the Age of Mercantilism. It is philosophy, ethics, political economy, and policy integrated in a government report that he wrote while executing a particularly heavy load of duties as Secretary of State.

Pointing out that men began by measuring everything in terms of their own bodies, Adams argued that the formation of society demanded that they get beyond this egoistic universe of the self. One's identity must be sustained through a sense of proportion based upon an acceptance of standards designed to order "the multiplying relations between man and man now superadded to those between man and things." Such "standards should be *just*" and "uniform" because of their great "influence upon the happiness and upon the morals of nations." The issue is of "momentous importance" because it affects such apparently disconnected elements as the safety of seamen and the welfare of the individual housewife. "The home, the market, the shop" have to trust each other: a contradictory, double standard "enters every house, it cripples every hand," and thus effects the "well-being of every man, woman, and child, in the community." No other philosopher or political economist in the world ever personalized and humanized the elementary problem of weights and measures—or any other mundane but vital element of their system—in a comparable manner. The document was, and remains, a magnificent triumph of the *Weltanschauung* of mercantilism that transcends its time and place.

THE MONROE DOCTRINE AS THE MANIFESTO OF THE AMERICAN EMPIRE

Adams also played a key role in formulating the Monroe Doctrine, a statement of the expansionism inherent in American mercantilism that was clearly the manifesto of the American empire. Though it is generally treated as the cornerstone of American diplomacy, most analyses of the doctrine emphasize its negative aspects. It is thus presented as a defensive statement of the territorial and administrative integrity of North and South America: no further colonization, no transfer or extension of existing claims, and in return America would not interfere in European affairs. This standard interpretation neglects three major facts: the men who formulated it were concerned as much with European commercial and economic expansion as with its schemes for colonization; they viewed it as a positive, expansionist statement of American supremacy in the hemisphere, and Monroe actually intervened in European politics with the very same speech in which he asserted that Europe should stay out of American affairs.

Aware that the political economy of the United States was established, and properly interpreting the results of the War of 1812 as being fundamentally favorable to its position in the hemisphere, American leaders reached an obvious conclusion. If they could exclude further European penetration as Spain's authority collapsed, then the United States would remain as the predominant power in the hemisphere. Monroe thus reasserted the expansionist thesis at the end of his message of December 2, 1823, which announced the doctrine. Having urged further support for manufactures and internal improvements, as well as warning Europe off Latin America while he encouraged the Greek revolution, he concluded with this well-nigh classic paraphrase of Madison's theory. "It is manifest that by enlarging the basis of our system, and increasing the number of States, the system itself has been greatly strengthened in both its [state and national] branches. Consolidation and disunion have thereby been rendered equally impracticable."

As one who was equally familiar with Madison's theory of expansion (he mentioned it specifically in his eulogy of Madison), Adams fully expected the United States to acquire Cuba, Texas, and other tidbits of territory in North America. But he was at least as concerned with establishing American commercial supremacy as he was with blocking further colonial experiments by European nations. This balanced expansionist sentiment behind the Monroe Doctrine was well revealed in the congressional discussions about Oregon which some thought was threatened by Russia as well as by England. Francis Baylies of Massachusetts might have been expected to concern himself with the "magnificent prospects" of the Pacific commerce, but he also quoted Napoleon to emphasize his support for territorial expansion: he "never uttered words of more wisdom than when he said, 'I want ships, commerce, and colonies.'" Robert Wright of Maryland called for expansion because "there is less danger of separatism in a confederacy of 20 or 30 States than in one of a smaller number."

Senator James Barbour agreed. "Our advance in political science has already cancelled the dogmas of theory. We have already ascertained ... that republics are not necessarily limited to small territories.... Whether America is capable of indefinite extent, must be left to posterity to decide." And speaking for a growing consensus, John Floyd of Virginia accurately concluded that "all contemplate with joy" continued westward expansion. It would provide land for farmers, "procure and protect the fur trade," "engross the whale trade," and "control the South Sea trade.... All this rich commerce could be governed, if not engrossed, by capitalists at Oregon."

Adams shared such commercial interest in the Northwest, and it contributed to his thinking about the Monroe Doctrine. Even more in his mind, however, was the importance of trade with Latin

America. By 1820, when Adams, in his instructions to American agents, described it as "deserving of particular attention," this trade had developed into a significant commerce that vigorous European intervention would curtail and perhaps even destroy. Baltimore specialized in flour and furniture, but Salem, New York, Philadelphia, and even New Orleans, shipped shoes, cotton textiles, fertilizer, pitch, and lumber into such cities as Rio de Janeiro. The carrying trade was also important. American shippers carried Asian goods to Chile, Argentine beef to Cuba, and European items to the entire region. British agents reported to Foreign Secretary George Canning that Americans controlled the Argentine flour market, that their tonnage in Uruguay was "greater than that of any other nation," and that Peru's commerce with Asia "has been entirely engrossed by the North Americans."

Aware of this strong position, Henry Clay predicted that in half a century Americans, "in relation to South America," would "occupy the same position as the people of New England do to the rest of the United States." The implications of Clay's remark unquestionably disturbed some southerners in 1820 as much as the validity of his prediction was to upset Latin Americans in the 20th century. His enthusiastic campaign to establish an American System embracing the hemisphere was important for several reasons. Promising "mercantile profits," an influx of Spanish gold, and markets for the farmers and other entrepreneurs of the Mississippi west, he also assured his countrymen that the expansion of America's ideological principles would provide military as well as economic security. Being like the United States, he argued, the new countries would not be prone to oppose its basic policies.

Adams was wary of Clay's rambunctious ideological assertiveness, but he was fully agreed on the importance of commercial activity. His instructions of May 27, 1823, to an American agent who was being sent to Colombia left no doubt about his basic strategy. The American political economy was now strong enough to take advantage of its great relative superiority over the emerging new nations. "As navigators and manufacturers, *we* are already so far advanced in a career upon which *they* are yet to enter," he explained, "that we may, for many years after the conclusion of the war, maintain with them a commercial intercourse, highly beneficial to both parties, as *carriers* to and for them of numerous articles of manufacture and foreign produce."

As he explicitly noted, Adams was aware that the United States had reached the point anticipated by Washington in his Farewell Address: the *Weltanschauung* and the political economy of mercantilism had built a nation strong enough to secure many of its objectives through economic power. And on becoming President he proceeded to act upon the fact, recommending in 1826 that the United States attend and take the lead in a proposed conference of the new Spanish-American republics. Explaining to the Congress what Washington had meant, Adams pointedly drew the obvious conclusion. "Must we not say," he asked rhetorically, "that the period which he predicted as then not far off has arrived?" The answer was obviously "Yes," and Adams proposed to adjust the nation's foreign policy to fit the new circumstances. Economic predominance would mean effective control without limiting America's freedom of action.

But Adams ran into stiff opposition. Southerners disliked his proposal on several counts. They understood the domestic implications of his remarks about a mature economy—it meant a weakening of their position. Many of them also coveted Cuba as new slave territory, and they were not interested in encouraging the general revolutionary fervor lest it triumph on the island in the form of a colored republic—or at home as slave revolts. Even more significant, however, was the criticism leveled at Adams by a good many northerners. They cornered him with his own earlier opposition to indiscriminate expansion. Far from representing merely a delaying action by the south, the debate over the Panama Conference was a fundamental argument about America's mercantilist foreign policy and its implications for future domestic affairs.

THE UNRESOLVED DILEMMA OF AMERICAN MERCANTILISM

Neither Adams nor other leaders could any longer evade the issue: Was expansion so absolutely essential to American democracy and prosperity that it had to be sustained despite the fact that it might well subvert the basic principles of self-government, and even the existence of the union? Adams might draw a distinction between territorial expansion and expanded trade connections but that did not enable him to wriggle free of the dilemma. For he wanted Texas and the Pacific coast, and he understood perfectly the political consequences of America's greater economic power in dealing with underdeveloped nations. Nor was he unaware of the implications of all the agitation to spread American ideas, principles, and institutions throughout the world.

As early as 1821, on the Fourth of July, in fact, he had delivered a devastating criticism of that kind of expansion. The true America, he warned, "goes not abroad in search of monsters to destroy.... She well knows that by once enlisting under other banners than her own, were they even the banners of foreign independence, she would involve herself, beyond the power of extrication, in all the wars of interest and intrigue, of individual avarice, envy, and ambition, which assume the colors and usurp the standard of freedom.... She might become the dictatress of the world; she would no longer be the ruler of her own spirit."

Having rendered this unequivocal judgment, Adams might well have squirmed five years later when Senator Levi Woodbury of New Hampshire rose in Congress to ask if the President still adhered to that standard. "Are we so moonstruck, or so little employed at home, as, in the eloquent language of our President on another occasion, ... to wander around abroad in search of foreign monsters to destroy?" Representative Alexander Smyth of Virginia spoke for still others who opposed any effort "to propagate our system on the other side of the Atlantic." "If there be a mode of destroying civil liberty," he echoed Adams, "it is by leading this Government into unnecessary wars."

The hour of decision had arrived. In one area, moreover, the mercantilists responded with great moral courage and *élan*. All the key leaders opposed the rising tide of laissez-faire aggressiveness against the Indians. Whatever the inherent "difficulty" or related political problems connected with dealing with them equitably, warned Madison, "it is due to humanity" to make such efforts. "They have claims on the magnanimity, and, I may add," Monroe agreed, "on the justice of this nation, which we must all feel." At least [Secretary of War John C.] Calhoun did, and vigorously asserted that "on every principle of humanity the continuance of similar advantages of education ought to be extended to them." For the doubters, he had extensive evidence gathered from experienced teachers. It was "almost uniformly favorable, both as to the capacity and docility of the youths. Their progress appears to be quite equal to that of white children of the same age; and they appear to be equally susceptible of acquiring habits of industry." Hence the nation should put an end to the "evil" of "the incessant pressure of our population, which forces" the Indians out of their homes despite treaties to the contrary.

Adams and Clay agreed, and made vigorous efforts to prevent

Georgia from uprooting Indians who were accepting the ways of American civilization. But confronted with a choice between federal troops in the south or the defeat of the Indians, Adams acquiesced. Georgia drove them west. It was a wrenching choice, and perhaps a fateful one; seeing one state defy the national government with impunity, Mississippi followed the same course and also succeeded. Far more than either the Kentucky Resolutions of 1799, or the South Carolina proclamation nullifying the tariff of 1832, it was the actions of Georgia and Mississippi that laid out the route to secession.

Perhaps Adams sensed this implication, for he ultimately concluded that domestic reforms took priority over further expansion. In that respect, at any rate, Adams proved capable of breaking free of the expansionist dogma of mercantilism. That had not been the case with Monroe. He had admitted that "so seducing is the passion for extending our territory" that it might destroy the union. But he had held fast to the concept of mercantilist empire, denying that expansion subverted republicanism. "On the contrary," he proclaimed on May 4, 1822, "it is believed that the greater the expansion, within practicable limits, and it is not easy to say what are not so, the greater the advantage which the States individually will derive from it.... It must be obvious to all, that the further expansion is carried, provided it be not beyond the just limit, the greater will be the freedom of action to both [national and state] governments." There could be no misunderstanding Monroe's choice. "There is no object," he asserted in his last annual message on December 7, 1824, "no object which, as a people, we can desire, which we do not possess, or which is not within our reach." In Monroe's mind, at any rate, expansion was one "of our institutions."

Clay came to doubt whether the beneficent results of expansion were so "obvious." He and Adams shared by 1828 a "great concern" over the implications of the expansionist thesis. But in fundamental respects it was Clay who made the most astute and devastating analysis of the danger and proposed the most relevant remedy. Even as early as 1820 he sensed that "a new epoch has arisen," and called America "deliberately to contemplate" the changed situation. "The call for free trade," he concluded in 1832, "is as unavailing, as the cry of a spoiled child in its nurse's arms, for the moon, or the stars that glitter.... It has never existed, it never will exist."

Clay understood that free trade defined in that manner was little more than a euphemism for a massive commercial empire. It was, "in effect," he concluded, "the British colonial system that we are invited to adopt." Then he quoted a British leader to make the point absolutely clear: "'Other nations knew, as well as [ourselves], what we meant by "free trade" was nothing more nor less than, by means of the great advantages we enjoyed, to get a monopoly of all their markets for our manufactures, and to prevent them, one and all, from ever becoming manufacturing nations.'" It was therefore a choice, concluded Clay, between making the home market "first in order" or embarking on a search "for new worlds ... for new and unknown races of mortals to consume this immense [surplus] of cotton fabrics."

Not only did Clay thus attack the very plan that Adams had advanced in 1823 for structuring America's future relations with Latin America, but he drew an amazingly accurate picture of the policy American manufacturers would advocate and help establish within less than 65 years. For by the 1890s, when they became deeply worried by precisely such surpluses, manufacturers of textiles and other goods turned to Asia and Latin America for markets, and to their own government for aid and assistance in exploiting their "great advantages" over the economy of underdeveloped countries. Both in its early part and at the end of the 19th century, their American system differed considerably from the one Clay had in mind.

Yet American mercantilists had built an economic and political system strong and flexible enough to survive 60 years of sustained exploitation and misuse by the advocates of laissez nous faire who triumphed in 1828. They even provided many of the central ideas that later Americans turned to in an effort to restore some balance, meaning, and purpose to their society. The accomplishments of the three Adamses, Madison, Jefferson, Washington, Gallatin,[6] Calhoun, and Monroe comprised a truly magnificent testimony to the relevance and the quality of the mercantilist *Weltanschauung*, and to the spirit and energy of the Americans who transformed it into institutions and an established political economy. In fundamental respects, and to an extensive degree, Americans have been, and still are, living off the intellectual and economic capital accumulated during the Age of Mercantilism.

This very durability of some of their ideas makes it easier to recognize and understand their failures. Perhaps the most apparent

6. Albert Gallatin (1761–1849), statesman, diplomat, and ethnologist, served as secretary of the treasury under Jefferson and Madison and later as minister to France and England.—ED.

weakness of their outlook lies in their argument that representative government, economic prosperity, and personal happiness all depend on expansion. They formulated this idea so rigorously and advanced it so vigorously and persuasively that Americans have never been able to examine it critically in an equally disciplined spirit. Until past the middle of the 20th century, at any rate, it became an integral part of their emotional and even psychological make-up. The power and persistence of ideas in the face of changing reality was never more amply documented. Whether cast in the overt form of slogans about an expanding economy or in the more complex ideology and myth of the frontier, the thesis that wealth and welfare hinged upon expansion provided daily a reminder of the Age of Mercantilism.

But the frontier theory of history was in reality only the most striking symptom of the basic failure of American mercantilism. It had been formulated as an answer to the crucial problem of controlling private property in order to achieve the general welfare. But it was in fact an evasion—and no very subtle or sophisticated one—of that central issue. For, given a continent easily conquered and ruthlessly exploited, it was not too difficult to accumulate the lowest necessary amount of public wealth while at the same time allowing private individuals and groups to acquire unlimited riches. For the same reasons, the expansionist thesis of the mercantilists also encouraged a nonintellectual approach to human affairs. Problems could be solved by growth. For men who valued intellectual achievement so highly, and knew it as vital in providing men with a sense of purpose and meaning, this was perhaps the greatest irony of their own labor and influence.

As the mercantilists knew, the construction of a successful economic system and the acquisition of personal fortunes was not the greater part of their *Weltanschauung*. Beyond those goals they were concerned with the *public* welfare and the spirit of a true corporate commonwealth. Hence the mercantilists were caught in their own argument: if property was essential to the individual's sense of identity, then it was by the same logic the basis of any public identity; the sense of *ours* was as vital as the sense of *mine*. But granted that the circumstances of world war and revolution were extremely difficult and the temptations of a continent extremely great, it is nevertheless true that the mercantilists never overcame their bias in favor of private property.

That they came as close as they did—and with men like Madison, Calhoun, and John Quincy Adams it was very close—is enough to justify high praise. They defined the problems so clearly that no one can ever know them and enter the plea of ignorance. A harsh judgment after the fact is perhaps unnecessary, for their failure brought its own consequences in the triumph of laissez faire. For them that was punishment enough. Unwilling in the final showdown to make a fuller commitment to social property in the name of a corporate commonwealth, they had no effective defense against the men who demanded that private property and interest be given full scope and unrestrained liberty in the name of individualism.

THE AGE OF
LAISSEZ NOUS FAIRE,
1819–1896

[from *The Contours of American History*, 1961]

Laissez-faire marketplace expansion and competition liberated the economic and political forces that dominated American society for most of the nineteenth century. Williams described the changes induced by the triumph of laissez-faire ideology, the opportunities and liberties it provided, and the successes enjoyed by Americans who benefited from the achievements of the marketplace. But he also called attention to inequities and contradictions in the system and noted, with pointed emphasis, that the rewards of laissez faire were gained at substantial cost. Social disorders, a wrenching civil war, and upheavals which accompanied America's rapid industrial growth exacted a high price. Individual failures rivaled successes. In the following selection Williams examined in particular the challenges of rising industrialism, the dilemmas posed by slavery, and the resulting tensions that confronted the theorists and practitioners of laissez faire in the years preceding the Civil War.

Our age is wholly of a different character, and its legislation takes another turn. Society is full of excitement; competition comes in place of monopoly; and intelligence and industry ask only for fair play and an open field.

Daniel Webster, 1824

221

A New Reality for Existing Ideas

[Government] was not intended to...create systems of agriculture, manu-facturing, or trade....Few men can doubt that....A system founded on private interest, enterprise, and competition, without the aid of legislative grants or regulations by law, would rapidly prosper.

Martin Van Buren, 1837

We are for leaving trade free; and the right to combine is an indispensable attribute of its freedom.

William Leggett, 1837

[A corporation] is, indeed, a mere artificial being, invisible and intangible; yet it is a person, for certain purposes in contemplation of law, and has been recognized as such by the decisions of this court.

Chief Justice Roger B. Taney, 1839

The Union, next to our liberty, most dear. May we always remember that it can only be preserved by distributing equally the benefits and burdens of the Union.

John C. Calhoun, 1830

If the State cannot survive the anti-slavery agitation, then let the State perish.

William Lloyd Garrison, 1836

THE THEORY AND THE REALITY OF THE MARKET PLACE

As generally presented and accepted, the *Weltanschauung* of laissez faire was based on what was presumed to be a simple if not obvious truth. Individualized free competition in an open and fair society would produce specific happiness and the general welfare. But the assumption of free competition was actually predicated upon three other unspoken premises: that domestic society was sufficiently balanced and unfettered to insure that such conflict remained crea-tive, that the market place continued to expand, and that other nations accepted and acted on the key axioms. All other things being equal, ran the argument, competition would generate progress.

Yet as Madison, Monroe, and other mercantilists often pointed out, these essential other things never were equal. Various individuals and groups were always insisting that they needed assistance, either to enter the game as an equal or to remain competitors. Often they did need it. Even under the most favorable circumstances, the very process of competition led to the destruction, failure, or bare survival of the less successful. While it promised a diversity of life, therefore, the dynamic of the system carried it toward a situation in which a few triumphant elements dominated the political and social economy. Hence the system always required a considerable amount of tinkering in order to keep it in working condition. Since these realities contradicted the central premise (and corroded the utopia) of the system, it was not unnatural that men were constantly on the lookout to find and eradicate the *one* evil—or to discover the *one* great equalizer—and thus establish the necessary conditions for uninhibited progress toward perfection.

Such troubled advocates of laissez faire faced still another difficulty. Usually thought of as a philosophy and a system of individualism, by which is meant the single human being, the competition and conflict of laissez faire actually occurred at many different levels. In addition to the individual, there were organized groups such as corporations, labor unions, and reformers; political subdivisions such as parties and the states; social and economic units which became self-conscious sections or regions; and, in the broadest sense, nations themselves in the world arena. These units also competed on several levels: economic, political, and intellectual-social. And given the argument that competition produced welfare, it should not be too surprising to realize that laissez faire served subtly (though persuasively) to condition men to accept armed conflict with righteous attitudes.

Hence [Martin] Van Buren's sanguine restatement of the principles of laissez faire as he became President did not match the realities he soon encountered. Government, he reminded the faithful, "was not intended to...create systems of agriculture, manufacturing, or trade." "Few men can doubt," he concluded, "that their own interest as well as the general welfare of the country would be promoted by...a system founded on private interest, enterprise, and competition [which], without the aid of legislative grants or regulations by law, would rapidly prosper."

Honoring the identical faith, Chief Justice Roger B. Taney, who had served earlier as [President Andrew] Jackson's attorney general, rendered a militant decision against monopolies in the Charles River Bridge case. Declaring that restrictive charters delayed progress, and that the country would be "thrown back...to the last century and be obliged to stand still" if they were not destroyed, he announced the new political economy and opened the market place to all competitors. But Taney's opinion also confirmed the corporation as a legitimate unit of competition. And that aspect of the court's decision amounted in the long run to a death sentence for individualized laissez faire, for the independent businessman proved incapable of holding his own against the corporation.

In the short run, however, it was Jackson's economic polity which brought on many of Van Buren's troubles. After destroying the national bank with his veto, Jackson transferred government funds to selected state banks. Already expanding their loans in competition with other local and regional banks, the favored institutions responded by further extending themselves. Accentuating his a priori commitment to hard money, the resulting economic orgy led Jackson to issue his specie circular of 1836, by which he lived up to his ancient preference for precious metal and at the same time sought to stabilize the wild boom. His return to the monetary principles of the Middle Ages would no doubt have pleased John Taylor of Caroline, but it had less happy effects on the political economy.

Unfortunately coinciding with a drop in exports and a poor crop season in 1835, the deflationary monetary circular counterbalanced the effect of distributing over five millions from the treasury surplus to the states (because it removed the specie from the banks), and played a key role in the development of a major crisis. As Jackson had joyfully anticipated, the maneuver toppled many of the speculators whom he thought selfish, unprincipled, and evil. But it also bowled over a good number of upright mechanics, farmers, and small entrepreneurs. Labor leaders such as [William] Leggett of New York had urged and praised the specie circular in the belief that it would give the mechanics an honest wage, undepreciated by inflation and the discounts on the notes of weak banks. But they soon found themselves confronted by increasing prices and growing numbers of unemployed in northern cities. Van Buren's cherished alliance between northern businessmen and mechanics, and southern planters, began to break apart under the pressure of class consciousness and regional economic conflicts.

Organized as the Equal Rights Party even before the shock of the Panic and depression, the more radical wing of New York politics provided an early example of the proliferation of political parties that was characteristic of the age of laissez faire. Often quick to criticize European countries for their multi-party systems, Americans seem prone to forget that between 1836 and 1896, they conducted their own politics in a very similar fashion. Economic and social conflict was the characteristic of the age, and it took political form as early as the 1820s, when a mechanics' organization held the balance of power in Philadelphia. Though with steadily decreasing significance, the phenomenon continued into the 20th century.

Standing for thoroughgoing reform in the tradition of laissez faire, the New York dissidents challenged the aristocratic governors of Van Buren's Regency machine and demanded more vigorous action against local and regional financial powers, a system of direct taxes, and election by direct popular vote. For a moment in February, 1837, when the depression struck hard, they turned to direct action. Urged on by posters that were blunt and threatening—"BREAD, MEAT, RENT, and FUEL! *Their prices must come down!*"—the response was militant. Crowds raided grocery stores and for a period of a few days led some conservatives to fear a general uprising. But the movement's respect (and ambition) for property checked them well short of a fundamental critique of the existing order.

Such conservatism also limited the effectiveness of leaders like Frances Wright, a striking and inspiring woman who combined femininity and social criticism in an explosive package. Mechanics and upper-class reformers responded to her appeals but did not take up her more basic reforms with equal enthusiasm. Indeed, they asked her to play down some of her more fundamental attacks on the system. And early proletarian leaders such as Mike Walsh of New York, who argued that the shift from Monroe and Adams to Jackson and Van Buren was "nothing but a change of masters," attracted an even smaller following. The shock of the panic passed and the labor movement remained an association of would-be entrepreneurs organized to secure reforms that would open the way for them to scramble to the top. Depressions only dramatized labor's commitment to laissez faire; lacking any firm conception of an alternative order, they responded to such crises by competing for the remaining jobs rather than by seizing the opportunity to change the system.

Buffeted by the gales of laissez faire, utopian experiments sank in the sea of continental property. They appeared irrelevant, if not stupid or dangerous, to men who assumed that welfare, and wealth, were a matter of time and labor. Albert Brisbane's image of an America organized in self-sufficient communities of 1,600 souls had little appeal to men whose immediate problem was to dispose of cotton and wheat surpluses. And while John Humphrey Noyes was undoubtedly correct in arguing that the jealousy provoked by property and sex caused a good share of men's troubles, the majority preferred the competition to pre-empt such rights over a disciplined struggle to sublimate their impulses in a co-operative common-wealth. As with [Walt] Whitman, most Americans evaded the challenge of Noyes's communal community at Oneida, New York, by blaming their troubles on other property holders or in joining the free-for-all for more property.

RELIGIOUS HERESY AND THE ASSAULT ON SLAVERY

Having destroyed the bank, that primeval monster in the garden of laissez faire, the Jacksonian safari in search of the secular and institutional evil that would explain the malfunctioning of the system began to converge with a moral crusade developing out of John Locke's definition of the natural (and unnatural) man, the break-down of Calvinism, and the philosophical ruminations of the trans-cendentalists. As the sustained vitality of the revival movement of 1799 and 1800 had suggested, religion in the age of laissez faire was in essence a series of variations on the Arminian heresy that had plagued Calvinism (and Jonathan Edwards) in the New England of the 1730s and 1740s. Encouraged by the secularization of God's will in the philosophy of Adam Smith and his followers, the religious advocates of free will soon reduced Calvin's social morality to a code of personal righteousness that paralleled and reinforced the individu-alism of Locke. The free man thereby became *ipso facto* the moral man. He was also the natural man.

A more portentous distortion of Calvin's corporate philosophy would be difficult to imagine, particularly in a society which had come to define freedom and liberty in terms of the right to vote and the right to become an independent entrepreneur. Here was the bedrock meaning of the transition to laissez faire. American history between 1828 and 1896 is largely the story of the multiple tensions among an attempt to apply the criteria of laissez faire, the realities of the situation, and a growing recognition that the implications of the effort were subversive of the very freedom it was supposed to create and guarantee. For if a man is free only if he holds property, then he is a mere product of material wealth. The new *Weltanschauung* liberated him only to set a horrible trap.

Nothing dramatizes the distortion of Edward's theology more ironically than the role of his brilliant and devoted student, Samuel Hopkins, in transmitting the spirit of the Great Awakening to men who had abandoned the corporate ethic for the Arminianism and secular laissez faire of Stoddard and Whitefield. For himself, Hopkins did not make the equation between morality and laissez-faire individualism. His attacks on slavery stemmed from a corporate philosophy that held all Americans responsible for slavery and hence obligated to devise a mutual and institutional solution. His approach pointed toward some form of emancipation compensated by the national government which would lead into gradual integration of the Negro with the rest of the political and social economy.

This institutional approach to slavery did not disappear with Hopkins. Even some of the transcendentalists like William Ellery Channing, for example, initially (1835) made a similar analysis. And while quite different in being New York businessmen instead of Unitarian ministers, Arthur and Lewis Tappan in the beginning also favored that kind of solution. In the short space of six years, however, both the Tappans and Channing had embraced the kind of individual moralizing that typified the convergence of laissez faire, the secular morality of natural law, transcendentalism, and Arminian Protestantism. As a preacher who took the evangelical fervor of Hopkins and Edwards but abandoned their corporate ethic in favor of individualized religion, Charles G. Finney was a key entrepreneur of that merger. Finney asserted that every man had a responsibility for helping to erect a framework within which every other individual had a chance to save himself. Until late in life, moreover, Finney also believed that he and his associates had the truth that could save anyone.

Religion thus embraced the task of reforming the moral world so that laissez faire could function in the political, social, and economic spheres. Theology had been adapted to the decline of mercantilism and the triumph of laissez faire. And having been so accommodated, it began to function as a powerful engine driving the change on toward its logical conclusion, the purification of the entire system. While ideological pioneers of the 1730s like Stoddard were probably aware that they were changing the essence of Calvin's doctrine to conform to their economic interests, it is unlikely that many Americans of the 1820s and 1830s realized that they were altering their religion. They were not hypocrites. They were simply men of their era who had never been trained or encouraged or led to examine— let alone question—the relationship between their interests and their ideas.

Just as Jackson had defined and asserted the essential supremacy of the national framework of the political economy against the freedom of a single element like South Carolina, so religious leaders like Finney and Theodore Dwight Weld asserted the moral imperatives of the order. Only moral men could attain the general welfare through the indulgence of their various self-interests. Since only free men could be moral, the slaveholder was by definition the most immoral. But free men had also slipped into evil ways. Having thus declared open season on the whole of human error (or as they termed it, sin), the moral reformers undertook a good many crusading expeditions into the jungle of man's fallibility. Their base camp was a privately recreated universe roughly comparable to the environment of the Old Testament—once again it was the Chosen People against all comers in a fight for righteousness.

Some reformers no doubt saw themselves as heroes in the romantic novels of Sir Walter Scott that enjoyed such tremendous popularity in the United States, but then many southern slaveholders did the same. Each group brought more to Scott than it took away. It seems more probable that they were men who either made the transition from mercantilism already possessing a strong moral system, or emerged in the world of laissez faire and proceeded, either by conviction or revelation, to define it in terms of religious morality. John Quincy Adams offers a good illustration of the first category which further suggests that the older group was strongly inclined toward an institutional resolution of the slavery issue.

Younger men like Finney and Weld were advocates of laissez faire. But being men of religious conviction, they could hardly be expected to become entrepreneurs in the ordinary sense. They saw themselves as trustees whose basic interest and responsibility in a laissez faire world was the business of reform. It appears more than coincidental, for example, that the Tappan brothers also established the first credit-rating system in the country. Their emphasis on the need for a set of fixed and well-defined rules by which to play the game does a great deal to explain the support they received from the middle class. Men of that group wanted guarantees that their enterprise would be rewarded. And the steady transformation of the abolitionist crusade into an antislavery campaign for free land suggests even more strongly that the underlying element in the situation was the *Weltanschauung* of laissez faire.

Seen through the prisms of religious forms and language, the secular principles of laissez faire appeared as a utopian revelation. Though fears of economic competition played an overt role to some extent, most of the violent and bigoted reaction against the increasing number of immigrants (7,912 in 1824, 76,242 in 1836, and 369,980 in 1850) was anti-Catholic in origin. It was grounded in the view of Catholicism as the worst of the old corporate and institutional religions headed by evil men who crushed liberty and violated freedom. The burning of a Massachusetts convent in 1834, the combined anti-Catholic and antislavery actions of men like Lyman Beecher, and the formation of the Native American Association in 1837 were thoroughly entwined aspects of the same outlook. A similar antagonism manifested itself in the anti-Masonic agitation of 1827–1831 in New York. Here again the relationship between the axioms of laissez faire and the definition of the enemy is apparent. Going rapidly into politics, the anti-Masons became the first third party to stage an open national nominating convention (1831).

Other reformers concentrated on the dangers of tobacco, alcohol, and meat-eating. While the crusades for temperance and a pure American race remained serious forces in American politics for nearly a century, the antislavery campaign soon became the dominant theme of the general drive to establish a proper moral framework for laissez faire. The sermon was appropriately simple: abolish slavery and the free system would flourish beyond all dreams. Along with Weld and Finney, William Lloyd Garrison completed the transition to a wholly individualized definition of the problem. Slaveholders became *the* evil, and nothing mitigated their sin. The trouble was bad *men*, not an institution.

Garrison hurled the absolute challenge. "If the State cannot survive the anti-slavery agitation, then let the State perish." Even though they were uneasy over slavery, the great majority of Americans drew back from such extreme abolitionists whose reform threatened the very system it was supposed to save. Garrison and others were physically attacked by northerners in several states, and leaders from all parts of the country, whatever their views on slavery, grew increasingly concerned to limit the impact of the agitation. But absolutist language finally provoked the irrevocable act: in 1837 abolitionist editor Elijah Lovejoy was murdered by a mob in Alton, Illinois.

Men like Garrison were exhilarated. The tragedy gave them a martyr and forced the country to confront the issue more directly. It also brought the abolitionists new converts like the wealthy and talented Wendell Phillips, some of them becoming key leaders in later transforming abolitionism into a more general political movement. Weld further stirred the fire by publishing his exposé of the evil, *American Slavery as I See It*, in 1839. As an indictment of the slaveholder, his tract typified the extreme individualist nature of the abolitionist movement. And despite the fact that Weld was willing to accept the Negro as a man capable of equal achievement, he offered no plan for dealing with the results of emancipation.

Perhaps nothing so reveals the crucial role of laissez-faire philosophy in understanding the abolitionists: whether they agreed with Weld about the capabilities of the Negro, or held him to be an inferior person, as most did, they simply assumed that he would take his place as a competitive unit in the system. Preferring to ignore the moral implications of the freedom to starve, the abolitionists also escaped the need to think seriously about their own responsibilities as liberators—or about the possibility that an institutional approach to slavery might produce more effective and more moral results. But the abolitionists were in the mainstream of what is generally called American radicalism. It was a radicalism that defined the individual's freedom from restraint as the crucial element of the good society. It rejected the idea of restrictions or discipline being accepted in order to establish and sustain the circumstances for individual and group creativity. That was dismissed as conservative or reactionary. Such a radicalism relied on expansion to underwrite its individualized freedom, and in keeping with that pattern the abolitionist movement soon embraced such a program.

In the meantime, the crisis generated by Lovejoy's murder marked the high point of the early abolitionist movement. In little more than a decade it had introduced and sustained the idea of direct action to resolve a national issue and had established an absolute definition of democracy that excluded many men, if not an entire section, on the grounds that it (or they) were evil. But it also strengthened the less extremist wing of the antislavery movement. Men who were appalled by Garrison's vulgarity, irresponsibility, and questionable sincerity turned to political action in support of a program to end slavery within a Constitutional framework. Organized in 1838–1839 around James G. Birney, an ex-Kentucky slaveholder, the Liberty Party won an immediate response in New York. Despite its more moderate tone and policy, it was interpreted by edgy southerners as a political force that might someday turn the power of the central government against them in favor of abolition. Northern purists, on the other hand, slandered it as an agent of the Devil.

THE EVOLUTION OF THE SOUTHERN PREDICAMENT

The impact of these early moral, ideological, and political attacks by the abolitionists was increased because they hit the south during a critical juncture in the area's development. The old seaboard south seemed to have entered the last stage of its decline as a center of commodity agriculture. Slave prices, for example, had fallen to $400 by 1828. This produced in Virginia, among other consequences, a new generation of leaders seriously interested in working out some program for ending slavery. Though largely upper-class conservatives, these men negotiated a tenuous alliance with western yeomen, a coalition that they hoped would give them the power to adjust Virginia's economy to the new industrial and agricultural order. They were opposed by established planters who feared a wholesale assault on property rights as well as upon their existing position, and who were appalled by the prospect of a sizable plurality of free Negroes. In many respects, therefore, the situation can be understood as the moment of truth for Washington's old idea that Virginia should diversify its economy and in that manner end slavery and maintain its position of national leadership.

The two groups clashed in the Virginia Constitutional Convention of 1830 in one of the crucial debates in American history. Erupting in the context of a depression in tobacco, cotton, and slave prices, the conflict seemed at first to veer in favor of those who proposed an institutional approach to emancipation. But entrenched in political and social power, and making effective use of the specter of abolitionism and a society dominated by free Negroes, as well as emphasizing the expense of compensated emancipation, the defenders of slavery finally won. The debate continued in the first sessions of the new legislature, however, because of the continuing strength of the antislavery group and in response to the crisis provoked when a free Negro preacher named Nat Turner sparked a slave uprising in 1831. Pointing to the key role of the free Negro in all slave revolts, and to the free-wheeling operations of others like William Johnson of Natchez (a barber who became a model of laissez-faire entrepreneurship), the proslavery group overrode its critics.

Antislavery organizations all but vanished from the south within five years. Slavery's victory was consolidated by the revival of commodity prices, the increasing intensity and vitriol of Garrison's attacks, and the developing division of the west into northern and southern sections. A good many commentators have concluded that the combination of the Erie Canal and the cotton gin produced the Civil War, and in a highly generalized sense the observation has validity. But it overlooks the crucial role of foreign markets for cotton and for the food crops of northern farmers, and it neglects the simultaneous expansion of the home market. That revival and expansion of the market was the key to the rapidly divergent development within the west between 1825 and 1846.

Little more than a fort in 1833, Chicago exploded into a city within a decade. What had been wilderness became $15,000 lots along the Illinois-Michigan Canal. In such a young and booming country (one foreign visitor recalled that he saw neither "an old man nor a gray hair") a man in Illinois could almost handcraft his career by reading law in a crossroads general store. But even so, many young men of the region, along with some of their fathers and grandfathers, were moving on to the black earth of the Iowa Territory and risking the tortuous struggle through the Indian country across the plains and mountains to make a claim in Oregon's lush Willamette Valley.

Already beginning to get the appropriate agricultural tools and machinery from American manufacturers, the upper Mississippi Valley was a region committed to the principles and myths of laissez-faire individualism with an ardor that was uncritical and unrestrained. Promising freedom and prosperity, the frontier was reinforced as the symbol of all that was good and necessary. And it did bring wealth, political freedom, and social acceptance to many men and women, and more particularly to their children. But it also produced a paradoxical mystique. One half of it was as hard-souled as any in the world, with one eye roving for the next unclaimed watering-place or likely looking acreage and one hand on a gun. Though the other half was in contrast warm and humane and cooperative, its fundamental nature was one that encouraged the evasion of the less obvious but subtly vital problems of social and personal relations. Indians were to be killed and the land was to be taken. By creating a mirage of an infinity of second chances, the frontier almost institutionalized everyman's propensity to evade his fundamental problems and responsibilities.

Yet in providing wealth and personal satisfaction for many, the frontier also worked its magic on easterners who never ventured west of Baltimore or Charleston—or Concord. Extending Rufus King's earlier appreciation of the importance of controlling the west, easterners began in the 1830s to stress the means of doing so through politics (Van Buren), economics (the absentee landowners), and education (abolitionists). Edward Everett, a Massachusetts leader who thought that expansion was "the *principle* of our institutions," argued that educational control would bring massive returns on the investment. "We can," he exhorted Boston capitalists, "from our surplus, contribute toward the establishment and endowment of those seminaries, where the mind of the west shall be trained and enlightened." A more candid definition of education as an instrument of social control would be difficult to find.

Tidewater planters harbored the same fears of the brawling southwest, but they had less of a problem: that part of the west adapted the political economy of the older south. Making his father's poverty-induced dream come true, Stephen F. Austin established a colony in Texas as the first step in capturing the Mexican and Pacific trade. It quickly attracted northern yeomen, eastern businessmen, southern planters, and freebooters from every region. But that venture was only the most dramatic example of the general process by which, without any plot or conspiracy but only the magnificent flowering of self-interest, the southwest saved the southeast.

By 1834 the new states along the gulf coast were producing more cotton than the Atlantic seaboard. Committed to a capitalistic commodity agriculture based on slave labor, the southwest began to import its slaves from South Carolina and Virginia. Old planters, and their sons, thus prospered with the new. By 1837, slaves in Virginia brought $1,000; from 17 cents a pound in 1820 and as low as 10 in 1827, the price of cotton jumped above 30 cents in the 1830s. Coupled with the antislavery agitation, this fantastic transformation of the old south into a new trans-Mississippi cotton economy and the concurrent extension of the old northwest frontier of Pittsburgh and Cincinnati into a trans-Mississippi west populated by merchants, manufacturers, and farmers produced vital political consequences.

As an area even more agricultural than the rest of the nation (90 per cent as against 70 per cent), the south became increasingly aware of its special circumstances. It had but a third of the white population and only a tiny fraction of the country's industrial production. Yet through its international cotton sales it earned much of the nation's needed capital. The paradox produced on the part of the south a steadily increasing self-consciousness compounded of pride in its achievements, nervousness over its difference, and sensitivity about the equity of national policies initiated by northern businessmen and western farmers. Concerned about its backwardness in matters of local internal improvements, educational investments, and political reforms, it initiated a movement to catch up in those respects. To a surprising degree, and one often overlooked by its critics, the south at first concentrated on its internal affairs despite the persistent vehemence of abolitionist criticism.

Reinforced by that attack from the outside, such self-consciousness sparked the beginning of a firm conception of the south as a separate and integrated region. Writers like William Gilmore Simms and Mark Littleton began to think as southerners despite their familiarity with the north. Simms, for example, became a great planter with 15 children, and his stories stressed the positive aspect of such a grand existence. So, too, the work of John P. Kennedy. One of Kennedy's novels, *Swallow Barn*, was an early version of the magnolias-and-maidens myth: its aristocratic whites and devoted blacks drifted about a feudal utopia so profitable that no one ever mentioned money.

More practical leaders began to talk about the need for a balanced southern economy. Ultimately leading to a revival of neo-mercantilist thinking, the first result of this outlook was a firm picture of the south as one competing unit within the national system of laissez faire. Rising in the Congress on December 27, 1837, [John C.] Calhoun [of South Carolina] presented six resolutions designed to establish the rules for competition at this sectional-national level. His restatement of the old Madisonian view that the Constitution had created a "feudal system of republics" was accepted. So was his protest against Garrison's propaganda. A majority could also agree that the national government should not be used by one element of the system to attack another. Even the safeguards for existing slavery were accepted in a modified form. But when it came to his proposal to denounce those who opposed expansion because it might extend slavery, Calhoun met defeat. That resolution was tabled.

In some respects, of course, Calhoun's effort to win a consensus on the expansion of the market place was blocked by outright abolitionists and others who feared the political influence of the slavery issue and by men who favored expansion but thought it unwise to raise the issue so bluntly. Jackson, for example, wanted Texas in the worst way but considered it dangerous to move too fast. The fundamental explanation of Calhoun's defeat, however, would seem to be found in an unorganized consensus of western agrarians and eastern businessmen who defined the market place in terms of individual free labor and the corporation.

THE EARLY STRUGGLE OVER DEFINING FREEDOM UNDER LAISSEZ FAIRE

Each of these major national units—the planter, the free individual entrepreneur, and the organized businessman—was beginning to define the national system in terms of the circumstances that favored his particular ability to compete. But laissez faire could also be defined as a system that gave all such elements equal freedom to compete throughout the nation. Calhoun asked for a consensus on that principle, even though he was well aware that the planter would never win in certain areas. But the rising leaders of institutionalized industrialism and the entrepreneurs of food-crop agriculture were already favoring a set of rules that gave them a basic advantage against their toughest competitor. Thus began a system-shaking argument about the first principles.

At the same time, moreover, a second basic issue was formulated when the corporation was openly accepted as a legitimate unit of competition. Jacksonian Democracy revealed its fundamentally laissez-faire nature in promulgating this view. Chief Justice Taney, the old Federalist crony of Jackson himself, and William Leggett, the left-wing leader of reform in New York, agreed completely that groups were legitimate competitive elements within the framework of laissez faire. "We are for leaving trade free"; Leggett declared in 1837, "and the right to combine is an indispensable attribute of its freedom." Taney handed down an identical ruling in the same year. In a decision that specifically opened banking to all citizens, he sanctioned the corporate form of organization.

"There is perhaps no business which yields a profit so certain and liberal as the business of banking and exchange," he explained (from his own experience); "and it is proper that it should be open as far as practicable to the most free competition and its advantages shared by all classes of people." Free banking acts in Michigan and New York extended the principle of general incorporation laws that states like North Carolina and Connecticut had adopted earlier. New York courts not only approved the form in 1838, but for purposes of competition in the market place explicitly equated such corporations with the individual. Taney added the final sanction. The corporation, he explained in an opinion of 1839, "is, indeed, a mere artificial being, invisible and intangible; yet it is a person, for certain purposes in contemplation of law, and has been recognized as such by the decisions of this Court."

Though not yet the predominant institution of business organization, partnerships remaining both more numerous and characteristic of the key segments of the economy, the corporation steadily gained favor. By 1860, for example, iron manufacturing was rapidly adopting the form, and other elements in the industrial economy of the north, such as railroads, were also moving in this direction. Further facilitated by the rationalization and acceptance of the factory system, the growth of manufacturing was revealed in many ways. Large capital investments, the integration of various phases of production, and mass output were ceasing to be unique or even unusual by the 1840s. Steadily expanding the market through and beyond their respective regions, the manufacturers gave a tremendous impetus to wholesaling, credit organizations, and newspaper advertising.

Perhaps the most striking aspect of northern industrial development, as well as the most crucial, was the establishment and extension of the railroad system. For in addition to being a business in its own right, railroading acted as an accelerator of other industries. Not only did it enlarge the market for manufactures, but it underwrote new construction work, facilitated and encouraged the filling up and mature settlement of the trans-Appalachian region, and provided the farmer with better connections with the cities and export centers. Recognizing these benefits, as well as responding to more direct entreaties, pressures, and enticements, both the states and the national government began subsidizing the railroads as early as the 1830s. Liberal grants of the right of eminent domain, cash gifts, and credit facilities were extended by Georgia and Virginia as well as by Indiana and Michigan. In a few states like Michigan, for that matter, the government built railroads and then disposed of them to private entrepreneurs. Congress did its part with rebates on iron duties (and later a general exception), land grants, and gifts of other raw materials.

This rising momentum of industrialism turned the economist Daniel Raymond completely away from mercantilism toward a theory of laissez faire based on the freedom of the manufacturing corporation. An even more striking illustration of the change was provided by Henry Carey, son of persistently mercantilist Matthew. Wealthy and socially acceptable at an early age—an appropriate symbol of the earlier successes of mercantilism—Carey presented his economic views in an essay on *The Harmony of Nature* (1836). Arguing a rather sophisticated version of Smith's laissez faire, he stressed three interrelated principles: happiness and the general welfare were most effectively produced by giving men of property the freedom of action that was theirs by natural law, and in particular by recognizing that even greater (and faster) rewards would be gained by encouraging and accepting the industrial corporation and other large business enterprise.

Carey's political economy provides an insight into the ideas and actions of Daniel Webster of Massachusetts, whose oratorical powers and abilities as a lawyer and general counsel for the upper class made him one of the key politicians of the northern business community. Webster did not follow Carey in the way that a young lawyer plagiarizes Blackstone—in that respect his mentors were the wealthy entrepreneurs who retained him—rather it is that Carey's views help to clarify the particular kind of nationalism which Webster advocated and represented after swinging over to support the tariff in 1828. It is often suggested that Webster changed his basic ideas as his constituents shifted from shipping to manufacturing. This interpretation explains him as a man of regional particularism and laissez faire who became a spokesman of government intervention, and coincidentally a unionist instead of a sectionalist.

Though such an analysis is correct in the sense that Webster shifted from free trade to protection, and dropped the rhetoric of regionalism for the metaphors of nationalism, it nevertheless produces a serious misunderstanding of the nature of his nationalism and that of the industrializing north. Webster denounced labor organizations and smeared those who questioned the wisdom of general incorporation laws as "un-American." Manufacturers and other industrial leaders wanted a national system, to be sure, just as they sought government aid in the form of tariffs or railroad subsidies. But they defined that system quite narrowly and explicitly because all they did was to extend their particular version of laissez nous faire to the entire society.

As such, therefore, neither they nor Webster advocated the inclusive, balanced kind of corporate nationalism that had been characteristic of the mercantilists, or that Daniel's resounding phrases implied. Primarily concerned with the freedom to industrialize the entire economy, such nationalists soon came to prefer overseas economic expansion to the acquisition of additional territory. Their opposition to the latter kind of expansion has led some commentators to conclude that they were anti-expansionist in general. But not only were they expansionists in the strict sense of foreign policy, but they were also expansionists in their relationship with other elements of American society. One of Webster's ostensibly nationalistic maneuvers, for example, was a grandiloquent gesture of defiance against the old regime during the Hungarian Revolution of 1848–1850; yet it in fact represented just such a policy of ideological and commercial expansion as he had advocated at the time of the Greek Revolution. And northerners of his outlook wanted to control the trans-Mississippi west under a similarly restrictive program.

Webster and his constituents wanted a national industrial system in which the government would provide direct and indirect subsidies to the favored element, and which would not limit that group's efforts to integrate the entire political economy on its own terms. Neither Webster nor large northern businessmen wanted the slavery issue to erupt in violence, but their concept of the Union offered a less than reassuring future to the south. It was Henry Clay, not Daniel Webster, who accepted industrialism and attempted to deal with it in a truly national manner. He tried very hard to adjust the ideology of laissez faire to the realities of America through reinvigoration of his mercantilist American System, and then to institutionalize that resolution in a political party. But he was defeated by the coalition of competing units that formed Jacksonian Democracy, even though that alliance was soon to disintegrate in civil war.

THE AGE OF
CORPORATION
CAPITALISM,
1882–

[from *The Contours of American History*, 1961]

The large corporation that came to dominate America's existence in the twentieth century was the central focus of Williams's portrayal of the third period that climaxed his interpretation of the national past. The functions of the corporation replaced the individualized, competitive practices of laissez-faire economics. An increasingly centralized, coordinated, and interrelated system promoted private property and marketplace expansion under corporate control and direction. Corporate leaders and their political allies took command of a national consensus that endorsed domestic growth fueled by overseas expansion in the wake of the crisis of the 1890s.

Williams sketched out the broad features of these developments and carried his discussion into the twentieth century. Tracing the substantial impact and achievements of corporate capitalism, he was however profoundly disturbed by the centralized, undemocratic control of economics, politics, and culture exercised by the corporate system in American society, and deplored the continuing reliance of the United States on imperial expansion abroad. It was time to initiate a new period in American history, he declared, a period in which Americans should seek an alternative, nonimperial way of life by creating a democratic, socialist society.

239

The modern stock corporation is a social and economic institution that touches every aspect of our lives; in many ways it is an institutional expression of our way of life.... Indeed, it is not inaccurate to say that we live in a corporate society.

William T. Gossett, Ford Motor Company, 1957

Lords Temporal rarely if ever make good Lords Spiritual.

Adolf A. Berle, Jr., 1959

The Triumph of the Rising Order

Independent capital persists as a force, but the units that compose it melt like bubbles in a stream.   *William J. Ghent, 1903*

A man who won't meet his men half-way is a God-damn fool.

Mark Hanna, 1894

Mr. Bryan said just one thing in his big [Cross of Gold] speech... that strikes me as true. He said that farmers and workingmen are business men just as much as bankers and lawyers. Well, that's true. I like that.

Mark Hanna, 1897

Mr. McKinley... undertook to pool interests in a general trust into which every interest should be taken, more or less at its own valuation, and whose mass should, under his management, create efficiency.

Henry Adams, 1918

We have a record of conquest, colonization and expansion unequalled by any people in the Nineteenth Century. We are not to be curbed now.

Henry Cabot Lodge, 1895

The extraordinary, because direct and not merely theoretical or sentimental, interest of the United States in the Cuban situation can not be ignored.... Not only are our citizens largely concerned in the ownership of property and in the industrial and commercial ventures... but the chronic condition of trouble... causes disturbance in the social and political conditions of our own peoples.... A continuous irritation within our own borders injuriously affects the normal functions of business, and tends to delay the condition of prosperity to which this country is entitled.

The United States to Spain, 1897

It is frequently asserted...that the output of factories working at full capacity is much greater than the domestic market can possibly consume, and it seems to be conceded that every year we shall be confronted with an increasing surplus of manufactured goods for sale in foreign markets if American operatives and artisans are to be kept employed the year round. The enlargement of foreign consumption of the products of our mills and workshops has, therefore, become a serious problem of statesmanship as well as of commerce.
The Department of State, 1898

Dependent solely upon local business we should have failed years ago. We were forced to extend our markets and to seek for export trade.
John D. Rockefeller, 1899

In the field of trade and commerce we shall be the keen competitors of the richest and greatest powers, and they need no warning to be assured that in that struggle, we shall bring the sweat to their brows.
Secretary of State John Hay, 1899

THE NATURE AND THE POWER OF THE LARGE CORPORATION

POWERFUL and productive in the world of things, and capable of sustaining and strengthening the oligarchies that created them, the large corporations (and their leaders) dominated American history from 1896 until past the middle of the 20th century. In its industrial and financial forms, the corporation transformed the fears of men like Madison and Jefferson, and the expectations of others like Seward, into a reality that crossed every economic, political, and social boundary, affected every branch of government, and permeated every aspect of the individual citizen's life. Ostensibly created to facilitate the rational and efficient production of goods to meet the needs of men, the corporation (like the sorcerer's apprentice) ultimately began creating in men the demand for goods they had never seen, observed in use, or even known they needed. And in many cases the original judgment had proved correct—they did not need them.

Undertaking a shopping trip in pursuit of an item first seen on the television screen produced by a corporation that very probably also provided the air time for the program, a housewife in the 1950s

242   A William Appleman Williams Reader

could easily have put on a dress made of synthetic fibers made by a corporation that exercised a large influence in the corporation that built the car (or bus) that she used for transportation. The insurance company that underwrote her trip may very well have financed the car itself, the garage in which it was parked, and the city streets upon which she drove. The gasoline that powered the car might have been produced by a corporation that could easily have had some share in the supermarket where she shopped. If not, the vegetables she purchased could have been grown on a contract farm owned by the corporation that also made the detergent or soap with which she washed the dishes from which the vegetables were eaten.

Even if he were, superficially, an independent businessman, her husband was still more intimately involved with these same, or similar, corporations. Most of the couple's entertainment was provided by corporations, as was the news they read in their newspapers and magazines, or heard and viewed over the television set that provided the starting point in the entire web of relationships. The political and economic issues in this news were defined largely by the policies and the programs of the corporations and their leaders. As man and wife, their own efforts to organize or participate in other functional groups that attempted to check or balance this power of the corporation were at best productive of little more than occasional minor victories, and more generally of an uninspiring and enervating stalemate that left the large corporation in its position of predominance.

The couple's fears for the future were centered on one of three major issues: upon their inability to break out of the pattern of installment living produced, packaged, and promoted by the advertising and public relations adjunct of the corporations; upon the possibility that the corporation economy might falter and flatten them along with its dividend payments; or upon the tension in foreign affairs that was very largely the result of the conflict between the expansion of those corporations and the opposition to them manifested by vigorous and militant rivals. With overseas direct investments of 29 billion dollars, sales of overseas agencies of 30 billion dollars (with an average profit of 15 per cent), and direct exports of between 15 and 20 billion dollars, the overseas economic empire of the United States in 1957 amounted to a total stake of twice the gross national product of Canada and was larger than the same total for the United Kingdom.

The problems of that empire provided most of the national

headlines in the 1950s, just as very similar foreign fears and antagonisms had greeted the new corporation system at the turn of the century. Writing in 1902 of *The Americanization of the World,* William Thomas Stead of England termed it the "greatest political, social, and commercial phenomenon of our times." "In the domestic life," echoed his countryman Fred Mackenzie in the London *Daily Mail,* "we have got to this: The average man rises in the morning from his New England sheets, he shaves with 'Williams' ' soap and a Yankee safety razor, pulls on his Boston boots over his socks from North Carolina, fastens his Connecticut braces, slips his Waltham or Waterbury watch in his pocket, and sits down to breakfast. There he congratulates his wife on the way her Illinois straight-front corset sets off her Massachusetts blouses, and he tackles his breakfast, where he eats bread made from prairie flour (possibly doctored at the special establishments on the lakes)...and a little Kansas City bacon....The children are given 'Quaker' Oats....

"He rushes out....[And] at his office, of course, everything is American. He sits on a Nebraskan swivel chair, before a Michigan roll-top desk, writes his letters on a Syracuse typewriter, signing them with a New York fountain pen, and drying them with a blotting-sheet from New England. The letter copies are put away in files manufactured in Grand Rapids....At lunch-time he hastily swallows some cold roast beef that comes from the Mid-West cow...and then soothes his mind with a couple of Virginia cigarettes. To follow his course all day would be wearisome. But when evening comes he...finishes up with a couple of 'little liver pills' [that were] 'made in America.' "

Germans and Frenchmen revealed similar uneasiness about American expansion, and the high Russian newspaper *Novoye Vremya* expressed its concern by pointing specifically to the example of Great Britain. "Everything," it lamented, "proves that Great Britain is now practically dependent upon the United States, and for all international intents and purposes may be considered to be under an American protectorate....The United States has but just entered upon the policy of exploiting the protected kingdom." While such estimates were obviously exaggerated as of 1900, the reality moved ever closer to them throughout the 20th century in the Western Hemisphere, in Europe, and throughout the rest of the world. Very candidily, and with considerable forethought, America pushed its way into the struggle for economic empire between 1895 and 1898. This involvement was dramatized and extended by the war with

Spain, and in 1899 and 1900 culminated in the famous Open Door Notes which demanded equal opportunity for America's tremendous economic power, a weapon that the nation's leaders felt confident would produce world economic supremacy without the limitations and dangers of old-fashioned colonialism.

Likewise, even as the nation emerged from the bloody strife and suffering of the depression of the 1890s, the inclusive nature and extensive power of the corporation was clearly revealed at home. Its triumph established a new political economy, a system of organized and controlled interrelationships and influence that was developed and put in operation during the presidential campaign of 1896. Whereas laissez faire had required at least two elections to establish its primacy under Jackson, the leaders of the age of the corporation scored an impressive victory in their first test. Organized and managed by Mark Hanna, one of the new order's more perceptive and effective spokesmen, this victory established the modern pattern of politics as an expensive, extensive, and centrally co-ordinated, high-pressure effort.

Despite the flamboyance and extremism of the rhetoric on both sides (itself a reminder of the campaign of 1828), and the emotional ardor of his supporters, [William Jennings] Bryan never seriously approached victory in the election of 1896. The rise of the large industrial corporation had given the urban manufacturing and commercial centers and their spheres of influence in the surrounding agrarian areas a predominance in the political economy that would never be successfully challenged by a purely and narrowly laissez-faire interest party such as the Democrats were under Bryan. For that matter, many western farmers responded to the Republican argument that overseas markets for surpluses would solve their particular problem while bringing general prosperity. The real issue was not whether the new order would triumph, but who was to control and direct it; that is, how it was to maintain an internal balance, accomplish the necessary domestic and overseas expansion, and in what way meet and master its political, economic, and philosophic competitors at home and abroad.

With considerable exaggeration, the beginnings of the age of the corporation might be dated from the first textile-mill town (complete with minister and teacher supplied on contract by the owner) established in New England early in the 19th century. But the foundations of the new system were actually started by the post–Civil War operations of men like James J. Hill in railroads and associated enterprises, the integrated organization of the Cambria Iron Works near Pittsburgh, and the development of the Rockefeller and Carnegie empires during the 1880s. After the adoption of favorable holding-company legislation by Delaware, Maryland, and New Jersey during the same decade and the concurrent consolidation of the House of Morgan, the rise of the large life insurance companies and such firms as the American Telephone and Telegraph Company made it clear that the corporation had moved rapidly into a position of predominance, a position that has never been challenged in a fundamental way.

None of the early firms, however large, revealed all the basic features of the corporation either in their specific organization and operations or in their impact upon the society at large. And in the case of [Andrew] Carnegie, of course, the overall characteristics represented a culmination of the laissez-faire entrepreneur. For this very reason, however, he and [John D.] Rockefeller, along with Hill, offer apt illustrations of how the corporation economy emerged as a function or consequence of laissez-nous-faire competition. But each of these enterprises did develop one or more of the essential aspects of the corporation that enabled it as an institution to create a distinctive new order once it came to control the key elements of the system. While the secondary characteristics and indirect ramifications of the corporation are numerous, even today not wholly known, its central features are clear.

Beyond the obvious fact of size, of authority and power as *one* unit over the rest of the economy, perhaps the main element introduced by the large corporation was a fundamental change in ideas about economic activity itself. Laissez-faire operators and spokesmen thought of the market place as a scene of individualized and somewhat random activity. But the spokesman and directors of the new order, though they accepted the traditional premise of private property and the vital role and necessity of an expanding market place, defined economic activity as making up an interrelated *system*. It was not just the sum of innumerable parts operating in an essentially casual and *ad hoc* fashion. The political economy had to be extensively planned, controlled, and co-ordinated through the institution of the large corporation if it was to function in any regular, routine, and profitable fashion.

This view developed in part from the narrow or interest drive of the corporation entrepreneurs to rationalize and control as much of the market place as possible—to make it *their* system. But it was soon generalized as the result of observation and reflection on broader issues. They concluded that Adam Smith's Hidden Hand was often so hidden that it failed to provide the guidance which should have prevented individual and general crises. Also, competition proved in practice to be inefficient, redundant, and wasteful. Finally, from being directly associated with both of these considerations, they grew more and more fearful that the end result of laissez faire would be economic breakdown and social revolution. "The panic of last year is nothing," warned Hill in 1894, "compared with the reign of terror that exists in the large centers. Business is at a standstill, and the people are becoming thoroughly aroused." Like the advocates of laissez faire, the corporation leaders feared social upheaval, but they provided a different answer to the question of how to avoid it. In their way, therefore, the proponents of a system based on the large corporation were capitalists who accepted, on the evidence of their own experience as well as their casual and distorted knowledge of his ideas, the analysis made by Karl Marx, and set about to prevent his prophecy of socialism and communism being fulfilled.

These broad ideas provided the background for understanding the nature and the ramifications of the corporation itself. It was and remains a form of organization designed to accumulate large amounts of capital, resources, and labor and apply them to the rational, planned conduct of economic activity through a division of labor and bureaucratic routine. Acting within this framework, corporation leaders directly and indirectly exerted several major influences on the political economy. They consolidated the main elements and processes of the economic system in a small number of giant firms. By the end of World War II (1947), for example, when the United States produced approximately 50 percent of all manufactured output in the world, a mere 139 corporations owned 45 per cent of all manufacturing assets in the country. These behemoths further centralized power within their own group and within specific corporations. Such centralization meant that the rights of the participants (directors and managers, as well as stockholders) were limited in a hierarchical fashion so that control over many units might be maintained with a comparatively small investment and a few firms dominate the general consolidation of the political economy.

In striving to achieve their various objectives, corporation leaders produced two kinds of integrated organization. One was horizontal, pulling together a number of operations at the same stage of production or service. Its purpose was to control the market. The other was vertical, several levels of production (from raw materials to distribution) being acquired and co-ordinated for becoming independent of the market. In later years, particularly after World War I and the Great Crash of 1929, such power was extended even further as giants like the House of Morgan, Procter and Gamble, and insurance companies began to acquire and operate various real estate (including farm) holdings.

In all its manifold features and enterprises, and in finance as well as in industry, the corporation operated within an oligarchic framework. Individual propertyholders (today stockholders) no longer enjoyed the kind of direct authority they had wielded in the age of laissez faire. And the labor unions neither sought nor received such power in the area of basic investment or operational decisions. This separation of literal ownership from practical control became progressively greater during the 20th century. As it did so, some observers concluded that corporation leaders were no longer guided by the philosophy and ideology of private property, but had in effect become dehumanized managers who abstractly kept the system going for its own sake. Another argument maintained that the managers had become public servants driven only by a desire to create the good society.

In the narrowest sense, these interpretations overlook two relevant factors. Up to World War I, and even later in specific cases, a bloc of voting stock large enough to sway key decisions was often held by one or two individuals. And in subsequent years the evidence has suggested strongly that however small their personal holdings, the directors and managers who staff the corporation still *think* and *act* as though the firm belonged to them. In an even more fundamental way, they have continued to define the system created and ordered by the corporation as one based on private rather than on social property. A typical sector of the corporation economy—say the automobile industry—would be a different phenomenon if it were organized and operated as a socialized enterprise. Such features as built-in obsolescence, indifference to safety factors, and redundancy of design would be avoided. For that matter, automobile production might be cut back very sharply in favor of a social investment in modern public transportation systems.

Though it may seem strange in view of the later inefficiency of the corporation system, the drive for efficiency was one of the motives that powered the merger mania of the period between 1889 and

1903. Capitalized at 25 millions, for example, the Illinois Steel Company of Chicago was organized with the claim of having a plant more efficient as well as larger than that of Carnegie. Rockefeller's Standard Oil Company abandoned the ambiguous partnership-trust form it had used after the reorganization of 1882 and became a gigantic holding company with clearly apparent corporate character-istics. And J. Pierpont Morgan successfully corralled the skittish and maverick railroad entrepreneurs in a consolidated and centralized railroad system in the east. "The purpose of this meeting," he bluntly told them, "is to cause the members of this association to no longer take the law into their own hands...as has been too much the practice heretofore. This is not elsewhere customary in civilized communities, and no good reason exists why such a practice should continue among railroads."

"Consolidation and combination are the order of the day," judged Walker Hill, president of the American Bankers Association in 1899; and the chief statistician of the Census Bureau verified this estimate in 1900. "A startling transformation" had occurred in the previous decade, he reported, one which "set at naught some of the time-honored maxims of political economy, which must readjust many of our social relations, and which may largely influence and modify the future legislation of Congress and the States." Joined by such men as August Belmont, and such firms as Lee, Higginson of Boston and Kuhn, Loeb of New York, Morgan's crusade for what he called a "community of interest" produced more than 300 consolidations between 1897 and 1903.

Morgan's own formation of the gargantuan United States Steel Company symbolized the entire epoch, but the appearance of the Amalgamated Copper Co., the American Tobacco Co., the Standard Distilling Co., the National Biscuit Co., the International Harvester Co., and the reorganization of the du Pont firm were just as important. And by 1900, the year after 1,028 firms had disappeared, the American Telephone and Telegraph Co. had become a $250 million corporation. Similar expansion and co-ordination completed the integration of such firms as Macy's, John Wanamaker's, and Woolworth's into the new political economy. Marshall Field and Sons exemplified the pattern with its wholesale purchasing, functional organization of the store, ownership of some supplying factories, and even in its benevolent creation of the Chicago Manual Training School.

THE CRISIS OF THE 1890S AND THE SPECTER OF CHAOS

Not only did the many business failures of the 1890s create circumstances favorable to such consolidation and centralization, but the crisis convinced most remaining doubters that laissez faire was unable to cope with the tensions and problems of mature industrialism. Beginning with Black Friday, the Panic of 1893 initiated an intense and double-cycle depression that lasted until 1898. Signifying the end of the easy investment opportunities and massive profits that had been provided since 1789 by the dramatic and once-over development of the continental west, and signifying also the completion of the basic steel, transportation, and power segments of the industrial economy, the depression of the 1890s profoundly shocked even the advocates of the new system.

Following upon the Haymarket Riot of 1886, the sequence of a general strike of Negro and white workers in New Orleans and bread riots and other disturbances throughout the south and the north reached a portentous peak of violence in the bloody and prolonged strike against Carnegie's Homestead plant in 1892. While willing to use troops in such emergencies, most capitalists realized that the economic system could not be operated on the basis of private and government soldiers maintaining production. Nor was the trouble limited to the east. Army units were also used during the same summer in the Utah copper strike. Then, coming after the depression had started, and seeming to verify the worst of the nightmares produced by the Homestead affair, the even more violent and extensive strike against the Pullman Company and the railroads in 1894 dramatized beyond question the need for a new approach.

Though in many ways the culmination of the old 19th-century pattern of company towns originated by textile mills, the circumscribed community and society founded and controlled by the Pullman Company was widely regarded before the upheaval as a model of, and for, industrial relations. More perceptive architects of the emerging corporation system such as Mark Hanna, the Ohio entrepreneur and politician, understood its weaknesses, but they did not immediately alter that general impression of the company. "Oh, hell! Model—!," he thundered to a group of industrialists and bankers. "Go and live in Pullman and find out." But most of his associates initially mistrusted him rather than the supposedly ideal solution to labor problems, and they did not begin to modify their opinions until the continuing crisis forced them to admit the need of a broader outlook. Hence their fears were further intensified by what they thought was a revolutionary march on Washington by Coxey's Army. The army was actually a rather pathetic and motley band of unemployed men who wanted relief rather than revolution.

Already prone to interpret such events in either-or terms, however, American leaders responded to the economic depression and its associated social unrest by intensifying their efforts to formulate ideas that would account for the crisis and provide practical solutions. As they developed such explanations and recommendations, they emphasized increasingly the role of foreign policy in solving domestic troubles and consciously initiated a broad program of sophisticated imperialism. For that matter, the triumphant corporation system rode in on the crest of what John Hay, in a revealing if indiscreet moment, called "a splendid little war." Underlying that expansion, and sustaining it on into the 20th century, was the central idea that overseas economic expansion provided the *sine qua non* of domestic prosperity and social peace. Gradually transforming this initially conscious interpretation of the crisis of the 1890s into a belief or article of faith—an unconscious assumption—Americans by the middle of the 20th century had established a network of investments, branch factories, bases, and alliances that literally circled the globe. Just as the sun had never set on the British Union Jack in the 19th century, neither did the Stars and Stripes know any darkness in the 20th century.

Also starting in the 1890s, Americans concurrently evolved a set of attitudes and ideas to rationalize and reform the political economy created by the large corporation. But even though they began with the urge to reform themselves, by 1917 they had concluded that such domestic progress depended upon first reforming the rest of the world. And despite periods of enforced preoccupation with domestic failures, this propensity to link improvements at home to conditions overseas remained an axiom with American reformers. Though the full development and convergence of these domestic and foreign programs did not occur immediately, it is nevertheless useful to preview the underlying assumptions and basic features of such new ideas.

For example, it is almost impossible to overemphasize the importance of the very general—yet dynamic and powerful—concept that the country faced a fateful choice between order and chaos. Not only did it guide men in the 1890s; it persisted through World War I, the

Great Depression, World War II, and emerged more persuasive than ever in 1943–1944 to guide the entire approach to postwar opportunities and problems. Only the anarchists and a few doctrinaire laissez-faire spokesmen seemed willing to accept the possibility of chaos. Arguing that it was both necessary and possible, most Americans reformulated and reasserted their traditional confidence in their ability to choose and control their fate. This romantic axiom had been a central theme of American history ever since the 1820s, and it carried over into the new age. But given a consensus on the sanctity of private property, and confronted by the increasingly obvious failure of laissez faire, this faith could be verified only by controlling the market place. While this tangle of ideas produced enough ideological rope for many a tug-of-war over who was to control the system and by what standard it was to be done, all such contests found the victors basing their program on overseas expansion.

THE INCEPTION OF AN AMERICAN SYNDICALISM

Within this framework, and originating largely as a reaction within the ministry against the failure of the church to sustain its old relevance and appeal as the source of values and inspiration, the idea of religion as the guide for creating an ordered and balanced system produced a movement known as the Social Gospel. Protestants as well as Catholics were influenced in such thinking by Pope Leo XIII's famous encyclical *Rerum novarum* (1891) on the nature and role of labor in an industrial society. Recommending the renewed study of St. Thomas Aquinas, and stressing the ideals of co-operation and equity between capital and labor, his ideas were particularly relevant to the political economy of the large corporation.

Even though in stressing the role of the Church it offered a different kind of unifying theme, such a fundamentally functional and syndicalist approach reinforced similar analyses provided by sociologists and industrial spokesmen. It also influenced the large number of American labor leaders who were Catholics, for it reinforced their preference for improving labor's position without attacking private property. Yet just as in earlier centuries, the advocates of a Christian solution for the problems of society divided over whether the commonwealth should be based on private or social property. While a minority asserted the stronger logic and the greater equity of Christian Socialism and exerted some influence in the early years of the century, the great majority in the Social Gospel movement favored Christian Capitalism.

Even within the ministry, such Christian Capitalists soon accepted the necessity and wisdom of American expansion and played a crucial role in reinvigorating the missionary movement. Arguing that it was necessary for effecting Christian reforms and for creating the circumstances in which men would turn to Christ, they also supported economic expansion. Reverend Francis E. Clark thought missionaries played a key role in "the widening of our empire." Robert E. Speer, secretary of the Presbyterian Board of Foreign Missions, reported that his church accepted commercial expansion and "welcomes it as an ally." And Henry Van Dyke of Princeton presented an argument that sounded like the expand-or-stagnate thesis of industrial prosperity. "Missionaries are an absolute necessity," he explained, "not only for the conversion of the heathen, but also, and much more, for the preservation of the Church. Christianity is a religion that will not keep."

Another persuasive idea was different in being a secular thought that became a religion, and in initially placing little weight on overseas expansion as such. Clearly arising out of the needs and desires of various interests to strengthen their own position within the corporation political economy, the idea that efficiency was crucially important to prosperity and the socially tolerable functioning of the system soon gained wide acceptance. Though some businessmen had stressed the axiom earlier, the general discussion was launched by engineering and scientific journals in the 1880s. Then it was adapted by Frederick W. Taylor to the needs of management. That in turn opened the way for a theory (and ideology) of rationalizing the political economy under the direction of the corporation that was evolved under the general leadership of Elton Mayo of the Harvard Business School. An initial stress of efficiency thus led to the view that the corporation was the feudal lord of a new corporate society.

Finally, and in a way that provided the foundation for all such thought and discussion, Americans came increasingly to see their society as one composed of groups—farmers, workers, and businessmen—rather than of individuals and sections. Almost unconsciously at first, but with accelerating awareness, they viewed themselves as members of a bloc that was defined by the political economy of the large corporation. Perhaps nothing characterized the new *Weltanschauung* more revealingly. For given such an attitude, the inherent as well as the conscious drift of thought was to a kind of syndicalism based on organizing, balancing, and co-ordinating different functional groups. In part a typical example of the way interests and experiences influence thought, but also the product of abstract analysis and interpretation, that kind of corporation syndicalism became by 1918 the basic concept of society entertained by Americans. That outlook provides the underlying explanation of the persistent conflicts between the units, and of the continued difficulty of developing any broad, truly inclusive program for balancing and directing the system. In one sense, the corporation was merely one of the functional units. But it exerted more power and influence than the others, and its approach to organizing and balancing the political economy remained an interest-conscious conception even though it did become progressively more sophisticated.

One of the best, as well as earliest and most widely read analyses of the syndicalist nature of mature industrialism and of the natural predominance of the large corporation within it, was provided in 1902 in a wry but essentially fatalistic study, *Our Benevolent Feudalism,* by William J. Ghent. Ghent thoroughly understood the essential feature of the new order: through its co-ordination of technology, capital, and labor, it could produce enough to provide plenty for everyone. But with the insight that provided the imagery of his title, he also realized that an economic, or political and social, decision by the giants would affect every citizen to a sizeable degree. While he concluded that the new system was too powerful to be destroyed and supplanted, and was likely to be moderately benevolent, he nevertheless pinpointed a central problem suggested by his analogy with feudalism: How were the vassals and the serfs of the new system to enforce the reciprocal obligations of the lords? This became a major issue that was never satisfactorily resolved.

In the meantime, several concurrent developments exemplified the kind of organization that Ghent anticipated would arise within the political economy. Often called by its advocates the "business form of government," the commission form of city rule was initiated in Galveston, Texas, in 1901. Devastated by a tidal wave, the city was re-established in line with the theory that "a municipality is largely a business corporation." Designed to break down the division between legislative and administrative functions, and thereby provide a way to plan and co-ordinate urban development, the commission system was opposed by special interests that wanted government amenable to them rather than responsible for a broader conception of the community. But mounting debts, inefficiency, and graft prompted reformers as well as corporation leaders to turn to various variations on the city-manager form, and by 1960 almost half of America's cities were organized on this plan.

In a similar way, trade associations became more active and extensive in co-ordinating various branches of the system and in exerting influence on the government as well as on the market. And rapidly expanding as a part of the general process of controlling the economic market place, advertising firms began to extend their services into the area of public relations. Men like Ivy Lee approached the ultimate objective by creating a favorable image of the corporation and fixing it in the mind of the general public. One of his early successes presented John D. Rockefeller as a man who distributed corporation profits by handing out dimes to children. By thus manufacturing a certain kind of news and organizing its mass distribution, the advertisers created a special function for themselves and at the same time began the now familiar process of defining the good society in terms of the corporation and the corporation in terms of benevolent efficiency.

Accepting the new system, Samuel Gompers assumed leadership of its labor sector. In theory, at any rate, Gompers could have dealt with the corporations in one of five ways. He could have ignored them (or gone along with the idea of company unions), tried to break them up through agitation for strong enforcement of the anti-trust laws, attempted to regulate them, turned to socialism (or co-operatives) and tried to change the property base of the whole political economy, or simply concentrated on organizing them while not challenging their basic predominance. He chose the last option. Then, in an act that was even more revealing of his outlook, he and his fellow labor leader John Mitchell of the coal miners joined Mark Hanna, Ralph Easley, August Belmont, J. Pierpont Morgan, George W. Perkins, and other corporation leaders on the board of directors of the National Civic Federation.

MARK HANNA AS THE ENTREPRENEUR OF THE CORPORATION SYSTEM

Conceived as a forum and institution for resolving industrial conflict through the co-operation of capital and labor, the NCF was organized by men who stressed the necessity of co-ordinating the various syndicalist elements to prevent crises (which would lead to socialism) or government intervention (which would lead to tyranny).

As typified in his wholehearted acceptance of the axiom that "organized labor cannot be destroyed without debasement of the masses," Hanna provided the new political economy with a vigorous, talented, and perceptive corporation leader. A businessman who took a Senate seat as his just reward for engineering the political victory of 1896, Hanna understood both the nature and the power of the new system. Exploiting both, but trying to do so in a way that took into account his awareness of the need for an attitude and an ethic that would promote a positive consensus among its various elements, he emphasized the need for order, for give-and-take, and for the necessity of running the system as precisely that, a system.

His superior understanding and sophistication prompted many economic giants of his own time to conclude that he was too liberal. They never bothered to hear him out, or simply could not follow him, on such issues as his candid evaluation of the Populist demand for nationalization of the railroads. Acknowledging its economic relevance in stabilizing a crucial element of the private-property market place, he merely commented that it was perhaps a good idea—provided it was not done until the corporations had extracted the first-run profits from building and establishing them. His calm estimate was based on economic logic and an astute perception of the basic loyalty of the reformers to private property—they were "useful citizens." His analysis also anticipated by half a century the reaction of British conservatives to the nationalization of the coal mines in England after World War II. Hanna understood that the same people would very probably run the railroads, and in all probability would hold a large share of the government securities that financed them.

Accepting the demise of the ruthless and callous individual entrepreneur, Hanna seems clearly to have realized that the "harmony of interests" which he sought depended upon the corporation executives, himself included, rising above interest-conscious leadership to the class-conscious outlook of an industrial gentry. For his background, time, and circumstances (which included opposition from reformers that was just as bigoted as that from interest-conscious corporation leaders), he progressed a long way up that difficult emotional and intellectual slope. As with mercantilists like Shaftesbury or the Adamses, Hanna understood that a system based on private property needed class-conscious leadership just as much as does a revolutionary movement. And he realized the crucial weakness of corporation leaders with an interest-conscious outlook. For even though the interest was a corporation which embraced much of the political economy, such men still viewed society from that interest base—stressing immediate opportunities or problems—rather than from the outside and with primary emphasis on its long-run, inclusive needs and equities.

In many cases, moreover, he revealed such class-consciousness in his actions. As a coal operator, he damned the militia for shooting a worker involved in a strike against his plant, and was immediately attracted to William McKinley, the young lawyer-politician who defended the union. Later, he played a major part in settling the bitter anthracite strike of 1900. Feeling that vigorous rivalry between various elements of the syndicalist system helped balance them, he encouraged the farmers to stand up for their rights. "Anybody abusin' you people now?" he would ask western audiences that were prepared to be critical. "All right, combine and smash 'em!" He was in turn capable of fighting with all the great power at his call to protect corporations when he thought they were being treated unfairly or limited to an extent that threatened their fundamental role in the system. And in some cases of that kind, his judgment was narrow and mistaken. Thus he never became fully class conscious.

But he did recognize the basic issue and did educate a good many leaders of his time, even though few of them ever admitted it. His courage and wisdom helped Theodore Roosevelt as well as McKinley, and his astute political sense put both of them into the White House. As might be expected, he organized political action as though it were a corporate enterprise. From collecting funds from corporations (and returning any that were given in anticipation of special favors or that were not used) to paying individuals to wear McKinley buttons for the bandwagon effect, Hanna established the modern political operation. He used carloads of Civil War veterans instead of bevies of titillating females, and dinner pails instead of straw hats, but his latter-day imitators added nothing essentially new. The politician as organizational man came in with Hanna.

But McKinley was far from the weak figure some have thought him. Even before he met Hanna, for example, he grasped the essentials of an equitable relationship between capital and labor and sensed the idea of the Presidency as the directorship of a corporate society. Hanna's tutoring strengthened and extended these insights and provided support and organization, but McKinley's reputation played a crucial role in winning labor to Republicanism in the 1890s. He was President in his own right and brought to the White House a firm conception of an integrated and balanced society based on private property and the large corporation.

In approaching the problems of the new political economy, McKinley laid great stress on ending social unrest and on the relationship between overseas economic expansion and domestic prosperity. Hence it is misleading to view him as a weak man who was pushed into expansion and war against his will by popular excitement and special interests. The issues were far more complex than that, as was the history, and revolved around the questions of how internal stability could be restored and how the most efficient kind of expansion could be initiated and sustained. Those were the basic issues. Spain's inability to restore order and routine government in Cuba was the catalyst in a dynamic equation formed of several potent elements.

History as a Way of Breaking
the Chains of the Past

I see what you are *not* making, oh, what you are so vividly not....
                              Henry James, The American Scene, *1907*

Imperceptibly, the function of nostalgia reduces the ability to function.
                              Wright Morris, The Territory Ahead, *1958*

We cannot begin until we have said farewell to the assumption that Utopia is in the old American frontier.   *Walter Lippmann, 1935*

I'm not concerned with the New Jerusalem. I'm concerned with the New Atlanta, the New Birmingham, the New Montgomery, the New South.
                              Reverend Martin Luther King, Jr., 1960

H ISTORY as a way of learning has one additional value beyond establishing the nature of reality and posing the questions that arise from its complexities and contradictions. It can offer examples of how other men faced up to the difficulties and opportunities of their eras. Even if the circumstances are noticeably different, it is illuminating, and productive of humility as well, to watch other men make their decisions, and to consider the consequences of their values and methods. If the issues are similar, then the experience is more directly valuable. But in either case the procedure can transform history as a way of learning into a way of breaking the chains of the past.

For by watching other men confront the disparity between existing patterns of thought and a reality to which they are no longer relevant, the outsider may be encouraged to muster his own moral and intellectual courage and discipline and undertake a similar re-examination and re-evaluation of his own outlook. Whether the student of history follows the responses of earlier men remains a matter of his own choice, and even if he accepts their views he is obtaining his answers from men, not History. History offers no answers per se, it only offers a way of encouraging men to use their minds to make their own history.

This essay in the review and interpretation of American history has suggested that several elements have emerged as the major features of American society, and that those have in turn defined the central issues faced by contemporary Americans. One is the functional and syndicalist fragmentation of American society (and hence its individual citizens) along technological and economic lines. The personal and public lives of Americans are defined by, and generally limited to, their specific functional role. To an amazing extent, they share very little on a daily basis beyond a common duty as consumers and a commitment to anti-communism. The persistent cliché of being "caught in the rat-race" dramatizes that alienation, as does the attempt to "play it cool" in order to maintain some semblance of identity and integration.

The second theme is the persistence of a frontier-expansionist outlook—a conception of the world and past American history—which holds that expansion (or "growth," as Walter Lippmann put it in 1960) offers the best way to resolve problems and to create, or take advantage of, opportunities. A third is a commitment to private property as the means of insuring personal identity, and of thereby guaranteeing democratic politics, and of creating material well-being. And finally, Americans have displayed a loyalty to an ideal of humanity which defines man as more than a creature of property; which defines him as a man by reason of his individual fidelity to one of several humane standards of conduct and by his association with other men in a community honoring those codes.

None of those themes is unique, or even of recent origin, in American history. One example will suffice to establish that. Bernard Baruch raised in 1944 the specter of a dangerous fragmentation of American society into functional groups bent on pursuing the short-run satisfaction of their interests to the detriment of the general welfare, and his report was followed by many related or separate comments on the same problem. But Herbert Hoover had discussed the same issue at great length in the 1920s; the founders of the National Civic Federation had been motivated in large part by a similar concern at the turn of the 20th century; Abraham Lincoln had come to stress the same issue after he became President in 1861; James Madison and other Founding Fathers had grappled with the identical problem in the late 18th and early 19th centuries; and Shaftesbury had struggled to provide a resolution of the same dilemma during the Restoration Era in England. Hence it was not the issues that were new in 1944. The crisis was of a different nature, being instead defined by the progressive failure of the approach that Americans had evolved to solve the problems. That approach no longer provided a satisfactory resolution.

From Shaftesbury's time forward, the solution developed by Americans had been compounded of two conflicting themes or answers. One was the interpretation of Christianity advanced by the Levellers during the English Revolution, and later reasserted wholly within that tradition by Karl Marx in the form of a secular socialism. It held that the problems raised by faction, interest, fragmentation, and alienation could only be resolved—and man restored to a true wholeness and identity—by de-emphasizing private property in favor of social property and through the co-operative building of a community rather than the mere construction of an organized collective system. Save for the first two decades of the 20th century, that outlook never played a large and direct role in American history. Indirectly, however, it did exert a sustained influence.

The other approach accepted private property as necessary and desirable. For guidance in defining and honoring the ideal of a commonwealth, its followers looked to different religious and secular traditions. One of these was Calvin's conception of a corporate Christian commonwealth in which the trustee accepted and discharged the responsibility for the general welfare; at the same time, all men were charged to honor the axiom that their choice between callings should be made in favor of the one that contributed most to the common good. Another tradition involved the ideal and practice of feudal *noblesse oblige*. That view had of course arisen within the Christian world, but by the 17th century had developed a secular life of its own. Finally, such men also relied upon a secular argument which held that expansion offered the only feasible way of underwriting private property while at the same time improving the general or collective welfare.

Put simply, the mercantilists such as Shaftesbury sought to integrate those three themes into a coherent and consistent *Weltanschauung*. That outlook on the world was, and remained, the essence of all class consciousness among upper-class groups in England and the United States from the Age of Elizabeth I. Thus Shaftesbury accepted the responsibility of those who enjoyed the possession of consolidated property for maintaining the general welfare and viewed the state as the natural and appropriate instrument for implementing that obligation. At the same time, he tried to organize political affairs on the basis of parties which included men of all functional interests (or factions) who accepted a broad conception of the general welfare and the means to achieve it. By thus coming together as men who shared an ideal of community—a Utopia— they would be able to override the tendency of functional activity to fragment and divide them—both internally (or personally)—from their fellow men.

Shaftesbury extended that outlook into foreign affairs. He accepted the necessity of expansion and acted vigorously to co-ordinate the various aspects of commerce and colonization. But he also sought to build such an empire as a mutually beneficial and responsible commonwealth. He had few qualms about waging war against outsiders to protect or extend the empire, and certainly intended to control its members; but he did have a strong sense of partnership that guided his actions toward the colonies. Shaftesbury and other mercantilists made many false starts, and they failed to control all factions (or to subordinate their own particular interests) at all times. It is nevertheless true that they did to a rather remarkable degree develop and act upon such a class-conscious outlook that combined a defense of private property with a belief in the necessity of expansion, and with an ideal of community and commonwealth.

That outlook was carried to America by the Puritans, by other emigrants, and by the empire directives prepared by Shaftesbury and his successors. It was thereby established, in various versions, in every colony. In many respects, moreover, it continued to mature and develop beyond its English origins and precedents. Indeed, Jonathan

Edwards integrated its various themes perhaps more successfully and infused them with a more noble vision of Christian community than any English or American philosopher either before or after his time. His corporate Christian commonwealth was one of the few American visions worthy of the name Utopia.

But in any of its versions, that outlook was a demanding *Weltanschauung*. As Frederick Jackson Turner pointed out three centuries after the colonies had become firmly established (and in doing so offered a revealing insight into his own generation), the urge to escape the responsibilities of that ideal of a corporate Christian commonwealth was powerful, persistent, and without regard for the direct and indirect costs of such flight. In England, for example, expansion offered a progressively more appealing substitute for the self-discipline and fidelity to ideal that was essential in maintaining the general interest against the factional. And in America the presence of a continent defended only by weaker souls made that solution even more convenient. Americans proceeded in the space of two generations to substitute the Manifest Destiny of empire for the Christian Commonwealth of Jonathan Edwards. Thomas Jefferson was the great epic poet of that urge to escape, to run away and spend one's life doing what one wanted—or in starting over time after time. [Andrew] Jackson, [Thomas Hart] Benton, and [James K.] Polk were but the type-cast protagonists of that dream, and through his early years even Lincoln was a man who charted his career by that same western star.

James Madison was the theorist of the outlook, and in offering expansion as the way of controlling faction, he articulated the guiding line of American history from the end of the 18th century through the 1950s. Yet unlike most who followed his theory, Madison recognized the grave implications of the solution; along with such men as Calhoun, Monroe, Clay, and especially John Quincy Adams, he sought to prevent the complete devaluation of the self-restraint and other ideals that Shaftesbury and Edwards had stressed. The continent was too much for them. By making escape so easy, it produced an unrestrained and anti-intellectual individualist democracy that almost destroyed any semblance of community and commonwealth. Even before the continent was filled up, the frontier had become a national Utopia and Madison's theory the New Gospel. Men largely ceased to think about problems, and merely reacted to them by reciting the frontier catechism and pushing the Indians off another slice of the continent. Following the general lines of Seward's reformulation of Madison's argument to fit the conditions of an industrial society, [John] Hay's Open Door Notes merely restated the principle in terms appropriate to the 20th century.

Less than 60 years later, however, the open door of escape was no more than ajar. Two forces had combined to all but close it: Russian and Chinese industrial and nuclear power and potential; and the growing refusal by societies that had formerly served as the frontier to continue in the role any longer. As a result, the frontier Utopia had ceased to offer a practical substitute for the more demanding *Weltanschauung* of class-conscious leadership and responsibility. *Expansion as escape meant nuclear war.* Yet the cold war was essential to those who still, consciously or unconsciously, saw expansion as the means of adjusting and controlling factions and at the same time providing some measure of welfare. In typical frontier fashion, such people saw defeat or war as the only other solutions.

Expansion of a vastly different character and drastically more limited nature was still possible, but even that could be sustained only by strengthening the self-discipline necessary to honor the commonwealth ideal that Shaftesbury, Edwards, and Adams had tried to sustain. Expansion of any sort was only possible without war, and that is to say, only possible if the frontier were abandoned as a Utopia. Expansion of that kind would of necessity be channeled through the United Nations, without political or economic strings, in an effort to help other societies solve their own problems within their own traditions. Hence the possibility of any full maturation of the class-conscious industrial gentry that had slowly been created by the corporation between the 1890s and the 1950s turned on one very simple test. Did that gentry have, or would it manage to muster, the nerve to abandon the frontier as Utopia, to turn its back on expansion as the open door of escape?

It is of course fair to ask whether any precedents exist for encouraging such a display of intelligence and courage. For while it is helpful to find examples in the past, it is too much to ask that contemporary corporation executives and political leaders model themselves on Shaftesbury or John Quincy Adams. Very few, if any of them, are men of sufficient empathy. Nor would it be wise for them to follow such a course even if they could. Not only are the circumstances different, but it is the attitude and the ideals that are important, not the personal styles or the specific policies. But there is no need to return to the past in that sense, for some of the very

Americans who restated the expanionist outlook in the 20th century also realized that there was another choice.

Brooks Adams, for example, admitted that America did not have to embark upon a program to control China and Siberia. It was merely the easier way out of the dilemma, and one which in his opinion offered more glory and riches. And as late as 1944, Dean Acheson acknowledged that he and his colleagues in government could invest an indefinite amount of energy and time in discussing alternatives to expansion as a way of building "a successfully functioning political and economic system." Acheson dismissed such approaches, however, on the grounds that they would weaken the rights of private property, require modifications of the Constitution, and limit the frontier-style liberties to which Americans had become accustomed.

Herbert Hoover and Charles Beard had more intellectual courage and imagination than either Adams or Acheson. They argued that it was possible to build a community—a commonwealth—based on private property without relying on imperial expansion. Whatever his other failings, Hoover did at least refuse to go to war for the Open Door in Asia, and did try very hard to change the character of America's overseas economic expansion. In some ways, at least, Beard advocated an even more rigorous effort to restore the ideal of a commonwealth as the American Utopia. But in its commitment to the frontier as a Utopia of escape, the American public refused to give that approach a serious or a fair trial.

Finally, the mid-century industrial gentry might draw even more encouragement from the example provided by the southern Negro. During approximately a century after the Civil War, the Negro modeled his aspirations and ideals on the white society in which he existed. Briefly at the end of the Civil War, again in the 1890s, and then with a rush during World War I, the Negro adapted the frontier-expansionist outlook to his own position. He defined northern urban centers as his frontier of escape from the conditions of survival in the south. For a generation or more, Negroes streamed into that supposed Utopia only in the end to discover that it was largely a mirage. Then, under the leadership of deeply religious and courageous men like the Reverend Martin Luther King, Jr., they broke with that traditional view of the frontier as escape and defined the south, the cities and the states where they lived, as the only meaningful frontier that existed.

Having made that magnificently courageous and deeply intelligent decision, they stood their ground and faced the issue in the present, reasserting as their solution the ideal and the practice of a Christian community or commonwealth. In a way that dramatized their abandonment of the frontier outlook, they organized themselves in such groups as "The Montgomery Improvement Association." No longer did they rally under the old slogan of the frontier, "Kansas or Bust," merely changing Kansas to read New York or Chicago or Detroit or Cleveland or Pittsburgh. They made no mention of the frontier: they simply talked about the here and the now, and set about to improve it guided by the Utopia of a Christian commonwealth. And to do so they chose the appropriate weapon—nonviolent resistance. Within one year they had effected more fundamental progress than in a century of following the white man's theory of escape through the frontier. Not merely did they begin to obtain food in formerly closed cafés: that was really a minor point. What they really won was respect for themselves as men who no longer ran away. The frontier never had and never could give a man that kind of self-respect.

But while Reverend King and the Montgomery Improvement Association offered the class-conscious industrial gentry inspiring proof that wealth and welfare were obtainable without running off to some new frontier, they also posed some crucial questions. Even if the gentry could regenerate such a Christian vision of a corporate commonwealth, would corporation capitalism be able to function if operated according to its precepts? Perhaps it would not. Perhaps the corporation economy could not function without the indirect but vital help of the citizen in the form of taxes paid to the government and then handed on to the corporation in the form of subsidies. If that were the case, then how and by what secular ideal and hierarchy of values—by what Utopia—would the class-conscious industrial gentry transform such double jeopardy into a system of true equity in which every citizen, along with the corporations, received a fair share of wealth and welfare? It might be rather difficult to convince the citizen that his sacrifices were worthwhile on the grounds that the gentry would then take an honest interest in him. For even under the best of circumstances, is having an interest taken in one a sufficient substitute for active participation in the present and future affairs of one's own society?

Those are fundamental and very difficult questions. Even to ask them is to understand why the frontier as a Utopia of escape has been so attractive in the past, and why it still exerts such influence in the middle of the 20th century. But to ask these questions is also to raise the issue as to whether Americans have any other traditions that are appropriate to the present. Is it really a choice between, on the one hand, a continuance of government by a syndicalist oligarchy relying on expansion or, on the other, a government by a class-conscious industrial gentry? To be sure, the choice does offer some measure of meaningful difference; for a class-conscious industrial gentry with the nerve to abandon the Utopia of frontier expansion would clearly provide at least the chance of a more equitable, humane, creative, and peaceful future. But if that is all Americans can offer themselves, then they are apt to become unique in the sense of becoming isolated from the mainstream of 20th-century development.

For the rest of the world, be it presently industrial or merely beginning to industrialize, is very clearly moving toward some version of a society modeled on the ideal and the Utopia of a true human community based far more on social property than upon private property. That is what the editors of *The Wall Street Journal* meant in 1958 when they candidly admitted that the United States was on "the wrong side of a social revolution." That socialist reassertion of the essence of the ancient ideal of a Christian commonwealth is a viable Utopia. It was so when the Levellers asserted it in the middle of the 17th century, and it remains so in the middle of the 20th century. It holds very simply and clearly that the only meaningful frontier lies within individual men and in their relationships with each other. It agrees with Frederick Jackson Turner that the American frontier has been "a gate of escape" from those central responsibilities and opportunities. The socialist merely says that it is time to stop running away from life.

And in Eugene Debs, America produced a man who understood that expansion was a running away, the kind of escape that was destructive of the dignity of men. He also believed and committed his life to the proposition that Americans would one day prove mature and courageous enough to give it up as a child's game; that they would one day "put away childish things" and undertake the creation of a socialist commonwealth. Americans therefore do have a third choice to consider alongside that of an oligarchy and that of a class-conscious industrial gentry. They have the chance to create the first truly democratic socialism in the world.

That opportunity is the only real frontier available to Americans in the second half of the 20th century. If they revealed and acted upon the kind of intelligence and morality and courage that it would take to explore and develop that frontier, then they would have finally broken the chains of their own past. Otherwise, they would ultimately fall victims of a nostalgia for their childhood.

THE CENTRAL UTILITY
OF MARX

[from *The Great Evasion*, 1964]

Williams had called attention to the ideas of Karl Marx in earlier work and had acknowledged the influence of Marx's thought on his own. In the essay *The Great Evasion* Williams applied aspects of Marx's analysis of capitalism he considered relevant and useful to an understanding of America's past development and current difficulties. Writing during the growing national turmoil of the 1960s, Williams attributed "the deepening crisis of increasing alienation, deprivation and frustration" to the failures of capitalist society and to the inability of Americans to confront the realities of these failures and the reasons for them. Instead, he said, Americans escaped the truth of their past and the realities of their present through expansionism at home and abroad that produced more troubles than it solved. He argued that Marx's insights could provide a basis for comprehending America's development which, Williams insisted, was not at all exceptional. Rather, it should be understood as the outcome of capitalist expansion which had begun in early modern Europe. Corporation capitalism represented the most recent stage of this long and complicated history.

The call to abandon [our] illusions about [our] condition is a call to abandon a condition which requires illusions.   *Karl Marx, 1843*

Finally, let us consider, by way of change, a community....
                                                              Karl Marx, 1867

The philosophers have only *interpreted* the world in different ways; the point is to *change* it.   *Karl Marx, 1845*

267

T HE central utility of Karl Marx for Americans in the middle of the twentieth century is that he is a heretic who helps us by bringing our capitalistic ego into a confrontation with our capitalist reality. As with the groom and the horse, the philosopher can lead us to the self-examination, but he cannot make us change our ways. Only we can do that. But there is no doubt as to the value of the philosopher—however we cope with his challenge.

When examined seriously and soberly, the evidence submitted by American capitalism fails to confirm either the popular stereotype or the official myth about Karl Marx. The United States has not proved that Marx was wrong. The overall achievement of American capitalism, even with the peacetime subsidies provided by the non-entrepreneurial taxpayer, and with the further direct and indirect assistance flowing from wars and cold wars, can at most be characterized as a high-level stalemate with the internal forces that Marx identified as driving capitalism toward breakdown under normal circumstances. And, in cybernated production, American capitalism would seem to have fulfilled its axioms and logic in a way that Marx saw as providing both the basis and the reason for a transition to a new order of political economy.

In its non-economic aspects, moreover, which Marx properly insisted were an integral part of the system per se, American capitalism offers countless examples, at both the individual and the group levels, of the harmful and dangerous devolutions that he feared and anticipated. The economic achievement has been purchased at very great costs in human and material resources. The Negro is still not integrated even into the marketplace, let alone the society, a full century after capitalism destroyed the neo-feudal Southern society based on slavery. And possessive individualism operating in a competitive marketplace has increasingly proletarianized and stratified American society.

The individual displays increasing signs, overt and unconscious, of alienation, disorientation, and anti-social behavior. The integrated personality, let alone the integrated group, is produced only in opposition to the status quo, rather than by and through a commitment to the avowed principles of the system. Perhaps the most disturbing evidence of all concerns the way Americans have denied the very conception and ideal of Utopia in the name of practicality, pragmatism, and realism. The metaphor of space, which was once a symbol of William Blake's cosmos that awaited man's fertile and creative and transcending genius, has been transformed into a literal area in which to repeat the old frontier habit of conquering a new and virgin territory and then making it over in the image of the old society.

In the realm of foreign affairs, meanwhile, Marx's analysis and predictions have withstood the test of changing reality in an even more dramatic way. From the seventeenth century to the present, the capitalist commitment to expanding the marketplace has guided and set limits upon American foreign policy. It defined relationships with Africa and the Negro, with the North American continent and the Indian (and even among the whites for control of the continent), and with the underdeveloped societies and nations (and, through them, with other industrial countries).

In each of these cases—the Negro, the Indian, the South, and the underdeveloped areas—the expansion of the American marketplace brought grave and painful consequences to the non-Metropolitan elements. After having been forcibly transferred from his home as a chattel colonial, the Negro was belatedly released from that condition only to be defined and treated as an unequal and hence unfree ego in the marketplace. The Indians who survived suffered a similar fate. The South is even today a depressed, backward, and unequal sector of the Metropolis. And the inherent inequality in the marketplace relationship between the Metropolis and the underdeveloped countries has led, as Marx forecast that it would, to increasing misery for the poor nations and to a determination on their part to break free of that inequitable imperial relationship.

Despite the flood of material artifacts constantly spewed forth by modern capitalism, therefore, these far more significant failures have produced an intellectual and moral malaise which confronts American capitalism with grave difficulties as it faces the clear and present need to initiate a graceful, generous, and dignified—*and effective*—transition to a post-capitalist order. This weariness has the effect of limiting even the most intelligent and concerned leaders to a range of choices which does not reach to the heart of the crisis. They propose and consider alternatives which, even at their best, never break through the conception of reforming and thereby saving the established system.

Such reform might be possible, at least for a time. The power and the momentum of the existing system will no doubt sustain it for a certain interval even without drastic reforms, and modifications of that nature might prolong its life for a significant period. This is not as certain, however, as the reformers hope and assert. The malfunctioning of the economic and political sectors is so serious and fundamental as to raise grave doubts about the viability of even an extensive repair job. And the social situation is so critical that it may, in and of itself, prevent such reforms from being instituted. Even if this is not the case, the proposed changes do not promise any creative transcendence of the present condition.

This unsettling truth is, of course, the most devastating commentary on the strategy of reforming and saving the system. It offers nothing to inspire a commitment to the effort. Hence it is imperative to confront the true nature and the full scope of the crisis and break sharply and finally with the strategy of preservation.

The crisis created by cybernated production is THE *crisis of capitalism as defined by Marx. The capitalist system has in cybernated production fulfilled its promise and potential, and has created the absolute necessity to transcend its inability to cope with its own success. But capitalist leadership literally does not know—it cannot conceive— what to do at this magnificent turning point in human history that was so accurately foreseen by Karl Marx. If left to its limited devices and cramped imaginations, the turn will not be made.*

This essential change of course can only be made by following Marx's insights and morality, and thereby undertaking the creation of a true human community. Instead of residing in defining Marx as an enemy or as a problem, wisdom lies in grasping the Marxist critique firmly so that it can be used as a fulcrum with which to move both America and the world. This makes it possible, first of all, to admit the finite nature of capitalism without denying either its achievements or its role as the creator of conditions and means for something better. It offers, secondly, the positive challenge of creating a better society rather than the negative task of prolonging an existing system that is increasingly caught up in its own difficulties and limitations. And it presents, in the third place, a meaningful guide for meeting that challenge.

Marx is, after all, the paradoxical prophet of affluence and of the irrelevance of affluence once it is attained. "The realm of freedom does not commence," he pointed out, "until the point is passed where labor under the compulsion of necessity and of external utility is required. In the very nature of things it lies beyond the sphere of material production in the strict meaning of the term." Capitalism has created in cybernated production the tool to provide such affluence, but it cannot employ that tool to build a truly free community.

For, grounded as it is in the principle and the practice of

possessive individualism, capitalism cannot break free of the conceptions and the institutions that define society as a marketplace system, and work as the process of alienating part of oneself in order to satisfy another part of oneself. Marx revitalizes, and offers for our consideration, the far more appropriate and classical conception of man as a social being, rather than as a competitive and alienated protagonist in the marketplace. "Only in association with others," Marx correctly insists, "has each individual the means of cultivating his talents in all directions. Only in a community therefore is personal freedom possible."

When Marx says that labor should cease to be "merely a means of life" and become instead "life's principle need," he is courageously substituting the classical meaning of work for the capitalist definition of man as a quantum of energy in the marketplace. He is saying that the central need of the individual is to fulfill himself in creative labor which produces relationships which humanize and strengthen and sustain his community with other individuals.

Marx did not define post-capitalist society—socialism and communism—as enlightened self-interest in a condition of gluttonous satiation. He was not primarily concerned with how much man possessed. He assumed that the problems of meeting material needs and providing a diversity of goods were quite capable of being solved—even that they would be solved in the technical sense during the last phases of capitalism itself. Marx was concerned with the way man defined himself and his relationships with other men, and how he used his creativity once his basic needs had been satisfied.

Instead of being derived from Hobbes, Locke, and Smith, therefore, Marx's outlook was grounded in the classical tradition. Elements of his thought can be traced back to Plato (as with Socrates in *Republic I,* and Glaucon in *Republic II*), to Aristotle, and to the Bible. The examples he repeatedly invoked were "the old Athens," the early Christians, and medieval feudal society. Marx's resulting *Weltanschauung* can be outlined in the following manner.

First. Man is a social as well as an egoistic being. Freedom is therefore defined as the reconciliation of the ego with the social, rather than by the unlimited exercise of the ego.

Second. The ego separates man from man. It makes him an exception to, rather than a member of, the human community.

Third. The objective is thus to end this separation between the egoistic interest and the common interest—or the community. This can only be done within the framework of the injunction to "love thy neighbor as thyself"; that is, by realizing that a man divided against another man is a man divided against himself. "Every man represents the other," Marx explained, "not through something else, which he symbolizes, but through that which he *is* and *does*." Individual dignity is thus defined by a situation "where we create independently within our own circle."

Marx's repeated references to feudal society have to be understood within this context. He saw feudalism as an order in which the egoistic and the social were linked through the relationships between people. To be sure, he idealized feudalism to some extent, but he did so knowingly, in an effort to provide a concrete example of the way in which the private and the public should be integrated. Whatever its failures, Marx explained, feudalism did involve a definition of *particular* interests and relationships in term of *general* interests and relationships. The individual's "private, particular activity and situation" was part of "a general activity and situation."

His own formulation transcended feudalism. "Human emancipation will be complete only when the actual existing individual man takes back into himself the abstract citizen, when, as individual man, he has become a generic social being in his everyday life, in his individual work and in his individual relations." When, in short, he defines himself in terms of, and acts on, the injunction to love thy neighbor as thyself.

Fourth. In the specific moral sense, Marx bases his *Weltanschauung* upon the classical and Old Testament distinction between good and evil. A *good* is internally coherent; it can work with all objects and be extended indefinitely. An *evil,* on the other hand, is internally incoherent and unstable. It conflicts not only with a *good,* but with itself. It is thus repressive and destructive. A *good* co-operates and creates a harmonious whole. An *evil* produces atomistic separation and, ultimately, destructiveness.

Fifth. Freedom, therefore, is neither the definition and the exercise of the ego in terms of possessive individualism in the marketplace, nor simply an illusion. Free love, for example, is not the uninhibited sexual conquest of a multiplicity of objects. It is love free in the far more fundamental sense that it does not rely on illusions or restraints (sexual and otherwise) to exist. It is the voluntary and unhedged acknowledgment, transcending the mere sexual, of interdependence. Free thought is that which explores the dynamism of its assumptions without subordinating itself to one particular interim set of conclusions in order to protect particular interests or authorities. And a free

society is that in which the individual defines himself, and acts, as a
citizen of a community rather than as a competing ego. In a very
real sense, therefore, the frontier for Marx is the space and resources
made available for human development by loving thy neighbor as
thyself.

Cybernated production has created the material base upon which
we can stand to accept and take up the challenge to act upon this
definition and vision of community. The effort will not be easy. It is
no commitment for those whose idea of Utopia is early retirement on
higher social security payments. But it is not impossible, and the
interrelated aspects of the process can be outlined with enough
clarity to reveal the broad kinds of action we will have to undertake,
and to define the dialogue through which we will guide our
continuing efforts.

We must begin by ceasing to limit our conception of humanity
and freedom by tying it to the possession of property. Property is the
night-light of the frightened and the banister for the immature. We
must abandon this crutch of identity and learn to walk on our own.
The point is not that we must abandon our possessions, but rather
that we must re-define the possessions as incidental to our functioning as humans, instead of as crucial to our existence as humans.
Once we recognize how little our property actually defines us today
(or what a meager definition it provides), and how cybernated
production can reduce property to an incidental if we use it to do so,
this crisis of definition can be surmounted.

*Hence the basic policy decision must be to undertake the planned,
controlled, and co-ordinated movement into full cybernated production.*

As we do this, we must initiate an open and sustained dialogue
concerning the problems of creating and maintaining a balance
between the non-economic and the economic, as well as among the
economic, consequences of such a move into full cybernation. In and
of itself, that is to say, the cybernation of the economy offers no
insurmountable problems, but the real issues involve deciding what
kind of a society we want when that has been done, and preparing
ourselves for that moment of achievement. For unless we are
prepared to act as true humans when we achieve full cybernation, we
will be unable to cope with the psychological challenge of having
either an identity or a creative purpose outside of the traditional
capitalist one of work in the competitive marketplace.

This suggests that we must very carefully co-ordinate the full
cybernation of the economy with a restructuring of the existing

political system, and with a vast and intense educational program. The central guideline for all of this is provided by two central truths. First, a true community is more easily obtainable, and more extensively developed, in small rather than in large units. Second, cybernated production makes it possible to honor this axiom about community and at the same time meet economic needs and desires.

Hence the issue is not whether to decentralize the economy and the politics of the country, but rather how to do so. The solution here revolves about the regional elements that make up the existing whole. These must be defined, and then established as economic and political units grounded in their own co-operatively owned and controlled cybernated productive systems. The existing states need not be destroyed, for they can continue to function as units within the new regional elements. It is conceivable, however, that the citizens of some states would decide, for economic and other reasons, to divide in order to join different regional communities. This should of course be permitted.

In and of itself, this process will open up a tremendous arena for intellectual and political action across the next decade. The exhilarating experience of constitution-making will be carried on within and between a minimum of eight to ten new communities. In addition, and concurrently, each new regional and cybernated economy will have to be constructed, and its interrelationships defined and established. In order to do these things, furthermore, the educational system will have to be simultaneously reoriented and extended to provide the leadership required.

This literal restructuring and rebuilding of American society offers the only physical and intellectual challenge capable of absorbing and giving focus to the physical and intellectual resources of the country during the next generation. Indeed, a planned move into cybernated production within this framework will still leave sufficient resources to provide vastly increased aid and assistance to the underdeveloped nations, and to continue the rational (as opposed to the political) exploration of space.

Throughout such a process, moreover, the participants will be educating themselves—formally and informally, and without restrictions as to age—for their membership in the truly human community they will be creating. In the end they will have built a physical America which will be beautiful instead of ugly, and which will facilitate human relationships instead of dividing men into separate functional elements. They will have evolved a political system which is democratic in form and social in content. And they will be prepared, as cybernated production is completed, to function as men and women who can define their own identity, and their relationships with each other, outside the confining limits of property and the bruising and destructive dynamics of the competitive marketplace. They will be ready to explore the frontier of their own humanity.

It matters very little whether one calls this socialism or civilization. The issue is what kind of people we want to be and what kind of a world we want to have. Hence the question is whether or not we have the will, and the integrity, to admit that Marx was right in insisting that these are the central problems, and also right in saying that human rather than marketplace answers are the only objectives worthy of our commitment and our energy. If we meet that test, then we can get on with the task of transcending Marx's prophecy by creating an American community that will be beyond even his noblest dreams.

A SURVEY OF
THE TERRITORY

[from *The Roots of the Modern American Empire,* 1969]

From the start of his research and writing, Williams had emphasized U.S. imperial expansion at the close of the nineteenth century as the defining event in the history of American foreign policy. He had also identified the principal actors in that development as leaders of the urban, industrial sector of the corporate political economy. In *The Roots of the Modern American Empire* he explored in considerable detail the role and significance of agricultural interests in American economic expansion overseas. The expansionist outlook of urban, industrial leaders during and after the 1890s, he concluded, was but the maturation of a process actually developed in agricultural terms by agrarian elements of the country between 1840 and 1893.

In coming to this judgment, Williams asserted as well that "the majority of the adult population played a vital part in the evolution and adoption of the imperial policy at the end of the nineteenth century." He thus denied that American imperialism was the consequence of conspiracy organized by the elite leadership of society or imposed upon an unwilling and passive majority. In order to change this policy, then, not only must the policymaking elite alter its outlook, but a broad, popular consensus must emerge to support such a change. When he wrote the book, Williams speculated whether expanding opposition to the Vietnam War might develop a fundamental reassessment of foreign policy and the system under which it functioned.

THE expansionist, imperial foreign policy adopted by the United States at the end of the nineteenth century was largely formulated in industrial terms by men who were leaders and spokesmen of that part of the political economy. They were primarily concerned with obtaining markets for surplus manufactured goods and venture capital, and with acquiring reliable access to cheap raw materials needed by the American industrial system. That industrial orientation of American foreign policy became increasingly clear during the twentieth century as American leaders struggled to build and maintain an international system that would satisfy the inter-related economic, ideological, and security needs and desires of the United States as they defined those objectives.

When the policy was crystallized in the latter years of the 1890s, and to an increasing degree in subsequent decades, the dynamics of the policy-making process centered in a relatively small group of economic, political, and intellectual leaders who characterized American interests and needs in those industrial-financial terms. Part of that centralization of power and authority was due to the inherent nature of government, particularly in a social system as large and as geographically extended as American society. Part of it was explained by the additionally inside, quasi-secret, and administrative character of foreign policy decisions in any government. Neither the majority itself nor a legislative assembly can handle policy matters on a routine basis. In the underlying sense, however, it was the result of the consolidation and centralization that accompanied the matura-tion of modern industrial capitalism in the United States, and which provided the industrial-financial leaders with their power base.

All of those factors have led historians to emphasize the industrial nature of the policy, and to stress the role of the small group of top policy makers. And, because of their power, authority, and influence in the political economy, those men have enjoyed and exercised a significant degree of sustained, unchallenged initiative. They have, of course, been subjected to pressures from various organized interest groups; and they have encountered resistance from other branches of the government, and from occasional upwellings of public feeling and opinion. Those forces have caused delays and shifts of emphasis in implementing the broad policy adopted at the turn of the century, but they have not produced major changes in the nature of the policy or a serious weakening of the power wielded by the leadership elite. In a great majority of instances, moreover, the more general opposi-tion to one or another aspect of the policy developed around a dissident faction of the leaders. Such was the case, for example, in connection with the defeat of President Woodrow Wilson's effort to establish the League of Nations on the basis of America's policy and power.

Much later, the opposition to the Vietnam war manifested some characteristics which suggested that movement might develop as an exception to the general pattern of criticism of American foreign relations in the twentieth century. It is possible that the resolution of the war could involve, or lead into, a reevaluation and change of the imperial policy first codified during the 1890s. Even if that possibility becomes reality, however, it is apparent that the origins of the opposition to the war involved members of the policy-making elite as well as outside critics. But it would also be clear under such circumstances that widespread support had developed for a more far-reaching shift in outlook and policy.

Whatever may happen in connection with the Vietnam war, the historical evidence makes it apparent that precisely such an involvement of the majority of the adult population played a vital part in the evolution and adoption of the imperial policy at the end of the nineteenth century. American imperialism was not forced on the majority by a domestic elite, any more than it was imposed on the country by outside forces or foreign nations. That presents what appears to be a paradox. For, on the one hand, the majority of the American people from 1865 to 1900 was associated with the agricultural part of the political economy. Yet, on the other hand, the policy itself was formulated in industrial terms by leaders of that section of the system.

II

The paradox is apparent rather than real. The resolution begins with a knowledge of the seventeenth-century colonists who produced a surplus of tobacco and exported it to Great Britain and other European nations; and, more particularly, with an understanding of their marketplace orientation and their marketplace conception of the world. The marketplace difficulties encountered after 1740 by the heirs of those early settlers defined the substance of the quarrel between the American colonies and the British metropolis. And the independence and freedom the American colonials felt they needed to solve their economic problems were the same freedom and independence they desired in their personal and social affairs, and which they worshiped in the abstract. The essence of political freedom manifested itself in the colonial assemblies (and in protest demonstrations) as the lack of it materialized in the marketplace.

The continued commitment to that outlook that tied freedom for individual men to the existence of a free marketplace exerted a steadily increasing influence on American foreign policy in the years after independence had been secured. Many men who feared a strong national government because of its power to restrict or control their activities nevertheless supported the Constitution on the grounds that the new, more centralized system would enable the United States to win advantages—and prevent losses—in the international marketplace. Such men also looked to a strong government to acquire more land needed to produce the surpluses they wanted to sell on the world market.

Whether in terms of the drive to possess more land, or in their pressure to protect and expand their position in the marketplace, the Northern as well as the Southern members of the agrarian majority exerted a strong and persistent influence on American foreign policy down through the War of 1812. In the direct sense, they demanded the defeat and expulsion westward of the Indians; they agitated the seizure of Florida, the trans-Mississippi region, and all or part of Canada; and they insisted that the government act to overturn the French and British restrictions that limited or closed their foreign markets. Their indirect influence was equally important. They created the products that in turn involved the processors, merchants, financiers, and shippers in the export trade. And they generated the assertive ideological argument that justified expansion as a policy that carried freedom to other men as well as being necessary for their own freedom and material well-being. They were first the harbingers, and then the militant advocates, of America's manifest destiny to lead and reform the world.

From the outset, moreover, the agricultural majority became increasingly conscious of the vital part that its surpluses played in the prosperity and growth of the entire American economy. Not only did they supply the food and fiber for the urban population that was thereby freed for other activities, but their exports paid for much of the foreign capital that went into manufacturing, banking, mercantile operations, and other nonagricultural enterprises. Neither the Southerners who chopped the cotton and harvested the tobacco, nor the Northerners and Westerners who cropped the grains and raised the livestock, had to wait for twentieth-century economists to conclude that they were the engine of American progress. For more than a generation after the War of 1812 the Southerners carried the bulk of the international payments load, and the brunt of the battle to secure the kinds of policies most appropriate to commercial, exporting agriculture. The farmers of the North and West were not inactive during that period, but most of their surplus was absorbed by the Southerners and by the increasing urban population at home, and they were preoccupied with developing a commercial agriculture west of the Appalachians.

Beginning in the 1840s, however, the Northern grain and livestock farmers again became more directly involved with foreign policy. They had begun to produce a surplus beyond the needs of the home market when the Panic of 1837 and the ensuing depression (which lowered land values as well as commodity prices) intensified that economic pressure to enlarge their overseas markets. Those difficulties also turned them toward the acquisition of virgin land at a time when the ecstatic reports about Oregon and California were reaching a crescendo. The epidemic of Oregon fever, for example, erupted first in Iowa and Missouri, from whence it spread quickly back across the Mississippi into Illinois, Michigan, Indiana, and Ohio. And some of those Northerners who wanted a chance to start over (perhaps for the second or third time), or a place to send their grown children, came to share the increasing interest of Southerners in acquiring the vast plains of Texas.

Some leaders of the Eastern metropolitan part of the political economy, such as William H. Seward, a key Whig politician of New York, read the Panic of 1837 to mean that the economy had reached the point where it needed an expanding foreign market to avoid further and even more serious depressions. And one group of urban entrepreneurs, which included flour millers and meat packers, were exporters intimately involved with (and ultimately dependent upon) the agricultural part of the economy. Their rising concern with overseas markets not only influenced metropolitan politicians on foreign policy matters, but helped increase the export consciousness of the farmers. From the time of the depression of the late 1830s and early 1840s, therefore, leaders like Seward labored to build a political alliance between Northeastern businessmen and agriculturalists by offering related benefits to both groups.

The Democrats were more immediately successful in the political arena, however, because they promised more land to the farmers of all sections of the country. The analysis underlying that strategy had first been propounded as an integrated argument by James Madison as early as 1786–1787, when he formulated his theory that republican government could be sustained only by "enlarging the sphere." That outlook provided the foundation upon which Madison formulated foreign policy, just as it did for Thomas Jefferson, James Monroe, and Andrew Jackson. President John Tyler and Secretary of the Navy Abel P. Upshur then applied it directly to the political situation created in the early 1840s by the expansionist demands to acquire Texas and all of the Oregon Territory. Tyler offered Texas to Southerners and Oregon to Northerners in a vain effort to control the Democratic party during the presidential campaign of 1844 and thereby remain in the White House.

Tyler failed, but the strategy was effectively used against him, and the Whigs, by James K. Polk. Along with other Democratic party expansionists like Senators Robert J. Walker of Mississippi and Stephen A. Douglas of Illinois, Polk aroused the party and the country with the imperial rallying cry of "the reoccupation of Texas and the reannexation of Oregon." The political success of their expansionist outlook and platform was due to the way they integrated several distinct themes into a coherent and dynamic whole. Most obviously, it was a straightforward promise to provide enough land, at least for the immediate future, for all Northerners and Southerners.

But it was also, particularly in the minds of men like Polk, Douglas, and some Easterners, a manifestation of the concern and determination to acquire the harbors on the Gulf and Pacific coasts that were crucial to America's overseas economic expansion. Madison himself had clearly understood that foreign markets were part of the sphere that had to be enlarged to insure the continuation of republican institutions and of prosperity, and his successors had not forgotten the lesson. The pressures for land and markets were complementary and reinforcing economic engines of expansion that were directly integrated, moreover, with the philosophical and ideological arguments that the expansion of the free marketplace was necessary for the preservation and the extension of political and social freedom. Polk was only voicing an outlook and a tradition that reached back into the eighteenth century, but he gave them classic form in his pronouncement that American expansion was justified because it involved "the expansion of free principles."

That kind of evangelical righteousness not only homogenized the economic and the philosophical forces that generate empires, but it created a powerful psychological drive that was quickly characterized by the protagonists themselves as America's manifest destiny to lead and reform—if not rule—the world. Already justified because it was necessary and fruitful, expansion became inevitable because it was the expression of a divine logic. The concept of The City on a Hill thus became The Empire of the Globe.

III

The growing conviction that the United States possessed irresistible power, and was the chosen instrument of an unsullied destiny, continued to be an important ingredient in the American imperial thrust long after the War against Mexico. And, however it was adapted by other nonagricultural groups, it evolved out of the ancient faith that men who worked the land were the bearers of primary virtue. In the short run, however, that righteous confidence was muted by the internal struggle for control of the empire that was acquired by force from Mexico and through the threat of force from Great Britain, and by the shifting outlook of the Northern agrarians. Both of those factors became apparent during the War with Mexico; the first in connection with the drive to go beyond the boundaries of Texas and take more territory in northern Mexico, and the second during the debates over the tariff in 1845 and 1846.

As they continued to increase their production of grain, cattle, and swine, Northern farmers grew more intensely concerned with foreign markets. Those American developments coincided with the agitation in Great Britain to repeal the legislation that protected British agriculture against foreign competition. The Manchester Anti-Corn Law Association was organized in 1838, and the Anti-Corn Law League followed in 1839. Agricultural leaders in the Northeast, as well as in the South and West, immediately recognized the favorable implications of such action for American farmers. The promise of the British market led some of them to moderate their militant demands for taking all the Oregon Territory north to 54° 40′ north latitude, and prompted even more to support modifications in the American tariff.

The argument that a lower tariff would promote American exports to Great Britain (and also to other countries) gained strength among Western agrarians as it became clear that the Corn Laws were going to be repealed. That turning point in British economic policy came on June 6, 1846. A short two months later, on July 30, 1846, the Walker tariff reversed the upward turn in American rates that had appeared in 1842. The coalition of Southern and Northern farmers that carried through that decision proved incapable, however, of resolving their differences over the disposition of the trans-Mississippi empire—or of agreeing on new imperial ventures.

Both groups wanted to control the western half of the continent, and the Northern agrarians became increasingly antislavery as they faced the prospect of competing against a forced-labor system. But favoring free soil did not mean agitating to free the black man. The majority of Western farmers were not abolitionists. They viewed the Negro as another rival for the bounty of the West. Their objective was to exclude both the white planter and the black man from the trans-Mississippi marketplace. That goal, and the attitude which produced it, gave Abraham Lincoln his victory over the abolitionist element in the newly rising Republican party, as well as his final triumph over Stephen Douglas. For Lincoln's policy of containing the slave labor system within its existing boundaries, without undertaking any direct action to free the black man, won him important support among Northwestern agrarians. And that strength was sufficient to check the abolitionists and simultaneously force the Easterners to promise free land to the farmers.

Douglas failed in his bid to unite and lead the country because none of his major policies spoke to either the immediate needs or the more underlying fears of the Northwestern agrarians. His argument that free labor would triumph over slave labor in the trans-Mississippi territory under the doctrine of popular sovereignty was rejected because it left too much open to too much doubt. The farmer wanted a sure thing, not the mere probability of ultimate victory after an arduous struggle. Douglas encountered similar resistance when he talked of the future rewards of expansion into areas like Cuba, or of the coming triumph of American exports in the markets of the world.

Northern farmers not only concluded that most of the immediate gains of taking Cuba (political as well as economic) would go either to Eastern businessmen or to the planters, but they had not reached the point in the commercialization of their agriculture at which export markets were regularly more important to them than the control of the free land across the Mississippi. They were businessmen, but businessmen oriented primarily to the domestic market. It is very probably true, as some modern economic historians have argued, that the Northern grain economy was committed to production for the foreign (and particularly the British) market by the end of the 1850s, but the Northern farmer did not think in those terms at that time.

For that reason, Douglas never reaped the strategic political victory he had anticipated in 1851 when he obtained the first federal landgrant subsidy for building the Illinois Central Railroad. Douglas conceived of the line not only as a way to tighten the bonds between the Northwestern farmer and his Southern customers, but as a method of projecting Northern surpluses out into the markets of the world as a major element in America's future economic supremacy. Douglas might well have been elected President on that program in the 1870s or the 1880s, but during the 1850s it was too much of an abstraction to be effective.

There was a surge of involvement and interest in overseas markets during the latter half of the 1850s, and particularly during the Crimean War and the Panic of 1857. Wheat exports, for example, jumped from 8.15 million bushels in 1856 to 14.57 million bushels in 1857. But the sporadic rise in such sales was not enough to turn the Northern farmer outward away from his deadly confrontation with the planter. In an ironic way, however, Douglas' loyalty to his vision of America astride the commerce of the world carried him to the side of Lincoln and into the camp of the Northerners who had earlier rejected him. For the secession of the South threatened the entire trans-Appalachian Northwest with the loss of egress to the open sea—and thereby its access to the world marketplace. Faced with that prospect, Douglas supported Lincoln and the Union.

Lincoln himself was quick to use the Douglas argument, moreover, when the outbreak of the Civil War dramatized the changes that had been taking place in the market patterns of the Northwestern farmers. Wheat and flour had begun to move directly eastward before the war, but large amounts of corn and pork were still consumed in the South. And Southerners also handled major quantities of the produce that was exported to Europe. The eruption of hostilities soon disrupted both of those activities, and the dislocation intensified the general derangement caused by the war. The President feared the Northwest might respond to the crisis by considering a settlement with the Confederacy. He countered that possibility with the argument that the great productivity of the agrarians had created a situation in which overseas markets had become essential. Compromise with the Confederacy was therefore impossible. The issue had to be settled unequivocally and for all time.

IV

Southern secession hit the Northern farmer severely and dramatically. At a time when he was becoming an increasingly efficient commercial producer, he lost a traditional and still significant domestic market and was simultaneously denied the use of the Mississippi for the cheap shipment of his surpluses to the East Coast and to foreign markets. The outbreak of the war also upset the economy of the Union, created a sharp depression, and thereby further decreased the market for agricultural goods. Those painful events served to unveil the full significance of the structural changes in Northern agriculture that had been taking place during the 1850s. The grain economy had become involved in the export of a rising surplus, and a similar pattern was emerging in flour and wheat.

The Northern agricultural businessmen did not recover until the combination of war orders and expanded exports to Britain (and the rest of Europe) created a boom. Then they improved their position despite the serious wartime inflation. They paid their debts, added new buildings and equipment, and bought more land. They also continued to expand their production, even though the overall rate of growth of the Northern economy decreased during the war. Compared with the Southern farmer, who turned to raising corn in order to feed himself and his army as his cotton rotted on the wharves, the Northern farmer reaped great gains from the war.

But in consolidating his new market orientation at the same time it increased his efficiency and surpluses, the war also created significant problems for the Northern farmer. As his commodities and produce went eastward for distribution to the domestic market, or transshipment to Europe, the Western farmer confronted the vital issues of transportation and control of the marketplace. He also became more concerned about the way the high American tariff rates, one of the prices he paid for the Homestead Act, which was supposed to give him cheap land, influenced the size of his foreign market. And the more agriculture became integrated and organized as a commercial system, the more the farmer was affected by the actions of his fellow agrarians and other groups in the political economy, by technological innovations, and by diseases and other natural phenomena that influenced his production.

The farm businessman very quickly focused much of his concern and agitation on the railroad system. He knew he needed reliable, fast, and cheap transportation to move his surpluses to market. For that reason, he generally urged and supported the construction of major east-west trunk lines and related feeder spurs, and directly or indirectly supplied many of the subsidies that speeded the work. Such action was a continuation of his traditional willingness to use the government for such broad economic purposes. But the agriculturalist also wanted an equitable return on his investment as a citizen, as well as reasonable treatment as an entrepreneur in the marketplace, from a transportation system that he viewed as a method of improving his competitive position. He supplied, as taxpayer, a large part of the cost of any and all internal improvements. He was not being given something for nothing by other segments of the population. The experiences of the war and postwar years, moreover, intensified the farmer's earlier awareness that the price he received for his surpluses was set on the Liverpool and London exchanges.

Such businessmen quickly and accurately recognized that the cost of transportation was one of the major overhead charges that affected their profits. It was also one of the factors of production that the farmer could reach and deal with directly. He naturally wanted low freight rates, but he also wanted rates that did not discriminate against him and rates that did not fluctuate arbitrarily and unfavorably with the time of the year and the market situation. The farmer's concern with transportation costs, which arose directly out of his routine business involvement with the foreign market, was the primary cause of his increasingly vigorous attack on the railroads.

To effect the changes he sought, the farmer assaulted the rails on the grounds that the subsidies they had taken from local and national governments defined them as quasi-public institutions, and that their arbitrary and selfish behavior posed a threat to the integrity of representative government. And he advanced the more general economic argument, taken from Adam Smith, that the railroad system, like the monetary system, was part of the structure of the marketplace itself, rather than merely another business operating in the marketplace. On that basis, the farmer maintained that the rails were subject to basic controls and regulations designed to guarantee the effective and equitable functioning of the marketplace for all entrepreneurs.

Such businessmen saw nothing radical, unreasonable, or illogical in turning to the government for aid in dealing with the transportation problem. Nor was there—despite the arguments advanced by contemporary critics and later observers in an effort to prove that the farmers were dangerous subversives, harbingers of socialism, or men incapable of accepting and adapting to the inevitable triumph of industrialism. The agriculturalist was acting wholly within the theories and traditions of marketplace capitalism when he demanded action to regulate rates and to provide competitive transportation alternatives by improving and extending the system of canals and navigable rivers.

Such immediate and fundamental concerns increasingly turned the Northern farmers away from the issues of Reconstruction after the Civil War. Whatever the individual exception, they had never as a group been actively concerned with freeing the slave and they did not provide any sustained positive support for the efforts of the Radical Republicans to extend large-scale assistance to the free black men. They were interested in blocking the resurgence of planter power in the national government, but that attitude was progressively weakened as they sought political allies against Northeastern urban leadership. For that reason, the Democratic party enjoyed a signifi- cant resurgence in the North by the end of the 1860s.

The Southern white farmer was initially preoccupied with the severe difficulties he faced as a defeated enemy in restoring produc- tion and reentering the marketplace as an effective operator. He found it necessary to combat many of the policies of the state governments that came into being under national Republican leader- ship. He had to struggle to maintain his position against the white business interest that took control of the cotton economy and pushed him into the role of a sharecropper. And he had to come to terms with the freed black man. He was thus more directly engaged in the politics of Reconstruction than his Northern counterpart. But the Southerner also steadily shifted his attention and effort to the issues that directly affected his position as a farmer in the marketplace. The prewar alliance between Northern and Southern agricultural busi- nessmen was revived on the basis of a common concern to check the power of the metropolitan businessman and to obtain internal improvements that would help all farmers.

As they became ever more involved in trying to deal effectively with the railroads, the farmers grew more intensely conscious that they composed a majority of the population that nevertheless regu- larly exercised significantly less power than a metropolitan minority composed of commercial, industrial, and financial groups centered in the northeastern part of the country. The agricultural sector of the

American political economy accounted for the majority of the population prior to the Civil War, and it continued to do so throughout the nineteenth century. The distribution of urban and rural population in 1870 was 9.9 million urban and 28.17 million rural; in 1900 it was 30.2 million urban and 45.8 million rural. And the true differential between the metropolis and the country was greater than indicated by those figures because not all of the urban centers were part of the metropolitan sector of the political economy. Many cities, even some as large as 100,000, were structurally and psychologically part of the country.

The farmers confronted the additional difficulty that both major parties emerged from the war dominated by metropolitan leaders. That was particularly clear in connection with the Republican party, but it was also true of the Democrats. And those farmers, Northern as well as Southern, who identified with and supported the Democratic party were denied substantial national representation and influence from 1860 until after the Panic of 1873. The agricultural majority of the country was thus effectively ruled by a metropolitan minority long years before the American political economy became industrialized.

The accelerating commercialization of agriculture intensified the farmer's awareness and understanding of his inferior position. The resulting consciousness of his predicament deepened his concern to win a greater share of economic, political, and social rewards. Whatever his more favorable view of the laws when they had been passed, he concluded well before the Panic of 1873 that the legislation voted by the wartime Union Congress had in practice balanced out in favor of nonagrarian interests and groups. His anger over that outcome was increased by the way many metropolitan spokesmen talked about the primary importance of the agricultural sector of the economy, and by the way many of their policies were predicated upon using the truth of that analysis for their own purposes. The theory about the primacy of agriculture was not simply a self-centered myth created and propagated by the farmer. Eastern financiers and other leaders spoke increasingly after 1870 of how the economy in general, as well as their particular operations, were dependent upon agriculture.

Such interpretations and arguments reinforced the agricultural businessman's traditional acceptance of and reliance upon the gospel of political economy according to Adam Smith. American farmers had been responsive as early as the end of the eighteenth century to all the main lines of argument advanced by Smith in *The Wealth of Nations*. They had taken his insistence that a free marketplace economy was essential to political and social freedom, and integrated it with the individualistic side of John Locke's philosophy. That produced an equation that causally linked the free marketplace with freedom per se. The true entrepreneur was a free producer who created plenty for all by operating freely in a free marketplace.

Smith likewise provided a solid critique of monopolies, and of the misuse of the government by special coteries of metropolitan interests. The farm businessmen were also aware that Smith offered careful and even sophisticated justification for government actions, such as those concerned with improving transportation or checking monopolies, that were designed to strengthen the structure and guarantee the freedom of the marketplace itself. And their own experience, particularly after the 1840s, steadily reinforced their understanding and acceptance of Smith's great stress on the necessity of the sustained expansion of the market as the dynamic engine of continued progress and freedom.

The farmers also extended their traditional appreciation of Smith's explanation of how the economy was inherently divided into a town and a country sector, and of his blunt judgment that the town or metropolitan sector enjoyed an inherent structural economic advantage over the country or agricultural sector. Given their internalized acceptance of the Smith-Lockean marketplace conception of the world and how it worked, the farmers' war and postwar experiences generated a steadily more intense consciousness of themselves as members of a country majority caught in an inferior, neocolonial relationship with the metropolitan minority.

The reinforcing interaction between that consciousness and the rising sense of urgency he felt as a commercial farmer to act effectively to improve his position turned the agriculturalist toward militant organization and action. Farmers had come together in various associations and clubs even before the American Revolution, but the spirit as well as the extent of such movements began to change during the 1840s. The shift became particularly significant during the Civil War, when farmers demanded government assistance against diseases that threatened their livestock, and opened a long campaign to win institutionalized recognition and influence for themselves in a federal department of government with representation in the Cabinet.

Then as the postwar boom began to dissipate at a time when they were encountering serious troubles with the railroads, the market system, and metropolitan political leaders, the agricultural business-men began to issue tough manifestos and declarations of independence. The movement became institutionalized on a national scale with the founding of the Patrons of Husbandry in 1867, and the ensuing rapid growth of the Grange and similar organizations during the next five years. Acting independently, as well as with other disgruntled businessmen like the merchants, the farmers moved to control the railroads, and to obtain other government action calculated to improve their position. By the time of the Panic of 1873 and the ensuing depression, therefore, the farmers were becoming a highly self-conscious, articulate, and increasingly militant majority in the United States.

V

The severe and baleful depression of the 1870s subjected the farmers to great adversity and suffering. Their response developed as a combination of several major alternatives. One of them, to hang on and somehow subsist and survive through individual courage and will power, and through mutual aid, was of necessity practiced by the great majority. However wrenching and painful it was, most farmers felt that course of action was more practical as well as preferable to the option of leaving the land. The travail of abandoning a personal business in which oneself and one's family had invested much psychological strength, as well as economic and physical resources, was compounded by the hardships involved in reestablishing oneself and one's family in the towns or larger urban centers that were plagued by unemployment and poverty.

The farmers revealed a similar disinterest in dealing with the depression and its consequences by making structural changes in the existing capitalist system. They did not respond to that choice as it was outlined and advocated by socialist and other radical workers and intellectuals in the cities, and they did not evolve a similar or related approach among themselves. Their commitment to market-place capitalism as defined and developed by Adam Smith, and to the philosophical system grounding political and social freedom in such a free marketplace economy, proved impervious and resilient enough to resist the impact of the worst depression that Americans had yet experienced.

One of the major sources of that strength was the conviction that the depression could be dealt with effectively by honoring the first principles of a free marketplace economy. Many farmers consequently embraced the alternative of reforming the system so that it could and would function as they thought and believed it should. Such efforts involved the agricultural businessmen in many organizations at the local and state levels, as well as in the nationwide Grange. They offered a great number of proposals, but their principal approaches can be grouped under a few main headings.

One such reform program concerned the land question. That issue was dramatized by the failure of the Homestead Act to provide a large number of people with good land at low prices, and some of the farmers concentrated on trying to revise and extend that legislation in order to accomplish the original intention. Others came to emphasize and attack what they considered the economically baneful and politically dangerous effects of the centralized ownership of vast acreages, and of speculative practices that denied anyone the use of the land.

Those approaches had the effect, directly or indirectly, of focusing more and more attention on the traditional assumption that American democracy and economic welfare were directly related to a surplus of fertile free land. Men had talked specifically about what they called the safety valve provided by the Western lands very early in the eighteenth century, and the discussion was revived during the depression of the 1870s. As a result, the famous frontier thesis began to be formulated at the grass-roots level by various agricultural spokesmen almost twenty years before it was stated by such intellectuals as Frederick Jackson Turner and Brooks Adams. Implicitly, if not overtly, that explanation of democracy and prosperity pointed toward the necessity of finding a new frontier. And that kind of reasoning, coupled with the impact of the depression, instilled the first sense of impending crisis, and even doom, that became steadily more intense and general through the 1880s into the 1890s.

All those results of the concern with land policy required time to mature, however, and in the meantime many farm businessmen were attracted to the idea of improving their competitive position in the existing marketplace. One such proposal, which appealed to Southerners as well as Northerners, advocated the organization of cooperatives to handle merchandising, and even some producing and marketing operations. The depression also intensified the existing concern to reform and regulate the railroads, to improve the system of water transportation, and to organize direct trade relationships between

American farmers and various European markets. The reformers also attacked the monetary system. They fought hard, and with temporary success, to block the policy of contracting the currency supply by withdrawing the Civil War greenbacks and resuming specie payments. They simultaneously opposed the centralization of power over the money supply among a few large financiers. And they opened what became a sustained and highly emotional effort to reverse the demonetization of silver that had occurred in February 1873, shortly before the first signs of the panic and depression.

The silver mining interest was of course a principal element in the coalition that agitated the remonetization of silver. And a significant number of metropolitan businessmen likewise supported the reform. But farm businessmen supplied the great strength of the movement. They gravitated to the issue and the campaign for several reasons. They felt that the act of demonetization provided a particularly gross example of the dangerous and selfish way the financiers used their vast power to control the political process as well as the marketplace, and thereby also illustrated the corruption of metropolitan politics. And, in truth, the farmers cut close to the bone when they made those charges. For the men who planned and carried through the demonetization of silver did engage in collusion over a number of years to insure the success of their efforts to place the United States on the gold standard.

The farmers advanced two principal arguments to support their demand for remonetization. One of them concerned the domestic marketplace. It asserted with considerable persuasiveness that the larger money supply created by coining silver was necessary to handle the business of a growing economy (and would therefore help generate recovery from the depression), and that the inflationary aspects of the move would help raise the standard of living for all Americans—including the farmers. The other argument for remonetization was directly related to the farmers' concern with overseas markets. The agricultural businessmen maintained first that the purely economic results of remonetization would expand their sales (and those of other producers). That would occur because the nations and individuals that sent silver bullion to America to have it coined into American dollars would have to spend the money on agricultural products, and on other goods and services. Even if remonetization did lower prices, as the gold advocates asserted it would, that effect would also operate to raise exports. Finally, the farmers pointed out that remonetization would make it possible for them to penetrate new markets in Latin America and Asian countries that based their monetary systems on silver.

In and of itself, the farmers continued, that effect of remonetization would serve to undercut the extensive power that Great Britain exercised in and over the world marketplace. That in turn would bring the metropolis and the country sectors of the world economy into a more balanced and equitable relationship; directly in connection with the English, and indirectly because weakening London was a way of weakening the New York money power that dominated the country sector of the American economy. The agrarians further maintained that remonetization would directly and significantly improve their position in the Liverpool and London commodity markets for grain and cotton. As long as silver was demonetized in the United States, they argued, British operators could and did buy the bullion cheaply in order to have it coined into Indian rupees. The profit on that operation enabled them to buy Indian wheat and cotton and undersell the American markets, or to improve Indian production and accomplish the same objective by cutting American sales in that fashion.

That multifaceted argument for the remonetization of silver on the grounds that it would enlarge the overseas market and at the same time improve the terms of trade quickly became an integral part of the farmer's case for recovering from the depression by expanding the overseas market for his surplus production. Such an export drive was a major alternative open to the agricultural businessmen, and they rapidly came to stress that solution above all others. As that happened, moreover, they increasingly related their attacks on the railroads (and their demands for improved water transportation) to the drive for foreign markets.

The antimonopoly campaign was affected in a similar, if also more complicated, manner. Some farmers stressed the argument that the big operators and trusts, by maintaining artificially high prices, prevented overseas market expansion. But others concluded that the meat processors and flour millers actually enlarged the market through their exports, and that analysis had the effect—directly or indirectly—of weakening the assault on the big operators. And, ultimately, the farmers moderated their antagonism toward established metropolitan political leaders as those men responded to the agrarian demand for larger foreign markets.

Several factors explain the consensus that developed in support of the export solution to the problems confronted by American farmers.

Their deep and positive commitment to the political economy developed by Smith and Locke made then unwilling to undertake radical changes, and that attitude reinforced the inherently expansionist logic of Smith and Locke. Their economic theory and beliefs turned them toward the overseas market. The pre–Civil War traditions of American agriculture further strengthened the appeal of that way out of the crisis, as did the direct experiences of the war and the postwar years.

But still another factor was crucial because it served to verify the theory, the beliefs, the tradition, and the past experiences in an intensely dramatic fashion. For with the fiscal year beginning July 1, 1877, rising agricultural exports rapidly improved the condition of the farmer and at the same time played a vital role in pulling the entire American economy out of the depression. The export of crude foodstuffs began to increase during fiscal 1876, moving from $79 million for fiscal 1875 to $94 million. Then they jumped to $155 million for fiscal 1877, $266 million by 1880, and remained at $242 million for fiscal 1881. Overseas sales of manufactured foodstuffs rose from $110 million for fiscal 1875 to $150 million in 1877, and then spurted to $193 million for 1880 and $226 million for fiscal 1881.

The primary cause of the boom was a five-year period of miserable weather, and widespread diseases affecting crops and animals, that drastically reduced the output of European agriculture. The secondary cause was the ability of the American farmer, and the related groups in the economy, to produce and deliver the food that was needed. The immediate economic results were threefold: Europe was fed, the American economy generated increasingly strong forces producing recovery from the depression, and the balance-of-trade position of the United States shifted to the positive side of the ledger. It is worth emphasizing, if only because it deeply affected the thinking of American leaders of that time, that *the agricultural businessmen, rather than the metropolitan industrialists, were responsible for the famous turn of the trade balance*. As some economists later pointed out, there were signs that the American economy had begun a slow revival from the bottom of the depression before the boom in agricultural exports; but the overseas market bonanza clearly played a crucial role in strengthening and sustaining the return to prosperity. American leaders of those years, moreover, were far less impressed with the role of nonagricultural factors in the recovery than they were with the importance of the exports of grain and meat. The effect on all American thinking, therefore, was to extend and deepen the orientation toward overseas markets as a crucial element in the nation's well-being.

That was particularly true of the farmers, naturally enough, but other groups in the political economy manifested the same kind of response. Such was clearly apparent, for example, among the producers intimately connected with the commodity crop farmers and the stockmen. Thus the meat processors and the flour millers extended their own efforts to penetrate and then enlarge their position in foreign markets. But the middlemen who handled the sales of the crops and the meat, and the railroad executives (and waterway operators) who moved the foodstuffs to the ports, revealed the same increased concern with overseas markets. So did the manufacturers of agricultural implements. They not only interpreted the boom in agricultural exports as the key to increased sales of their equipment in the domestic market, but they intensified their own overseas marketing campaigns. And, finally, the Southern manufacturers of rough cotton textiles, who in many cases had a particularly close relationship with the cotton farmers, formulated their strategy of growth in terms of the export market.

The impact of the boom in agricultural exports was not limited, however, to the farmer and other businessmen whose operations tied them directly to the agricultural sector of the economy. Metropolitan leaders responded to the export bonanza by increasing their emphasis on the general importance of agriculture, by beginning to transfer the significance of the export market to their own particular situation, and by thinking more of the importance of the overseas market in the functioning of the entire economic system. In a similar fashion, key politicians of both major parties became export-oriented to a far greater degree, and on a far more permanent basis, than they had been before the depression. And some of them, like James Gillespie Blaine, reacted by making overseas economic expansion a central element in their basic program for the nation (and their own political success). Those men, along with some industrial and financial leaders, began to think less in terms of special-interest groups and more in terms of all such groups as interrelated parts of an integrated system that would come to depend more and more on exports.

Secretary of State William Seward had of course formulated his policies on that kind of analysis, and his ideas continued to be felt through men like Commodore Robert W. Shufeldt of the Navy.

Shufeldt was no doubt concerned with increasing the influence and improving the condition of the Navy, and with fulfilling his personal ambitions. But his strategy for achieving those objectives was based upon strengthening the Navy as the advance agent and defender of a vastly larger strategic perimeter. Schufeldt pointed to the central importance of agricultural exports in the general economy as proof that America was becoming irrevocably involved and committed in the world marketplace, and argued that the Navy was the only military instrument capable of dealing with the new situation.

A similar though more sophisticated economic analysis was offered by civilian intellectuals. David A. Wells, who had edited the *Pennsylvania Farm Journal* in the 1850s before becoming a government economist, was one such figure. Another was Edward Atkinson, who was particularly knowledgeable about cotton textiles. They were steadily effective in promoting a growing awareness and acceptance of the export orientation among metropolitan leaders. Directly and indirectly, therefore, the agricultural businessmen played a central part in redefining the strategic boundaries of the United States from an essentially defensive concept based on the continental limits to a far more dynamic and activist conception tied to the actual and desired position of the economy in the world marketplace. In some respects, at any rate, that was the most subtle yet far-reaching influence the farmers exercised on American foreign policy.

The great surge in exports also had the important effect of generating a growing certainty about the strength and power of the American economy. That was especially noticeable among the farmers and their spokesmen, who interpreted the boom as proof of their ability to control the markets of the world, as well as convincing evidence of their major role in the American economy. But a number of other businessmen also read the bonanza to mean that the United States was rapidly becoming the most powerful nation on earth. They agreed with the agriculturalists that the nation could begin to use that strength to control more markets, and to achieve other objectives of a political and ideological nature. That conviction was particularly significant in determining the response of the farmers to the end of the boom and the related decline of their economic welfare.

VI

The recovery of European agriculture was the primary cause of the end of the bonanza export market. The cycle of bad weather came to an end, the crop and livestock diseases ran their course or were brought under control, and production revived. There were other factors in the change, however, and they contributed to the continuing challenge to American farmers. One of those was the rising competition provided by the return of Russia to the international commodity markets, and by the increasing grain production in India. Another involved the anti-American restrictive policies devised and adopted by almost all European nations in response to the flood of American exports.

The overseas market boom of the late 1870s created the paradoxical situation in which the American farm businessmen, who were in a quasi-colonial position inside their own national economy, functioned as economic imperialists whose exports shook the political economies of European nations. The vast surpluses of cheap American food seriously disturbed the agricultural, and hence the political and social, organization of Germany, Austria, France, and Great Britain. *The American farmer, rather than the American manufacturer or financier, alerted the rest of the world to the power and the dangerous challenge of the American economy.* The specter of an Americanization of the world, as it came to be called in the 1890s, was initially created by the sodbuster, the swineherd, the cattleman, and the cotton-chopping sharecropper.

The immediate European response of fear and anger was swiftly translated into various measures designed to prevent the American giant from overwhelming—and controlling—their economies. One countermeasure involved encouraging alternate sources of supply in Argentina, as well as in Russia and India. Another emphasized efforts to improve the productivity of European agriculture. Russia, for example, soon began to provide government assistance in storing and transporting the wheat crop. And a third consisted of various restrictions calculated to decrease or halt the importation of American agricultural products.

The policies that raised barriers against American pork and beef were carefully explained and defended on the ground that American livestock, and the related meats, were extensively diseased. The argument had some substance. The prevalence of pleuro-pneumonia among cattle, and the extent of cholera and trichinosis among swine, were significant. And there is no reason to doubt that some European officials had a sincere regard for the public health of their countries. But it is highly questionable whether American meat was more diseased than the European product, and there is no question that the habits of food preparation and use in Europe contributed extensively to the amount of sickness and death. The evidence is clear, moreover, that much of the action against American exports was generated by very powerful and effective pressure from deeply interested economic groups that had no desire to be driven out of business. That opposition remained highly effective long after the health argument had been met by a vast improvement in the condition of American livestock. The result was a rising bitterness among American agriculturalists that contributed very greatly to defining major European nations as a direct threat to the national necessities—and hence vital interests—of the United States.

The American response to the end of the boom in agricultural exports had an extensive effect on the nation's attitudes toward foreign policy. That was the case not only because the downturn involved the fundamental assumptions, analyses, and beliefs of the great majority of the people of the United States, but because those people undertook a sustained and increasingly militant campaign to solve their problems through the recovery and expansion of the overseas markets for their surpluses. Their battle for markets was not predestined to evolve into imperialism, but their ideas, beliefs, and practices did carry them to the point where they confronted a choice between embracing imperialism or changing their domestic political economy in fundamental respects. They resolved that dilemma in favor of imperial expansion because their marketplace philosophy, traditions, and actions all combined to persuade them that such an imperial policy was the only workable solution, and that it was likewise the only approach that would sustain and even enlarge the area of freedom.

The end of the boom initially shocked American farm businessmen with a realization that their problems had not been solved for all time. It likewise reminded them forcefully that Adam Smith's free marketplace economy did not function automatically. All the old problems reappeared once the boom ended. The railroads were still powerful and still controlled by metropolitan leaders, and the system of water transportation was still unable to provide a satisfactory and competitive alternative. The money system remained under the control of metropolitan gold contractionists, and the anger over that situation was intensified by the realization that farm exports had underwritten the resumption of specie payments on a gold standard. And the flour millers and meat processors, along with the merchants and other middlemen, were more firmly entrenched at crucial crossroads of the agricultural economy.

Each of those aspects of economic reality reinforced farm awareness of metropolitan power over the country. So did the political parties. The Democratic victory in the congressional elections of 1874, which had raised hopes that a restoration of two-party politics would bring significant benefits to the farmers, did not produce such results. The leadership of both major parties continued to deal with the problems of the nation from the point of view of the metropolis, and on such issues as the money question identified the interests of the American metropolis with those of Great Britain and other Western European countries.

The long-standing resentment against that attitude and its practical consequences was further intensified because the end of the boom coincided with three developments that extended and deepened the earlier challenge to the traditional assumptions about a surplus of easily available land. The question, as many historians and economists later pointed out, was not whether the continent was literally full of people, or even whether all the nonmarginal land had been turned to cultivation. Neither of those conditions existed. But the great majority of Americans did not approach the issue in those terms between 1876 and 1896. They viewed the problem from within the tradition that defined a surplus of easily available and productive land as a necessary condition for American prosperity and freedom. And they interpreted the situation that existed after 1880 as one that threatened that classical foundation of American progress and liberty.

They first pointed out that while such land was not wholly occupied, it was nevertheless clear that the reservoir of cheap, good land was being rapidly depleted. Then they argued that another significant acreage was held by relatively few large domestic or foreign owners, and was thus effectively withdrawn from use by American homesteaders. And, finally, they correctly noted that profitable cultivation of much of the remaining open land required more capital (and other assistance) than was available to the average American. That analysis produced many proposals calculated to sustain the reality of the tradition that linked American welfare to a surplus of good land. One group continued to approach the problem largely or wholly within a domestic context, and was concerned either to return some of the best land held by large American operators to the public domain, or to help Americans sustain themselves on the land that was difficult to farm. But another response was directly related to the evolution of foreign policy attitudes and proposals.

There was first of all the militant antiforeign feeling and agitation that arose among farmers of all sections against Europeans (and particularly the British) who controlled vast acreages from Texas northward to the Canadian border. That produced an anticolonialist movement of major proportions that was directed against American metropolitan leaders who were associated—indirectly as well as directly—with the foreign owners, as well as against the aliens themselves. The practical result was a movement for the nationalization of such land in order to make it available to American farmers.

The alien land issue reinforced the existing agrarian anger against the British and other Europeans over the demonetization of silver, and the restrictions raised against American agricultural exports. Those reactions were in turn generalized as well as intensified by the explicit and implicit conclusions drawn from the confrontation with the tradition that linked American well-being with a continuing surplus of land. For what happened during the late 1870s and early 1880s can only be understood as a broad grass-roots formulation and acceptance of the frontier thesis explanation of American history.

That analysis carried the farmers (and the other Americans who accepted it) into an even greater emphasis on the necessity of overseas markets. Such markets appeared as the only frontier that could sustain prosperity and freedom. The agricultural businessmen ultimately came to argue that they had to defeat the European metropolitan centers of power not only to win those markets, but also in order to realize their rightful majority rights and influence against the power of the American metropolis. The farmers who were quasi-colonials in the domestic economy thus became anticolonial imperialists in foreign affairs as a strategy of becoming equals at home.

VII

The expansionist-oriented outlook that the farm businessmen developed by the end of the export boom produced several consequences that progressively affected their actions during the decade of the 1880s. It led them to become steadily more skeptical and angry toward the majority of metropolitan leaders who responded indifferently or slowly to agricultural alternatives and pressures. That in turn extended and strengthened the development of farm leaders and organizations. Finally, the farmers concentrated ever more specifically—and militantly—on programs and policies calculated to regain the position they had enjoyed during the export boom, and to penetrate and hopefully dominate new markets in Latin America and Asia.

Cattlemen concentrated their efforts on reopening and enlarging the European market. They first demanded retaliation by the government against the British regulation that required the slaughter of all live cattle imports within ten days of arrival. In general, however, metropolitan leaders opposed that strategy. An important group of the cattle raisers then began advocating a program of inspection and control to eradicate pleuro-pneumonia. That caused conflicts with the meat processors who resisted such regulation, and led to intensified demands for antitrust legislation. Still other cattlemen turned to the remonetization of silver, or to exporting live cattle through Canada, as a way of counteracting the British refusal to remove their restrictions.

The swine feeders composed a larger group because many grain farmers began to raise hogs as a way of obtaining more profits from their corn surpluses. They tended to be more persistent about retaliation against European restrictions on pork, and continued to press for barriers against French and German exports even after they began supporting a meat inspection program. Their troubles in the hog market affected their corn problems, furthermore, and they soon agitated for government activity to enlarge the exports of that commodity.

Some of the hog producers, along with one group of cattlemen, were less militant critics of the meat processors. They argued that the big firms—Armour, Swift, and Morris—made great efforts to enlarge their exports of preserved and refrigerated meat, and expressed great skepticism that smaller companies created by antitrust action could do as well in the ruthless international competition. On balance, however, and largely because conditions did not improve in any sustained way, the drive for foreign markets during the 1880s strengthened the campaign for an antitrust law just as it continued to augment the push for federal regulation of the railroads. The battle for overseas markets had the ironic result, moreover, of improving the meat eaten by Americans.

The campaigns to reopen European markets increasingly converged with, and reinforced, the general economic nationalism manifested by the farm businessmen. The attack on foreign land-owners and speculators was broadened to include British and other investors in cattle raising, meat processing, flour milling, and railroads. The arguments for the remonetization of silver steadily won more adherents in the South, as well as in the North and the West. And Southerners developed an analysis that quickly produced a proposal to store surplus commodities like tobacco, rice, and cotton in government warehouses. One of the objectives of that subtreasury plan, and the one that most historians have stressed, was to obtain short-run credit advances for the surpluses while they were held off the market. But the farmers based their argument for the program on the proposition that holding the surpluses, or controlling and manipulating the supply, would enable the American agricultural businessmen to dominate the commodity marketplace of the world—and, more specifically, to break the economic power of Great Britain. The entire approach was a product of the export orientation of the farmers.

The failure of metropolitan leaders to respond to such proposals for reopening the European markets produced several results. Farmers became increasingly angry and militant, particularly as the depression of the 1880s intensified and extended their difficulties. Some turned back toward their earlier effort to cut their losses in the existing marketplace, and to win a larger share of those rewards, by reforming the system. Their inability to win any quick or dramatically productive victories, however, reinforced the feeling that the domestic American metropolis operated as part of an international metropolis that controlled their markets and kept them in an inferior position. Such an analysis strengthened their already assertive economic nationalism and pointed them once again toward the export solution. And that extended the pressure to find and open new markets.

One element of metropolitan leadership centered in the Republican party had tried ever since the 1860s to deal with the overseas market orientation of the farm businessmen by defining the home market that would be produced by industrialization behind high tariff walls as a new and better export market. Beginning in the 1870s, and continuing with growing vigor during the 1880s, those Republican leaders sought to counter the antimetropolitan feeling among farmers by depicting men who advocated low tariffs or free trade as un-American agents of the British who wanted to dominate the American economy. Their propaganda, which ranged from wild and crude accusations of conspiracy to sophisticated and clever syllogisms, had the related objective of sustaining the Civil War image of the Democratic party as a hothouse of sedition and treason. The Republican tariff argument was thus a strategy of continuing to wave the bloody shirt to retain political power.

Three factors progressively undercut that attempt during the 1880s. One was the increasing number of metropolitan leaders who adopted and adapted the traditional export orientation of the agricultural businessmen. Various elements of the industrial part of the economy, including relatively small hardware factories as well as giants like Standard Oil and the largest agricultural implement manufacturers, produced increasing surpluses. They had to be exported if they were to be sold at all. The hard times of the 1880s not only dramatized that truth to those companies, but turned other metropolitan entrepreneurs toward the foreign markets. As a result, Republican leaders began to modify and then to change their position on the tariff.

The second factor involved the way the Democrats increasingly emphasized the export argument in behalf of low tariffs. Southerners had stressed that point before the Civil War, but it gained new attention as political leaders such as Representative Roger Q. Mills of Texas began to employ it after it had been reformulated by intellectuals like David Wells. They also added a clever argument developed by standing the Republican high tariff logic on its head. Low tariffs would not only enlarge the market for agricultural surpluses, the Democrats asserted, but by expanding the market for manufactured goods they would create a big home market for the farmer. In adopting that approach, Grover Cleveland stressed the benefits to metropolitan interests, but his vigorous advocacy nevertheless attracted farm businessmen away from the Republican high tariff position.

The Democratic agitation of their new thesis on low tariffs reinforced the general agricultural drive for new markets, which in itself was the third element that weakened the Republicans. The convergence of those themes was at first particularly apparent in the South, where the traditional concern over markets for raw cotton was extended during the 1880s by the expansion of a rough-cotton textile industry geared to production for foreign markets. The Southern campaign was especially vigorous because it was a manifestation of a militant desire by a section that had been defeated in war to overthrow Northern domination, as well as the product of a close relationship between many of the cotton producers and the textile mills.

VIII

The Southern push for new markets came to be symbolized by Senator John T. Morgan of Alabama, who waged a ceaseless struggle to penetrate Africa, Latin America, and Asia. His battles in behalf of an isthmian canal, and to enlarge the Navy, generated growing support among farm businessmen throughout the country, and were a significant part of the dynamic process by which they increasingly defined America's strategic perimeter in terms of the world market-place. Morgan's arguments also strengthened anti-British feeling, and contributed to the agitation for the remonetization of silver. The Southerners also exerted an important influence on Northern metro-politan leaders. Part of that effect grew out of the challenge that the region's textile mills presented to the New England firms. The latter first responded by supporting the South's bid for the export market in rough cottons, and then gradually turned in the same direction as the economy failed to generate sustained prosperity after the depression of the 1880s. Some railroad leaders, most notably James J. Hill of the Great Northern, also came to view cotton exports to Asia as an important part of a strategy to create a continuous flow pattern of transcontinental freight traffic designed to increase profits on a regular basis.

Southern concern with overseas markets also affected Northern Republican leaders like Blaine who had not abandoned the hope of building a viable political movement in that section. Along with a few others, Blaine realized early in the 1880s that the export approach offered a promising way of holding the Western farmers while adding Southern support. Such men were aware that the meat and wheat producers of the vast trans-Appalachian region had become increasingly concerned with new markets in Latin America, and that they were beginning to talk about Asia as still another place to sell their surpluses.

The flour millers of the West, along with the meat packers, had first turned to those markets during the downturn of the late 1860s. Their interest intensified during the depression of the 1870s. Then railroad men like Hill and Stuyvesant Fish of the Illinois Central added their pressure. By the mid-1880s all elements of Western agriculture were becoming increasingly vigorous in demanding government action to open and control alternate markets. More and more farmers, for example, wanted the remonetization of silver to facilitate the direct penetration of Latin American and Asian economies, and to weaken Great Britain's position in those markets.

The farm businessmen also accepted the need for a larger Navy and for an isthmian canal. Agricultural attitudes on those issues have often been misunderstood because their critique of specific proposals has been misread as unequivocal opposition to the programs. In the case of the canal, for example, they concentrated their efforts on influencing the plans for financing the operation. They wanted it built by the government in order to avoid a repetition of the subsidies given to the railroads, to involve the government in extending the marketplace, and to insure that they would be able, through the Congress, to influence future decisions.

Their approach to enlarging the Navy (and the merchant marine) was even more subtle and complex. They were primarily determined to establish the program on the cornerstones of an advanced American technology and effective government control. They were secondarily concerned to make a sound decision about the composition of the new fleet, and at various times did disagree among themselves as well as with metropolitan leaders over the relative weight to be assigned to cruisers and battleships. Those attitudes and positions had the effect of delaying somewhat the construction of a large battleship Navy. But the Navy Department's own plan for growth called for phased development of a battle line, and the effect of the agricultural critique can easily be exaggerated. Furthermore, the policy of the farmers unquestionably contributed to the building of a better Navy, and they clearly supported its deployment and use in behalf of American economic expansion.

The agricultural pressure for markets advanced rapidly toward a climax after 1886 as continued economic difficulties interacted with the slowness and ineffectiveness of metropolitan leadership. While President Cleveland's belated emphasis on low tariffs as a way of enlarging exports added to the pressure for foreign markets, for example, his purist laissez-faire attitude prevented him from acting quickly and effectively on that proposal. That increased the impatience of the farm businessmen. Their organizations, including the Northern and Southern Alliance movements as well as the reviving Grange, persistently stressed the need to find new and larger markets.

One of the more revealing indications of the progressive integration of all the expansionist themes and policies appeared in connection with the long-standing campaign to improve the Department of Agriculture and raise it to Cabinet status. One indirect tactic employed by the agriculturalists involved attacks on the Department of State as a refuge for incompetent and aristocratic metropolitan leaders, and assaults on the appropriations for the department as a way of forcing it to use personnel to expand exports. The direct strategy called for unrelenting pressure for markets to create a Cabinet spokesman to defend and advance their interest overseas as well as at home. When that objective was finally gained in 1889, moreover, the farmers merely redirected their pressure for markets to the new official.

In a similar way, the long struggle by Western agriculturalists to win statehood for the territories became intimately involved with the rising demand for more vigorous market diplomacy. Their inability to obtain satisfaction from metropolitan leaders deepened their consciousness and resentment concerning their own inferior and quasi-colonial position as the country sector of the political economy. The farmers not only sought more home rule in their own areas, but they wanted additional votes in the Congress and the related influence in the councils of the major parties where the basic alternatives were so often formulated.

Their attitudes and activities made it apparent by 1887–1888, moreover, that they might well organize their own political party if existing Republican and Democratic leadership continued to be unresponsive and ineffective. Some metropolitan Democrats were by that time beginning to fear, with reason, that they were losing control of the party to the farmers headed by such fast-rising militants as William Jennings Bryan of Nebraska. And the more perceptive Republican leaders recognized that their party could be reduced to a metropolitan minority by the defection of angry agricultural businessmen to such a reoriented Democratic organization or to a new party.

IX

The Republicans reacted to the challenge more quickly and with greater success than the Democrats. They did so largely because Blaine understood the seriousness of the danger, and together with a few other metropolitan leaders, devised a strategy that ultimately retained the loyalty of the Western farmers. Blaine also hoped to win enough support among Southern cotton interests to extend the party's power base in that region. That effort failed, but his attempt nevertheless had the effect of strengthening the general consensus on economic expansion. It was clear by the end of the first Cleveland Administration in 1888 that the agrarians had two major options. They could exploit Cleveland's weaknesses and try to take control of the Democratic party, or they could unite to form their own organization. The farmers are often blamed, and during those years attacked each other, for falling between those two stools. That judgment overlooks two crucial factors. First, they were at the very least as much concerned with a foreign policy solution to their problems as they were involved with domestic answers to their difficulties. Secondly, and in that context, Blaine was one of the few people in those years to enjoy and exploit an understanding of that overseas market emphasis among the farm businessmen. Blaine's astute appeal to the farmers on that basis thus accounted for much of what has been termed their indecision or blind loyalty to party. In a real sense, Blaine defined the issue as a choice between alternate methods of market expansion and persuaded a determining group of farmers that his policy would be more effective.

Benjamin Harrison shared Blaine's insight into the crisis and rapidly committed the Republicans to an expansionist strategy in foreign affairs after he defeated Cleveland in the presidential election of 1888. He did so on the broad grounds that the entire economy required foreign markets, and because they offered a way to hold on to a crucial bloc of agrarian votes. In that respect Harrison was acting for specific metropolitan interests that had accepted the export thesis and for the intellectuals who had generalized that analysis to the entire political economy. And in many ways he was himself an intellectual, even though he was not an academic or a New England man of letters.

Thus to conclude that Blaine and Harrison were actuated by a political motive is to miss the crucial part of the story. Since politics is defined by the acquisition and retention of power, there is no doubt at all that Harrison and Blaine were politically motivated. Once over that twig in the analytical path, it is possible to deal with the more significant obstacles of determining the outlook that guides various men in attempting to secure the power, and defines the purposes they intend and try to achieve. Blaine and Harrison did not want the power for its own sake, or to fulfill a psychotic need to control other people. They sought it in order to act upon a broad policy of overseas economic expansion that they considered necessary and desirable for the entire political economy, as well as for specific interests within it; and they concluded they could win the power by offering that program to the agricultural businessmen who had done so much since 1866 to generate both the idea itself and the pressure to act upon the idea.

Thus Harrison not only overrode his political and the personal reservations to appoint Blaine as Secretary of State, but he carefully chose an expansionist to fill the newly created post of Secretary of Agriculture. Jeremiah M. Rusk of Wisconsin was an enthusiastic and untiring advocate of overseas markets for dairy farmers, livestock raisers, wheat growers, and corn producers. Harrison's other close associates, like Whitelaw Reid, shared that outlook. The widening and deepening of the agricultural unrest that occurred between the election and Harrison's inauguration only intensified their commitment to an expansionist program. The convergence of many Southern and Western farmers into the Alliance and Populist movements made it clear that the Republicans would have to act very quickly if they were to survive as anything more than a local and regional force. Harrison and Blaine were so concerned that they accepted the grave risk of splitting an already weakened party in order to save it by embracing overseas economic expansion. The showdown came early in 1890 when Blaine openly challenged the protectionists led by Representative William McKinley of Ohio for control of tariff policy.

McKinley had long been a champion of high tariffs, and regularly used the continuing industrialization of Ohio as proof of the way that protection created a home market for a diversified agriculture. He had realized from an early date, however, that foreign markets would become important when a mature industrial system had been created. In that sense, subtle but fundamental, the fight between McKinley and Blaine was over timing rather than principle. And since McKinley was intelligent, sensitive, and shrewd—as well as politically ambitious—he ultimately concluded that Blaine was correct about the crucial issue.

Blaine's strategy was a theoretical and practical work of art. Sometime during the 1870s, and perhaps a bit earlier, he had realized that the principle and practice of reciprocity offered the best of protection and free trade. He no doubt also understood, since the Grange and other farm groups had discussed and supported the policy during the mid-1870s, that reciprocity appealed to agricultural businessmen as a way of enlarging their foreign markets. And he had done much to keep the issue alive during the 1880s. Reciprocity was (and remains) a policy based on an honest marketplace exchange. The United States, as in Blaine's approach, lowers tariffs on products that it needs in return for a reduction of tariffs by another country on surplus goods that Americans want to sell. In order to open markets for Western and Southern farmers (flour, meat, and rough textiles), and for metropolitan manufacturers (oil, dry goods, and such items), Blaine confronted McKinley with a demand to revise the staunchly protectionist bill that McKinley had produced by 1890.

The ensuing battle was bitter and bloody, but Blaine won. His victory was primarily due to Western support for a strategy that promised to open new foreign markets and at the same time lower the cost of sugar. For Blaine argued powerfully that a reduction of the American tariff on sugar would not only break the barriers against flour and meat in Latin America, but that it would open the German market for American pork. And, once adopted as policy, the principle could be used to reopen and enlarge the markets of France, Great Britain, and other European nations.

Secretary of Agriculture Rusk was not idle while Blaine (and Harrison) fought McKinley. Rusk was a Union veteran who believed in direct action, and the domestic battle for reciprocity absorbed but a part of his energy. Anticipating victory there, he pressured Germany and France to arrange final surrender terms on pork, and simultaneously nagged the British to admit live cattle from the United States. In the third ring, he campaigned to expand corn exports. That effort, supported in particular by agricultural businessmen in Iowa and Minnesota, produced a major attempt to combine altruism and overseas market expansion in a private and official program of foreign aid. The strategy was to donate corn to Russia in order to relieve that nation's famine and demonstrate America's humanitarianism, to illustrate the superiority of the American free-market system, and to create a new market by changing Russian eating habits. The classic objectives of expanding markets and the area of freedom would thus be achieved.

Blaine's reciprocity program and Rusk's corn-to-Russia aid proposal established approaches that became institutionalized as central features of American foreign policy in the twentieth century. Both plans were also effective in the short run. The Harrison Administration's vigorous expansionist efforts generated a growing overseas interest in corn, reopened the German market for pork, and cleared the way for rising agricultural exports to Cuba and other Latin American economies. The widespread support for those actions made it clear, moreover, that the growing farm pressure for overseas markets was creating an increasingly deep and persuasive consensus in favor of such expansion. The movement had generated a momentum that was becoming ever more powerful.

Nothing demonstrated that more effectively than the congressional elections of 1890. On the surface, of course, it appeared that the overseas market strategy of Harrison, Blaine, and Rusk was a colossal failure. Angry farmers returned a congressional majority composed of Democrats, Populists, and dissident Republicans. But those new men were in truth at least as expansionist as the office-holders they replaced—and very probably more so. Party labels quickly proved a poor guide to foreign policy attitudes. The Populists provided the most dramatic evidence of that truth. Nebraska Senator William V. Allen bluntly told his colleagues, for example, that his supporters wanted more militant action in behalf of expansion, and promised to give them what they asked. Senators William A. Peffer of Kansas and James H. Kyle of South Dakota verified Allen's reading of the foreign policy attitudes of the dissenting farmers. And Representative Jeremiah Simpson of Kansas, crying out that "we are driven from the markets of the world," launched a campaign for overseas markets that ended several years later in a wrenching confrontation with imperialism.

Secretary of State Blaine and President Harrison were of course deeply distressed by the Republican defeat in 1890. But they had two insights into the situation that proved to be correct, and in acting on those perceptions they laid the foundation for a strategic Republican victory based on a foreign policy of overseas economic expansion. Harrison and Blaine realized that the 1890 defeat was due to three factors. Given the onrushing anger of the farmers, the Republicans lost because their expansionist program had not been put into operation quickly enough to produce tangible results, and the fight between Blaine and McKinley had divided the party and weakened the campaign effort.

They also understood, finally, that much of the Populist program (as with the proposals of other unhappy farmers) derived from agriculture's long emphasis on foreign markets. The mounting fury for the remonetization of silver (which had not been slaked by the Sherman Silver Purchase Act of 1890), the agitation for a subtreasury system of storing surplus commodities to control the market, the continuing demands for railroad regulation, and the sustained pressure for more improvements in the network of water transportation (including an isthmian canal), all evolved out of the farmers' practical and intellectual commitment to the overseas market.

On the basis of that analysis, Blaine and Harrison sustained their effort to pull the agricultural businessmen back into the Republican party by stressing just such expansion. The President's cross-country tour in 1891, for example, was a succession of speeches that explained his actions to enlarge foreign markets, and pleaded for support to sustain and extend such activities. In the narrow sense, and in the short run, the Harrison-Blaine approach appeared to fail in 1892 just as it had in 1890. The Democrats elected Grover Cleveland and maintained control of the House of Representatives. Those appearances proved to be misleading, however, because the consensus on expansion that had been so largely created by the agriculturalists proved to be more consequential in determining American foreign policy than the differences between the parties.

X

Nine events that occurred between the elections of 1892 and 1896 deepened, extended, and consolidated the expansionist outlook that the agrarian majority of the nation had evolved prior to 1892. The two that opened the sequence, the Hawaiian Revolution of January 1893, and the wracking depression of the 1890s that began with a panic in the spring of 1893, also exerted a particularly significant influence on the final integration of all the themes in that imperial *Weltanschauung*, and on the broad policy formulations that it produced.

The Hawaiian Revolution was the culmination of a century of American economic and ideological expansion into and throughout the life of the islands. The resulting power and influence excited the jealousy of other nations, and engendered persistent native resistance. The island opposition threatened to become more than merely troublesome after it won a narrow victory in the Hawaiian elections of 1890, and it was further strengthened when Queen Liliuokalani ascended the throne in January 1891. She immediately acted in ways to give meaning to her belief that Hawaiians ought to control Hawaii; and the depressing effect of the reciprocity provisions of the American tariff law of 1890, which handicapped island sugar exports to the United States, deepened her determination to implement her conviction.

Secretary of State Blaine attempted to counter the economic difficulties between 1890 and 1892 by making Hawaii a protectorate, but anti-American groups blocked the proposal. He then encouraged the pro-American interests that staged a successful coup against the Queen in January 1893 with the aid of American naval forces and a contingent of Marines. President Harrison promptly collaborated with the new rulers in an effort to annex the islands before he left office. Many farmers agreed with the President on the necessity and desirability of annexation, but enough opposed the move in the spring of 1893 to prevent action. That group favored de facto American control of the islands to facilitate marketplace expansion across the Pacific into Asia, but they were also concerned to honor the axiom of self-determination that was part of the free marketplace philosophy. Their confidence in the power of an American presence in the islands was the crucial factor that allowed them to formulate a policy that seemed to uphold ideological virtue at the same time it promised economic success.

That same attitude provoked their great and sustained anger, however, when President Cleveland proposed to return Queen Liliuo-kalani to her throne (and power). The majority of farm businessmen interpreted that recommendation as involving an even more flagrant violation of the principles and practices of freedom and self-determi-nation that was contained in the proposal for annexation. The result was a coalition of metropolitan and agricultural expansionists, sym-bolized by Republican Senator Henry Cabot Lodge of Massachusetts and Populist Senator Allen of Nebraska, that demanded the deploy-ment of the Navy to maintain the kind of true freedom that the pro-American coup had ostensibly established in the islands and to insure effective American domination of those stepping stones to the markets of Asia. Cleveland's policy also had the result of further stimulating agricultural anger against him as a particularly short-sighted and selfish metropolitan leader.

The farmers were not merely insisting that the freedom defined by the free marketplace political economy was true freedom. They were also asserting that the right of self-determination had to be judged in that light—at least in cases where the issue involved the expansion of America's free marketplace system. That was a momen-tous and far-reaching resolution of the contradiction between com-mitment to the freedom of self-determination and an equally strong commitment to the necessity of expansion in order to insure one's freedom and prosperity. It was the last step in transforming the long and urgent agricultural pressure for expanded exports into imperialism. The farmers stopped short of embracing a policy of colonial annexation, but they revealed an implacable determination to dominate and set limits on the Hawaiian political economy, and to define the islands as an element in their own expansionist program.

The grave depression that began in 1893 reinforced that response to the Hawaiian Revolution. Pervasive and continued economic difficulties heightened the farmers' already great concern for overseas markets and increased their militance in fighting for that objective and in battling metropolitan leaders who were slow to accept or act on that policy. The resulting upsurge in unrest, reinforced by a similar dissatisfaction among workers in the cities, was a major factor in completing the acceptance by metropolitan leaders of the overseas market approach that the farmers had been pushing for a generation. The other element was the direct economic pressure of the depression. Manufacturers and financial giants rapidly concluded that the industrial sector of the economy needed foreign markets at least as badly as the agriculturalists.

That ever-widening metropolitan concern for economic expansion led within five years to the general and final acceptance of the traditional agricultural outlook. That rapidly developing consensus did not prevent the eruption of serious and embittered arguments, however, over the best methods of expansion, or over which groups should formulate and execute the policy. Just such a fight, indeed, was the third important event of the period between the elections of 1892 and 1896. The issue concerned which monetary system—gold or silver—provided the best basis for economic development and expansion.

Cleveland and other determined defenders of gold monometallism launched an aggressive campaign to repeal the Sherman Silver Purchase Act of 1890 immediately after the panic of 1893. The case they advanced for gold rested largely on the necessity of maintaining the gold reserves of the Treasury in order to preserve America's international credit standing, and on the argument that gold monometallism was the standard of the world marketplace, and for that reason the United States had to operate on that basis if it wanted to expand exports.

Agrarian and other silver advocates exploded in opposition. They vigorously pressed their powerful theory that the full remonetization

of silver would produce a vast expansion of American exports—
industrial as well as agricultural—and asserted that result would in
and of itself generate recovery and guarantee permanent prosperity.
They also claimed that remonetization would accelerate and extend
domestic capital formation, and thereby further strengthen the forces
of economic revival at the same time it created more equity and
balance in the marketplace.

The agricultural businessmen lost the battle. Treasury purchases of
silver were stopped at the end of 1893. The defeat sustained the fury
that the fight aroused, however, and the silverites wholly committed
themselves to reversing the decision. The struggle also greatly
intensified the existing economic nationalism of the farmers and
focused it even more sharply against Great Britain and American
metropolitan leaders who supported British policies. Similar though
less highly charged conflicts shortly developed over the merits of
reciprocity as against low tariffs, over the most effective kind of
Navy, and over the priorities of expansion.

The men who became the major protagonists in the evolving
struggle actually formulated their positions long before 1896. William Jennings Bryan argued as early as 1893 that the combination of
silver and low tariffs, reinforced by the power created by the
productivity of the American farmer, would give the United States
supremacy in the world marketplace and the opportunity to spread
freedom around the globe. William McKinley took his stand on a
program that combined Blaine's argument for reciprocity with a call
for an international agreement to use both gold and silver. He
became so persuasive in behalf of that expansionist strategy that the
Southern and Northern delegates to the founding convention of the
National Association of Manufacturers gave him an ovation in 1895.

Long before that date, however, some Democrats had recognized
the appeal and effectiveness of Blaine's reciprocity approach, and had
begun to respond to the support that it generated. But the man who
was probably the key figure in that development, Walter Quintin
Gresham of Indiana, was a Republican who supported Cleveland in
the election of 1892 on the tariff issue. Gresham was deeply concerned about the agricultural and urban unrest throughout the
country, and won the support of many farmers (including some
Populists) because of his sympathy with their predicament. He
concluded that the depression had created a potentially revolutionary
situation, and argued that overseas economic expansion offered a way
of resolving the crisis.

After he took office as Secretary of State under Cleveland in 1893, Gresham became a central actor in the fourth and fifth events that helped crystallize the agrarian and metropolitan consensus on market expansion. One of those episodes involved American diplomatic and naval intervention of 1893–1894 against a Brazilian revolt whose leaders opposed the nation's recently negotiated reciprocity treaty with the United States. They feared it would make Brazil an American vassal. Metropolitan business interests exerted the most direct pressure on Gresham and Cleveland to deploy the Navy against the rebellion (though the flour millers and meat packers were also active), but that in itself revealed how rapidly the urban groups were adopting the outlook of the farm businessmen. And the agriculturalists generally supported the militant display of force on the grounds that it weakened the British, and because it might improve access to markets throughout Latin America.

The farmers were more positively engaged when Gresham next moved against the British in Nicaragua during 1894. Much of that approval grew out of Senator Morgan's long agitation for an isthmian canal routed through that country, and his specific proposal in 1893 to involve the United States government in constructing the waterway. Gresham's tough and shrewd diplomacy, which significantly reduced Great Britain's influence in Nicaragua, won applause from Populists as well as from more conservative farmers and metropolitan interests. It also strengthened the existing confidence among the agriculturalists that the United States was powerful enough to achieve its marketplace objectives without having to fight any wars.

That sense of certainty exercised an increasing psychological influence on the farmers after 1894. It deepened their anger against metropolitan leaders like Cleveland who appeared cautious or timid in situations like the Nicaraguan confrontation, and it generated a momentum that carried them into making demands that ultimately provoked a war with Spain. At that point, not too surprisingly, the confidence was merely transferred to the problem of winning the war and became self-reinforcing—and therefore even more persuasive and consequential. That process was accelerated by other events during 1894–1895. Those incidents (the sixth and seventh in the overall pattern) involved the tariff bill finally produced by the Democrats in 1894, and the Sino-Japanese war of 1894–1895. Whatever the intentions and hopes of some Democrats, the Wilson-Gorham tariff of 1894 had two negative effects on overseas market expansion. By restoring sugar to the duty list, it abrogated the reciprocity treaties concluded by Blaine after 1890, and made it impossible to renegotiate such pacts. The schedule did provide free entry for a few raw materials, but even Cleveland recognized that those exceptions would not produce any significant rise in exports.

The most telling impact of the Wilson-Gorham measure came in the upper Middlewest because it destroyed the basis for the deal with Germany permitting the import of American pork products, and because it demolished the great and growing Cuban market that the flour millers and meat processors had created for those surpluses. The reaction was swift, negative, intense, and cumulative. Astute members of both parties realized, particularly after the Republicans scored a massive victory in the congressional elections of 1894, that the upper Mississippi Valley had become the pivotal region for the presidential campaign of 1896. And by that time the Wilson-Gorham tariff had served as the catalyst that touched off a revolution in Cuba that became the focus of agrarian pressure for a militant foreign policy.

Finally, the Wilson-Gorham measure also created support for the export program advocated by David Lubin of California. Lubin was a wealthy merchant who became a wealthy farmer, but he discovered in the process of that transition that the unrest and anger of agricultural businessmen were based on real rather than imagined difficulties. He proposed to meet the crisis by using government funds to pay the farmers a bounty on their exports. The California Grange was the first group to endorse his scheme, and he slowly won more backing across the nation. Lubin's greatest influence came later, however, after World War I, when the pressure for an export-debenture plan based on his idea reached a climax.

The Sino-Japanese War produced ńo such dramatic consequences in the development of American foreign policy. But while its effects were more indirect and subtle, they were nonetheless extensive. Most importantly, it extended the concern that various groups of agriculturalists had already manifested in the Asian (and particularly the Chinese) market, and had a similar, and probably greater, effect on the attitude of metropolitan leaders. The integration of Latin America and Asia in American thinking about overseas market expansion, a synthesis that became progressively more general during 1896 and 1897, was a quietly portentous result of the war. The conflict also moved the farmers further along in their acceptance of the need for a powerful battleship Navy.

Most political leaders recognized during 1894 that the expansionist outlook for the agriculturalists, which so explicitly combined the economic and ideological themes of the free marketplace philosophy, had become a major factor in the political situation. The continuing severity of the depression accentuated that impact, and simultaneously created more urban support for the same program. All those elements, metropolitan and agrarian, economic and political, affected Cleveland's decision in 1894 to take a militant stand against Great Britain's effort to acquire more Venezuelan territory.

The resulting crisis, the eighth event of the years 1892–1896, sustained the movement of the farmers toward imperialism. Once again, the crucial effects came indirectly through the reinforcement and deepening of an existing attitude. First of all, the idea of using foreign policy action to satisfy or distract the agriculturalists was publicly as well as privately recommended by a significant number of leaders. That of course enhanced the expansionist orientation, as well as sharpening its focus. The approach was so openly discussed, for that matter, that many farmers (and particularly Populists) became highly skeptical that Cleveland would translate his tough rhetoric into action. They interpreted the bombast as a desperate political maneuver.

But that in itself produced a second vital effect. The farmers concluded that even more pressure would have to be exerted before the agricultural majority would obtain its rightful influence in making policy decisions and thereby realize its objectives. And finally, the ultimate retreat by Britain again heightened agricultural confidence in America's ability to win its victories without war. In that respect, the outcome of the Venezuelan crisis significantly extended the feeling that the unilateral remonetization of silver would give the United States effective control of the world marketplace.

The final event of those momentous four years was the Cuban revolution that erupted in February 1895. In an ironic and perhaps even poetic way, moreover, the outbreak of the revolution was directly connected with a measure conceived to further such expansion. For the shock to the Cuban economy caused by the dramatic disruption of American-Cuban trade when the Wilson-Gorham tariff law ended Blaine's reciprocity jolted the Cubans into rebellion. In an eerie preview of a pattern that would become commonplace during the twentieth century, the farm drive for export markets had established a superior-inferior relationship with another political economy that created all the classic problems of imperialism.

At the same time, moreover, that relationship generated the final and self-sustaining convergence of interests and ideas that produced the overt decision for imperialism. The central elements of that dynamic process had become wholly apparent—and deeply consequential—before the opening of the conventions called to nominate presidential candidates for the election of 1896. The economic impact of the depression, and its effect in producing a real fear of extensive social unrest or even revolution, had completed the long and gradual acceptance by metropolitan leaders of the traditional farm emphasis on overseas market expansion as the strategic solution to the nation's economic and social problems.

And the agricultural campaign for the extension of freedom and global enlargement of export markets reached its own crescendo in a demand for the election of a President and a Congress that would use American power to remonetize silver, to free Cuba, and to reform the world by applying the principles of the free marketplace political economy. That mighty surge of farm businessmen captured control of the Democratic party and handed its presidential nomination to William Jennings Bryan.

The direct and indirect influence the agriculturalists exerted on the Republicans was less dramatic, perhaps, but it was no less extensive. Encouraged by strong pressure from Midwestern leaders as well as metropolitan spokesmen, William McKinley made the restoration of reciprocity (in general, as well as with Cuba in particular) a major element in his program to revive prosperity. He likewise promised to support Cuban freedom. And despite his formal commitment to the gold standard, he carefully and extensively presented himself as a man who would use American power in an effort to win agreement from Britain and other European nations to create an international monetary system based on silver as well as gold.

XI

To an extensive degree, indeed, the presidential campaign of 1896 was waged within the framework of analysis, policy, and national psychology that had been created after 1860 by the agricultural majority of the country. That was largely the case in connection with domestic affairs, and it was wholly true in the realm of foreign policy. In that pervasive sense, the farm businessmen emerged triumphant even though their candidate was defeated by a leader who transposed the agricultural outlook into industrial terms and gave it a metropolitan emphasis. The domestic victory of the farmers did not become fully apparent or effective until the Progressive movement flowered after the turn of the century. The result in foreign affairs, however, was clear even during the campaign, for the confrontation between McKinley and Bryan involved primarily a dispute over which methods of market expansion would most promptly and permanently restore prosperity and thereby resolve the social and political crisis.

Three factors swung the battle to McKinley. His stress on reciprocity treaties and the remonetization of silver through international agreement proved effective against Bryan's heavy-handed emphasis on the unilateral remonetization of silver to carry crucial Midwestern states. Second, McKinley used a combination of arguments for the protective tariff and for reciprocity treaties with great skill to hold labor as well as business groups in the Eastern metropolis. And, finally, the jump in wheat exports (and the associated rise in prices) that occurred late in the summer seriously weakened Bryan's argument that the depression could not be overcome without the remonetization of silver. Western farmers (and Eastern businessmen) reacted to that traditional index of economic activity just as they had since the early Civil War depression. The farm businessmen—and their role in the economy—had transformed what was originally an analysis into a pattern of response that affected the nation's politics as well as marketplace expectations and behavior. As a result, a significant number of them became sufficiently optimistic to turn away from Bryan and vote for McKinley.

Those expectations, which were shared by many metropolitan businessmen, were not promptly fulfilled. Recovery from the depression had in truth begun by the time McKinley was inaugurated in March 1897, but the gains remained diffused and uneven. The resulting disappointment first produced grumbling and impatience among the farmers and uneasiness in the metropolis, and then generated a rising pressure for action in Cuba and a growing concern to implement a program of overseas economic expansion. McKinley thus confronted a gathering storm even as he moved into the White House. Agricultural interests clamored for action to reopen the Cuban market, and metropolitan interests demanded protection for their property and investments in the island. Other spokesmen who analyzed the problem in terms of the economy as an interrelated system argued that the Cuban crisis had to be resolved so that the government and all businessmen, including farmers, could proceed with general market expansion. Metropolitan leaders particularly stressed that approach, but a significant number of agriculturalists offered the same recommendation.

Populists and other militant farmers took the lead in demanding that McKinley intervene to free the Cubans. Their action had the effect of renewing and intensifying the traditional integration of the economic and ideological themes in their expansionist thought and argument. Firm intervention to force Spain to retreat in Cuba, they cried with growing anger and impatience, would reopen the markets they needed, extend freedom for the Cubans (and thereby create an even larger market), and strike a resounding psychological blow against Great Britain and other European nations in all the markets of the world. That assault on McKinley created a political crisis involving a challenge to metropolitan authority in general, as well as to the position of the Republican party in particular.

McKinley had recognized the potentially dangerous results of such dissatisfaction even before he was inaugurated, and clearly hoped that Cleveland could terminate the Cuban crisis before he left office. Cleveland publicly warned the Spanish in December 1896 that the United States would move more forcefully if the rebellion was not handled promptly and effectively, but the problem was simply beyond the abilities or the power of the government in Madrid. Some metropolitan businessmen began at least as early as May 1897 to encourage McKinley to act more vigorously to restore peace on American terms, and the President moved to increase direct American pressure on the Spanish in June.

Neither metropolitan nor farm businessmen wanted war at that time. For one thing, they were not bloodthirsty. But a more important factor was their vast confidence that America was strong enough to free Cuba without having to go to war. And that assumption was very largely a product of the long campaign of argument and assertion by the agriculturalists that had been reinforced and seemingly proved by American victories in European markets, in controlling Hawaii, and in weakening Britain's position in Latin America. McKinley himself shared that happy belief in the efficacy of American power. That confidence was significantly challenged, however, by two developments during the latter half of 1897. One was the increasing evidence that Spain was not going to buckle under American demands—and pressure—to deal with Cuba in the way specified by McKinley. The second was the growing indication that Japan and the European powers were going to preempt and then divide the great market frontier of China. The interrelated implications of those two events were immediately recognized and discussed by farm leaders, as well as by key metropolitan decision makers.

The flour millers, meat packers, and cotton exporters (particularly the Southern textile men) promptly called for government action to protect their existing and anticipated market. Farm spokesmen talked seriously of changing the diet of the Chinese, as well as of clothing them in American cotton. In a similar way, railroad men like Hill and other industrial leaders mounted their own campaign to avoid being excluded from what came to be discussed as the next bonanza market for American surpluses.

The China crisis was the decisive factor in shifting the locus of power in formulating foreign policy from agricultural businessmen to the metropolitan leaders. Not only were urban groups more directly and intensely concerned about Asia, but the metropolis had produced an intellectually powerful and politically influential group of leaders who enjoyed direct access to McKinley. The farmers did not lack all leverage, for Secretary of Agriculture James Wilson of Iowa was a militant expansionist who enjoyed a deepening personal friendship with the President. And the growing possibility that the agricultural spokesmen in the Congress might wrench the initiative from McKinley provided them with indirect but powerful influence. In one major respect, of course, that pressure for action in Cuba was the force that finally pushed McKinley and key metropolitan businessmen into an acceptance of war.

But a war to extend classic marketplace freedoms to Cuba was neither logically nor inherently a war to accomplish that objective and at the same time project American economic power into a free Asian marketplace. Yet the second war was the war that the United States fought in 1898–1899. The agriculturalists ultimately accepted that second war, and embraced the policy evolved to harvest its rewards, but they were not directly responsible for defining the conflict in those terms. Metropolitan intellectuals, businessmen, and politicians were the principal authors of that strategy. Congressmen and Cabinet members were talking with McKinley at least as early as September 1897, for example, about controlling the Philippines as a springboard into Asia if it became necessary to go to war against Spain to end the Cuban mess. The government had developed its own military plans for such a two-front war, moreover, before

Assistant Secretary of the Navy Theodore Roosevelt put his similar ideas into operation one afternoon after his superior had left the office early. Roosevelt was given a mild rebuke, but his basic orders were not revoked. They were improved. Agricultural influence was not absent even from that episode, however, for Roosevelt and other metropolitan leaders were acting upon the frontier-expansionist thesis of American prosperity and welfare.

It is highly unlikely that President McKinley was affected directly by the version of the frontier thesis developed by intellectuals like Frederick Jackson Turner and Brooks Adams. But those men did influence metropolitan leaders like Roosevelt to whom McKinley regularly exposed himself. And the President continued to discuss the problem with other men who argued the wisdom of fighting a war against Spain over Cuba, if it proved necessary, in a way that would provide a base for American economic and military power in Asia. He was also subjected to ever more insistent pressure from his political advisers to act against Spain over Cuba before the angry farmers took control of the country.

That became an increasingly real threat after January 1898 because Spain remained adamant in response to American pressure. The campaign led by key Populists became so directly challenging by March that it convinced reluctant metropolitan leaders that war was necessary to preserve the proper organization (and control) of the American political economy. At that point, if not before, McKinley opted for war. In all fundamental respects, therefore, historical as well as immediate, the war against Spain was a war of the majority of the American people.

The agriculturalists also supplied a classic moment of truth when Populist Jerry Simpson looked boldly into the implications and the consequences of the long campaign by farm businessmen to expand the free marketplace. He recognized the harsh validity of Thomas Jefferson's earlier warning that a commitment to ever expanding export markets would lead first to war and then to war again. Simpson concluded that imperial wars were more destructive of freedom than the failure to capture more export markets. He also sensed, if indeed he did not fully comprehend, that everything after the decision to go to war to extend the free marketplace to Cuba would be an ultimately unsuccessful rear-guard action to prevent those unhappy consequences.

So it proved.

The farmers fought hard to make certain that American expansion was not institutionalized in the form of traditional colonialism. For one thing, neither the Northerners nor the Southerners wanted to become involved in more problems with black men. Nor did they relish the moral and practical difficulties involved in ruling and training people who had yet to understand and accept the truths of a modern marketplace political economy. In the fundamental sense, of course, their victory against colonialism was due to their long fight in behalf of free marketplace expansion. They had created a consensus in support of an overseas economic expansion that attacked colonialism in the name of self-determination and freedom. But they also effectively opposed those Americans who flirted with orthodox colonialism between 1897 and 1900. They insured that Cuba was not annexed, and committed the United States to freeing the Philippines even as those islands were taken to provide a base for the penetration of the China market.

On all counts, therefore, the long battle of the agricultural businessmen for overseas marketplace expansion played the principal role in the development and adoption of an imperial outlook and policy. The occupation of the Philippines was viewed and accepted as a regrettably necessary—and temporary—means to the realization of an ultimately just and progressive end. Once past that unfortunate exception, the way lay open for the application of the classic marketplace philosophy. The Open Door Notes of 1899 and 1900, which committed the power and the prestige of the United States to the principles of self-determination and the open marketplace, were the formal expression of an outlook and a policy that the agricultural majority had advocated since before the Civil War.

But the policy of expanding the free marketplace led unfortunately to wars: wars to apply the principles; and wars to defend the freedom and the prosperity that the expansion of the principles had ostensibly produced for Americans. Finally, after long years, it became clear that the expansion of the free marketplace had failed to bring freedom and prosperity to all Americans, let alone to all the people of the world. Yet at that moment the difficulty was compounded in a truly tragic way because the view of the world that had produced the crisis was an outlook that had been created and accepted by the majority.

There was thus no elite or other scapegoat to blame and replace. There are only ourselves to confront and change.

If we can understand how we became an imperial metropolis in the name of the freedom and prosperity of the country, then perhaps we can free our minds and our wills to achieve freedom and prosperity without being an imperial society.

WHAT THIS
COUNTRY NEEDS . . .

[from *Some Presidents: Wilson to Nixon*, 1972]

Ostensibly a critique of *The Shattered Dream: Herbert Hoover and the Great Depression* by Gene Smith, this book review was actually used by Williams as a platform from which to reexamine the ideas and programs of Herbert Hoover whose presidency was routinely condemned by historians and political commentators. Hoover's vision of America, Williams countered, deserved better understanding and serious consideration. A conservative loyal to capitalism, Hoover was nonetheless dedicated to a nonimperial community of self-governing citizens and groups cooperating to build a better life within the existing system—"a people's capitalism," as Williams described it.

At the time Williams was one of a few historians, following the lead of Richard Hofstadter, who offered a revisionist perspective of Hoover. He portrayed the former capitalist engineer, secretary of commerce, and president as aware of the need to "overcome the classic inequities of capitalism" and acutely sensitive to the dangers and negative consequences of centralized "bureaucratic statism." Williams also reminded his readers that Hoover opposed the use of imperial power "intent upon dominating the destinies and freedom of other people." He was, Williams stated, quite simply "against the Empire." His failures notwithstanding, Williams concluded, Hoover compared favorably with his successors whose unwillingness to honor the principles of self-determination Williams deplored.

This essay about Hoover was one of several in a small volume of revised articles in which Williams discussed books about American presidents from Woodrow Wilson to Richard Nixon. In an introduction to the collection he remarked that in the twentieth century the president had become the "key figure in the effort to construct a corporate system that would function effectively." The ever greater

324

difficulties of doing this, and the challenges to the system domestically and from abroad, led to increasingly centralized power in the executive branch of government. In turn this produced an accumulation of presidential transgressions and usurpations. Public confidence and trust correspondingly deteriorated. "The presidency," Williams concluded, "is thus in crisis because the system is in crisis." And, he went on to say, "the only way to resolve the crisis is to build a social movement" capable of "asserting public power against Presidential power."

HERBERT Clark Hoover almost never laughed, or so Gene Smith tells us; but I have one of those visions that historians occasionally allow themselves: if one arose very early (sometime during that missing hour 'twixt four and five) and moved very quietly along the upper reaches of the McKenzie River east of Springfield, Oregon, there Hoover would be, just barely visible in the mist—in his waders, standing tit-high in that damnably cold water, a string of trout drifting downstream from his suspender button, one hand with a fly rod and the other with the latest *New York Times Book Review* section, his head and cigar tilted high, roaring at the latest historical account of his failures. His belly laugh would override the rapids because he would already have read a story about voluntary communes in Iowa, Idaho, and Indiana, and another about Julius Lester's beautiful blast at white radicals for having to learn the same thing over and over and over and....

Back in the real world one would naturally assume that old-mod Charlie Michelson* killed Olde Herbie dead between 1929 and 1933. As a kind of live-ammunition training exercise for the subsequent massacre of Alfred Landon.

Not quite. Professor Richard Hofstadter raised him from the grave in a memorable chapter of his fine book *The American Political Tradition*.

But then Professor Schlesinger devoted an entire volume to a counterattack on Hoover as a tune-up job for levitating Godfather

---

*Michelson was the Democratic Party's publicity agent who mounted a powerful smear campaign against Hoover based on the classic techniques of the false choice and the false syllogism (very similar to the current advertising for Winston cigarettes).

Franklin. And Izzy Stone can hardly let an issue escape him without swinging his scimitar at what he assures us is the ghost of Hoover ensconced in the White House as clandestine adviser to Richard Nixon and Billy Graham.

But why?

Why so much labor to exorcise a cold and feeble failure? And why so much reliance on analogy to put down Nixon, a man who has generously stockpiled a public arsenal accessible to all critics?

Smith gives us a clue or two but never uses them. So the place to start is with Julius Lester's wryly devastating comment: "The inability to move beyond a politics of reaction has been detrimental to the growth of a white radical movement." For to discuss Nixon in terms of Hoover, and to define Hoover in terms of the Michelson (and textbook) myths, is to display the mind (and politics) of the knee-jerk. The way to get at Hoover, as well as Nixon, is to pick up on two more of Leser's remarks. The first is his accurate observation that white radicals persistently react to specifics instead of seeing the specifics as part of an integrated system that must be dealt with as a system. The second is his call for "a positive revolutionary program."

Now at this point we must go very slowly because we are so confused (as Harold Cruse pointed out a year ago) that, given a problem, we tend to duck into a cloud of quick-frozen New Deal rhetoric for the solution. Hoover was not a revolutionary. He was not even a modern liberal. And he does not deserve uncritical acclaim. But he was an unusually intelligent, and often perceptive, conservative who understood that the system was a system; that it was based on certain clear and not wholly absurd axioms, and that it would work only if the people acted in ways that honored those principles.

"I want to live in a community that governs itself," Hoover explained very simply, "that neither wishes its responsibilities onto a centralized bureaucracy nor allows a centralized bureaucracy to dictate to that local government." "It is not the function of government," he continued, "to relieve individuals of their responsibilities to their neighbors, or to relieve private institutions of their responsibilities to the public." "You cannot extend the mastery of the government over the daily working life of a people," he warned, "without at the same time making it the master of the people's souls and thoughts."

If you are Hoover, that is to say, then your moral imperative demands that you let the system come apart at the seams rather than violate the principles by saving the system *for* the people. One of your principles is that the system is *their* system, and hence the moment *you* save it *for* them you kill the dream. For when you do that you *rule* the people instead of serving the people. And the commitments to honoring principles, and to service, are Quaker creed. Perhaps, even, *the* Quaker faith. And Hoover was a Quaker.

So is Nixon. Of course. So there we have a case of no difference with a fantastic distinction. For Hoover held the dream as if it were the Holy Grail, while Nixon has the Holy Grail carried around in a black box by an aide as if it were the daily code for Armageddon.

Back to Gene Smith and his book. His title is *The Shattered Dream,* yet he shows little if any recognition of Hoover's dream. For Hoover did *not* dream that the system would always function properly; or that, in the crisis of the Great Depression, it would right itself automatically and roll on beyond poverty. Hoover's dream was that the people—the farmers, the workers, the businessmen, and the politicians—would pull themselves together *and then join together* to meet their needs and fulfill their potential by honoring the principles of the system.

That dream defined both the basis and the nature of his anti-depression program. In his view, the government could.

> ...best serve the community by bringing about co-operation in the large sense between groups. It is the failure of groups to respond to their responsibilities to others that drives government more and more into the lives of the people.

Thus he offered ideas, his own influence, the services of the national government, and increasing monetary help short of massive federal intervention. But he could not go beyond his commitment to the principle that the people were responsible—"this is the people's problem"—and embark upon what he considered the "disastrous course" of centralized, irresponsible, and increasingly irresponsive and manipulatory bureaucracy.

As it happened, he did provide more federal aid than had been offered in any other depression, and would have supplied far more if the Democrats had not defeated or spiked a long list of proposals after their victory in the 1930 Congressional elections. And he did in truth block out the basic shape of the New Deal. But he simply could not give over and admit through his actions that he had abandoned his commitment to an American community and to the spirit and the will of the people.

And that faith had its useful side. Led by Gerard Swope of General Electric, some corporation giants pushed him to endorse a plan, presented as a cure for the Depression, that would have given them official sanction to exercise vast powers over the entire political economy. Hoover erupted in angry opposition. It was "the most gigantic proposal of monopoly ever made in history" and "a clock for conspiracy against the public interest"—a long step toward fascism. It later became, of course, the blueprint for the NRA of the New Deal.

You have to take Hoover whole. He should have given more direct relief and he should have blocked Swope and his cronies. He should have offered more of himself sooner to the people and he should have held fast to that beautiful faith in the people. The visceral truth of it all is that Hoover was done in by his faith in the dream of a cooperative American community, and by his ruthless intellectual analysis of what would happen if the dream was not honored.

Either the people save their country or it does not get saved. It may get stuck back together. It may get managed well enough to remain operational. It may even get shoved into the next historical epoch. But it does not get saved. Meaning it does not get purified by the people demanding that it operate according to its principles.

Hoover was traumatized by the failure of the people to take charge of their immediate lives and then join together in cooperative action, and by his terrifying insight into what the future would be if the people continued to duck their obligation—or if they settled for less.

Do not laugh. Hoover outlined our future in 1923. We are living in it now. We do not like it. And even yet we have not taken charge of our immediate lives so that we can then come together and create an American community. *We* have *let* the future that Hoover foresaw in 1923 *happen to us*. Hoover *did not do it to us*.

To fully comprehend this, we must understand that Hoover knew modern American industrial society better than *any* other President. It takes one to know one. And he had been one. And had become increasingly disturbed and concerned. Let us begin in 1909, with the chapter on labor in his famous (and still used) exposition of the *Principles of Mining*. "The time when the employer could ride roughshod over his labor is disappearing with the doctrine of *'laissez faire,'* on which it was founded." Indeed, unions were "normal and proper antidotes for unlimited capitalistic organization." The good engineer "never begrudges a division with his men of the increased profit arising from increased efficiency." And the good engineer took an honest "friendly interest in the welfare of the men"; and further understood that

> ...inspiration to increase exertion is created less by "driving" than by recognition of individual effort, in larger pay, and by extending justifiable hope of promotion.

Of course it is capitalistic. And of course it has a tinge of paternalism. But it is personal, it is moral, and it reveals an awareness that the past is past—and that the corporation poses a serious danger to community.

The Bolshevik Revolution extended Hoover's awareness of such matters; in part because, as he noted, it "was a specter which wandered into the [Versailles] Peace Conference almost daily," and he dealt with it as an adviser to President Wilson. He naturally opposed communism as being destructive of individuality *and* true cooperation among individuals and groups. But he did understand that the revolution was the work of men and women striving to realize their potential. Misguided as they might be, he acknowledged that they, too, were reaching for the dream.

Even more important, perhaps, Hoover saw and understood the rise of fascism long before most other American leaders. During those same years of the early 1920s, moreover, he extended his awareness of what the corporation was threatening to do to America. The

> ...congestion of population is producing subnormal conditions of life. The vast repetitive operations are dulling the human mind.... The aggregation of great wealth with its power to economic domination presents social and economic ills which we are constantly struggling to remedy.

He then pulled it all together in a perceptive (though horribly mistitled) essay called *American Individualism* that he wrote as he entered upon his long service as Secretary of Commerce (1921–1928). From experience and observation, Hoover concluded that capitalistic industrial society (and specifically America) had become functionally divided into three major units, and that the society was poised on the threshold of becoming a syndicalist system. One group was composed of capitalists, including agricultural entrepreneurs as well as industrial, banking, and commercial operators. The second functional bloc was labor.

The third was defined by a rather tricky concept, that of the public per se. It was in substance, though neither in form nor in rhetoric, a class. That is, it was all the small and middle-sized independents and their dependents—along with labor. Meaning most of us. Hoover was in effect making an analysis of the giants, on the one hand, and the rest of society, on the other: those with national power and those who had to cooperate if they were to avoid manipulation.

> The American people from bitter experience have a rightful fear that great business units might be used to dominate our industrial life and by illegal and unethical practices destroy equality of opportunity.

From this it followed that two criteria had to be met if the dream was to be fulfilled. First: the government had to act, simultaneously, as umpire of the actions of the three groups *and as leader of the public in coming together in cooperative action.*

Beautiful. And damnably difficult.

It is beautiful because if perfectly describes the dilemma of trying to govern a continent without a social movement that represents the common interest of various special interests, and that is engaged in the process of redefining those separate groups as equal elements of a commonwealth. Honest and intelligent public servants offer the only hope under such circumstances. But Hoover also knew that such government from the top down was difficult because bargains between market place interest groups that were arranged or regulated by the government did not define the true common interest, and because the procedure could so easily slide into manipulation by the government and the strongest interest groups.

Even so, Hoover maneuvered some of it almost beyond belief: As in his successful battle to define broadcasting as a public forum. And as in his use of brain power and moral power to keep wages high in 1929 and 1930.

Compare that with Nixon.

No problem. Nixon has no moral power.

On with Hoover's second imperative: the people had to accept and discharge their responsibility to come together in cooperative action to create "a community that governs itself." Then came the eerie part. The future map. What would happen if the people gave up on the dream? If the corporations took over—fascism. If job-oriented labor leaders took over—a mutant, mundane, and elitist corruption of socialism. If government per se took over—an elitist, bureaucratic, and community-destroying hell-on-earth.

So right it shakes you.

It is easy to say that Hoover's dream involves an unresolvable contradiction: that a people's capitalism of the kind that he envisioned is like a round square. And the criticism is deadly if you see Hoover as nothing more than a Quaker Rockefeller. But when a man talks seriously about the need for grass-roots cooperation in order to secure and maintain the opportunity for individual fulfillment, then he is not discussing orthodox capitalism. He is headed, however cautiously and even unknowingly, toward a transitional kind of political economy. It might indeed be impossible to realize that kind of a society, and certainly we have not created it, but Hoover was correct about the other options if we did not break out of our traditional *Weltanschauung*.

If the people abdicated their responsibility for realizing the dream, and instead relied on the government, Hoover projected a period of increasingly unsuccessful bureaucratic pseudo-socialism. And then, "in the United States the reaction from such chaos will not be more Socialism but will be toward Fascism."

So what we have now is a horrible combination of what he saw as the three possibilities.

But he *must* have failed beyond giving too little relief, beyond waiting too long to give more of himself, and beyond being bull-headed about his dream.

True.

His mishandling of the Bonus Army.

That story is the best thing in Smith's book. He describes it very well, but he does not tell us what it means. To understand that, you have to know the dream. And then face the truth that by 1932 the people had not taken charge of their immediate lives and begun to come together to create a community. Instead, they had begun to petition the government for salvation.

For the feel of how Hoover reacted, do not waste your time ransacking the archives. Just listen to The Doors doing the first verse of "The Soft Parade." His dream was crumbling, dribbling down into Washington by ones and twos. Then by thousands. And he drew the traditional American civilian conclusion. People marching pose a military problem. The explanation for that response is basically simple: the people have done little serious marching except on the way to war.

Now the American military have the patience that begets great power: wait for the civvies to come to us and then we are in charge. And so they were. MacArthur and his minions. The third-person types. MacArthur to an aide: "MacArthur has decided to go into active command in the field."

But the key was Hoover's trauma. That shut him off: confused the desperation of the people with the willful intent of the people. He mistakenly thought they wanted what we have today. So he gave over to MacArthur. And Douglas did his thing. Bayonets, sword-drawn cavalry, tear gas (a baby died), and fire. (And then another failure. For MacArthur usurped power, went beyond his orders, and Hoover did not strike him down.)

But the people only wanted what they thought was the New Frontier—help from the Metropolis for the country. Help from a few of the people for most of the people. In Hoover's view, however, that was impossible. He was correct. The Metropolis is not a few of the people helping the rest of the people. The Metropolis is managers and directors ruling the people. In reality the New Frontier was simply the Metropolis as the center of The Empire, lording it over us at home and abroad with increasing indifference (even contempt) for what Hoover understood as the principles of the system—and for Hoover's dream. If the Metropolis saves the country, it does so by changing what Hoover believed in as the people and the community into The Empire.

Hoover was against The Empire. That was the Quaker. Not Nixon-Quaker. Just Iowa-boy-Hoover-Quaker. Meaning that he Honest-to-God-and-to-the-people simply wanted us to exchange the things we create for the things we need. And to give of ourselves to each other in times of well-being as well as in times of crisis. If we did that, then there would be no government intervention and management in our honest exchange, and we would remain masters of our lives, and we would create an American community.

Once again, of course, Hoover can be damned for not breaking free of capitalism. He can be faulted, for example, for not realizing that it was impossible to depoliticize trade and investment in a market place system. But I have the thought that one measures capitalist leaders not by how socialist they are, but by the extent to which they understand and try to overcome the classic inequities of capitalism without at the same time moving toward fascism or bureaucratic statism. As Joan Hoff Wilson convincingly demonstrates in two forthcoming books—a perceptive biography of Hoover

and a keen study of the business community and foreign policy—
Hoover was willing to work toward a largely self-contained economy, and he was consistently opposed to the assumptions and
attitudes that produced the cold war. He told President Harry S
Truman in May, 1945, for example, that the United States should be
content "to persuade, hold up our banner of what we thought was
right and let it go at that." One wonders how many liberals, let alone
radicals, would be content with that basic policy; but the crucial
point is that the history of the world, and our present condition,
would be drastically different if Truman had followed Hoover's
advice.

So we come right down on it. The trouble with Hoover was that
he believed. Not just in us. But in the very best in us.

To get straight on that is to understand the great strengths of his
foreign policy along with his weaknesses during the Depression. The
guiding axiom was to act, as a people, in ways that would build an
international community. To be a good neighbor. "We have no hates;
we wish no further possessions; we harbor no military threats." That
meant, *ipso facto,* that he "absolutely disapproved" of the concept of
the United States as Big Brother to the world.

Hoover was keenly aware that "a large part of the world had
come to believe that they were in the presence of the birth of a new
imperial power intent upon dominating the destinies and freedom of
other people," and he recognized the necessity for non-imperial—
and anti-imperial—action. The Quaker knew it was not enough
simply to say that Dollar Diplomacy was "not a part of my
conception of international relations."

First things first. Control the bankers. The government, he
asserted bluntly, "has certain unavoidable political and moral responsibilities to guide and control such loans." "No nation should allow
its citizens to loan money to foreign countries unless this money is to
be devoted to productive enterprise." Otherwise the government
would be drawn ever deeper into the maelstrom of intervention.
That meant no loans to prop up Potemkin-like governments, no
loans for military purposes, and none for "political adventure." And
it meant no government underwriting because that "placed the risk
on the taxpayer and not upon the private banker."

The financiers and their allies were too powerful, and Hoover
could not win a clear victory in that battle. He needed help from the
people which they never gave. But he blocked the bankers when and
as he could, kept the issue before the public, and refused to be drawn

into intervention. Thus, when he became President, he promptly published J. Reuben Clark's memorandum on the Monroe Doctrine, a document that President Calvin Coolidge had buried because it destroyed the grounds for using the policy as a sanction for such interventions. Thus he returned to the policy of recognizing Latin American governments without demanding that they satisfy U.S. criteria. And thus he withdrew the Marines from Nicaragua and Haiti, and refused to send them into Panama, Honduras, or Cuba.

Of course, all that principle poses a problem. If you cannot properly intervene for the bankers, neither can you intervene to reform the backward or to block the difficult and the bothersome. Once again the trouble with Hoover was his damn stubbornness about that dream. He was all the time trying to play it straight.

Hoover resolved the dilemma by cutting through to first principles on military policy. The armed forces of the United States had the one purpose of guaranteeing "that no foreign soldier will land on American soil." "To maintain forces less than that strength is to destroy national safety, to maintain greater forces is not only economic injury to our people but a threat against our neighbors and would be a righteous cause for ill will amongst them."

That meant that the Chinese had to meet the Japanese attack of 1931 with their own resources and will. The assault on Manchuria was of course "immoral," but "the United States has never set out to preserve peace among other nations by force"—and Hoover was not about to begin. "These acts do not imperil the freedom of the American people, the economic or moral future of our people. I do not propose ever to sacrifice American life for anything short of this." To intervene in China, moreover, "would excite the suspicions of the whole world." And, finally, a sense of history: "No matter what Japan does in time they will not Japanify China and if they stay long enough they will be absorbed or expelled by the Chinese."

Reminds one of John Quincy Adams. "America goes not abroad in search of monsters to destroy.... She might become the dictatress of the world; she would no longer be the ruler of her own spirit."

Herbert Clark and John Quincy: too bad they are gone. Spiro Agnew could spend the rest of his life chasing after them, screaming all the while that it was time to take care of those effete radical-liberal snobs who are undermining and destroying the nation and its rightful place in the world.

So we come back to what the man Julius Lester says: if we

concentrate on destroying Hoover, then "ultimately we will destroy ourselves."

What I mean is that Gene Smith tells us that Hoover, in the depths of the hell of 1931, said that "what this country needs is a great poem. Something to lift people out of fear and selfishness."

If you kill a Quaker engineer who came to understand that—and to believe in and to commit himself to that—then you have murdered yourself.

CONFESSIONS OF AN INTRANSIGENT REVISIONIST

[from *Socialist Review*, 1973]

This selection differs from all the others in this book. It was Williams's statement of the purposes of his historical research and how he approached it. His remarks were also a reply to those who attacked his work, including some who questioned his scholarly credentials. Originally delivered as a paper at the annual meeting of the American Historical Association in 1973, the "confessions" revealed, in a manner rarely displayed by scholars in a public forum, autobiographical information about Williams's intellectual and professional development. Professor Thomas McCormick, one of his students and colleagues, later observed that this was an example of Williams's way of "demystifying the process of creation while taking [the audience] into his confidence."

Allow me first to comment directly on the prospects of revisionism.

Go back fifty years.

You will find a youngish doctor in New Jersey who is writing poems, essays, and novels during the moments between-and-after treating his patients. One of his books is a collection of subtle Freudian commentaries on key figures in early American history; and perhaps the best of those pieces, entitled "The Virtue of History," is a revisionist interpretation of Aaron Burr.

The doctor's name is William Carlos Williams. The work is called *In the American Grain*.

Now return to the present.

Go across the river from New Jersey. There you will find an extremely talented gentleman named Gore Vidal who has platinum-plated his literary reputation by offering a brilliant revisionist novel about Aaron Burr. Mr. Vidal does not mention the once-young-and-now-dead poet in New Jersey.

So go the prospects of revisionism.

Well, not quite.

After all, Korea, Cuba, Vietnam, Cambodia, and Chile did happen. So did Jackson State and Kent State. And now we have Watergate and San Clemente, and the cruel games being played in the name of national security and the energy crisis. There is no way to deny the revisionist insight into any of those issues.

Beginning with my first appearance before this honorable trade association as a freshman PhD, I have responded to many critics in candor and in length: orally and in writing, and directly and indirectly. I have not answered others because they have been redundant or incidental; because their primary thrust has been non- or anti-intellectual; or because in general I have been more concerned with getting on with my life.

I am here today in the hope that we can open a dialogue about History, as well as about particular parts of history: a dialectic involving our different strategies of intellectual inquiry. I have chosen the idiom of confession because it offers the most direct way of confronting three important matters: acknowledging mistakes, bearing witness to the truth, and stating one's considered view of the world.

I. ON ADMITTING MISTAKES

Having taken notes on thousands of primary and secondary documents (and during interviews with hundreds of protagonists), and having many times revised my first drafts, I assume as part of being human that I have made these kinds of mistakes:

1. I have miscopied, or incorrectly transcribed, such documents;

2. In making summaries or abstracts, I have used language that became unclear or ambivalent when I returned to my notes; and

3. I have not always perfectly transferred an initially accurate note or summary into my final draft.

I am also certain, for two reasons, that I have not corrected all those mistakes during the process of publication:

1. I respect my own typing, linotype operators, computer print-outs, and copy editors, but I also know that each makes his own kinds of mistakes; and that all of them make mistakes correcting mistakes (and thereby produce some very strange results).

2. I am a poor proofreader. By the time I receive galley proof (let alone page proof) I am satiated with the sight of my mind as it existed eight to twelve months earlier. I cope with that situation as I learned to deal with the blindness of the egg checker. After you have candled so many eggs, they all look good or they all look bad. So you turn the job over to someone else while you go off to plow a field, lay in the hay, or catch some catfish. But all of us are susceptible to the blindness of the egg checker—thus there are some mistakes in my work that can be interpreted by those who do not understand such human frailty as proof of crimes that never entered my head, and would in any event be utterly beyond my interest or my patience.

I have always become intellectually excited in the course of any project—researching and writing history has been one of my favorite highs. That has probably led to a higher incidence of the kind of mistakes that I have just described, and has certainly prompted me to present much of my work too cryptically. I have too often written to myself, so to speak, during moments of intellectual exhilaration.

Moving on to a different kind of mistake, and given the orthodoxy that guides this trade, I have erred in not devoting my life to one subject or to one period. Thus all that I have written is subject to modification simply because I do not know everything about every-thing that I have written about. I have wandered as an historian because I explored many aspects of life before I became an historian, and because I think that it is only rarely that the belated discovery of new documents revolutionizes some part of history.

Here we come in a preliminary way to the heart of the matter about revisionism. *The revisionist is one who sees basic facts in a different way and as interconnected in new relationships.* He is a sister and a brother to those who use old steel to make a zipper, as contrasted with those who add new elements to make a better steel.

I have also mistakenly assumed that everyone engaged in the serious study of human affairs understands that the urge to power is a significant, but nonetheless routine, element of life. Hence I have considered it more important to concentrate on why individuals or groups want power, what happens when they get it and use it for their purposes, and how they respond to changes in order to keep power. It is of course important to study the special case of those who seek power for its own sake; but neither my personal nor historic experience has convinced me that mankind—and hence History—can be understood in those terms.

In a similar way, I have mistakenly assumed that we all know that some psychological orientation informs the work of every historian; but that if psychology is your thing, then you become a psychologist. I am obviously a Gestaltian who does not think that Freud or Jung or Adler wiped the slate clean of Dilthey or James—or even Marx.

I have likewise been mistaken in assuming that my personal dedication to freedom and equality *within a community* is unequivocally documented in my teaching, my writing, and in the way that I live my life. I disagree with those who assert that such a commitment can only be established by perpetual outrage against the faults of other societies. It is easy to construct an academic (even public) career by moralizing about the failures of other countries. It is also a cheap shot—*bush*. There are moments when serious protest promises consequences, and in those instants I have signed my name, written a private letter, walked the streets, or sent my money.

But whether I am writing about American History, or typing as a citizen to change America, I must first understand America. And I confess that in my lifetime—from the Great Depression to Watergate—that task has absorbed most of my intelligence, my guts, and my energy. I do not approve of imperial actions by Russia *or* by Israel, and I do not approve of repression in Brazil *or* in France; but most of all I like them least by and in my own America.

Finally, I am sure that I am mistaken, *within my chosen framework,* in some of my reconstructions, analyses, and interpretations. I take it as given that most of you who look at the world from another perspective think that I am mostly wrong. Neither truth traumatizes my ego. I learned a lifetime ago that I could not sink every shot or make every finesse, read every book in every library, memorize every document in every archive, or answer every question that I asked myself in the first light of dawn to the satisfaction of myself—let alone to the plaudits of everyone else.

Yet, granted such mistakes, and speaking very softly, I confess that I must say these things:

1. I do not think that my mistakes subvert the value of my work;
2. My critics have yet to respond to fundamental issues that I have raised; and

3. I am sure that a number of my reconstructions, analyses, and interpretations—granted their weaknesses—have informed and challenged your minds. I never entertained the slightest thought of doing more.

2. ON WITNESSING TO THE TRUTH

Here permit me to be blunt.
1. I have never engaged in an intellectual conspiracy.
2. I have never wilfully distorted a document.
3. I have never invented evidence.
4. I have protected the confidentiality of primary sources in the United States, Russia, England, and Cuba. I will continue to protect them until they choose to enter the public arena with their information.

3. ON CONFESSING ONE'S CONSIDERED VIEW

Here we confront the central questions, how one perceives the evidence, and how one presents one's perceptions. For the primary issue between me as a revisionist and my serious critics involves our different theories of knowledge—our antithetical conceptions of reality. An honest and potentially creative conflict.

I came to History after ten years of sustained involvement in mathematics and the physical sciences. That education and experience inherently included the serious study of such giants as Aristotle, Descartes, Spinoza, Leibniz, Kant, Whitehead, and Russell. Confronted with such conflicting theories of knowledge, I was inexorably drawn into the process of choosing how I would make sense of the world.

Surprising as it may seem, I did not follow Descartes into a universe composed of discrete positivistic and atomistic elements sometimes connected to each other in a mechanistic fashion. Instead, I chose Spinoza. I thought he was far more realistic in positing one organic world in which seemingly separate parts are in reality always internally related to each other; a universe in which an ostensibly positivistic fact is in truth a set of relationships with all other facts and therefore with the whole.

From the moment I encountered him, therefore, I responded to Marx. For, despite his extensive empirical research, which gives him the appearance of being a super-positivist, I recognized him as a fellow Spinozian. Hence I read him then, as I read him now, as a genius in social history and political economy—and not at all as an early computer offering the date for the birth of Utopia.

I remain exhilarated by his capacity for seeing in one piece of evidence a set of relationships that reveal an economic truth, a truth about an idea, a social verity, and a political truth. I also think that there is more psychological insight in his analysis of our alienation from our Humanity under western capitalism than there is in all but a one-foot shelf of contemporary psychohistory.

Spinoza and Marx proceed from the assumption that everything is internally related to everything else. Thus the problem is not whether or how *a* may be related to *d* or *p* or *v*, but instead the question of how *a* and *d* and *p* and *v* reveal as microcosms the nature of the macrocosm. Or, conversely, how the macrocosm reveals the character of *a* and *d* and *p* and *v*. Reality is not an issue of economics versus ideas, or of politics versus either; it is not even defined by coefficients of correlation between voting records and geographic location, or by a mathematical model that proves that what was done was wrong. Reality instead involves how a political act is also an economic act, of how an economic decision is a political choice, or of how an idea of freedom involves a commitment to a particular economic system. Lukács said it all in three sentences.

> It is not the primacy of economic motives in historical explanation that constitutes the decisive difference between Marxism and bourgeois thought, but the point of view of totality. Whatever the subject of debate, the dialectical method is concerned always with the same problem: knowledge of historical process in its entirety. This means that "ideological" and "economic" problems lose their mutual exclusiveness and merge into one another.

Granted all that, my confidence in the Spinozian-Marxian strategy of intellectual inquiry was severely tested by Fred Harvey Harrington. He pushed the positivistic, interest-group approach to its furthest limits. He could dissect any decision, event, or movement into its constituent parts with a subtle, loving ruthlessness that earned him the nicknames of Mr. Cold, and The Fish Eye. And he understood the techniques of quantification and statistical correlation, though he chose to translate them into the King's English.

After a time, however, the mathematician in me realized that neither he nor anyone else of his persuasion had developed either a scale for weighing the various atomistic factors, or a system of differential equations that could reintegrate the parts into the whole. In the usual course of events, that is to say, discrete atomism, or sophisticated scientism, does nothing more than turn Carl Becker on his head: every historian becomes his own man, and hence there is no dialectical encounter between theories of knowledge. There is only an endless argument about which factor is most important—or endless evasion in the name of multiple causation.

At this point, Hans Gerth took me by the hand. As a brilliant (though neglected) member of the Frankfurt School, he teased and pushed me into a confrontation with the central theory of reality into a manageable intellectual tool? Which is to say: who mediates between our ordinary selves and genius?

Guided by Gerth, I became deeply involved with Hegel, Dilthey, Adorno, Horkheimer, and Lukács. I enjoyed the ensuing dialectical tension: that coming apart at the seams at midnight, and then the stitching it back together in a sentence or two at 3 A.M. Dilthey ultimately taught me the concept of *Weltanschauungen,* the sense of three dialectically interacting world views: a workable version of Spinoza's organic reality, and a realistic limit on relativism.

Foreign relations seemed to offer the most promising arena for the deployment of that intellectual strategy. Indeed, if there is a Spinozian whole for an historian, then it has to involve foreign policy and the periodization of history. My first book was the result of an effort to lay an empirical foundation for developing a set of internal relations that would make it possible to conceptualize the organic sense of reality entertained by American policy-makers (and, by indirection, by the American body politic). I chose relations with Russia because it struck me that such a *Weltanschauung* was apt to reveal itself with particular clarity during a confrontation with a different view of the world.

Out of that effort came my concept of Open Door Imperialism as the *Weltanschauung* of twentieth-century American foreign policy. I began with three atomistic documents: Secretary of State Hay's circular letters of September 6, 1899, and July 3, 1900, and his note to the Germans of October 29, 1900. I next conceptualized those documents as the basic formulation of a general outlook that was amplified and applied to other areas of the world, as in Secretary of State Root's instructions of November 28, 1905, to the American delegation to the Algeciras Conference.

I concluded, at the end of that intellectual voyage, that the Open Door Policy was a vast network of internal relations in the sense meant by Spinoza and Marx—and therefore a *Weltanschauung* in the sense meant by Dilthey. Viewed in that way, it is a conception of reality that integrates economic theory and practice, abstract ideas, past, present and future politics, anticipations of Utopia, messianic idealism, social-psychological imperatives, historical consciousness, and military strategy.

As formulated by the protagonists at the turn of the century, the *Weltanschauung* of the Open Door was an integrated set of assumptions that guided elitist *and* popular thinking (and responses), and that defined bureaucratic perceptions and actions. It then became an ideology (even theology), and ultimately a reification of reality that is finally being subverted by a new reality.

It is so easy to illustrate this with the likes of Hay, Conant, Root, Wilson, Culbertson, Hughes, Hull, and Stimson that the challenge lies with those like Hoover and Acheson. Hoover is fascinating because of his instinct to transcend the orthodoxy. Acheson is particularly revealing because he crystallized the discussion of the 1890s in his 1944 testimony before the congressional committee on postwar planning and policy.

To avoid "a very bad time," Acheson warned, meaning "the most far-reaching consequences upon our economic and social system," "you must look to foreign markets." True, "you could probably fix it so that everything produced here would be consumed here, but that would completely change our Constitution, our relations to property, to human liberty, our very conceptions of law. And nobody contemplates that. Therefore, you find you must look to other markets and those markets are abroad...."

The issue here is not economic motives, and certainly not the kind of economic determinism that Marx would have scorned as absurdly simplistic. The first point is the network of internal relationships in Acheson's mind between foreign markets and everything that he treasures. Or, conversely, the inability to imagine freedom and welfare in a non-capitalistic framework. Secondly, we have a conception of markets that involves American predominance. That is not trade in the classic sense of give-and-take. It is the imperial dynamic of we need, you give.

Having crystallized, Acheson began to reify. As in National Security Council Document No. 68: freedom and welfare can be secured only through "the virtual abandonment by the United States of trying to distinguish between national and global security." And then the ultimate distillation: "We are willing to help people who believe the way we do, to continue to live the way they want to live." Acheson was not present at the creation of a policy—he merely presided over the reification of a *Weltanschauung*.

All of which brings me back to Spinoza. Acheson provides us with a fact that contains the whole, and a whole that contains every fact. So if I condense the evidence about Russian policy on reparations at Potsdam into one introductory paragraph that summarizes Moscow's comments of earlier years, and at the same time provides a preview of the Kremlin's final posture, I have not distorted history. I have done my best to encapsulate the history that I then explore: that is the definition of an essay.

Just as when I seem redundant in *The Roots of the Modern American Empire,* it is because I am trying to explore and reveal all the internal relationships that give meaning to a group of positivistic facts.

Ah, so.

I make my final confession. I have fallen between upteen stools. So be it. All I can do is to echo Wright Morris: *What a Way to Go!*

But, in a final effort to explicate the text, let me offer you a proposition taken from William Carlos Williams' essay on Aaron Burr.

> Near the end of his life a lady said to him: "Colonel, I wonder if you were ever the gay Lothario they say you were." The old man turned his eyes, their lustre still undiminished, toward the lady—and lifting his trembling finger said in his quiet, impressive whisper: "They say, they say, they say. Ah, my child, how long are you going to continue to use those dreadful words? Those two little words have done more harm than all others. Never use them, my dear, never use them."

That is why, warts and all, I remain, faithfully yours, an intransigent revisionist.

LET US MAKE
OUR OWN FUTURE
WITH THE HELP OF
THE PAST

[from *America Confronts a Revolutionary World, 1776–1976,* 1976]

The later writings of William Appleman Williams were increasingly concerned with the ethics of power, the honoring of principles of self-determination, and the replacement of the American empire with a federation of regional communities. The book from which this selection is taken involved Williams in an extended discussion of how the United States subverted its original commitment to self-determination and revolution to become a counterrevolutionary power opposed to domestic structural change and convinced of its mission to make the world over in its own image. Americans, Williams claimed, evaded truths about their past and shunned the possibilities of the future. Thus they remained isolated in the present, trapped in the illusory belief that the United States is unique, an example the rest of the world wishes to imitate. But, Williams observed, America from the outset of its existence "and unto this day has faced a revolutionary world that increasingly challenged its claim—and self-image—as the dynamic instrument (and symbol) of human fulfillment." The U.S. response to this challenge, ever more violent in the twentieth century, violated the "bedrock principle" of self-determination that had been at the center of the American revolutionary experience. Williams called on Americans to recover the tradition.

We are all inextricably locked into the past, and the choice is between imprisoning oneself in the past and taking rational, innovatory steps into the future.   *Historian Moses I. Finley, 1975*

You must abolish the system or accept its consequences.
                                              Orestes Brownson, 1840

He who desires but acts not, breeds pestilence.
            William Blake, The Marriage of Heaven and Hell

Thou wilt find rest from vain fancies if thou doest every act in life as though it were thy last.   *Marcus Aurelius Antoninus,* Meditations, *II, 5*

WE have been playing hide-and-seek for two centuries on the basis of a gentleman's agreement never to run off into either the Past or the Future. That has nevertheless left us with a large playground, perhaps best epitomized in this motto: "Limbo Is Our Way of Life."

Prospering in limbo *is* an unusual achievement. Perhaps, as Bismarck commented, we have enjoyed a special dispensation from God. Those inclined to that explanation would do well to remember, however, that the German Prince linked us with fools as being the two particular concerns of the Lord. And also to recall Jefferson's somber remark about trembling for us because he knew that God was just. On the other hand, we may owe it all to nothing more mysterious than vast resources, fortuitous circumstances, and superior firepower.

Explain it as you will, America has until recently defied Time. We have been so effective in preserving the Present, however, that we have failed to realize that it is rapidly becoming archaic. Even more disturbing, we have hardly noticed that we have paid in the coin of our heritage. We have forgotten what it is to self-determine ourselves.

It may well be too late. I do not say that with finality, but as a citizen and as a historian I have to admit the possibility. And if all that the rumors of catastrophe mean (à la Acheson) is that the barbarians will land at Plymouth Rock, I can only say that I will give over in peace. They would move us off dead center. But I see no true barbarians on the horizon: certainly not the Russians. Everyone with the interest in conquering us, or the power to do so, is lusting for our Present. A dreary prospect.

Which confronts us with the challenge of being our own barbarians. Viewed superficially, as bombs assembled in the basement and then secreted in toilets on the thirtieth floor, or as shooting Presidents and other factotums, that is not a meaningful choice. That is silly self-indulgence. But taken seriously, as an effort to create for the first time an American Future, it is an exciting challenge. To be a contemporary barbarian is to use our revolutionary right of self-determination to create a community in place of a marketplace; to replace the impersonal logic of possessive individualism with the morality of helping each of us cherish the other.

I

Let us begin by saying simply that James Madison was a highly intelligent person who was as wrong as anyone can be. He argued that expansion underwrites freedom, but the truth is that expansion is nothing more than a polite word for empire. And empire is the end of freedom. At home as well as abroad. John Quincy Adams finally got it right: to embark upon an effort to save the world is to destroy ourselves as well as many parts of the world. Probably all of it.

Let us next admit that Lincoln (*and* Wilson *and* Acheson) were giants who fudged the central issue. Once we began to hedge the right of self-determination in the name of our Present, we began to take our rewards in the goodies of the imperial marketplace and in the false coin of self-righteousness. It is not pleasant to root out and then turn away from the deadly weaknesses and evasions of those we have trusted and honored. But so be it if it is so revealed. We have no choice but to self-determine ourselves or die.

So we must face the question of how to begin, what to seek, and how to continue the voyage. Let us first go back to Madison and turn him inside out. Instead of enlarging the sphere, let us work our way toward the goal of creating several small spheres that will be communities. The very idea of an imperial community is, upon even the most cursory examination, a contradiction in terms—a denial of the premise in the program to realize the premise. If the objective is to govern a continent under one system, then it can only be done as an empire. Consider not only America. Look at Russia, India, and Brazil. Even China, although we can learn important things from Mao's efforts to devise a way out of the dilemma.

Hence we must move another step into the Past beyond Madison. Unlike Lincoln, we must seek to honor rather than to supersede our revolutionary forefathers. That means evoking and using the Past to create a Future that honors our primary commitment to self-determination. We must return therefore to the Articles of Confederation. That document offers us a base from which to begin our voyage into a human Future; a model of government grounded in the idea and the ideal of self-determined communities coming together as equals when and as it is necessary to combine forces to honor common values and realize common objectives.

Many years ago I argued that the Articles were unsuited to their time. I would stick with the essence of that judgment: newly independent societies require a sustained and coordinated effort to survive, develop their own identities, and establish their political economies. That is the underlying explanation of the rise of mercantilism during the latter part of the sixteenth century. It also goes far to account for the distortions of socialism and communism in the twentieth century. They were conceived as postcapitalist models for an industrialized community, not as a way of transcending economic weakness and the social fragmentation generated by modernization.

But I have become steadily more impressed with the vision that produced the Articles. They represented a profound perception that the human dilemma is not defined by a simple choice between survival or honoring one's ideals. They speak to the truth that we struggle to honor our ideals. Otherwise we become the walking dead. And deadly.

Viewed in that light, the Constitution deserves our respect as an unusually sophisticated statement of the argument that we honor our ideals only as we survive. Our respect, but neither our agreement nor our veneration. For survival at the price of institutionalizing domestic and global empire, *and internalizing empire as a way of thought and life,* is to rob our soul to feed our belly.

II

Harsh words. I stand on them. The Constitution, to borrow a telling phrase from Jean-Paul Sartre, is a room with no exit. If you accept its essential philosophy because you want to preserve the Present, then you cannot change its essentials because that would be to risk the Present. Thus, to paraphrase Warren Susman, you endlessly redecorate the room because you dare not move to another.

The image of robbing the soul to feed the belly can also be interpreted as defining one as an idealist rather than a realist. Some might enjoy the witty thrust that I am using Christ against Marx. It is a clever but essentially irrelevant comment. Both systems, like the one created by Freud, are grand and noble metaphors describing the human condition and offering ways to realize our full potential. The central problem, however, has never been to reconcile Freud and Marx, or Christ and Marx, but rather to integrate the Marx of the Old Testament and the Marx of the New Testament. For otherwise our souls are full and our bellies empty, or our bellies full and our souls empty.

There is in the Old Testament Marx a candid recognition and acceptance of the truth that we humans cannot get enough soul food if all we concentrate on is feeding our bellies. It is as important to be free and human, and to deal with others as equal members of the community, as it is to be satiated with yummies from the store. *Any* store. The New Testament Marx never recants that truth, but he is more than a bit bedazzled by the material wonders of capitalist industrialism.

He more than occasionally sounds euphoric: we now have the power to fill *all* bellies *all* the time *and* to be free. But if one overlooks the exaggeration of exuberance one must give him his due: he just might have squared that circle. A challenging case can be made that if Western Europe and the United States had turned to socialism during the 1870s, then the world would have enjoyed an equilibrium between the soul and the belly, and that the Socialist ethic would have enabled us to deal with the problem of finite resources in an equitable and humane fashion.

But that did not happen, and we are today confronted with honoring the Old Testament Marx by imagining and then creating our own New Testament. It may sound a bit disrespectful—some will no doubt say irreligious—but I think he would enjoy a bit of blunt talk. If his First Coming failed to meet its schedule (and was thereby distorted by those who tried to force it past its time), then we will have to arrange the Second Coming on our own. I think Marx would not only approve but feel betrayed if we failed to try.

III

We must begin, each of us, with ourselves. I do not mean psychoanalysis or group therapy or transcendental meditation. Each of those is helpful for some people in some circumstances at some time. But I am talking about acting as thoughtful and militant *citizens*. That is not only excellent therapy, but it is the essence of liberation and community—of self-determination.

The true destructiveness of our concern to preserve the Present lies in the way it has limited and confined our basic sense of self-determination. It is not simply that males have defined females as housewives and sex objects. Or that whites have viewed colored people as inferior. It is equally deadly for females to accept (implicitly or otherwise) the male definition of self-determination as *macho* success in the marketplace, or for Blacks and Reds to seek fulfillment in putting the whites down on the mud sill. All that is understandable and natural, and some of it is necessary and healthy; but none of it is meaningful as a definition of citizenship in a community.

A citizen is a person who knows—and honors—the truth that he or she can fulfill himself or herself only as a member of a community. In the end, therefore, we have to say no to empire, for it is a contradiction in terms to talk about being a citizen in an empire. Some people feel that ending the war in Vietnam and driving Nixon from office created a momentum for change. But it is impossible to end the empire, either at home or abroad, by winning occasional dramatic victories. Particularly when they are in truth but marginal victories. The structural determinants of another imperial war, and for another effort to consolidate total power, remain essentially as strong as ever. A massive and centralized empire absorbs such setbacks, even calls them defeats, as a sponge absorbs water. It is all very well to argue that enough water will saturate the sponge, but that will also very probably inundate us along with the leaders of the empire.

Therein lies the problem. We can benefit from external pressures on the empire, or gross abuses within the empire, only if we are ready to act at home. So we are back with the importance of being citizens. If that begins, as I think it does, with a commitment to community and to the best of our heritage, rather than to the mirage of a free marketplace or the narcissistic dream of self-selected and self-sufficient cadres, then it moves next to acting as a citizen in one's own neighborhood. That means, as a start, nothing more dramatic than opening oneself to know other people. First to learn their names, and to use them at every opportunity. Then to learn their concerns, and how they think and feel about dealing with those difficulties. Finally, to understand their dreams and visions and to talk with them about how to translate them into reality.

It all sounds very elementary and time-consuming, and it *is* very elementary and time-consuming. But it has to be done if one is to be a citizen embarked upon the adventure of building a self-determined community. After that, moreover, the labor grows even more difficult. Moving out of a neighborhood in which you have earned your way as a citizen into the city or the state is a demanding experience. It is going back to being alone and in today's America made even more painful because there are so few neighborhoods sure enough of themselves to welcome a stranger as a fellow citizen. But it has to be done. Not by all of us all of the time, but by all of us some of the time. It cannot be left to the politicians simply because it ceases to be self-determination if we delegate it to someone else.

The saving grace is that each of us has his particular way of moving to and fro between our own neighborhood and the larger society. All of us have that ability. The issue is to use it. Some of us write, not just books or articles, but, even more important, letters to friends and to newspapers and magazines to discuss the issues involved in building a community. Others have different skills which open the way to becoming fellow citizens. There are those who create that feeling and reality with few if any words: they bring alive the reality of community simply by helping countless people. And there are those gifted few who publicly personify the ideal. They know and respect our concerns, our ideals, and our visions. They become leaders, and so long as they honor the community they deserve to be treasured and supported. Otherwise send them back to the neighborhood to begin again.

IV

I have been trying, of course, to describe the process whereby you and I as individuals benumbed by the empire begin to function as citizens and then come together with countless others to create a social movement strong enough to leave the Present for a better life of our own creation. We cannot do it any other way.

It is possible, of course, to change the rulers of an empire by staging a coup. But, even if the new leaders want to alter the structure, they cannot do so *democratically* unless they represent and are supported by a social movement. If they substitute force, then they dishonor their avowed ideals and become another group of imperial overlords. Christ, for example, did not make his revolution by assassinating Pontius Pilate and installing his disciples as the top bureaucrats of the system.

Neither did Lenin, despite all the talk (including his) about the seizure of power by a minority of a minority. Lenin and the Bolsheviks took power as the vanguard of a broad social movement committed to changing the structure of Russian society. The subsequent failure to respond to the various elements in that movement— and the consequent necessity to substitute force for community —does not change the essential nature of the Revolution. Lenin acted in the name of a social movement that had been developing since 1825 and which survives today through such courageous and thoughtful people as Roy Medvedev.

The central point has been made many times since the Russian Revolution. One thinks immediately of the Chinese revolutionaries led first by Sun Yat-sen and then by Mao Tse-tung. They saw themselves as expressions and agents of a vast upwelling of people who knew that a better life depended upon changing the structure of Chinese society. Mao understood the two essentials better than almost anyone. The right of self-determination is in truth an ongoing revolutionary process that must be honored into the Future. But it is not another name for anarchy, and hence we have to agree upon limits. That poses an extremely difficult problem, but then that is the definition of life.

Then one thinks of India and Cuba. India is turning toward despotism because Gandhi's successors failed to recognize the difference between the political party and a social movement. A party rules people, whereas a social movement creates a community. Castro sensed that crucial distinction and has tried—with increasing success—to use his power to create a community. The "Maximum Leader" has a vision of making himself incidental: of using his charisma to insure his ultimate irrelevance.

Hence it is important to understand the nature of a social movement. It is, to begin with, not an interest group, not even a large one, for the members of such a group are concerned primarily (if not exclusively) with their particular objectives. Nor is it a group of people who come together from different backgrounds to accomplish one specific task.

The project to put a man on the moon illustrates the different nature of such activities. The people in the space program shared a common interest, compromised various conflicts in order to realize one objective, and enjoyed a limited kind of camaraderie. But they were not united by a common concern with the nature and quality of life, and most of them spun off to other things when the particular job was finished.

The struggle to end the war in Vietnam involved more of the elements that define a social movement and for a short period gave promise of transcending its immediate objective. One dynamic and imaginative group of people in the coalition was unquestionably concerned with developing an alternate conception of America,* and it proved able for a time to work with other groups who were not initially or primarily interested in that objective. That crucial capacity to function as a citizen working with others to evolve a mutually self-determined future was aborted by a combination of impatience, elitism, the lack of any real consequential sense of history, and the failure to offer even a meaningful outline for a different America. The antiwar coalition thus became a single-issue pressure group that began to disintegrate even before the war was actually terminated—though it clearly made an important contribution to that result.

By contrast, a social movement generates its own objectives rather than coming into existence to implement or oppose decisions made by others and is deeply involved with the fundamental issues of the political economy. It may (and often does) begin in the herky-jerky dissatisfactions of unassociated people about their existing circumstances and their anger toward those they hold responsible for their unhappy predicament. But to become a social movement, those people must agree to compromise their different immediate interests and lifestyles *in order to create a different way of life.*

Hence we must develop a vision. The term *vision* sounds romantic, even mystical, but it is essentially practical. The Monroe Doctrine and the Open Door Policy, for example, were visions, but they were also very earthy conceptions of how to organize the world. A vision is an ordering of values in an ideal way. An organization of reality as we would like it to be. Hence it is a religious experience. Once again, as when in the introduction I defined *structural,* I go to the dictionary: religion involves a "code of ethics." To be religious, therefore, means to acknowledge, and to do one's very best to honor in practice, a system of values. Such a structure of ideals may or may

*While the Students for a Democratic Society are usually noted at this point, it is important to realize that *there were many other students and nonacademics* who were initially excited by and involved in the exploration of specific and vague alternatives to the existing imperial system.

not invoke the name of God in the biblical sense, but it must provide *some* injunction to do certain things and not to do other things.

It all means, and sooner rather than later, that we who want to move beyond the Present must commit ourselves to a new ethical system. The private gain and private pleasure of possessive individualism must give way to helping other people. Must give way, that is, to being citizens of a community.

Such an alternate conception of life involves three major elements. First, a combination of new values and a revised ranking of the old values that are considered important to honor. Second, new institutions and rules (and modifications of the old ones) designed to implement the new hierarchy of values. Third, a continuing willingness to tolerate and compromise secondary differences in order to translate the vision into reality—into a community.

Creating a social movement in contemporary America poses an extremely difficult challenge even if we assume that a significant number of people begin to act as citizens in their neighborhoods and the immediately larger units of the existing empire. Once people stop saying, "Oh, hell, *I* can't do anything," because they have discovered that they *can* affect and change their existing life and environment, they soon begin to ask, "What can we do about the *real* causes of our troubles?" I do not think that there is any consequential answer— theoretical or practical—to that question within the existing system.

We have been reforming America since it was consolidated as a Constitutional empire, and we have ended in an imperial mess. Our rulers are unable to disengage from even the most obvious mistakes in foreign policy with any intelligence and morality, or grace and dignity, and they continue to pout and whine about (and intervene in the affairs of) most of the people with whom we share the globe. They do not offer their ostensible fellow citizens at home any meaningful work despite a list of vast and pressing needs that requires countless books to enumerate. And what we call our social fabric is so sundered by conflicts of color, sex, and class that much of the time it reminds one of the emperor's new clothes. It is fair enough to blame *Them,* but the truth of it is that *We* continue to allow a tiny minority to control our political economy (and hence our lives) as their private pastime. The system survives through inertia and even more because no vital alternative has been proposed and agitated.

V

So once again let us return to the Articles of Confederation. I suggest that we embark upon a sustained effort to organize a social movement dedicated to replacing the American empire with a federation of regional communities. No euphemisms and no talk about reform. The objective is to create a federation of democratic Socialist communities.

The politics of that proposal are difficult for two reasons. It is impossible to begin by organizing a continental social movement. At the same time, we all know that the boundaries of the states have almost no ultimate relevance to the basic problems that have to be dealt with in order to change the existing structure and create a more humane society. Even so, I see no other place to initiate a radical strategy. Thus I suggest that we learn something from the Old South about how to practice the theory of self-determination.

Each of our states now retains a significant sense of identity despite a century of domestic imperialism that has centralized and consolidated power in Washington in the name of efficiency, reform, and mission. I have experienced that self-consciousness in Iowa, Texas, Wisconsin, and Oregon and have observed it in many other states. That spirit, and the related anger about further encroachments upon self-determination, can be encouraged in the name of democratic Socialist communities just as Georgia and South Carolina built upon it to create a movement for southern independence.

Radicals seem forever unable to understand that states' rights can be invoked and honored to create a Socialist community as well as to defend slavery (or other conservative and reactionary objectives).* That provides a sad but nevertheless revealing example of America's general lack of a true sense of history. But there is no reason, for example, why the citizens of any state whose political economy is dominated by a few corporations cannot muster their will and transform the monsters into instruments of community welfare. Orestes Brownson had it right: "You must abolish the system or accept its consequences." The point is to stop wasting one's time trying to housebreak a beast that inevitably conditions or intimidates its ostensible trainers.

Two political strategies can be pursued simultaneously, much as

---

*For example: petroleum and its related products (such as gas) are a *social* resource. So, also, are railroads. Hence such means to our human welfare should be managed by people elected by those who define the need.

Sam Adams and others did during the decade prior to the Revolution of 1776. There is no rational argument against using the existing electoral system *if* it is done openly in the name of a federation of democratic Socialist communities and *if* it is undertaken, not with a desire to be defeated, but with a desire to attract non-Socialist support on the basis of a positive vision of the future.

But it is also essential to create alternate institutions that maintain constant pressure on the imperial bureaucracies. It matters far less what they are called than that they do the homework and display the will required to force the system on the defensive. None of us likes to be nagged, particularly by people who have their facts straight and who keep on coming, and for that reason such nagging is an effective tactic in a prerevolutionary situation. Consider, as an illustration, the achievement of a group of students at Oregon State University (considered by most radicals as well as most conservatives to be a cow college that will still be there after all the others have jumped over the moon). Initially concerned only with ecological issues, they gradually became an extralegal standing Ways and Means Committee concerned with all primary issues affecting the people in the state. They are inspiring in their effectiveness and perhaps even more so because of their total lack of fear for the future.

Such groups will continue to be essential in the Future. Just as it is impossible to create a democratic Socialist community without tough and committed citizen involvement, so will it be impossible to sustain that better life without the same kind of determination to maintain the reality of self-determination. The price of liberty is not so much vigilance as it is involvement. If you want to rest, vote for a dictator.

VI

The crucial arena for such citizen groups is and will remain the states. That is where social movements have to be built, and they are the units for building coalitions to deal with regional and federal issues. Some existing boundaries will need to be modified as we create regional commonwealths, and the largest cities should become regions in their own right, but even then the subdivisions that we think of as states will remain essential to democratic socialism.

In the meantime, moreover, social movements within the states can accomplish far more than has generally been attempted since the heyday of Georgia, South Carolina, and Mississippi. The environmental laws and programs in California and Oregon illustrate the practicality of that logic, as does the recently enacted election law in Texas that requires those who make illegal campaign contributions to compensate the opponent over whom they sought criminal advantage.

The vitality and power of such community politics provide the only way to prevent regions from becoming bureaucratic morasses and to insure that the decisions of those dealing with federal matters will not be abstract and elitist. The decentralization of the existing American empire does not provide a guarantee of democratic equity, it only offers a human scale for action and government within which a social movement can operate effectively to create that kind of community. With that ever in mind, let us explore the outlines of one such region—a Pacific Northwest Community—that is eminently feasible.

We begin with the states of Washington, Oregon, Idaho, and Montana. Assume that we have created in each of those states a social movement that is capable of dealing with many problems and exploring many opportunities within those limits. Which is to say that we are willing and able to confront the power of corporations, the issue of priorities for the use of resources, the question of our relationship with other regions in the world, and have evolved a hierarchy of values to guide us in our life together. And, because names are important, let us, in honor of the Americans who first lived here, call our region *Neahkahnie* (Nee-ah-*kahn*-ie).

We citizens of those states are now aware, and will know even more intimately at that point, that the lives of all of us in the Pacific Northwest are irrevocably intertwined and mutually dependent upon each other. We do have common problems and share a way of life, and those provide us with the basis for developing a vision of a meaningful future. As part of that awareness, we know that some of us, particularly in Oregon and Montana, have potentially more affinity with other regions.

Parts of Oregon have a natural association with a community that reaches into California and Nevada, and perhaps even into other existing states. In a similar way, Idaho and Montana will probably divide: some sections will join us while others will find a more congenial affiliation east of the Rockies. Nor can we gloss over the need for *Neahkahnie* to evolve a close relationship with British Columbia. Therein lies a dynamic element in realizing Marx's vision of international solidarity. Once we begin to end the empire in

America, we will exert pressure for similar reorganizations throughout the world. People working out their relationships with a new
America will be influenced not only by our example, but by the
practical necessity of acting in different ways.

That will also be true of the regional communities within America. The new federalism will be based on three kinds of fundamental agreement. The first concerns a firm commitment to basic rights
as a condition of membership in the federation. We can begin with
the Bill of Rights and move on through other political, and social
and economic, foundations of a democratic Socialist community. The
second involves procedures for reaching and implementing federal
decisions. The third is defined by the ongoing negotiations between
such regional communities as they deal with routine economic
relationships. Each of us can and must offer suggestions in each area,
but that can become meaningful only as we begin to create a social
movement dedicated to the basic objective.

Even as we gather strength, we will face three kinds of criticism
which will often be offered by the same people. The first is that
socialism inevitably means less rather than more self-determination.
I can reply only that yes, it will mean less self-determination for
those who now exercise monopoly power over most aspects of life for
the rest of us. But the kind of socialism that I am advocating is based
upon the replacement of the existing empire by regional communities of a human scale governed through democratic procedures. We
will require plans, but we now live (if that is the word) under plans
devised by a tiny elite: I am proposing plans suited to our respective
conceptions of community. Finally, I do not advocate the total
nationalization of the economy. Once we set our goals and establish
our priorities, I think we should rely heavily on cooperative action to
realize our objectives.

Second, we will be attacked for advocating or condoning violence.
Here again I can only respond by saying, yes, there will be some
violence. But not mindless or irrelevant violence. There is a vital
difference between advocating violence and reluctantly accepting
violence. When one is concerned, as I am, to build a social movement
to change the structure of one's own society, one does not advocate
violence. One seeks instead to persuade one's fellow citizens to
participate in the enterprise, to join in the adventure, to walk arm in
arm into the Future. To murder a President is to give up, admit
defeat, surrender, commit suicide. And to murder fellow citizens

with bombs placed in random toilets in random banks is to file a petition of moral, political, and intellectual bankruptcy.

But inevitably there will be some violence. How much will depend upon how many people remain actively opposed to the ideal of a self-determined community. If you are determined to prevent the creation of that kind of life, or if you think that you have the answer for all the rest of us and are determined to impose it upon us, then so be it: I will meet you on the barricades.

Third, we will be told (as even orthodox reformers are told) that our revolution will weaken America's power in the world. Again, I answer yes. If you judge power only by contemporary imperial criteria, then America will become weaker. Indeed, that is implicit in the proposal for a social movement to create the new federation. Such an America will not try to police the world, or even any part of it, and it will not attempt to expand the area of freedom by subverting the self-determination of other peoples.

But I am not saying, as so many critics charge, that a new America will be isolationist or indifferent to its security. As suggested by the example of a Pacific Northwest Community developing a close relationship with British Columbia, such an America will evolve alternate and more equitable associations with other societies. And such a new America will have considerable power and influence of a different and more consequential kind than that displayed by the existing imperial system.

That does not mean it will be eternally safe. Anyone who tells you that about any society is either a fool or a knave. Hence all I can say to you is that I prefer to die as a free man struggling to create a human community than as a pawn of empire.

So make *your* choice. Continue the treadmill exercise of trying to preserve the Present, or accept the challenge of creating our own Future. But at least make it as the decision of a consciously self-determined human being who understands what is involved and is ready to accept the consequences.

Let us together find rest from vain fancies.

THE EMPIRE AT BAY

[from *Empire as a Way of Life*, 1980]

By 1980, when Williams wrote *Empire as a Way of Life*, the final chapter of which is represented here, the United States was attempting to reorder its domestic affairs and reassert its power and influence throughout the world after a decade of dramatic reversals. Williams reviewed the situation in terms of the theme he had pursued for more than twenty years, declaring that empire as *the* American way of life, "a smashing success when it is going well," was now in deep distress. He expressed astonishment at the continuing inability of Americans to understand their past, whatever the chosen idiom, suggesting however that the current difficulties provided a major opportunity: confront and acknowledge the choice of empire and seek ways of limiting and improving life in it, or reject empire for community, his preferred alternative.

We are the most ambitious people the world has ever seen:—& I greatly fear we shall sacrifice our liberties to our imperial dreams.
> *Henry J. Raymond, Editor of the New York Times,*
> *to Secretary of State William Seward, 1864*

Our frontiers today are on every continent.
> *John Fitzgerald Kennedy, 1960*

No single nation however big and powerful can dominate a world of some 140 interdependent nations and embracing some four billion people.
> *R. S. Rajaratan, Singapore Minister of Foreign Affairs, 1979*

IN a rare moment of candor, Secretary of State Dean Acheson admitted in 1953 that he and Harry Truman might not have been able to sustain their grandiose imperial policy if the North Koreans

360

had not "come along and saved us." Actually, Acheson did not even say "North Koreans." He said "Korea." Given his reputation for sometimes shading the truth so finely as to render it indistinguishable from an ordinary lie, that remark prompted some observers to reopen the question of whether or not South Korea, with the overt or tacit approval of the United States, provoked the North Korean attack of June 1950.

On balance, however, it was simply one of those wars that anybody could have counted on to erupt some time. Both halves of that divided country were dying to start dying to unite themselves. That old deb'l nationalism raised to fever pitch by very strong shots of mutually exclusive theologies. In any event, the debate about who bears ultimate responsibility obscures the fundamental issue of the response by Truman and Acheson.

Clearly, when the Secretary acknowledged that Korea "saved us," he did not mean in the sense of preventing the defeat or the destruction of the United States. He meant only that it allowed the government to implement the apocalyptic imperial strategy of NSC-68.* Primed and ready, armed (or driven) psychologically as well as with the heady rhetoric of that document, they simply went to war. They by-passed the Congress and the public and confronted both with an accomplished fact. A few phone calls, and it was done. Go to bed at peace and wake up at war.

It was even more dramatic than the subsequent intervention in Vietnam as a demonstration of the centralization of power inherent in empire as a way of life. The State had literally been compressed or consolidated into the President and his like-minded appointees. In a marvelously revealing description, underscoring Truman's earlier lecture to the cabinet, the war without a declaration of war was called a "police action." Ironically, the most succinct commentary on Truman's remark was provided by the editor of the *New York Times*. "We are the most ambitious people the world has ever seen," noted Henry J. Raymond on May 30, 1864, "—& I greatly fear we shall sacrifice our liberties to our imperial dreams."

*National Security Council memorandum No. 68, circulated secretly and approved by President Truman in April 1950, escalated the cold war by militarizing U.S. containment strategy. It followed on the heels of two portentous events: the successful detonation of an atomic bomb by the Soviet Union in August 1949, and the conquest of China by the Communists (the People's Republic was proclaimed in October 1949). NSC-68 called for a vast rearmament of the U.S. and a jump in the defense budget from $13 billion to $50 billion.—ED.

I

The military containment and subsequent rout of North Korean forces (by the end of September 1950) created a moment of imperial euphoria. American leaders were high on NSC-68. The United States undertook to liberate North Korea by conquest and integrate it into the American Empire. It was assumed in Washington that such action would accelerate the process of disintegration within and between Russia and China and so finally create an open door world. Then came the moment of truth, and the empire suddenly found itself at bay. The Chinese entered the war with massive force on October 26 and drove the Americans southward to the line that originally divided Korea.

Once again one thinks of how American leaders failed to comprehend the willingness of black citizens to settle for promises of future equality and freedom at home. They had first misread and misapplied that episode in their dealings with the Russians; then with the Chinese; and finally, with increasing frequency, in Latin America, Africa, Southeast Asia, and the Middle East. The mistaken assumption that other poor and demeaned peoples would display similar forbearance was the cosmic cost of such prejudice and racism.

The Roosevelts, the Trumans and the Achesons, and most of their successors, fundamentally misconceived the deeply patriotic—even loving—commitment of American blacks to what Martin Luther King called The Dream of America. And because they could not acknowledge the existence of an American Empire, they could not comprehend—let alone understand—that other so-called inferiors felt the same love for their cultures; and that, viewing America as an empire which threatened the integrity and existence of their cultures, they would ultimately fight rather than accept indirect destruction.

The empire had been brought to bay. Dwight David Eisenhower understood that essential truth, and further realized that the future character of American society depended upon how the culture responded. His first objective after he became President in 1952 was to end the Korean police action before it spiraled into World War III. That accomplished, he set about to calm Americans, cool them off, and refocus their attention and energies on domestic development. He was a far more perceptive and cagey leader than many people realized at the time—or later.

The image of a rather absent-minded, sometimes bumbling if not incoherent Uncle Ike was largely his own shrewd cover for his serious efforts to get control of the military (and other militant cold warriors), to decrease tension with Russia, and somehow begin to deal with the fundamental distortions of American society. He clearly understood that crusading imperial police actions were extremely dangerous, and he was determined to avoid World War III. When Britain, France, and Israel attacked Egypt in 1956 over the nationalization of the Suez Canal, the President called British Prime Minister Anthony Eden and scolded him sharply: "Anthony, you must have gone out of your mind."

When the moment came, Eisenhower could be just as blunt with Americans. A good many of them were probably shocked when, in his farewell address of 1961, he spoke candidly and forcefully about the military-industrial complex that since 1939 had become the axis of the American political economy. That was such a catchy phrase that not many of them noticed that he went on to assault the distortion of education involved in that consolidation of power. The historically free and critical university, he noted, "the fountainhead of free ideas and scientific discovery, has experienced a revolution in the conduct of research.... A governmental contract becomes virtually a substitute for intellectual curiosity."

The speech was not an aberration: Eisenhower had become ever more deeply concerned with those issues after retiring from the army. Thus, while it is true that he was not an intellectual, and was conservative in many ways, it is also true that he had a firm sense of how The State had gradually taken over the very process of creating and controlling basic ideas—the ways of making sense of reality. Or, in a different way, how The State used its extensive control of information, and its ability to make major decisions in the name of security, to create an ideology ever more defined in content as well as rhetoric as an imperial way of life.

Eisenhower's most serious weakness did not lie in his fidelity to a rudimentary version of marketplace economics, or even in his excessive caution about how quickly and how far he could move the American citizenry away from its imperial obsessions with Russia, China, and other revolutionary movements. It was defined instead by his unwillingness to translate his valid perceptions into strong policies and active sustained leadership. He lacked Hoover's (let alone Churchill's) toughness about accepting the limits of American power, and the former President's knowledge that the only way to deal with the costly and unhealthy consequences of empire was to begin creating a different way of life. Given his charisma, Eisenhower could have initiated that process and perhaps even created an irreversible momentum.

Failing to do that, he left no dynamic legacy. The militant advocates of the global imperial way of life quickly reasserted their power and policy. They, too, recognized that the Chinese counterintervention in Korea had brought the empire to a critical juncture. Their response was to reassert American power and get on with policing the world in the name of benevolent progress. Led by John Fitzgerald Kennedy, and calling themselves the New Frontiersmen, they perfectly expressed the psychopathology of the empire at bay and its consequences. Onward and outward in the spirit of NSC-68. "Ask not what your country can do for you," intoned Kennedy in his 1961 inaugural address, "ask what you can do for your country." By country, of course, they meant *their* government.

Kennedy and his advisers had the brilliant perception to talk about the empire in the classic idiom of the frontier. That propaganda gem is of itself almost enough to justify honoring them as the cleverest imperial leaders of their generation. The best that Henry Kissinger could do a few years later, for example, was to blurt out a crude reference to the same idiom—presenting himself as Gary Cooper in *High Noon*. The excessively self-conscious Dr. Cowboy will ride on stage in good time, but for the moment let us concentrate on those Kennedy hands who were born and bred to empire.

"Our frontiers today," cried Kennedy, "are on every continent." America has "obligations," he explained, "which stretch ten thousand miles across the Pacific, and three and four thousand miles across the Atlantic, and thousands of miles to the south. Only the United States—and we are only six percent of the world's population—bears this kind of burden." He understandably neglected to mention that the burden on the metropolis was somewhat eased by the benefits of controlling a grossly disproportionate percentage of the world's resources. He was more concerned to create the psychological mood of impending doom: "The tide of events has been running out and time has not been our friend."

The failure of the effort early in 1961 to overthrow Fidel Castro's revolution in Cuba intensified that trauma. Not only did the rhetoric become ever more apocalyptic ("this time of maximum danger"), but Kennedy immediately began a massive military build-up in the spirit of NSC-68 (three special requests for extra funds during 1961). Then he indulged himself in a truly arrogant and irresponsible act. Knowing that the United States enjoyed a massive superiority in strategic weapons, Kennedy publicly goaded, even insulted, the Soviet Union by gloating about its gross inferiority.

He scared the Russians viscerally; and in the process not only prompted them to launch a desperate effort to correct the vast imbalance, but very probably touched off the internal Soviet dialogue that led to the confrontation in 1962 over Russian missiles in Cuba. The more evidence that appears about that moment on the edge of the abyss, the more it seems probable that the Soviets never had any intention of going to war. Taken with all appropriate skepticism, for example, Premier Nikita Khrushchev's account very likely contains the essence of truth: Moscow was less concerned with the possibility of a second invasion of Cuba than with somehow—even at sizable risk—jarring Washington into a realization that, if pushed to the wall, the Russians would fight rather than surrender. Given their grave inferiority, the only way they could make that point was by creating a situation that would dramatize for Americans the threat as experienced daily by the Soviets.

Kennedy's understanding of that message was limited. He spoke of the need to avoid further such crises, but he clearly felt that America had regained the initiative; that he was now free to deploy American forces to prevent or control further change that might weaken the American empire. He did talk about accepting diversity among the poor and developing nations, and about programs to facilitate some social and economic improvements in Latin America and other countries. And he did make some efforts, as in the Alliance for Progress and the Peace Corps, to act on that rhetoric. But he also embarked upon an obsessive campaign to murder Castro, and he deployed between 15,000 and 20,000 American troops (many of them in the field as advisers) to intervene in the revolutionary civil war in Vietnam. Those frontiers on every continent were going to remain frontiers in the traditional American meaning of a frontier—a region to penetrate and control and police and civilize.

II

This essay, an effort to review our development as an empire and to encourage a searching dialogue among ourselves about the character of our culture, has never attempted to offer a detailed reconstruction of American foreign policy. Hence it would be a contradiction in terms to wander off into a blow-by-blow account of recent events. But it does seem useful to explore some of the contemporary aspects of our imperial way of life.

Let us begin with the relationship between NSC-68 and the civil rights movement of the 1950s and 1960s; and let us assume that American leaders, whatever their prejudices or racism, believed that the empire would provide blacks and other disadvantaged groups (including poor whites) with greater opportunities and rewards. Their most popular euphemism for empire—*growth*—was invoked on the grounds that the same share of an ever larger pie would produce improvement for everyone. And elitists like Acheson had reason to believe that the minorities and other poor would continue to be patient until the fruits of empire were harvested.

But the war in Korea, and the related increase in military spending, revealed the true priorities of the empire and hence dramatized the discrepancy involved in talking about empire in terms of liberty, freedom, equality, and welfare while denying those benefits to large numbers of people at home. That contradiction was further highlighted by the nonviolent nature of black protest against being denied elementary equity on the buses of Montgomery, Alabama, in 1955, and in the eating places of Greensboro, North Carolina, in 1960. Some white Americans recognized and became upset about that contrast, but neither Eisenhower nor Kennedy devised an effective response. The former was socially and politically too conservative and cautious, and the latter was more concerned with standing up to the Russians all along America's global frontier.

But Lyndon Baines Johnson did make a brave—and in the end tragic—effort to resolve that visceral contradiction in the imperial way of life. He tried to make major improvements in the quality of life for the poor and disadvantaged of all colors (and therefore for all other Americans), and at the same time secure the frontier in Indochina. That proved to be impossible because by 1964–65 the dynamics of empire as a way of life left him no room for maneuver. Given the legacy of prejudice and racism, and the global definition of America's political economy and its security as formulated in NSC-68, Johnson was trying to swim in the sky. But at least he tried.

Stated bluntly, the President could not muster the votes to help the poor at home unless he honored the imperial ethic in Vietnam. He simply did not enjoy the personal and political advantages that enabled Eisenhower to move quietly toward a less grandiose foreign policy. That meant that any effort to make structural reforms at home would provoke a militant reaction around the classic imperial theme of "Who Lost Whatever Wherever?"

Johnson first tried to finesse the war issue. Therein lies the stuff of great drama. A modern Shakespeare might well do it this way: if only Johnson had gone with his instinct as a Southerner to recognize in the Vietcong the American blacks driven to violence, then he might—just might—have begun the process whereby Americans said no to empire and yes to the vision of community. But the imperial North had forever scarred the South. Left it resentful and determined to prove its valor and its equality. There is a great play in that old fear of the South transformed into a recognition of the truth that one either frees the slaves or confronts a rebellion. But the North had failed to learn that lesson during Reconstruction after the Civil War, and so Johnson had no allies to help him redefine the truth of America.

So from finessing the war Johnson moved to lying about the war. His effort to stand firm on the frontier while effecting reforms at home led him to create enormous inflationary pressures within the economy, and to engage in ever more serious self-deception and public dissembling to sustain popular support for the imperial war. In the end, that is to say, Johnson was the victim of the basic fear, so candidly expressed in NSC-68, that America was fundamentally threatened by *any* disorder in the world. (A fear also revealed in the President's intervention in Santo Domingo.)

That fog of trepidation and dread continued to influence the conduct of foreign affairs by President Richard Milhous Nixon and Secretary of State Henry Kissinger. Their bone marrow anxiety provides the key to resolving the apparent paradox in a diplomacy that sought to stabilize relations with the Soviets while simultaneously recognizing the communist government of China, falsifying official records to hide an illegal and devastating expansion of the Vietnamese war into Cambodia, launching an effort to subvert an *elected* socialist government in Chile, and supporting a dictatorship in Iran that was instrumental in raising oil prices.

No one yet knows the precise nature of the relationship between Nixon and Kissinger. But Kissinger could not have functioned as he did without the support of the President. The Secretary of State has provided the most information about the assumptions that underlay their policies, and it seems apparent that they recognized that the grand objective of NSC-68—the subversion of the Soviet Union—was no longer realistic. Kissinger had long agreed with Churchill,

A William Appleman Williams Reader

for example, that the United States should have negotiated a broad settlement with the Russians in 1947–48, and concluded during the 1950s that American policy had "reached an impasse."

Thus it was necessary to stabilize the existing balance between the two superpowers. The first step on that road, at least in their view, was to assert their power over the bureaucracies in the State Department and other branches of government; a task Kissinger undertook with great relish as an exercise of his own ego in the service of his great-man interpretation of history. That done, Kissinger could begin the effort to order and balance the world.

He now and again admitted the impossibility of doing that without a clear conception of a limited American imperial system, and likewise spoke of the importance of justice; but he never provided either the vision or the definition of justice. Indeed, Kissinger had little patience with anyone who was concerned with the character of the world order he invoked so often. In one classic instance, for example, he dismissed such people for "confusing social reform with geopolitics." Yet his favorite word to define geopolitics was "equilibrium"—little more than a fancy synonym for order. As for justice, Kissinger might usefully have remembered the rabbi's wisdom about Deuteronomy 16.20: "Justice, justice shalt thou pursue." Asked why the word justice is repeated, the rabbi explained that it was done to emphasize the necessity of pursuing justice *with* justice.

Given the Nixon-Kissinger willingness to settle for controlling nothing more than the world outside Russia and Eastern Europe, their policy of detente and strategic arms control was a rational first step toward that objective. And it is certainly arguable that their approach to China (despite their tactics of secrecy and shock) was on balance a positive and stabilizing maneuver as long as it was not allowed to become part of a new strategy of containment designed to destabilize the Soviet Union. And that caveat applies to subsequent American leaders as well as to Kissinger and Nixon.

The weaknesses of the Nixon-Kissinger approach became clear in their dealings with the rest of the world. On the one hand, they defined stabilization as allowing the United States to decide what was permissible and impermissible beyond the Soviet sphere. But, on the other hand, they lacked any significant comprehension or understanding of the dynamic, causal inter-relationships between economics, politics, and social affairs within the poor regions of the world, or between the global rich and poor. Hence they mistakenly linked any changes not approved or controlled by the United States to the influence of the Soviets. The unhappy results became most apparent in Cambodia, Chile, and Iran.

The unconstitutional bombing of Cambodia, which clearly did more to destroy the fabric and morale of that society than the incursion of the North Vietnamese which Kissinger used to justify the monstrous act, is in some respects less revealing of their diplomacy than their actions in Chile and Iran. The American ambassador to Chile began his report on that nation's presidential election of 1970 in these words: "Chile voted *calmly* to have a Marxist-Leninist state, the first nation in the world to make this choice *freely and knowingly*."* In keeping with the primary responsibility of a foreign service officer, that is an essentially factual report; although adding the term *Leninist* to Marxist has long been the routine ploy used by those in power in America to turn an avowed socialist into a communist pawn of the Kremlin. The ambassador then offered, in a wholly legitimate way, his evaluation of the evidence: it was in his view "a grievous defeat" for the United States.

Kissinger's account of America's subsequent efforts to prevent Salvador Allende from becoming president of Chile, and later to destabilize and subvert his government, is remarkable for its conscious and unconscious revelations about the Nixon-Kissinger conduct of foreign affairs. Before Allende became president, for example, Kissinger presents the man as a doctrinaire communist in the Russian mould. Once Allende becomes President, however, Kissinger talks about the *possibility* that he will *become* such a puppet. In a similar way, the Secretary of State stresses Allende's narrow plurality in 1970 without once noting, even in a footnote, that Allende increased his vote in the next election, which was held in accordance with Chile's Constitution.

All that tells us more than Kissinger intended us to know, but he is even more illuminating when he insists that "our concern with Allende was based on national security, not on economics," and proceeds to emphasize "American interests in the hemisphere." There are three responses. First, Kissinger cannot seriously expect the observer to believe that Washington was worried about the Russians' turning Chile into a base for a strategic—geopolitical—military attack on the United States. Even he admits that the issue had been settled during the Cuban missile crisis; and, for that

*Italics added.

matter, refined during his tenure in the basement of the White House.

Second, if Kissinger did in truth not consider economic interests as an integral part of national security ("America's interests in the hemisphere"), then one must conclude that he was stunningly obtuse and probably not qualified to be Secretary of State in the world's premier capitalist political economy.* Third, in view of Kissinger's presentation of himself as a realist, he wholly ignores the feasibility of working with an elected socialist government as a hard-headed as well as moral strategy to counter the Soviet appeal in the Third World and to give hope to all democratic reformers in the poor nations. American leaders seem to be limited in their sight to the left by *benevolent* dictators like Tito of Yugoslavia.

The Secretary's performance in dealing with Iran offers support for all those criticisms. Give him his due: he has quietly and cryptically admitted that his comprehension of the relationships between economic, political, and social development was less than sophisticated. Hardly even rudimentary. But that is only part of the explanation of his failure in Iran. For it is extremely doubtful that any one nation could control events in the non-Soviet world. Asked for his comment on the matter, Karl Marx would have laughed aloud in the reading room of the British Museum.

Still and all, it is difficult to imagine how anyone of Kissinger's intelligence could combine more errors of perception, understanding, analysis, and policy in dealing with Iran. Neither he nor Nixon exhibited any sense of that nation's history, or even of its intensely religious and nationalistic pride. And they obviously assumed that Iranians had accepted or forgotten that the United States had grossly intervened to control the resources and the government of that country even before overthrowing an elected government in the 1950s.

Given all that, it is not surprising that they embarked upon a policy doomed to failure. In embracing and arming the Shah, in truth a petty despot, they committed America's geopolitical interests to a government guaranteed to generate ever growing internal opposition to its pretensions. And in supporting, even encouraging,

---

*It is possible, of course, that Kissinger made his disavowal in the hope of defusing the criticism that economic concerns were involved in the effort to subvert an elected government. If so, his sensitivity to the charge is revealing in its own right; and, in any event, he would have been better advised to be candid to avoid the thought that he was incompetent.

the despot to raise the price of oil to pay for his tinkertoy regime they undercut the foundation of the American imperial way of life they sought to preserve.

In the fundamental sense, the Americans held captive in Iran through and beyond the winter of 1979–80 were hostages to the American Empire. Prisoners taken in payment for the United States treating Iran and other weak countries (in that region, but also elsewhere) as vassals laboring at low wages for the welfare of the imperial metropolis. The story goes back far beyond the 1953 coup that put the Shah back on his throne, let alone the intervention at the end of World War II that played a significant part in the intensification of the Cold War. The tale has its origins in the 19th-century penetration of the region by American traders and Christian missionaries, and becomes a major (if neglected) theme of imperial diplomacy with the advent of Zionism and the importance of oil reserves during the 1920s and 1930s.

Our limited sense of History denies us any significant understanding of how trade, religion, oil, and revolution have converged to create a crisis in the Middle East. Simply put, the hostages are centerpieces carefully placed to dramatize our imperial way of life. They were seized to italicize the imperial nature of the American Way of Life. It would be a mistake to dismiss the religious point being documented by that act (the imperial nature of Christian missionaries), but here I would like to concentrate on the distortion of religion known as Zionism and the economics of oil.

The American inability to distinguish the difference between self-determination for a society of Palestinians (of whatever religion) and a geographical area populated exclusively by self-proclaimed pure Zionists may well generate the Apocalypse. Even if it does not, that confusion has already told us all that we should need to know about *any* people confusing themselves with the Lord. One thinks here of Winthrop, Jefferson, and others confusing metaphor with reality. Of not understanding that a metaphor is a cookie that when held too long in the hot fist will crumble into disaster. Of coming to believe that the City on the Hill has the right to expect to control the world.

Not at all after all, indeed in the beginning, the Palestinians are surely every bit as qualified as human beings as the Zionists. Leave it at that. One does think here of how we Americans honored the First Americans only after they had lost. It does not take too much imagination to visualize [Menachem] Begin dedicating a graveyard to

[Yasir] Arafat, intoning the usual Western pieties. The point is not to damn Begin. The point is to awaken our own conscience. Think of how we have treated our Begins and Arafats. And we, the happy citizens of the empire, respected American blacks only after they committed their imaginative pacific terrorist acts. They went to eat where they had a perfect legal imperial right to eat even if the imperial citizens beat them bloody. They went to church where they had a perfect legal imperial right to worship the God of their choice even if we bombed them taking communion.

Who is the terrorist?

It simply will not do for Zionists to define themselves as the benevolent, progressive policemen of the Middle East. No more than it will do for us to present ourselves in that idiom on the global scene.

And so to oil. The truth of it is that nobody believes us when we talk about oil as if we were socialists committed to internal equity. The world knows that we are imperialists dedicated to controlling all the oil we can funnel into our bellies. Oil is not the primary cause of empire. It is not even the principal definition of contemporary empire. But it is the slickest way we now lie to ourselves about the nature of empire. Let us risk confronting a bit of history.

Americans began to produce oil near Titusville, Pennsylvania, on August 27, 1859. Fifty years later the United States pumped more than the rest of the world combined. The political economy of capitalism shifted away from coal and neglected to explore other sources of energy. There was a short but intense oil scare between 1917 and 1924: a hullabaloo created by the navy shifting to oil-firing turbines, the Mexican Revolution, the boom in automobiles and airplanes, the beginnings of the petrochemical industry, and the struggle for market supremacy (and survival) among American petroleum corporations.

That crisis disappeared in the cloud of confidence puffed up by the finding of new reserves abroad (as in Venezuela), by new discoveries at home (as in Texas), by more efficient exploration and production at home, and—most particularly—by gaining access to the vast reserves in Saudi Arabia and other poor and weak countries in the Middle East. No better example ever of the rewards of empire as a way of life. But make no mistake, we also came to rely on other cheap materials from the provinces.

The United States continued to produce half the world's oil until, in 1948, it became a net *importer* of oil. True imperial dependency upon the natives. But that phrase I quoted earlier, John McCloy saying we *should* "have our cake and eat it too," perfectly captures the euphoria of the imperial way of life as applied to oil. Americans, citizens as well as leaders, simply assumed that they could sell their oil abroad for a good profit while importing it from the provinces at *pennies a barrel*.

The imperial way of life was disrupted by OPEC in 1973-74. But the oil-fired empire, once symbolized by the navy and now by intercontinental bombers, could not talk about the problem in a realistic way simply because it had never come to terms with its imperial way of life. The euphemisms began to dissolve. The United States supported the creation of Israel for three reasons: a commitment to the principle of self-determination, the financial and political power of Jews in domestic American politics, and the imperial usefulness of Israel as a client state in the oil-rich Middle East. The problem was that the Palestinians also had a right to self-determined nationhood, and oil was a most effective way to make that point.

And so the crisis deepened. Kissinger said it all in one sentence: The United States must somehow "shape events in the light of our own purposes." A marvelously subtle definition of empire. But note particularly that *somehow*. What a delightful way of avoiding any coming to terms with the reality of empire. But to evade that moment of truth means again going to war.

No candor, more flight from reality. More flight, no peace. No chance finally to confront the central challenge:

Is the idea and reality of America possible without empire?

Or define the issue in these ways.

Is America *even imaginable* only on a global scale?

Are we unable, *intellectually*, to do any better than to sermonize on the theme that endless growth is crucial to our social-psychological health; and are we unable, *morally*, to share the world (say with the Palestinians as well as the Zionists) on an equitable basis?

If you answer "yes" to those questions, then hunker down for what James Baldwin once called The Fire Next Time. We will suffer what we did unto Hamburg, Dresden, and Tokyo. We will suffocate, sizzle, and fry. All in the name of defending the proposition that democracy is impossible without empire.

But consider another question. Is it possible to create and sustain a democratic culture without conquering or otherwise controlling and wasting a grossly inequitable share of social space and resources?

If you answer "yes" to *that* question then you declare yourself a pioneer on what Carl Becker might have called the ultimate American frontier. Meaning you are prepared to challenge your assumptions and join John Adams in accepting the "irksome" annoyances involved with asserting a "measure of independency."

Come along. It is certain to be more challenging than walking along the Indian trails with Daniel Boone. And surely we can do better than Jefferson or Lincoln, those heroes of the morality of having it every which way while evading the truth of empire as a way of life. It *is* time to turn in the credit cards and stop passing the buck on to the next generation.

If you are ready to bestir yourself to face that issue, we can take comfort and courage from that impressive, and delightfully variegated, group of Americans who created the tradition of speaking truth to empire. We need to stop here for a moment to avoid confusion. To be honest, History must tell the story of those who won: why they won and how they intended to exploit their victory. But also History must tell us about those who offered an alternative vision and discuss the value of their different views.

So let us think about the people who lost. Now is the time to learn from them. Truth to tell, an impressive lot. Those people who said *no* to empire as the only definition of democracy: a delightfully unclassifiable collection of women and men. There are slave owners like John Taylor of Caroline County, Quaker abolitionists from Pennsylvania, and descendants of slaves like William E. B. DuBois and A. Philip Randolph. There are thrice-over certified conservatives such as John Quincy Adams and Herbert Hoover. There are radicals of your choice: say Eugene Debs or the Women's League for Peace and Freedom. And there are liberals like Robert La Follette, Carl Becker, Charles Beard, or Helen G. Douglas.

The exciting and profoundly important thing about all of those human beings is that they began as advocates of a system based on empire and then became, through their experience and reflection (the essence of *doing* history), people who questioned and challenged that conventional relationship between democracy and empire.

It works, it happens, down the line. I live in a nonacademic community. You have to earn your way in. My way is pool. I like the game and play it well. Professors playing pool with loggers and truck drivers and gippo fishermen properly go through an apprenticeship. You beat us at our game and we will try your game. Now my game at pool is to play the capitalist machine tables in such a way as most nearly to duplicate the real game of pool. No slop, no errant ball counts. You call your shots and bank the Eight Ball. The fascinating thing is that people like to be challenged to play the best they can in the most difficult circumstances. *They like the tough game.*

And that is where we are in the relationship between empire and democracy. So back to Taylor and Adams and Debs and straight pool. We come down to these questions.

1. Who makes policy on the basis of what perceptions and interests? I think here of Herbert Hoover trying to control the bankers. We have a right to know. Hoover lost in the 1920s and we have lost. *We do not know.*

2. Assume empire is necessary: what is the optimum size of the empire; and what are the proper—meaning moral as well as pragmatic—means of structuring, controlling, and defending the empire so that it will in practice produce welfare and democracy for the largest number of the imperial population?

3. What is the minimum effective size of the empire?

4. What happens if we simply say "no" to empire? Or do we have either the imagination or the courage to say "no" to empire?

It is now *our* responsibility. It has to do with how we live and how we die. We as a culture have run out of imperial games to play. Assume the worst. Empire as a way of life will lead to nuclear death. Community as a way of life will lead for a time to less than is necessary. Some of us will die. But how one dies is terribly important. It speaks to the truth of how we have lived.

THOUGHTS ON THE COMPARATIVE USES OF POWER

[The George Bancroft Lecture, United States Naval Academy, September 1986]

The last two items in this collection are previously unpublished essays. Each was composed within the remaining five years of Williams's life, and both focused on the responsible uses of power. In these pieces he provided illustrations from the American past and from another culture affirming national traditions of nonimperial and moral behavior, and suggesting them as models for contemporary American society.

In the first article Williams drew upon the experiences of China in the two centuries before the discovery of the Americas, recounting how Chinese leadership of the time rejected the lure of empire in favor of a program of internal improvement and promotion of the general domestic welfare. Williams contrasted this development to a very different outcome in the United States. There was, however, also an American tradition of anti-imperialism, Williams noted, represented by John Quincy Adams in the nineteenth century and by Charles Evans Hughes in the twentieth. Williams invoked this legacy and urged its renewal.

THE Standard Operating Procedure in this situation is to assert that one owes everything to the Alma Mater, and then complain that The Place Has Gone to Hell. But I think that it will be more fun to tell you a few tales before we enter upon our serious conversation.

First, I was bored to distraction during my first fifteen months here at what we used to call the Navy's School for Wayward Boys. Having been a Rat at Kemper Military School, I considered the hazing on the Severn to be unimaginative and intellectually feeble. And I could work that basic hand-held calculator, the double-log slide rule, even while sleeping at parade rest. Hence I took to listening to jazz, reading history and politics, and novels and poetry. As a result,

Second, I almost flunked out. Ultimately I was challenged sufficiently to raise my grades enough to graduate near the top of the bottom third of my class; and along the way I learned the bilge smarts to volunteer for the amphibious corps rather than become a messenger boy on a battleship.

Third, and particularly as a First Classman, I had fun tweaking the ideology of the Authorities to learn whether or not they honored in practice all the rhetorical broadsides they fired at us. There was the time, for example, when I persuaded the members of my section in thermodynamics that we should roller skate to class in order to demonstrate the principle of the conservation of energy. The professor thought it a delightful application of his wisdom, gave us 4-os, and dismissed us early.

The radar watch had picked us up, however, and the Officer of the Day awaited us upon our return. He had recently returned from the battles for Guadalcanal and walked with a bit of a limp. He also had a marvelous sense of humor and a flair for leadership. We confronted each other and burst out laughing. He did not put us on official report. He merely had us do double-time, with the skates banging around our necks, out to the laboratory and back. Fair enough.

I hope you understand that the story does speak to my primary theme: namely, the comparative uses of power. The question of how one acquires power, and the purposes for which one uses power, are at the center of our individual morality and our public virtue. There is no great secret about the nature of power. Power is the capacity to persuade or force other people to do what you want them to do. Once you comprehend that central matter, then you understand the famous aphorism by Lord Acton: "Power corrupts, and absolute power corrupts absolutely." That means that if you get too much power you are tempted to persuade or force other people to do things *that even you know are wrong.* You act against your own integrity, as well as against the public welfare and the public virtue. That is in truth the ultimate corruption. You begin to play at being God.

In the minds of its creators, the purpose of the United States Naval Academy was as much to discipline power, to prevent the abuse and corruption of power, as to provide a professional education. Along with others, perhaps most particularly Lieutenant Matthew Fontaine Maury, George Bancroft was a man dedicated to the principles of responsible democracy, and hence particularly aware of the dangers of the corruption of power.

Bancroft was fully aware of the disgraceful behavior of Commander Alexander Slidell Mackenzie aboard the brig *Somers*. He was a tyrant who in 1842 played God in ordering the execution of Midshipman Philip Spenser, Bos'n Samuel Cromwell, and Seaman Elisha Small. They had dared to criticize Mackenzie's performance as a commanding officer and to suggest that he lacked a sense of the limits of power and an understanding of public virtue.

Bancroft was by no means perfect, but when he shortly thereafter became Secretary of the Navy he determined to create an institution that would train midshipmen in the principles of public virtue as well as in ordnance, seamanship, and navigation. His dream was to graduate gentlemen as well as officers of the line. Bancroft understood that the attempt to combine the idea and the ideal of an officer of the line and a gentleman defined a paradox that might never be resolved. After all, it *is* difficult to be a razorback drill sergeant *and* a nice guy. But it is one of the great challenges of your heritage, and you are heirs to the effort to resolve the paradox.

A handful of novelists and script writers have attempted with varying degrees of success to address the problem. But let us make no mistake about Bancroft. He would be appalled—if not outraged—by the practice of allowing graduates of this Academy to parlay their publicly funded education into hundreds of thousands of dollars of private profit by playing various professional sports while ostensibly serving full time the public welfare and the public virtue. Bancroft would instead give his blessing to the man who met his service obligations and *then—and only then*—became a world-class quarterback.

It is impossible to resolve the paradox of being an officer of the line and a gentleman by doing whatever one *can* do. That is certainly the abuse—if not the corruption—of power. We move closer to the truth if we think in terms of what an officer and a gentleman *will not do*.

II

As Bancroft understood, this issue of power involves far more than being an Academy officer. It is at the center of defining a culture. In what ways, that is to say, will we acquire power, and in what ways for what purposes will we use it? Bancroft confronted that challenge when the Democratic party, which had appointed him secretary of the navy, refused to condemn slavery and begin to end that inhuman institution. He broke with the party and turned his energy, intelligence, and morality to writing the first overarching history of this country.

Every individual and every culture faces that kind of choice, that moment when one says No instead of Yes—or worse, when one just does it because one can do it. Let us think about that visceral issue by examining how two cultures have used their power in the form of open sea navies. Such ships, individually or gathered together in squadrons or fleets, were humankind's first intercontinental missiles. They were (and remain) capable of transferring goods, ideas, values, and people from one continent to another without recourse to overland transport. Such missiles are especially potent instruments for the projection of power. Marco Polo made that point when he reported that in 1290 he was returned from China in a convoy of fourteen "great ships, everyone of them having four masts.... (And) in every ship there were 600 men, and provisions for two years."

Until very recently, however, and even largely today, most historians have presented the development and deployment of such intercontinental missiles as the unique achievement of Western European genius. This is history at its ethnocentric worst. The Arabs, for example, built their ships with far more sophisticated sails—and reached India and China long before Prince Henry the Navigator created his school of oceanography and navigation at Sagres. Indeed, the graduates of Henry's academy needed an Arab navigator to guide them to India.

Define the comparison this way. The Portuguese reached the Cape of Good Hope in 1488; ten years later Vasco da Gama made a landfall in India; and then came Alfonso de Albuquerque, one of the most ruthless and bloody commanders of Western European intercontinental missiles. Between 1506 and 1515 he took Goa and Malacca and, on the second try, captured Hormuz.

Long before that, between 1405 and 1433, the Chinese Admiral Zeng He organized and led seven voyages that reached (if not went beyond) the Cape of Good Hope—and mapped that area more accurately than the Portuguese. The Chinese fought no wars of conquest and established no colonies.

One of the weaknesses of my generation's education here at Annapolis involved the failure to give us an appreciation of the complex process which created such intercontinental missiles, and of the dialogue behind the decisions about their use. It is worth a few moments to consider those complexities.

First come the raw materials. Not just the iron and wood and copper, but also the food to feed the workers. Next the supplies to house and clothe the women and men. Then the transport to assemble all those necessities at the center of construction. If we were describing Western Europe, we would invoke the idiom of an industrial revolution. Yet the Chinese were doing all those things as early as the thirteenth century, if not before.

And so to the creation of an educational system. Education to find and transform raw materials. Education to sustain a surplus agriculture. Education to design and build the transportation network. Education to imagine and design the missiles. Education to make the tools to make the missiles. Education to assemble the missiles with care and precision. And education to navigate the missiles.

The Chinese were not unique in creating that kind of infrastructure, but they did it far earlier than Western Europeans. The ships that Zeng He commanded on his seven great voyages were at least 350 feet long with five masts and carried center-hung rudders of about 400 square feet that could be raised and lowered to serve as centerboards.

Beyond all that, the Chinese were also experts in watertight compartment construction, the use of the compass, the ability to determine latitude, the making of charts, the capacity to determine speed at sea, the design and control of sails, knowledge of meteorology, and keeping records of tides, currents, and soundings. Quibble as you will, Zeng He made seven voyages through the Indian Ocean to the east coast of Africa with a total of about 900 ships and some 188,000 people. All together, the Portuguese mustered fewer than 66 ships. Their crews were small, and many died.

Here it is easy to become diverted by the delights of technology. But we must return to the issue of education, and in particular the education concerned with knowing what to do with such power. To speak bluntly, what is the purpose of such power?

I suggest that it is useful to think in terms of what I call the

Three C's: Curiosity, Commerce, and Conquest. Zeng He did fight some battles, and established a Chinese presence in Malacca, Sumatra, and Ceylon. But a presence is not a colony, not even a satellite or a client state. The Chinese never used force to create a territorial or ideological empire.

We are left, therefore, with Curiosity and Commerce. Surely what we tend too often to describe too simply as the Chinese sense of being the Center of the Universe contributed significantly to their disinterest in overseas empire—just as a certain kind of xenophobia in the United States has periodically produced opposition to imperial misadventures. In any event, unlike Caesar, the Chinese came, saw, and went home.

With all that power at their command, the Chinese nevertheless said *No*. There were several reasons, and historians will argue forever about which one was the most important. They had reopened the great inland Grand Canal, an accomplishment which diverted need and attention from open sea transport. There was corruption and bureaucratic intrigue within the government. But all of those factors dramatized the question of *who and what is China?*

In that sense, we are not so far as you might think from George Bancroft's paradox about being an officer of the line and a gentleman. And I would suggest that the key factor in the Chinese decision was a revival of neo-Confucianism heavily influenced by Buddhism. Herewith an excerpt from a powerful memorandum of 1426:

> Arms are the instruments of evil which the sage does not use unless he must. The noble rulers and wise ministers of old did not dissipate the strength of the people by deeds of arms.... Your minister hopes that your majesty... would not indulge in military pursuits nor glorify the sending of expeditions to distant countries. Abandon the barren lands abroad and give the people of China a respite so that they could devote themselves to husbandry and to the schools.

That was a powerful answer to a visceral question. It was echoed four centuries later by an American secretary of state shortly to become president. We need not digress into the relationship between neo-Confucianism and neo-Puritanism to recognize the affinity of wisdom offered by John Quincy Adams on the 4th of July, 1821. "America goes not abroad in search of monsters to destroy.... She well knows that... she might become the dictatress of the world; [but] she would no longer be the ruler of her own spirit."

Adams was no less concerned about the territorial integrity and domestic welfare of the United States than the forgotten adviser to the Chinese court. But both of them understood the dangers of defining their respective cultures and security in terms of the world. In that fundamental sense, Adams and his Chinese counterpart agreed that a truly great culture should be an *example* of civic virtue and community rather than a camp of warriors eager to do violence in the name of abstractions and profit. You might think on the possibility that it has something to do with being a gentleman as well as an officer of the line.

Adams lost his battle. The United States soon deployed squadrons of intercontinental missiles on station in the southeast and southwest Pacific Ocean. That makes a bit of a joke of the current flurry of talk in the United States about the Pacific Rim. Today's discussion largely ignores the truth that the Pacific Rim begins at Cape Horn and runs north around Alaska and then southward along Japan and China to Australia and New Zealand and on to Antarctica. The Pacific Rim encompasses at least half the world.

Americans opened their activities along that rim with trade with China in 1784. A bit later the United States claimed the Columbia River. Next, in the name of Curiosity and Commerce, President Thomas Jefferson dispatched Meriwether Lewis and William Clark to secure that claim. That was the beginning of the end for Curiosity. As Thomas Hart Benton remarked, "Access to Asia becomes a symbol of freedom....It was a boundless field, dazzling and bewildering the imagination in its vastness and importance." Asa Whitney topped Benton: "We reach out one hand to all Asia, the other to all Europe, willing all to enjoy the great blessings we possess, claiming free intercourse and exchange of commodities with all, seeking not to subjugate any, but *all*."

The rush to marry Commerce and Conquest in the name of Freedom had begun. America's intercontinental missiles were not so silent partners in the Opium Wars, played a key role in the war against Mexico that directly and indirectly conquered the Pacific Rim from San Diego to Puget Sound, and simultaneously projected American power in Peru, Sumatra, Fiji, and Samoa. Those increasingly heavy swells became a tsunami—Commodore Matthew C. Perry in Japan, others in China, Fiji, Samoa, and Chile, culminating in the formal conquest of the Philippines and Hawaii. The telling symbol of all that activity is not Theodore Roosevelt charging up San Juan Hill in his wire-frame spectacles but rather the intercontinental missile known as the *USS Oregon* racing from San Francisco to Cuba to help defeat the Spanish fleet at Santiago.

It was all very exhilarating. The intercontinental missile had become the magic wand that turned conquest into freedom. There came a moment, however, when the ghosts of John Quincy Adams and his unknown Chinese ancestor evoked an instant of sanity. That happened at the end of World War I when the United States and Great Britain, recently allies, appeared to be embarking upon a mad competition to build the world's greatest fleet of intercontinental missiles.

Truth to tell, two high-ranking army officers seemed to comprehend the inherent insanity of it all better than, or at least earlier than, either naval officers or civilian leaders. General John Joseph (Black Jack) Pershing said it was time to stop the "plunge headlong down through destructive war to darkness and barbarism." His most sophisticated aide, General Tasker H. Bliss, insisted that the United States had a moral responsibility to offer a "reasonable proposition tending to remove mutual fear."

Down the line various civilian leaders picked up on that theme. One of them, President Warren G. Harding, was a most unlikely candidate for imaginative leadership. And yet, on a cold November day in 1921 he spoke these words: "We are but freshly turned from the burial of an unknown American soldier.... Whether it was spoken or not, a hundred millions of our people were summarizing the inexcusable cause, the incalculable cost, the unspeakable sacrifices, and the unutterable sorrows, and there was the ever impelling question: How can humanity justify or God forgive?"

You must remember that those words—"How can humanity justify or God forgive?"—were not spoken at a showcase ceremony in Arlington National Cemetery. Harding was opening a major disarmament conference initiated by the United States to reduce and control intercontinental missiles. Harding was a vain man, but on this occasion he was content. He passed the torch to Secretary of State Charles Evans Hughes, probably the closest we have come to the reincarnation of John Quincy Adams.

Hughes evoked that tradition. He did so on the basis of having done his homework, and because he had discussed the fundamental issues with the brightest and the best of the United States Navy. They had educated him, and he had educated them, and they had reached a consensus about the best policy for the United States. It may not have been a unique moment, but it surely is one to remember and reflect upon.

We are here, Hughes began, to respond to "humanity crying for relief and craving assurances of lasting peace. A world staggering with debt needs its burdens lifted." Then he turned the screw. "Is it not plain that the time has passed for mere resolutions?... We can no longer content ourselves with investigations, with statistics, with reports.... The essential facts are sufficiently known. The time has come for action.

"Competition will not be remedied by resolves with respect to the method of its continuance. One program inevitably leads to another, and if competition continues, its regulation is impracticable. There is only one adequate way out, and that is to end it now."

That proposition is so tightly argued that it bears repeating:

"Competition will not be remedied by resolves with respect to the method of its continuance. One program inevitably leads to another, and if competition continues, its regulation is impracticable. There is only one adequate way out, and that is to end it now."

As with John Quincy Adams a century earlier, Charles Evans Hughes was echoing that Chinese minister's advice of 1424: "Give the people a respite so that they could devote themselves to husbandry and to the schools." Think of Bancroft's challenge, his paradox of being an officer of the line *and* a gentleman, as being applicable to the entire culture—civilians as well as the military. If we do that, then perhaps Hughes and Adams, along with their Chinese counterpart, offer us a way to resolve the paradox and further the security, the welfare, and the public virtue of the Commonwealth.

THE ANNAPOLIS CROWD

[1987, unpublished]

Honoring and fulfilling obligations and upholding standards of moral conduct was a responsibility Williams did not take lightly. An emphasis on accountability formed the backdrop for his condemnation of the naval officers who were key participants in the Iran-Contra affair during the administration of President Ronald Reagan. This scandalous episode, Williams elaborated, was but the most recent, if a highly dangerous, illustration of an assault on the public trust and an abuse of power to which, he argued, the country's political system had become ever more susceptible. For Williams, himself a graduate of the Naval Academy, the wholly unacceptable conduct of the naval officers was an ironic display of the unethical consequences of the empire he had opposed in his lifetime.

THE popular image of military leaders in high politics is defined by army officers. From the Revolution to the Civil War, moreover, the picture is one of a citizen-politician who became a general and then led the nation as a civilian: George Washington, Andrew Jackson, and Zachary Taylor. That idea lingers on in the nostalgic fondness for Harry S Truman, the World War I artillery officer who had no qualms about using the atomic bomb, stood up to the Russians, and then sent troopers to Korea to teach the Evil Empire a lesson it would never forget.

The Civil War professionalized the perception, however, hence the honors awarded to West Point graduates like Robert E. Lee, Ulysses S. Grant, Douglas MacArthur, and Dwight David Eisenhower. Even George C. Marshall is included in that group because of his

A declaration of interest: I was graduated from Annapolis in 1944 and served as the executive officer of an LSM in the Pacific theater through the end of World War II.

385

education at Virginia Military Institute, which generally has been viewed as the Southern version of West Point.

A few citizen naval leaders have been allowed into the back rows of the pantheon of American heroes. One is sometimes inclined to think their acceptance is due to their ability to coin a memorable phrase. John Paul Jones: "I have not yet begun to fight." Oliver H. Perry: "We have met the enemy and they are ours." David G. Farragut: "Damn the torpedoes. Full speed ahead." And Matthew C. Perry's comment on the purpose of his Black Squadron as it entered Tokyo Bay in 1853: "Japan should change her policy." As we know, Japan did change policies; and thereafter the United States and other nations invested much blood, treasure, and persuasion to induce changes in that original change.

But Annapolis, founded in 1845 (forty-three years after West Point), has never produced a group of graduates generally recognized and honored as political leaders by the public. Admiral George Dewey, the naval hero of the Spanish-American War, did become a celebrity and indulged himself in visions of a political career. That cruise in the spotlight ended when he was nominated for the presidency in 1900 by the fourth annual convention of Hoboes. He served out his time as president of the general board of the Navy Department.

Jimmy Carter technically qualifies as the exception that makes the point. He was commissioned from Annapolis in 1946 and ultimately served at sea as an engineering officer in nuclear submarines before leaving the service in 1953 and embarking on his voyage through Georgia politics to the White House. But in truth Carter never informed his public life with either the substance or the style of an Annapolis officer of the line. That may appear to be a contradiction in terms, but it is actually a paradox that contains an important truth that tells us much about other academy graduates who have exercised extensive power within the government. Hence it is useful to explore the point with some care.

The first clue is provided by Carter's adamant refusal, even as president, to take pride in using his full name—James Earl Carter, Jr. Particularly as he has praised his father with affection as well as respect. Beyond that, naval officers have earned nicknames associated with their performance and temperament, but none involves the diminutive of a given name; and all publicly identify themselves with their full name. Carter's behavior in that area offers firm evidence supporting his persistent presentation of himself in politics as an outsider. But an officer of the line is most certainly not an outsider. He has been educated to be, and knows himself to be, one of the consummate insiders.

Next consider Carter's extremely weak understanding of strategy and tactics. He instead defined himself as an engineer, and appropriately (and typically) immersed himself in details. As a result, he was unable to delegate that work to others while he considered and defined the broad purposes of power. Hence he became trapped in the flow of often marginal information and earned a reputation for vacillation—even irresolution.

All of those characteristics were neatly summarized *before* Carter became president by an officer of the line under whom Carter had served. "Well, if I were going to commission a new nuclear sub, I would ask specifically for Carter as my senior engineering officer. But I would not want him on the bridge. So, as president—no, I don't think so." Pause. "No, definitely not."

II

We are confronted, therefore, with the question of precisely how a Naval Academy education prepared its graduates for public service. For, after all, the root meaning of the word *officer* defines a person working to capacity to fulfill and honor a public duty or obligation.

From its origins under the careful eye of George Bancroft, a Harvard graduate who earned his Ph.D. in Germany and became a major historian, diplomat, and cabinet officer, Annapolis has traditionally offered a broader and more demanding intellectual and cultural curriculum than West Point. History, literature, geography, and classical politics were required along with electrical engineering, thermodynamics, navigation, seamanship, and gunnery. Thus, though it is not generally remembered, the academy produced major intellectual leaders in such varied fields as exploration, ocean cartography, science, political commentary, military strategy, and even literature. Consider only Nobel Laureate Albert A. Michelson and the prolific Isaac Asimov. And even George Westinghouse, the great inventor and capitalist, attributed much of his success to his training in the regular navy.

And there are many others. Probably the most striking example is Alfred Thayer Mahan. He gained public as well as inside acclaim and influence for his geopolitical theory about the primacy of sea power as the means to security, prosperity, and social well-being. Mahan influenced Theodore Roosevelt and other American leaders, and affected the thinking of all major powers. He provided the foundation for Admiral Chester W. Nimitz's strategy of island-hopping against Japan in World War II (a concept mistakenly attributed to Douglas MacArthur); and the advocates of air power as the solution to all military problems offered little more than an adaptation of Mahan's ideas to the technology of airborne battleships, cruisers, and destroyers (and more recently of stealth machines as flying submarines).

Mahan was also important because he tried to infuse his global and implicitly imperial strategy with a sense of moral and civil responsibility—a *noblessse oblige* to be honorable and generous. Looking back at him across one of the most ruthless, lying, violent, and destructive centuries in recorded history, that may seem naive or romantic—if not quixotic. It is nevertheless true. Hence to comprehend the outlook that Naval Academy graduates brought to politics it is necessary to understand the sources of that commitment. While Carter's approach to such issues was certainly influenced by his family upbringing, he also brought some of that tradition to the White House in his concern for human rights and his inclination to allow other cultures to find their own way to Truth and Beauty.

The most revealing way to explore the Academy doctrine, orthodoxy, or secular theology is by way of the handbook assigned to all entering midshipmen as the basis of the formal and informal indoctrination of the plebe. Known informally as the "Pocket Bible," it opens with the blunt statement that it provides the essentials of the "outlook" which is the "foundation" of Academy education. It then presents the oath taken as the heart of the process of entry into the Naval Aristocracy. Here it is vital to stress one point.

The oath is not taken to a person or an office. The oath is to "honor and uphold and defend the Constitution of the United States of America."

Within that very specific framework, the purpose of the Academy is defined as producing "educated gentlemen" dedicated to "honor, uprightness, and truth," men committed to "impartial justice" and sufficiently in control of their egos to practice "a frankness to admit mistakes and profit thereby." In sum, the Academy is charged to educate and commission "an officer of the line and a gentleman."

A warrior, that is to say, and not simply a man trained and

authorized to kill in the name of the state. In one form or another, every society has developed its particular version of this distinction between the warrior and the killer. One of the classic examples comes from China, the first culture to develop massed intercontinental seapower. It did so beginning during the Tang dynasty and continued through the Ming dynasty (c. 1127–1433), culminating in the awesome voyages of Zeng He, the admiral of what the Chinese called the Star Raft....

Zeng He came west as a warrior rather than as an imperial conquistador or killer. His purpose was exploration, trade, and civil intercourse between cultures. If attacked, he fought with courage and skill and defeated the enemy. Then he returned the leaders who challenged him to their seats of power. Neither the founders and shapers of the Naval Academy, nor any other Westerners, knew about Zeng He until the middle of the twentieth century. But the concept of "an officer of the line and a gentleman" evolved around a similar ideal of the warrior. Part of that came from George Bancroft and the New England sense of the patrician gentleman. Other elements emerged from the Southern aristocracy, and in the more specifically naval reality and romantic images of Captain James Cook and Viscount and Admiral Horatio Nelson of the Royal Navy.

The language itself, "an officer of the line," goes back to the eighteenth century when wooden men-of-war engaged each other in a broadside line at distances often no more than a hundred yards. It was terrifying close-quarters combat with guns more powerful than either Napoleon or Wellington mustered at Waterloo. Officers of the line were the men who trained and inspired their men to close with the enemy, men who were there with their crews as deck and gunnery officers to face the horrors of dealing and being dealt death.

Nelson was the Anglo-American personification of the officer of the line. Courageous almost to a fault, he lost an eye off Calvi but went on to win the Battle of the Nile (1798) and the Battle of Copenhagen (1801) before his great victory at Trafalgar (1805). He was also a gentleman. (Oh, yes, a gentleman is permitted one grand passion—his with Lady Emma Hamilton.) He was known for his character as a religious, generous, and affectionate officer who trusted his men and fought his ships alongside them. One of those compatriots summarized it this way: "Nelson was the man to *love*."

In some respects, however, Captain Cook defined more clearly the essence of the officer of the line as a gentleman. A man of low birth, he became a superb navigator who prepared the way for the British capture of Quebec during the Seven Years War. His subsequent achievements at sea were characterized by his commitment to humane principles and the acceptance of other cultures—and indeed respect for them. As for his leadership, there is the marvelous story of how he persuaded his crew to eat the foul-smelling and -tasting sauerkraut as a preventive measure against scurvy: he assembled the crew to watch his officers eat the stuff.

Cook's truly world-class skills as a navigator and ship handler and cartographer (it required a satellite to make *minor* corrections in his chart of New Zealand) have tended to obscure his character as a gentleman. He respected his crew, the Pacific people he encountered (he understood that they stole things as a sign of respect), and believed deeply that the Elizabethan tradition of a Great Chain of Being involved all human beings.

Those are the elements of the tradition of an officer of the line and a gentleman that the United States Naval Academy sought to adapt and institutionalize. And to a surprising degree the effort succeeded. Even the caustic and acerbic social commentator Thomas Nast paid tribute to part of that style in an 1882 cartoon for *Harper's Magazine*. Using a remarkably modern exhortation, he depicted the navy flying a pennant from the mainmast which read "Keep Cool."

And many officers from ensigns to admirals, nicely symbolized at both ranks by Ernest J. King, did understand and honor the essentials of the concept of a gentleman. There are certain things that one *always* does whatever the danger or personal inconvenience, and other things that one simply *never* does under any circumstances. That brings us to the crucial right and responsibility—yes, even the duty—of an officer of the line and a gentleman to challenge an order that violates his oath to the Constitution and his tradition. It is indeed the ultimate act of honoring that oath and that tradition. It is not to be undertaken lightly. It requires a courage beyond the bravery of combat. It is the ultimate act of saying *No* to something that is wrong. It can lead to a court martial. It can also open the door to truth.

It does have the great virtue of keeping one from saying that he would go stand in a corner or sit on his head if his commanding officer told him to do so. And thereby confusing loyalty with honor.

III

And so this voyage brings us to Oliver North, John Poindexter, Robert McFarlane, and James Webb. We now have the chart that enables us to consider and judge those graduates of the United States Naval Academy. They are the men who were trained in the tradition of an officer of the line and a gentleman. They could have said *No.* They played central roles in the Iran-Contra operation which, far more than Watergate, created a fundamental threat to constitutional government in these United States. And which may still do so. All of them either lied openly or covertly ("I don't remember"), or turned two blind eyes to their sworn responsibilities. Nelson and Cook would have turned on their heels.

It would be convenient to conclude that the curriculum and related indoctrination at the Naval Academy somehow suffered a catastrophic decline after World War II. Two kinds of evidence tell us otherwise. A significant number of Oliver North's classmates, for example, were so outraged by his behavior (and his being treated as a hero) that they went so far as to discuss returning their graduation rings to the Academy or to Secretary of the Navy Webb. Other graduates—and their wives—became wholly disgusted when they were unable to evoke *any* response when they wrote or called Webb. The tradition had not died; it had simply been dishonored.

McFarlane is the only one of the group who seems to have any vestige of the commitment to honor the concept and the reality of being an officer of the line and a gentleman. However belatedly, he seems to have realized that he and the others should have refused to obey orders that violated their oath to "honor and uphold and defend the Constitution of the United States of America." At least they should have resigned their commissions and gone to the Congress. At best they should have publicly demanded a formal board of inquiry by the secretary of the navy into orders that violated their oath and their tradition.

But then Secretary of the Navy James Webb should have done *his* duty. He came into his high office when the basic elements of the truth were known. Here we tread cautiously into the no man's land, or into that barely charted estuary. Webb and North were classmates at the Naval Academy. Webb lost to North in the fight for the boxing championship of their weight division. He also chose service in the Marine Corps and displayed courage at least equal to North's in the hellish horror of combat in Vietnam, and won even higher decorations. He then became a justly acclaimed novelist who wrote, of all things, a story about the Naval Academy called *A Sense of Honor.*

But as Secretary of the Navy under President Ronald Reagan *after* the lies became known, Webb did not initiate action (say a board of inquiry) under the provisions of the Uniform Code of Military Justice.

Neither did he answer letters or phone calls. His proxy reported that "we have had many complaints about this matter, but the secretary is not available."

But the tradition is not yet dead. One of Webb's ostensible subordinates, Chairman of the Joint Chiefs of Staff Admiral William J. Crowe, Jr., did have the will and the courtesy and the candor to respond to a letter from an outraged widow of an Academy officer.

"I do not think that Lieutenant Colonel North is a hero."

Neither are the others.

As for Ronald Reagan, he could not even act the part of an officer of the line and a gentleman.

AFTERWORD:
SAYING NO TO EMPIRE
AND YES TO COMMUNITY

And this is the way of the world. No, rather, this is the way we have made
the world.   *Anonymous*

Not to choose is to choose.   *Albert Camus*

What shall it profit a man, if he shall gain the whole world and lose his
own soul?   *Matthew 16:26*

If everyone elsewhere *does* deny us the chance to realize ourselves by
changing them...we can finally confront the question of what we are going
to make of America.
   William A. Williams, Preface to History as a Way of Learning, *1974*

We largely define ourselves in terms of the world. The point of socialism in
America is to define ourselves as Americans.
   William A. Williams, Letter to The Nation, *1981*

THE controversial ideas expressed in these selections from the
writings of William Appleman Williams earned him a reputation as a revisionist historian, a reputation he clearly welcomed. No
study of the history of American foreign relations can now ignore his
work, and his ideas continue to influence new interpretations. He
was, in the judgment of another historian, "the most influential
American diplomatic historian of his generation."[1]
   But Williams not only proposed alternative explanations of the
American past; he also offered a different vision of the American
future. "I think...history does help us face vital questions about our

   1. Gary R. Hess, "After the Tumult: The Wisconsin School's Tribute to William
Appleman Williams," *Diplomatic History,* 12 (Fall 1988), 499.

393

future as a people," he wrote in 1974.[2] While others, including American leaders, may hold that the nation's success, mission, and ultimate significance depend on a triumphal advance into the world's frontiers, Williams persistently argued that such an organizing principle of American society was a grave mistake, one that has produced tragic consequences that outweigh its benefits. Locating the meaning of the nation in terms of others represents a labored escape by America from itself, Williams insisted. In deploring the choice, he was not advocating isolationism, a charge often made by his critics. Rather, he argued, Americans have for too long avoided confronting the basic question of what they intend to do about America, *in* America. Instead, he said, they have chased after empire in the name of professed ideals of freedom, well-being, and security, believing they can achieve their national destiny by trying to change and save the rest of humanity instead of relating to it; of being *in* but not *of* the world.

The result, in Williams's estimation, has been imperial behavior (the means) to assure the benefits (the ends) of an American-created empire. Moreover, he argued, the American empire has become both a declared virtue and a habitual way of life for its inhabitants. The costs, he believed, are too great to justify the effort. Not only are many excluded from the promised rewards of empire, but others must be overcome, coerced, or even killed because they stand in the way; most important, our avowed ideals are subverted and our freedom and humanity compromised and diminished.

Williams objected that Americans have gone to great lengths to deny or ignore the facts of their imperial past while celebrating it as affirmation of proclaimed ideals. How Americans perceive their imperial past, how they might yet confront it, and how they should face their future differently by creating an equitable, moral community were his passions. He had no formula for achieving this community. "I have no list of answers," he confessed in his last book. "Only a fool unrolls blueprints and specifications for changing a way of life."[3] But he knew that Americans must first confront what he saw as their imperial past and present. In that judgment, as well as in much of his morally fired historiography, Williams was influenced by the American historian whose work he so respected, Charles A. Beard.

2. Williams, *History as a Way of Learning* (New York: New Viewpoints, 1974), p. xvi.

3. Williams, *Empire as a Way of Life* (New York: Oxford University Press, 1980), p. 224.

For the better part of almost forty-five years Williams explored the American past—"discovering America, almost like Columbus," as Warren Susman recalled—trying to come to terms with the American present.[4] This unapologetic, unconventional historian roughed up the discipline, raised unorthodox questions, challenged established script, and proposed often disconcerting assessments and ideas about American history. His interpretive reconstructions of the past eventually commanded the attention of critics as well as admirers.

Because he was a committed radical activist as well as a historian, Williams advocated a transformation of American priorities and commitments toward the world and within America itself. He believed he had discovered disturbing and destructive patterns of conduct in American history, and he wanted, in his own words, "to break free of the past." In that sense, understanding and learning from history was a liberating and creative act, preceding and informing the building of an alternative future. The process involved facing the past, Williams repeatedly demanded, retaining aspects of yesterday as one moved on to tomorrow.

He never wrote in detail about this part of his political philosophy, but one who reviews his writings has a sense that Williams struggled to legitimate an American radicalism to a wider audience within the context of the American experience. He was also speaking to the political left, admonishing it to avoid "becoming more like what we find so unacceptable" and to acknowledge the value of what had been positive in the past, just as he urged radicals to engage in "a tough, honest, and thoughtful dialogue with first-rate conservatives."[5]

That had been one of the central and controversial thrusts of *The Contours of American History*, in which his debt to Beard was so clearly evident. In a new preface to the 1966 edition of the book, Williams joined conservative contributions to a radical future: "I see," he wrote, "a greater urgency...to honor those of our traditional ideals, values, and practices that remain creative, and a more insistent necessity to create new visions, virtues, and procedures to replace those that have reached their potential and survive only as

4. Warren Susman, "The Smoking Room School of History," in Paul Buhle, ed., *History and the New Left: Madison, Wisconsin, 1950–1970* (Philadelphia: Temple University Press, 1990), p. 44.

5. Williams, *The Roots of the Modern American Empire* (New York: Random House, 1969), pp. 452–453; Williams, "My Life in Madison," in Buhle, *History and the New Left*, p. 267.

connections and rationalizations that impede the building of an American community."[6]

The disputes with serious critics of his work were over his reading of the evidence on the nature of the American past. But for those who shared in varying degrees his analysis of American history and contemporary society, there was by no means agreement that fundamental change was possible.

Yes, they agreed, it may well be that some Americans had "created the tradition of speaking truth to empire," and had "questioned [the] conventional relationship between democracy and empire." But they had lost in the effort, as Williams himself conceded.[7] "A new America, like a new world order, is unlikely to stray very far from its discursive origins," Marilyn Young, a historian sympathetic to Williams's work, argued recently. Which means to say, among other things, that the system is simply too powerful, too resistant, and too ingrained to break the strong grip of existing habit over the national ethos.[8]

Williams understood the power of the system. He knew that the alternative democratic, decentralized socialist community he envisioned would not arrive soon. In the immediate future he could only hope that an enlightened conservative leadership, "acting on a radical analysis," would set limits on the size and behavior of empire. Toward the close of America's military intervention in Vietnam, Williams acknowledged that conservatives had not done this. It was clear from interviews and writings late in his life that he saw short-run limits and long-run change as possible only through the efforts of citizens themselves, based on an understanding of the nation's past and its political culture. The effort would require a will to act—and not merely in response to a crisis or agenda created by others. Williams was convinced that examples and opportunities for such actions existed while frankly admitting the possibilities of failure.[9]

Williams was faulted for entertaining hopes of change. At first glance the doubters appear to have the better of the argument, despite the end of the cold war and the apparent cessation of the

6. Williams, Foreword to *The Contours of American History* (Chicago: Quadrangle Paperbacks, 1966), p. 6.

7. Williams, *Empire as a Way of Life,* pp. 211–212.

8. Marilyn Young, "To Empire or Not to Empire," paper presented at "Rethinking the Cold War," a conference at the University of Wisconsin in honor of William Appleman Williams (Madison, Wisc., October 1991), pp. 4–5.

9. See, for example, "William Appleman Williams," interview by Mike Wallace in Henry Abelove, Betsy Blackmar, Peter Dimock, and Jonathan Schneer, eds. *Visions of History* (New York: Pantheon Books, 1984), pp. 135–140.

nuclear arms race. Alarmed and agitated by unpredictability, instability, and an inability to manage developments in the aftermath of the collapse of the Soviet Union and its empire, and fearing these conditions endanger U.S. interests in the world, American leaders have proclaimed the need for a "New World Order." It is a perspective that bears a remarkable similarity with the past, echoing, for example, phrases from National Security Council memorandum No. 68, the cold war tocsin of 1950: "Even if there were no Soviet Union, we would face the great problem...of reconciling order, security, the need for participation, with the requirements of freedom."[1]

The truth is that American abilities to command developments in a fragmenting world have diminished. Trends perhaps reminiscent of the interwar years—as, for example, the formation of economic blocs and the prevalence of shifting political coalitions, not to mention religious and ethnic reassertions—have produced uncertainty and flux. With substantial problems at home, the United States fumbles to reclaim power in a world transformed.

Once upon a time, in the flush of victory over its World War II enemies, the United States was confident that it could and should exert its will on behalf of proclaimed virtues shared and accepted by others. "We are willing to help people who believe the way we do, to continue to live the way they want to live," Dean Acheson, arguably the most influential American foreign policymaker in the postwar years, declared in 1947.[2] Revealing in its frankness, Acheson's remark simultaneously expressed the character and the misconception of America's approach to the world. Even in 1947 the reality was more complicated; the attempt to define others did not go unchallenged and produced much agony. Upon the signing of the nuclear arms reduction treaty in December 1987, a leading Soviet official is reported to have said to his American counterpart, "We Russians are about to do something terrible to you. We are going to deprive you of an enemy." The cold war between the United States and the Soviet Union thus ended when one side decided to stop fighting it. The origins and costs of the crises and abuses of power generated by the conflict have yet to be acknowledged, let alone confronted.

William Appleman Williams believed that "people do understand,

1. "A Report to the National Security Council on United States Objectives and Programs for National Security—N.S.C. 68," Washington, D.C., April 14, 1950, p. 34.
2. Dean Acheson quoted in Williams, *The Tragedy of American Diplomacy* (New York: Dell Publishing, 1972), p. 14.

feel, sense that the crunch is here."[3] He may have hoped for too much in thinking this would lead to "saying no to Empire in order to say yes to community," but surely the history he sought to understand, and urged others to rethink, may yet bring us to ponder anew the fundamental purpose of America, to imagine and then begin to create a more humane, a more equitable, a more rewarding way of life. That, after all, was the ultimate spirit of his commitment to "doing history."

3. "William Appleman Williams" in *Visions of History,* p. 139.

Bibliography

WRITINGS BY WILLIAM APPLEMAN WILLIAMS

Books

The International Impact of National Economic Planning. Leeds, England: University of Leeds (1948).
American-Russian Relations, 1781–1947. New York: Rinehart (1952).
The Tragedy of American Diplomacy. Cleveland: World Publishing (1959). Revised 1962, 1972.
The Contours of American History. Cleveland: World Publishing (1961).
The United States, Cuba, and Castro. New York: Monthly Review Press (1962).
The Great Evasion: An Essay on the Contemporary Relevance of Karl Marx and on the Wisdom of Admitting the Heretic into the Dialogue About America's Future. Chicago: Quadrangle Books (1964).
The Roots of the Modern American Empire: A Study of the Growth and Shaping of Social Consciousness in a Marketplace Society. New York: Random House (1969).
Some Presidents: Wilson to Nixon. New York: A New York Review Book, Vintage Books (1972).
History as a Way of Learning. New York: New Viewpoints (1974).
America Confronts a Revolutionary World, 1776–1976. New York: William Morrow (1976).
Americans in a Changing World: A History of the United States in the Twentieth Century. New York: Harper and Row (1978).
Empire as a Way of Life: An Essay on the Causes and Character of America's Present Predicament Along with a Few Thoughts About an Alternative. New York: Oxford University Press (1980).

Edited Works

The Shaping of American Diplomacy, 1750–1955. Chicago: Rand McNally (1956). Revised 1972.
America and the Middle East: Open Door Imperialism or Enlightened Leadership? New York: Rinehart (1958).
From Colony to Empire: Essays in the History of American Foreign Relations. New York: John Wiley and Sons (1972).

America in Vietnam: A Documentary History (with Walter LaFeber, Thomas J. McCormick, and Lloyd C. Gardner). Garden City, N.Y.: Anchor Press/Doubleday (1985).

Contributions to Compiled Works

"Introduction" (with Harvey Goldberg) and "Charles Austin Beard: The Intellectual as Tory-Radical," in *American Radicals: Some Problems and Personalities,* edited by Harvey Goldberg. New York: Monthly Review Press (1957).

"The Age of Mercantilism: An Interpretation of American Political Economy, 1763–1828," and "The Legend of American Isolationism in the 1920s," in *Essays in American Diplomacy,* edited by Armin Rappaport. New York: Macmillan (1967).

"Rise of an American World Power Complex," in *Struggle Against History,* edited by Neal D. Houghton. New York: Simon and Schuster (1968).

"The Vicious Circle of American Imperialism," in *Readings in U.S. Imperialism,* edited by K. T. Fann and Donald C. Hodges. Boston: F. Porter Sargent (1971).

"Raymond Robins," in *Dictionary of American Biography,* Supplement 5, 1951–1955, pp. 578–580. New York: Charles Scribner's Sons (1977).

"Amerikas 'idealistischer' Imperialismus, 1900–1917," in *Imperialismus,* edited by Hans-Ulrich Wehler. Konigstein: Althenaum/Dusseldorf: Droste (1979).

"The City on a Hill on an Errand into the Wilderness," in *Vietnam Reconsidered: Lessons from a War,* edited by Harrison Salisbury. New York: Harper and Row (1984).

"William Appleman Williams," interview by Mike Wallace in *Visions of History,* edited by Henry Abelove, Betsy Blackmar, Peter Dimock, and Jonathan Schneer. New York: Pantheon Books (1984).

"My Life in Madison," in *History and the New Left: Madison, Wisconsin, 1950–1970,* edited by Paul Buhle. Philadelphia: Temple University Press (1990).

Articles

"A Frontier Federalist and the War of 1812," *Pennsylvania Magazine of History and Biography,* LXXVI (January 1952), 61–85.

"Brooks Adams and American Expansion," *New England Quarterly,* XXV (June 1952), 217–232.

"A Second Look at Mr. X," *Monthly Review,* 4 (August 1952), 123–128.

"Moscow Peace Drive: Victory for Containment?" *The Nation,* 177 (July 11, 1953), 28–30.

"A Note on the Isolationism of Senator William E. Borah," *Pacific Historical Review,* XXII (November 1953), 391–392.

"The Legend of Isolationism in the 1920s," *Science and Society,* XVIII (Winter 1954), 1–20.

"Raymond Robins, Crusader—The Outdoor Mind," *The Nation,* 179 (October 30, 1954), 384–385.

"Cold War Perspectives—A Historical Fable," *The Nation,* 180 (May 28, 1955), 458–461.

"The Historical Romance of Senator Neuberger's Election," *Oregon Historical Quarterly,* LVI (June 1955), 101–105. Reprinted as "Neuberger Ducked the Basic Issues," *Frontier,* 6 (October 1955), 5–6.

"The Frontier Thesis and American Foreign Policy," *Pacific Historical Review,* XXIV (November 1955), 379–395.

"Babbitt's New Fables," *The Nation,* 182 (January 7, 1956), 3–6.

"Great Boomerang: The Irony of Containment," *The Nation,* 182 (May 5, 1956), 376–379.

"Challenge to American Radicals," *Frontier,* 7 (June 1956), 5–6.

"On the Restoration of Brooks Adams," *Science and Society,* XX (Summer 1956), 247–253.

"Reflections on the Historiography of American Entry into World War II," *Oregon Historical Quarterly,* LVII (September 1956), 274–279.

"A Note on Charles Austin Beard's Search for a General Theory of Causation," *American Historical Review,* LXII (October 1956), 59–80.

"Taxing for Peace," *The Nation,* 184 (January 19, 1957), 53.

"Latin America: Laboratory of American Foreign Policy in the 1920s," *Inter-American Economic Affairs,* 11 (Autumn 1957), 3–30.

"China and Japan: A Challenge and a Choice of the Nineteen Twenties," *Pacific Historical Review,* XXVI (August 1957), 259–279.

"The American Century, 1941–1957," *The Nation,* 185 (November 2, 1957), 297–301.

"A Note on American Foreign Policy in Europe in the 1920s," *Science and Society,* XXII (Winter 1958), 1–20.

"The Age of Mercantilism: An Interpretation of the American Political Economy, 1763–1828," *William and Mary Quarterly,* XV (October 1958), 419–437.

"Needed: Production for Peace," *The Nation,* 188 (February 21, 1959), 149–153.

"Take a New Look at Russia," *Foreign Policy Bulletin,* 38 (April 15, 1959).

"Samuel Adams: Calvinist, Mercantilist, Revolutionary," *Studies on the Left,* 1 (Winter 1960), 47–57.

"On the Origins of the Cold War," in "The Origins of the Cold War—An Exchange," *Commentary,* 31 (February 1961), 152–153.

"Protecting Overseas Investors," *The Nation,* 193 (August 26, 1961), 100–101.

"The Irony of the Bomb," *Centennial Review,* V (Fall 1961), 373–384.

"Foreign Policy and the American Mind: An Alternate View," *Commentary,* 33 (February 1962), 155–159.

Contributor to "American Socialism and Thermonuclear War: A Symposium," *New Politics,* 1 (Spring 1962), 40–45.

"Cuba: The President and His Critics," *The Nation,* 196 (March 16, 1963), 226ff.

"Historiography and Revolution: The Case of Cuba," *Studies on the Left,* 3 (Summer 1963), 78–102.

"American Intervention in Russia, 1917–1920," *Studies on the Left,* 3 (Fall 1963), 24–48; (Winter 1964), 39–57.

"Cuba: Issues and Alternatives," *Annals of the American Academy of Political and Social Sciences,* 351 (January 1964), 72–80.

"The Vicious Circle of American Imperialism," *New Politics,* IV, (Fall 1965), 48–55.

"The Cold War Revisionists," *The Nation,* 205 (November 13, 1967), 492–495.

"An American Socialist Community?" *Liberation,* 14 (June 1969), 8–11.

"How Can the Left Be Relevant?" *Current,* 109 (August 1969), 20–24.

"Notes for a Dialogue with Messrs. Harrington, Schlesinger, and Zinn," *Partisan Review,* XXXVIII (January 1971), 67–78.

"Confessions of an Intransigent Revisionist," *Socialist Review,* 17 (September-October 1973), 89–98. Reprinted as "A Historian's Perspective," *Prologue: Journal of the National Archives,* 6 (Fall 1974), 200–203.

"Understanding Intervention," *The Nation,* 228 (June 9, 1979), 654–655.

"Is the Idea and Reality of America Possible Without Empire?" (an adaptation from the forthcoming *Empire as a Way of Life*), *The Nation,* 231 (August 2, 1980), 104–119.

"Notes on the Death of a Ship and the End of a World: The Grounding of the British Bark *Glenesslin* at Mount Neahkahnie on 1 October, 1913," *American Neptune,* XLI (1981), 122–138.

"Thoughts on Rereading Henry Adams" (presidential address to the Organization of American Historians), *Journal of American History,* 68 (June 1981), 7–15.

"Regional Resistance: Backyard Autonomy," *The Nation,* 233 (September 5, 1981), 161, 179–180.

"Radicals and Regionalism," *democracy,* 1 (October 1981), 87–98.

"History as Redemption: Henry Adams and the Education of America," *The Nation,* 234 (March 6, 1982), 266–269.

"Procedure Becomes Substance," *democracy,* 2 (April 1982), 100–102.

"Missile Ban in Washington: 1921," *The Nation,* 237 (November 26, 1983), 530–533.

"Thoughts on the Fun and Purpose of Being an American Historian," *OAH Newsletter,* 13 (February 1985).

"Thoughts on the Comparative Uses of Power," George Bancroft Lecture, United States Naval Academy (September 1986), published here for the first time.

"The Annapolis Crowd" (August 1987), published here for the first time.

Book Reviews

"Collapse of the Grand Coalition," *The Nation,* 179 (November 6, 1954), 408–409. Review of *America, Britain, and Russia: Their Cooperation and Conflict, 1941–1946* by William H. McNeill.

"The Age of Re-forming History," *The Nation,* 182 (June 30, 1956), 552–554. Review of *The Age of Reform* by Richard Hofstadter.

"The Convenience of History," *The Nation,* 183 (September 15, 1956), 222–224. Review of *Russia Leaves the War* by George F. Kennan.

"The Empire of Theodore Roosevelt," *The Nation,* 184 (March 2, 1957), 191–192. Review of *The Imperial Years* by Foster Rhea Dulles and *Theodore Roosevelt and the Rise of America to World Power* by Howard K. Beale.

"Schlesinger: Right Crisis, Wrong Order," *The Nation,* 184 (March 23, 1957), 257–260. Review of *The Crisis of the Old Order, 1919–1933* by Arthur M. Schlesinger, Jr.

"The 'Logic' of Imperialism," *The Nation,* 185 (July 6, 1957), 14–15. Review of *The Coming Caesars* by Amaury de Riencourt.

"Loss of Debate," *The Nation,* 186 (May 17, 1958), 452–453. Review of *The Ordeal of Woodrow Wilson* by Herbert Hoover.

"Fire in the Ashes of Scientific History," *William and Mary Quarterly,* XIX (April 1962), 274–287. Review of several books on historiography.

"The Acquitting Judge," *Studies on the Left,* 3 (Winter 1963), 94–99. Review of *Imperial Democracy: The Emergence of America as a Great Power* by Ernest R. May. Reprinted in James Weinstein and David Eakins, editors, *For a New America: Essays in History and Politics from 'Studies on the Left,' 1959–1967.* New York: Vintage Books (1970).

"Last Chance for Democracy," *The Nation,* 204 (January 2, 1967), 23–25. Review of *Overtaken by Events: The Dominican Crisis from the Fall of Trujillo to the Civil War* by John Bartlow Martin.

"Officers and Gentlemen," *New York Review of Books,* XVI (May 6, 1971), 3–8. Review of nine books "From MacArthur to Mylai."

"Demystifying Cold War Orthodoxy," *Science and Society,* XXXIX (Fall 1975), 346–351. Review of *Aid to Russia, 1941–1946: Strategy, Diplomacy, and the Origins of the Cold War* by George C. Herring and *Soviet-American Confrontation: Postwar Reconstruction and the Origins of the Cold War* by Thomas G. Paterson.

SELECTED COMMENTARIES ABOUT WILLIAMS'S WORK

Clifford Solway, "Turning History Upside Down," *Saturday Review* (June 20, 1970), 13ff.

Carl N. Degler, review of *The Roots of the Modern American Empire,* in *American Historical Review,* LXXV (October 1970), 1780–1782.

Robert W. Tucker, *The Radical Left and American Foreign Policy.* Baltimore: Johns Hopkins University Press (1971).

Robert James Maddox, *The New Left and the Origins of the Cold War.* Princeton: Princeton University Press (1973).

Christopher Lasch, "William Appleman Williams on American History," *Marxist Perspectives,* 3 (Fall 1978), 118–126.

Richard A. Melanson, "The Social and Political Thought of William Appleman Williams," *Western Political Quarterly,* 3 (September 1978), 392–409.

John Lukacs, review of *Empire as a Way of Life,* in *New Republic,* 183 (October 11, 1980), 31–33.

Edward S. Shapiro, "Revisionism R.I.P.," *Intercollegiate Review,* 17 (Fall/Winter 1981), 55–60.

William Marina, "William Appleman Williams," *Dictionary of Literary Biography,* 17, *Twentieth Century Historians.* Detroit: Gale Research Company (1983).

David W. Noble, *The End of American History.* Minneapolis: University of Minnesota Press (1985).

William G. Robbins, "Doing History Is Best of All. No Regrets"; Ivan R. Dee, "Revisionism Revisited"; and David W. Noble, "William Appleman Williams and the Crisis of Public History" in *Redefining the Past: Essays in Diplomatic History in Honor of William Appleman Williams,* edited by Lloyd C. Gardner. Corvallis: Oregon State University (1986).

Bradford Perkins, "The Tragedy of American Diplomacy: Twenty-five Years After," *Reviews in American History,* 12 (March 1984), 1–18. Reprinted in William Appleman Williams, *The Tragedy of American Diplomacy.* New York: W. W. Norton, paperback edition (1988).

Gary R. Hess, "After the Tumult: The Wisconsin School's Tribute to William Appleman Williams," *Diplomatic History* (Fall 1988), 483–499.

"Excerpts from a Conference to Honor William Appleman Williams," edited by Dina Copelman and Barbara Clark Smith, *Radical History Review,* 50 (Spring 1991), 39–70.

Index

Abolitionism, 226–238, 283, 373
Acheson, Dean, 102, 263, 343, 344, 360; quoted, 134, 397
Acton (Lord), 377
Adair, Douglas: quoted, 11
Adams, Brooks, 19, 82, 89–104 et passim, 120, 126, 128, 263. See also Frontier thesis; *America's Economic Supremacy*, 127
Adams, Henry, 82, 94, 120; quoted, 240
Adams, John, 183, 194, 198, 200, 374
Adams, John Quincy, 25, 202–212 et passim, 334, 374; as anti-imperialist, 347, 376, 381–382, 384; and Calvinism, 207; and Monroe Doctrine, 212–215; and private property, 215–220; quoted, 201, 202; *Report upon Weights and Measures*, 211
Adams, Samuel, 164, 183, 186, 187–200 et passim, 356; quoted, 163
African-Americans, 268–269, 362; and frontier thesis, 263–264
Agnew, Spiro, 334
Agriculture: distribution of urban and rural population, 288; and expansion, 276–323; exports, 294; and silver, 292–293
Agriculture Department, 306
Aleksandrov, 154
Alexeev, Mikhail, 53, 55, 56–57
Alfonso de Albuquerque, 379
Algeciras Conference, 342
Alien land issue, 300
All in One Life (Byrnes), 147
Allen, William V., 310, 312
Allende, Salvador, 369
Alliance for Progress, 365
Alliance movement, 308
Amalgamated Copper Co., 248
America-China Development Co., 130
America Confronts a Revolutionary World (Williams), 27, 345
American Asiatic Association, 122
American Bankers Association, 248
American colonies, 162–202 et passim; and agriculture, 278–279; demographics, 187–188
American Diplomacy, 1900–1950 (Kennan), 69–74 et passim
American Empire. See Imperialism, American
The American Frontier (Truman), 101
American Historical Association, 90, 336
American Indians, 175, 269, 279; and Puritans, 180–181
American Individualism (Hoover), 83, 329
American Insurance Co. versus Canter, 211

American Magazine, 187
The American Party Battle (Beard), 112
American Philosophical Society, 177
The American Political Tradition (Hofstadter), 325
American Radicals: Some Problems and Personalities (Williams), 105
American Railway Union, 92
American Revolution, 118; forces leading to, 162–220 et passim; ideology, 190–198; and indebtedness, 190–198
American-Russian relations. See Soviet Union
American-Russian Relations (Williams), 16–17, 37–67, 89
American Slavery as I See It (Weld), 230
"American System," 205–212, 214, 238
American Telephone and Telegraph Co., 245, 248
American Tobacco Co., 248
Americans in a Changing World (Williams), 30
America's Economic Supremacy (Adams), 100
Annapolis, Md., 13, 169. See also U.S. Naval Academy
"The Annapolis Crowd" (Williams), 33, 385
Anticatholicism, 229
Anti-imperialism, 116–132, 376–384 et passim
Antoninus, Marcus Aurelius: quoted, 346
Appeal to the Toiling, Oppressed, and Exhausted Peoples of Europe (Lenin), 80
Appleman, Mildrede Louise, 12
Apprenticeship schools, 196
Aquinas, Thomas (saint), 251
Arabs, 379
Arafat, Yasir, 372
Architecture, Southern, 167
Argentina, 214; as alternative to U.S. agriculture, 297
Arminian heresy, 226–227
Armour and Co., 301
Arnold, G. L., 139
Articles of Confederation, 348, 355
Asia, 382; and anticolonialism, 122–132 et passim; as market for U.S., 304; relations with U.S., 218
Asimov, Isaac, 387
Astor, John Jacob, 124
Atkinson, Edward, 296
Atlantic, Ia., 12
Atlantic Conference, 100, 140–142
Austin, Stephen F., 233
Austria: and American agriculture, 297
Automobile industry, 129, 247

405

Jesus Christ, 351
Joffe, Adolf, 58
John Wanamaker's, 248
Johnson, Lyndon, 158, 366–367
Johnson, Thomas, 169, 171
Johnson, William, 231
Johnston, Eric, 146, 146n
Jones, John Paul, 386
Jones, Willie, 170
Journal of Commerce, 122
Judson, William V., 38, 43n, 47, 49, 51–53, 59
Junto, 177
Jusser, Jules J., 44

Kaledin, Alexei, 53, 54, 56–57
Kellogg, Frank B., 88
Kemper Military Academy, 13
Kennan, George Frost, 17, 68–74, 91, 103, 148; quoted, 134
Kennedy, John F., 364; quoted, 360
Kennedy, John P., 234
Kennedy, Robert F., 158
Kentucky Resolutions, 217
Kerensky, Alexander, 37, 39, 44
Kerth, Monroe C., 47, 49
Khrushchev, Nikita, 365
Kilburn, Lawrence, 173
King, Ernest J., 390
King, Martin Luther, Jr., 263, 362; quoted, 257
King, Rufus, 202–203, 211, 232
King's College, 173
Kissinger, Henry, 364, 367–369, 373
Klein, Julius, 84
Knaplund, Paul, 15
Knox, Alfred, 51, 51n
Kolchak, Aleksander, 40
Korea, 360–361
Kornilov, General Lavr, 54, 57
Kropotkin, Sasha, 45
Kuhlmann, Richard von, 58
Kuhn, Loeb and Co., 41, 248
Kyle, James H., 310

La Follette, Robert, 374
Labor: and frontier thesis, 92; and Marx, 271; and syndicalism, 251–254
Labor strikes, 249–251, 256
LaFeber, Walter, 16–17, 23
Laissez faire, 221–238, 328; and freedom, 235–238. *See also* Free trade
Lamb, John, 194
Lamont, Thomas W., 47, 55, 87
Lansing, Robert, 41–67 *et passim*, 70; quoted, 38
Latin America, 218; and anticolonialism, 122–132 *et passim*; and Good Neighbor Policy, 100; and Herbert Hoover, 334; as market for U.S. 304, 310; and *Pax Americana*, 85; programs under John F. Kennedy, 365

Latvia, 141
Laurens, Henry, 168, 170
The Law of Civilization and Decay (Adams), 94, 96
League of Nations, 75–88 *et passim*, 98, 278; Article X of the Covenant, 83
Lee, Higginson and Co., 248
Lee, Ivy, 254
Lee, Richard Henry, 170
Lee, Robert E., 385
Leeds University, England, 28
Leggett, William, 224, 235; quoted, 222
Lengerke Meyer, George von, 42
Lenin, Nikolai, 39–67 *et passim*, 80, 352
Leo XIII (pope), 251
Leopold, Richard W., 79
Lester, Julius, 325, 326, 334–335
Levelers, 186, 188, 195, 259, 265
Lewis, Meriwether, 382
Liberty party, 230
Liliuokalani (queen), 311
Lincoln, Abraham, 26, 259, 283; and expansion, 347
Lippmann, Walter, 258; quoted, 257
List, Frederick, 206
Lithuania, 141
Littleton, Mark, 234
Liverpool, Lord: quoted, 202
Liverpool exchange, 286
Livingston, Robert, 194, 199
Livingston, William, 172
Locke, John, 185, 192, 226, 289
Lockhart, Robert Bruce, 55, 67
Lodge, Henry Cabot, 76, 78, 79, 82, 94, 96, 120, 126, 312; quoted, 240
London exchange, 286
London Foreign Ministers Conference, 154
Louisiana Purchase, 81
Louisville Canal, 208
Lovejoy, Elijah, 229
Lubin, David, 316
Lukács, Georg, 341

MacArthur, Douglas, 332, 385
Mackenzie, Alexander Slidell, 378
Macy's, 248
Madison, James, 118, 167, 259, 261; and expansion, 280–281, 347; and frontier thesis, 117–118; influence on Charles A. Beard, 109–115 *et passim*; and Missouri Crisis, 204; quoted, 116; theory of expansion, 212–215
Madison, Wisc., 14, 23, 29
Mahan, Alfred Thayer, 97, 387–388
Main, Jackson Turner, 15
Malin, James C., 98
Manchester Guardian Weekly, 12
Manchukuo, 88
Manchuria, 39–40, 88, 152; and Herbert Hoover, 334
Mandeville, Bernard: quoted, 162

A NOTE ON THE EDITOR

HENRY W. BERGER was born in Frederick, Maryland, and studied at the Ohio State University, Mexico City College, and the University of Wisconsin, Madison, where he was a student of William Appleman Williams and received a Ph.D. in history. He has since taught American history at the University of Vermont and at Washington University, St. Louis, where he is now associate professor. He has written on a variety of subjects in the history of American foreign relations.